PAN-SLAVISM

Its

History and Ideology

PAN-SLAVISM

Its
History and Ideology

· BY ·

HANS KOHN

SECOND EDITION, REVISED

New York: Vintage Books
A DIVISION OF RANDOM HOUSE

· 1 9 6 0 ·

VINTAGE BOOKS

*are published by Alfred A. Knopf, Inc. and Random House,
Inc.*

*Reprinted by arrangement with University of Notre Dame
Press.*

FIRST VINTAGE EDITION

To my friend and colleague

Joseph E. Wisan

The nations accept ideas like a mould into which they throw all the instincts, sentiments, knowledge, prejudices and mistakes which derive from their incomplete education, their incoherent experiences and the accumulated influences of family and country.

Albert Sorel
L'Europe et la Révolution Française

Preface

THE FOLLOWING PAGES present the first attempt at a
comprehensive survey and analysis of the history
and ideology of Pan-Slavism in the English language.
They originated in a series of lectures which the
Committee on International Relations of The University of Notre Dame invited me to deliver there.
I wish to thank the Committee and the University
of Notre Dame Press for their co-operation in making the appearance of the book possible. It may
help toward a better understanding of the complex
problems which the emergence of the Slav nations,
above all, of Russia, to full political and cultural participation in the life of the nineteenth and the twentieth centuries created, for them, for the other peoples, and for Western civilization. Perhaps the twentieth century may confirm the proud faith of some
of the fervent Slavs of the preceding century, who
regarded the Slav problem as the most important
that mankind faces. Though this may be a typical
nationalist exaggeration, there can be little doubt
about the need for a deeper study of Slav history
and aspirations. The student of "the Slav world,"
who is familiar with other forms of nationalism,
especially in central Europe and in Asia, will note
that Slav attitudes are in no way unique but fit well
into the general pattern of the age of nationalism.
Above all, there is no clearly defined or unified Slav
attitude. The aspirations and trends of the different
Slav peoples are varied and often contradictory. Even

Pan-Slavism itself has meant different things to different Slav groups: and there have been many Slavs who rejected Pan-Slavism or any separation, on racial or linguistic grounds, from the general course of Western civilization.

During my work on this book, I received much help from my friends, Mr. Wallace Sokolsky, my colleague at The City College of New York, Mr. Ruben Weltsch, of the Cincinnati University Library, and Dr. Hugo Knoepfmacher, of Washington, D. C., with whom I started to study Russian literature and history in Siberia thirty-five years ago. Having been brought up in the Czech environment of the ancient city of Prague, perhaps the principal battleground of German and Slav nationalism, I found my contact with the warmth of Russian civilization and the vastness of Russian nature a fascinating experience. The problems of the Austrian monarchy and the expanse of the Russian dominion decisively influenced me in the study of nationalism as the preponderant factor in modern history.

H. K.

New York, Fall 1952

Introduction

PAN-SLAVISM, a movement in which nationalist elements were mingled with supra-national and often imperialist trends, was a product of the political awakening of the intellectuals in central and eastern Europe, which was brought about by the French Revolution and the Napoleonic Wars. But even more potent was the influence of German romanticism and of a linguistic Pan-Germanism as represented by Arndt and Fichte.[n] Pan-Slavism proclaimed the affinity of various peoples, in spite of differences of political citizenship and historical background, of civilization and religion, solely on the strength of an affinity of language. It could thus arise only at a time when under the influence of Johann Gottfried Herder the national language, the mother tongue, was regarded as a determining factor for man's loyalty—and his intellectual and spiritual life.

But Herder did more for the rising Slav consciousness than to emphasize the vernacular as the only true foundation of civilization. In the few pages of the fourth chapter of the sixteenth book of his "Ideas for the Philosophy of the History of Mankind" (1784) he gave the Slavs the consciousness of a unity based upon the community of high morality and glorious destiny. He proclaimed the Slavs the coming leaders of Europe. A disciple of Rousseau, he compared favorably the rural and backward Slavs with the highly civilized Romance and Germanic peoples, whose very degree of civilization implied

their alienation from the state of nature and therefore their approaching decadence. The proud Germans with their aristocratic warrior tradition had
from Charlemagne on oppressed and humbled the
Slavs who with their primitive democratic organization and their natural disposition toward peace had
cultivated music and poetry instead of war. Herder
was convinced that the nineteenth century would
bring the vindication and the leadership of the Slavs.
He admired and collected their folklore and folksongs, and admonished their few intellectuals to develop the native tongues instead of abandoning them
for German and French. These words of the great
German writer were balm for the often-hurt pride
of the Slav intellectuals. Their civilizations, backward in the eyes of Europe, were praised and extolled by one who had been the teacher of Goethe.[n]

Only at the beginning of the nineteenth century
did Herder's teachings begin to penetrate to the
Slavs. He insisted on the rights of their nationality
and language at a time when the Bohemians, Slovenes or Croatians had no consciousness themselves
of their nationality or of any possible future for the
Slavs. He taught them that "a people, and especially
a non-civilized one, has nothing dearer than the language of its fathers. Its whole spiritual wealth of
tradition, history, religion, and all the fulness of life,
all its heart and soul, lives in it. To deprive such a
people of its language or to minimize it, means to
deprive it of its own immortal possession, transmitted from parents to children." The picture which
Herder drew of Slav life and character, a picture
conditioned by his philosophical convictions rather
than by history and reality, deeply influenced Russian and Polish, Czech and Croat thinking about
themselves and their position in the world. Their historians labored to provide historical foundations for
this lofty metaphysical view and their politicians

based their claims upon these "findings" of history. Thus a second basis was created for Pan-Slavism. To the undisputed affinity of language from which was deduced a doubtful common descent, there was added the rather nebulous affinity of a Slavic *Volksgeist*. Just as German political and social thought of the War of Liberation against Napoleon was influenced by the West and showed little originality in spite of its claim to profound originality, to a mythical German *Eigenart*, so the corresponding Slav thought, in spite of its anti-German attitude and its insistence on Slav originality or *samobytnost*, was deeply indebted to the Germans.

German scholars laid the foundations of Slav historiography and Slav linguistics. Gerhard Friedrich Müller (1705–83) and August Ludwig Schlözer (1735–1809) devoted much of their time to the exploration of Russian history. While the former lived in Russia, Schlözer after a few years in the east returned as professor to Göttingen where he became one of the most influential publicists of the period. At the time of his retirement in 1804 he was ennobled by Emperor Alexander I of Russia. Like Herder, he was extremely friendly to the Slavs and did not extol the Germans. He started his *Allgemeine Nordische Geschichte* (General History of the North, Halle, 1771) by saying of the Slavs: "This is the great, renowned, ancient, powerful and widely spread people (Völkerstamm) in the north, of whom very little is still known." Thirty years later, in the first scholarly edition of the Russian chronicles ascribed to St. Nestor (*Nestor: Russische Annalen in iher slavonischen Ursprache verglichen, gereinigt und erklärt*, Göttingen 1802, 1809) he wrote: "Hardly has another people in the world expanded its dominion or its language further than the Slavs. From Ragusa on the Adriatic Sea to the Baltic Sea and the Arctic Sea in the north and to Kamchatka and the proximity of Japan in the east, one finds everywhere Slav populations." [n] Johann Christoph Adelung (1732–1806) and Jakob Grimm (1785–1863) became the teachers of the Slav grammarians and lexicographers. Karl Gottlieb Anton (1751–1818) set the example for research in Slav antiquities and folklore. His *Erste Linien eines Versuchs über der alten Slaven Ursprung, Sitten, Gebräuche, Meinungen und Kenntnisse* (First Outline of an Essay about the Origins, Customs, Habits, Opinions and Knowledge of the old Slavs, Leipzig, 1783) showed a deep sympathy with the Slavs.

These intellectual influences would hardly have aroused Pan-Slavism without the profound changes which the century between 1750 and 1850 produced in the economic and cultural status of the Austrian Slavs and in the political and military positions of Russia. The enlightened policy of the great Habsburg rulers, Maria Theresa, Joseph II and Leopold II, much improved the material well-being of the Slav peasants in their dominions and opened for them the way to modern education and to a rise in social status. Joseph II removed the restrictions on the Protestant minority among the Slovaks and Czechs. Through their affinity with German Protestantism, the young Protestant generation among the Slavs first became susceptible to the influence of the new German nationalism. Russia had nothing to match this systematic and steady improvement of the Slav masses in Austria, which by assiduous and hard work, initiative and disciplined co-operation achieved their integration into the rising liberal middle-class society of the West. But it could offer the fascination of success and power. From the wars against Napoleon Russia had emerged as the greatest continental nation; its soldiers occupied Paris; its Emperor dominated the peace conference. Suddenly the world became conscious of Russian and Slav might. Were not the Slavs the most numerous people in Europe and was not their number fast growing?

Was not the Russian Monarch planning to push the frontiers of his realm far westward?

The more Russian power was feared in the West, the greater became its potential attraction for some of the non-Russian Slavs who looked to the "big brother" for protection and help. Russia was not only the largest and most populous state in Europe with a population estimated at 55 to 60 millions and a yearly increase of about half a million,[n] she was the only independent Slav state, if one disregards the tiny Free State of Cracow with its population of 108,000 according to a census of 1821, and the barely known and distant little mountain region of Montenegro. One of the few forerunners of modern Pan-Slavism, the Croat priest Juraj Križanić (1618–83), went to Russia to preach there the unity of all Slav peoples under the rule of the Tsar of Russia and the religious guidance of the Catholic Church. With Western eyes and a perspicacity unusual for his time, he recognized the backwardness of Russia and some of its fundamental causes; his proposals for reform made him equally unpopular with the ruler and with the church of the land which he regarded as the head and center of all Slav peoples.[n]

Križanić remained without any influence in his own time. The traces of his life and thought were quickly lost until a much later generation of scholars rediscovered them. Pan-Slavism made hardly any impression upon Russia even at the beginning of the nineteenth century. The only Slav people who attracted Russian attention then, the Poles, was a hostile people. Conscious of their strength, the Russians were much too occupied with themselves and their relation to the great Western nations to pay much attention to the non-Russian Slavs who appeared to them, if they thought of them at all, as poor and rather uninteresting relatives. The principles governing the Russian policy from 1815 to 1850 were those of religion and of legitimacy as the

safest bulwark against the threat of revolution. The
principles which governed the Pan-Slav movement
in its first or Western stage from 1815 to 1850 were
the very opposite principles of nationalism and liberalism. The influence which awakened the educated
classes among the Slav peoples, including the Russians, to national consciousness in the first half of the
nineteenth century did not emanate from Moscow
or St. Petersburg, but from the French Revolution,
romantic poetry, and the German idealist philosophy.

In Russia it was a Pole who in the interests of
Poland hinted at a potential role for Russia among
the Slavs. Prince Adam Czartoryski (1770–1861), the
friend of Emperor Alexander I, wrote from Tilsit on
May 23, 1807, to Count Pavel Aleksandrovich Stroganov in London that a federation of the Slav nations was a great and unique goal towards which
Russia must of necessity aspire.[n] A few years later,
under Western influence, a group of young men in
Russia founded a Society of United Slavs. In gran-
diloquent dreams characteristic of the generation
which participated in the secret societies preparing
the Decembrist uprising of 1825, Peter Ivanovich
Borisov and his brother Andrew drew up in 1823 a
"Catechism" which demanded the union of all Slavs
who had been separated from each other by ignorance of their common ancestry. The emblem of the
society consisted of an octagon to represent the eight
Slav nations (Russians, Poles, Slovaks, Czechs, Serbo-
Croats, Bulgars, Lusatians, and Slovenes) and of four
anchors to represent the four Slavic seas (the Black
Sea, the White Sea, the Dalmatian Sea, and the
Arctic Sea). Every member had to take an oath
swearing that he would brave one thousand deaths,
overcome one thousand obstacles, and devote his
last breath to the liberty and brotherly union of the
noble Slavs.[n]

Pan-Slavism did not originate as an imperialist
movement with the Russians. Russian expansion in

the eighteenth and early nineteenth centuries was
motivated by Great Russian demands and drives and
by the ideology of the Orthodox religion, not by any
feeling of Slav community. It was the non-Russian
Slav world in its national awakening which felt the
need of closer co-operation. In 1848 two of the Slav
peoples had hardly shown even the first traces of a
national awakening: the Byelorussians in the Russian Empire and the somewhat more advanced Bulgarians in the Turkish Empire. The Poles lived divided up among the Russian, Prussian, and Austrian
states; the Ukrainians were subjects of Russia and of
Austria; the few Lusatians inhabited parts of Prussia
and of Saxony; the Croats and the Serbs occupied
territories under Austrian and Turkish domination;
only the Czechs and Slovenes found themselves entirely within Austria, and the Slovaks within Hungary. Thus the Slav world, apart from the Great Russians, offered the spectacle of subjection and multiple
division. Their national consciousness was weak and
still in the process of formation, except in the case of
the Poles. The same held true of their national languages. The first foundations of modern literature
in the various vernacular tongues were just being
laid. Under these circumstances, the urge for added
strength and security by union and unity was understandable. Pan-Slavism arose as a defensive movement of the Western Slavs. At the beginning its
emphasis was on language, literature, and culture,
for in the central European situation before 1848—
the political stillness of the Metternichian era and
the influence of German idealist philosophy—national movements were the concern of writers, poets,
and scholars. The word Pan-Slavism was first used
by a Slovak writer in 1826 in a Latin treatise on Slav
philology."

The mutual contacts engendered by Pan-Slavism
strengthened the nascent national movements among
the Slavs. But this growing nationalism itself be-

came an obstacle to the realization of Pan-Slavism. The more the various peoples became conscious of their individuality, their historical traditions and their own language, the less they were inclined to sacrifice them for some fervently proclaimed but non-existent Slav culture or language. The affinity of the Slav languages and the belief in a very doubtful common ancestry in prehistoric times offered no solid foundations for unity. On the contrary, political and historical realities, differences of religion and civilization, ran counter to the Pan-Slav aspirations. Nor did proximity create good neighborly relations. The Greek Orthodox Russians and the Roman Catholic Poles have lived for the last three hundred years in a state of almost unbroken hostility. The Poles regarded themselves as the defenders of Europe against a Byzantine–Tartar world. The Czechs and Slovaks were both predominantly Roman Catholic, with Hussite traditions surviving among the former and the Protestants representing a strong minority among the latter, and although both spoke closely related dialects, their historical development had been different, the Czechs forming part of the Holy Roman Empire and of the Austrian dominion, the Slovaks of the Kingdom of Hungary. As a result they have shown an enduring incompatibility of temperament and aspirations. The Croats and the Serbs speak the same language. But the Croats came under German and Italian influence and are Roman Catholics; the Serbs lived for five centuries under Turkish domination and are Greek Orthodox. The oft proclaimed unity of these two people scarcely existed in reality. Macedonia has formed the battleground between Bulgars and Serbs as the Ukraine has been disputed for centuries between Poland and Russia. Memories of a distant past, revived by nationalist historiography, have created contradictory claims to territories which at one time or another belonged to one or the other Slav people at a period of its expansion and

imperial greatness. Since the national awakening of
the Slavs in the first part of the nineteenth century,
Slavs have fought and hated other Slavs at least as
bitterly and consistently as they have fought and
hated non-Slavs.

Nevertheless, Pan-Slavism, though it has so far not
become a political or cultural reality, has for the last
one hundred and fifty years moved many Slav minds
and has given rise to a number of interesting and
influential theories; at certain times it has enthused
the Slav masses, has become an instrument of Russian imperialism, and has preoccupied and frightened the statesmen and political observers of other
nations. With its temporary resurrection by the Russian communist government in 1941, it has after
some decades of somnolence re-entered upon the
political stage as a potential actor. But whatever its
effectiveness among the political and social factors
which have shaped Europe in the age of nationalism,
the history of the Pan-Slav idea in all its changing
forms throws much light upon the thought and
aspirations of the Slav peoples and thus helps to
clarify a problem which began to alarm Europe a
century ago and has since grown in urgency.

Contents

Contents

PART I

Pan-Slavism and the West

1815-1860

I am by education a European. I want to
tell you that the culture of Europe and
America is spiritually adequate for me. I say
this to those Slavophiles who see something
in Russia and the Slavs which is above
Europeanism. The best Russians are also
admirers of the Occident.

T. G. MASARYK TO KAREL ČAPEK

1

Romanticism and Realism Among Czechs and Slovaks

THE MODERN MOVEMENT of Pan-Slavism started in the 1820's among the Western Slavs under the influence of the romantic movement, which was at the height of its influence throughout Europe. In its origins, among the Lake poets in England and in the circle around the brothers Schlegel in Germany, romanticism opposed the libertarian and rationalist tendencies of the French Revolution. In its later stage romanticism presented a more complex attitude, its imagination turned simultaneously to the fascination of the past and the Middle Ages and to the appeal of the future happiness of free men. Under the quiet surface of the Biedermeier the unrest of the Napoleonic wars continued to arouse in the educated young generation a longing for change, for activity, for a new sense of self-fulfillment. This new liberalism had little of the enlightened rationalism of the preceding generations; it was filled with mystical fervor and a semi-religious enthusiasm. In this climate of ill-defined hopes and dreams nationalism took hold of two young Lutheran Slovaks who may be regarded as the fathers of early Pan-Slavism, Jan Kollár (1793–1852) and Pavel Josef Šafařík

(1795–1861). Kollár became its first poet, Šafařík its first scholar.

At that time the Czech and Slovak national consciousness had not yet crystallized. The Slav-speaking people of Bohemia called themselves Czechs but in the Czech language this term included all the inhabitants of Bohemia of whom a large part spoke German; east of Bohemia was Moravia where the Slav-speaking people called themselves Moravians and learned only slowly to identify themselves with the Bohemian Czechs as a Czech people; east of Moravia, separated by the Carpathian chain of hills, around the foot of the high Tatra Mountains, lived the Slovaks speaking several dialects closely akin to the Moravian. Bohemia and Moravia had a common past; until 1526 or 1627 they had formed an independent kingdom which then was united with Austria under the Habsburgs. Under the Bohemian King Charles IV of the House of Luxemburg, who was also Holy Roman Emperor (1346–78), the Bohemian capital of Prague became one of the cultural centers of the West. Jan Hus (1369–1415) started there the first Reformation movement. The Czech historians of the romantic nationalist awakening were to look back to the Hussite 15th century with the reign of George of Podebrady (1457–71) and the rise of the Unity of Czech Brethren as the high point of Czech history. Different was the fate of the Slovaks; after the brief existence of the Moravian-Slovak Empire of Rostislav (846–70) and Swatopluk (890–94), they had fallen under Magyar domination. Their country formed an integral part of the Hungarian kingdom for more than one thousand years, from 905–1918. Thus the closely related two branches of the Western Slavs had known an entirely different development.

The numerically much inferior Slovaks, living under infinitely more backward economic and social conditions, were at the time of their national awaken-

ing the first to feel the need of support from the
Czechs. Among the Slovaks, the Lutheran minority,
emancipated under Joseph II, established connections with the German Protestant universities. German scholars and writers had just started to proclaim that the Germans of Prussia and Bavaria, of
Hanover and Austria, though speaking various
dialects, formed one nation and had one language.
Did not the Slavs in a similar way, though living in
various lands, in Russia and Austria, in Prussia and
Turkey, form one nation? Were not the languages
they spoke dialects of one Slav language? This fiction
of one Slav nation and one Slav language dominated
the thought of Kollár and Šafařík.

Kollár, like Palacký and Štúr later, studied at the
Lutheran Lyceum in Pressburg. The language of
instruction there was Latin, at that time the official
language of the kingdom of Hungary, but the government had established a chair for Slav language
and literature. This chair was occupied by Jiří
Palkovič (1769–1850) who like all Protestant Slovaks
at that time used Czech as the literary language.[n]
Kollár and Šafařík were in touch not only with the
Czechs; Pressburg, then the capital of Hungary,
gave them the opportunity of meeting also with
Croats and Serbs who lived in the southern part of
the state. The close relationship between Czechoslovaks and Serbo-Croats was established at the very
awakening of national consciousness. Kollár noted
later that his encounter with southern Slav students
in 1812 made him dimly realize for the first time the
need for a change in the condition of the Slavs. He
became aware of the fact "that we all form one nation." [n] Šafařík himself was called in 1818 as director of the Serb Lyceum in Novi Sad (Neusatz) in
southern Hungary where he stayed until 1833 when
he moved to Prague, which had become the center
of Slav studies.

The Grand Old Man of that newly born discipline,

the Catholic Abbé Josef Dobrowský (1753–1829),
represented the enlightened scholarship of the eighteenth century. His main works were a History of the
Czech Language and Literature (*Geschichte der
Böhmischen Sprache und Literatur*, 1729) and a
Grammar of the Czech Language (*Ausführliches
Lehrgebäude der Böhmischen Sprache*, 1809).
Twice, however, he attempted to publish periodicals
(in German) which in the new fashion were de-
voted to the supposedly one Slav language and
literature. The first one, in 1806, he called *Slawin.
Botschaft aus Böhmen an alle Slavischen Völker,
oder Beiträge zur Kenntnis der Slavischen Literatur
nach allen Mundarten* (Slawin. Message from
Bohemia to all Slav Peoples, or Contributions to the
Knowledge of the Slav Literature according to all
Dialects). He followed it in 1814 by *Slowanka, für
Kenntnis der alten und neuen Slavischen Literatur,
der Sprachkunde nach allen Mundarten, der Geschichte und Altertümer* (Slowanka, for the knowledge of the Old and New Slav Literature, of Slav
Linguistics according to all Dialects, of Slav History
and Antiquities).[n]

Šafařík's scholarship, under the influence of romanticism and nationalism, lacked the sobriety of
his great predecessor. His fame was established by his
History of the Slav Language and Literature
(*Geschichte der Slavischen Sprache und Literatur*)
which he published while he was still teaching in
Novi Sad in 1826, and his Slav Antiquities (*Staro-
žitnosti slovanské*, Prague, 1837). His research and
his many publications fertilized Czech and south
Slav scholarship. He declined calls to chairs in
Moscow, Berlin, and Breslau. As a romantic nationalist he idealized the past character of the Slavs.
He wished not only to be a scholar but the prophet
of the national awakening of his race, which he
glorified, stressing apologetically its unique character

and mission. To his scholarly Pan-Slavism Kollár
added the inspirational superstructure.

The turning point of Kollár's life was in the years
which he spent between 1817 and 1819 as a student
of theology at the University of Jena. The small
Thuringian town in the Grand Duchy of Saxony-
Weimar had at the turn of the century been the
home town of Friedrich Schiller, Johann Gottlieb
Fichte and August Wilhelm Schlegel. When the
young Slovak student came there, Jena was the
center of romanticism and nationalism among professors and students. The nationalist student fraterni-
ties, the Burschenschaften, celebrated in October,
1817, the famous Wartburg Festival in commemoration of the third centenary of Luther's reformation
and of the fourth anniversary of the Battle at Leipzig. Kollár participated in the festivities and caught
the contagion of the youthful enthusiasm. His teachers, the historian Heinrich Luden (1780–1847), the
romantic natural scientist Lorenz Oken (1779–1851)
and above all the philosopher Jakob Friedrich Fries
(1773–1843), were among the leaders of the nationalist student movement. Fries, who had become popular through his two recent publications "On the
Threat Presented by the Jews to the Germans" (*Über
die Gefährdung des Wohlstandes und Charakters der
Deutschen durch die Juden*, Heidelberg, 1816) and
"Of the German Confederation and the German
Constitution" (*Vom Deutschen Bund und Deutscher Staatsverfassung*, Heidelberg, 1817), called his
participation in the Wartburg Festival "the most
excellent (*ausgezeichnetste*) moment" of his life.
His nationalist revolutionary enthusiasm displeased
the authorities who suspended him for five years
from his teaching job.

This whole atmosphere excited Kollár. Under the
romantic influence, the distant past of the country-
side between the Saale and Elbe rivers, when these

lands had been inhabited by Slav tribes which had long since disappeared, was evoked by him and was fused in his imagination with his love for Frederike Wilhelmine Schmidt, the daughter of the Protestant minister of the nearby town of Lobeda. The name of this small town dreaming quietly in the shadow of the ruins of the ancient Lodaburg, recalled its Slav origin. The young woman, who was neither pretty nor remarkably intelligent according to general standards, appeared to him to surpass in beauty and wisdom the Jenaan girls; her uniqueness could be explained by the fact that she was the daughter of the Goddess Slava and the embodiment of all the past Slav generations with their heroic struggles and sufferings. Mina, as he called his fiancée, became his Laura to whom he sang sonnets as Petrarch had done and his Beatrice who guided him through the Slav Valhalla as her greater predecessor had guided Dante through the Christian heaven. Imitating the German patriotic poetry of the wars against Napoleon, Kollár sang the ancient glories of the Slavs, grieving and embittered about the defeats and humiliations they had suffered at the hands of the Germans, but comforting himself with the still imposing vastness of the Slav realm which reached from the Elbe to the Pacific Ocean. In 1824 when Kollár had returned from Germany to become pastor of the Lutheran Slovak church in Budapest, he published the poems under the title "The Daughter of Slava" (*Slávy Dcera*) which immediately established his fame throughout the Slav world. In later editions he added, though with an ever diminishing poetical talent, many new sonnets. But the value of the book did not lie in the realm of poetry. It was a nationalist sermon which soon lost the freshness of the youthful amatory experience and became overburdened with archeological scholarship. Its spirit, however, remained the same throughout: an illusionist idealization of the Slav past in the spirit of Herder whom

Kollár acknowledged as his teacher, and an excessive
optimism about the Slav future. Both these attitudes
made the book the national bible of early Pan-
Slavism.[8]

The elegiac mood bewailing a past apparently lost
forever is relieved more and more as the poem
progresses by flourishes of trumpets announcing
future triumphs. The composition of the whole is
poor, much remains nebulous, and in the later parts
the poetry is drowned under a display of bookish
learning. Raising his eyes from the past to the immense resources of the vast Slav nation, the poet
looked hopefully to the future. If only the Slavs
would learn a lesson from the past and gain strength
in unity, they would become indestructible. As
Byron's Childe Harold mourned the present-day decay of the Greeks and tried to reawaken them by
singing of their past glories, Kollár called upon the
Slavs to become conscious of their strength and
mission. "It is true that we came somewhat late,
but so much the younger we are." In a century, the
poet is certain, "everywhere the Slavs like a mighty
flood will extend their limits; the language which
the Germans wrongly consider a mere speech of
slaves will resound in places and even in the mouths
of its rivals. The sciences will flow through Slav
channels; our people's dress, their manners and their
song will be fashionable on the Seine and on the
Elbe. Oh, that I was not born in that great age of
Slav dominion; or that I may not rise from the grave
to witness it."

Kollár was deeply influenced by Herder. He glorified him as the priest of humanitarianism but even
more as the friend of the Slavs.

Kant and Wieland have no nationality.
Schiller is cold to us, Klopstock mute,
Not thus you, priest of humanitarianism.
Contrary to custom, you were the first

To defend and highly praise the Slavs.
For that accept from them honor and thanks.

The Slav poet borrowed from Herder the identification of the Slavs with peace, democracy, and humanitarianism, with the archetype of pure humanity and pure Christianity. While he accepted the words of Herder's enlightened eighteenth-century humanitarianism, its substance disappeared in Kollár's own new romantic-nationalist climate, which often carried national resentments, claims, and exclusivism to an extreme unknown to Herder. Rhetorically Kollár admonished the Slavs to regard the nation merely as an expression of humanity. "And always when you call 'Slav!', let it be man who answers." "In other nations humanity comes after nationality," he wrote. "Among the Slavs nationality comes after humanity." But the famous words of Terence, "I am a human being, and nothing human I consider alien to me," which would have sounded natural in Herder's mouth as it did in that of Cicero, Kollár changed into: "I am a Slav and nothing Slav I consider alien to me."

The Goddess Slava—a word often derived from *sláva*, glory, and often from *slovo*, word, indicating the Slavs as the natural masters of the word, of poetry and song—calls upon her children to become conscious of All-Slavism (*Všeslavie*), to unite and to become highly cultured; then they will soon be the first nation on earth. "Scattered Slavs, let us be a united whole, and no longer mere fragments. Let us be all or naught." Mother Slava advises her children to learn the right answer when asked who they are:

"Who art thou? A Russian; and thou? A Serb; and thou? A Czech; and thou? I am a Pole.

"My children: Unity! Speak not so but say: I am a Slav."

Yet in spite of these grandiose illusions and dreams, Kollár, like the whole Slovak generation of his period, remained little interested in political goals. He lacked Herder's serene objectivity in judging nations but he was concerned as Herder was with culture and language, not with states and politics. He naturally admired Russia of which he knew practically nothing, but like Šafařík he was loyally attached to his legitimate state and ruler." What he demanded was the literary and cultural solidarity of the Slavs. Similar thoughts were then widespread but Kollár lent voice to them, not only in his poetry but in his famous *Über die literarische Wechselseitigkeit zwischen den verschiedenen Stämmen und Mundarten der Slavischen Nation* (On the literary solidarity between the various peoples and dialects of the Slav nation)." "The Slavs have counted themselves," Kollár wrote, "and have found that they are the most numerous people in Europe. This knowledge has made them conscious of their strength. But their strength is rooted not only in their material preponderance. Their intellectual faculties reveal the greatest variety and their language unites all the virtues of the ancient and the modern languages." The suggestions which he made were modest in their scope. The educated Slavs should learn the principal four languages, Czech, Illyrian, Polish, and Russian. "Each dialect should draw new vitality from its contact with the others for its own rejuvenation and enrichment but without infringing upon the others nor allowing itself to be infringed upon." Bookshops should distribute books of all Slav "dialects," Slav scholars and writers should meet in frequent congresses, the works of the various Slav literatures should be translated into the other "dialects." Kollár explained the leadership assumed by the Slovaks by the very fact that "the Tatra Slavs had so far almost no literature of their own, therefore they first opened their arms to embrace all Slavs. Their dialect stands grammatically and geographically in the center of all Slav dialects: for the Tatra mountains are the nest and cradle of all Slavs. Therefore the idea of solidarity, if it did not first originate with the Slovaks in Hungary, at least took root there faster and deeper than anywhere else." Kollár was convinced that the Slavs formed one nation. "For the first time after many centuries the various dispersed Slav tribes (Stämme) regarded themselves as One great nation and their various dialects as One language. They awaken to a national sentiment and long for a close tie (*Aneinanderschliessen*)."

Even this limited Pan-Slav appeal for a revival of Slav literary creativeness through linguistic and cultural unity remained ineffectual, if measured by reality. True, various literatures in the Slav languages flowered in the next one hundred years to a degree which in 1830 few would have thought possible. But insofar as this was due to outside influences, these influences were not the result of Slav solidarity; they were not Czech or Polish in the case of Russia or Russian or Serb in the case of Bohemia, they were German or French or English, and they expressed the solidarity of Western civilization infinitely more than solidarity based upon similarity of language or race. At the beginning of the twentieth century it was easier to buy in the Czech bookshops of Prague, German or French books than Russian books. The educated Croat or Slovak read French and German; few were the individuals who read Russian or Polish.

Nevertheless, in visualizing the Slavs as a unified body with a great future, the fathers of literary Pan-Slavism helped the awakening of the national consciousness of their own Slav-speaking peoples. In Western Europe modern nationalism was the work of statesmen and political leaders; the political reality and the social-economic transformation came first and created the frame in which the young nation could develop with a sense of social reality and political responsibility. In Central and Eastern Europe, it was the poet, the philologist, and the historian who created the nationalities. From the Elbe to the Volga, from the Eider to the Tiber, from Flanders to the Morea, intellectuals began to cultivate their mother tongue and to study the past with a new feeling of pride, and they aroused the peasants to aspirations and demands never felt or voiced before. Europe east of the Rhine and the Alps seemed, in the stillness imposed by Metternich and Nicholas I, to slumber in the provincial drabness of small towns and in the idyllic satiety of the Biedermeier. But underneath, the foundations were being undermined, much less by any actual change of the social structure than by the dreams of the intellectuals. The seed of the French Revolution after lying dormant for many years seemed to bear sudden and surprising fruit in 1848.

The two Slovak spokesmen of Pan-Slavism found a willing echo in all the Slav peoples. For they expressed, in the familiar mood of the period, a general belief in historical progress, in a bright future, in the advent of some great spiritual manifestation, of a new era for mankind which would establish forever the basis of liberty, peace, and happiness. The Slavs seemed young, untouched by all the dissensions and conflicts ravaging the older nations: were they not destined to be the messengers of the new age? What they needed was only an assurance of their strength which, except for the Russians, was only a promise of the future. This promise was brought to them by Šafařík and Kollár.

Upon the appearance of Šafařík's Slav Ethnography (*Slovanský národopis*, Prague, 1842), which contained a map and statistics of the Slav peoples, Stanko Vráz (1810–51), one of the leaders of the Illyrian movement, wrote from Zagreb to Prague:

"When I brought a copy of this map, the local patriots and even the non-patriots almost tore it out
of my hands. All of them cannot get over the fact
that the Slav nation is spread so far. The map arouses
more patriots here than a whole literature could
do." [n] The greatest Ukrainian poet Taras Shevchenko
(1814–61) dedicated to Šafařík his poem "The
Heretic" in which he glorifies Jan Hus. The dedication expressed the poet's dream of a union of the
Slavs in which all would be truly free (and the oppression of the Ukrainians by the Russians ended).

> Brothers clasped the hands of brothers
> And they promised loudly
> Oaths of quiet love and friendship
> Ever and for Ever!
> Into one great sea there gathered
> All the Slavic rivers.
> Glory be to you, o wise man,
> Czech and Slav together . . .
> Your mighty ocean
> Of the Slavs, reviving,
> Will be full again, 'tis certain
> And the boat goes sailing.
> With its mighty sails wide spreading
> And a helmsman noble
> It will sail on a free ocean
> O'er the boundless waves.[n]

The great Polish poet Adam Mickiewicz opened his
first lecture in 1840 at the Collège de France, where
he inaugurated the chair of Slavic languages and
literatures, with Kollár's words: "Tous les peuples ont
prononcé leur dernier mot; maintenant, Slaves, c'est
à notre tour de parler."

While Kollár and Šafařík proclaimed the solidarity
and integration of the Slavs, other Protestant Slovaks
took the lead in denying that Czechs and Slovaks
were one nation and that Slovak was only a Czech
dialect. The Catholic Slovaks who formed the large

but less active majority of the people had maintained such a position for some time, partly out of distrust of Hussite tendencies among the Czechs. But in the 1830's the Slovak Protestant youth, aroused by the July Revolution in France and by the Polish uprising of that year, had been enthusiastic supporters of Kollár. Their leader was Ludevít Štúr (1815–56), mediocre as a writer and thinker but full of the typical sentimentalism and lyricism of the period, a man who like many at that time devoted all his life to the cause of his people and spent himself in its service.[n] He consumed his life in writing innumerable articles and poems, founding short-lived periodicals and societies, and glorifying the theme which then resounded in so many languages, the duty to love the fatherland and to cultivate the mother tongue. He joined a students' society at the Protestant Lyceum of Pressburg where the members obligated themselves to converse only in Czech and to prepare every month a paper in Czech on a literary subject. He became assistant to Palkovič and taught his course on Slav grammar, using for the first time Czech instead of Latin as the language of instruction. He participated on April 24, 1836, in the Slovak students' festival in the ruins of Devin, a castle at the confluence of the Morava and the Danube where the great Moravian ruler Svatopluk had resided. There in the spirit of the Wartburg Festival and of the romanticism of the then widely celebrated Polish exiles, they sang the new popular songs recalling the very few years when a Slovak nobleman, Pribina, of whom practically nothing is known, ruled around 830 from the city of Nitra (Neutra) before he became subjected to the Moravian princes—the one and only episode of Slovak independence. Though himself a heathen, Pribina built the first Christian church in Nitra. But the less authentic knowledge nationalists have of their heroes the greater they seem to them. Captivated by the melodious language of the Slavs commemorating "the dear and high Nitra," one could even overlook the fact that the times of its flowering, conjured up by the song, were very distant, extremely short-lived, and on the whole unknown."

From 1838 to 1840 Štúr studied at the University of Halle where he was influenced by Hegelian philosophy. After his return he again taught Czech as assistant professor at the Pressburg Lyceum. But he was dismissed in 1844 in the course of the Magyarization of the Hungarian Lutheran Church which Count Karol Zay started as inspector general with the rather strange motivation that it was the duty of every loyal citizen, lover of freedom, and reasonable man, to support the Magyarization of Hungary. In this situation Štúr decided that the survival of the Slovaks depended on the unity of the Catholics and Protestants and on the establishment of Slovak nationality in Hungary upon a firm and popular foundation. In 1845 he began to publish a political periodical in the middle-Slovak dialect which now became the Slovak literary language, the *Slovenské Narodnje Novini* (Slovak National Newspaper) and the next year he followed it up with a book "The Slovak Dialect or the Need of Writing in this Dialect," which he dedicated to his two friends, Michal Miloslaw Hodža (1811–70), Pastor in Liptovský Sv. Mikuláš, and Josef Miloslaw Hurban (1817–88), Pastor in Hlboké near Nitra. These three Slovak Protestants, united in friendship and common aspirations, became the leaders of the Slovak cultural revival and the people's spokesmen in the stormy events of the revolutionary year 1848."

In 1847, in a meeting of the publishing society Tatrin, founded three years before, the Slovak Catholics and Protestants established a common national front. Five years later appeared a "Short Grammar of the Slovak Language" written by a priest, Martin Hattala, and sponsored by the three

Protestant leaders and three Catholic priests. The
Slovak nation, with its own literary language, was
definitely established. Immediately writers began to
justify its existence by an "ideology." It was not only
claimed that the new language fulfilled a practical
need by uniting Catholics and Protestants, intellectuals and peasants, but Slovak intellectuals began to
regard their people as the central and original Slav
nation, and their language as the purest Slav tongue.
The Carpathian Tatra mountain, on the slopes of
which the Slovaks lived, was proclaimed the cradle
of Slavdom. The Czechs, on the other hand, had
pushed westward away from the racial roots, and
their character and language were deformed by German influences. It seemed more advisable for the
Czechs to find true Slavdom in the clear sources of
Slovak inspiration than to ask the Slovaks to drink
the "polluted" waters of Czech customs and speech.
Herder's description of the Slav children of nature
fitted the Slovak peasants better than the rising
Czech middle class. As happens among nationalists,
the Czech nationalist leaders showed little love or
understanding of the aspirations of the Slovak nationalists. Though the Czechs eagerly asserted their
folk-originality against the Germans, they could not
see any reason for the Slovaks to claim the same
rights against the Czechs. The disputes of the
1840's between Czechs and Slovaks ran counter to
"Slav solidarity." Since then they have disturbed for
a whole century the relations between these two
closely related Slav neighbors.

The year 1848 brought, as we shall see, the first
great manifestation of Pan-Slavism which the realistic and responsible Czech leaders of the 1840's
channeled into Austro-Slavism, aligning the Austrian
Slavs with the general Western movement of liberalism and political emancipation. Štúr from the beginning opposed this moderate trend. Disillusioned
with the failure of the 1848 Revolution, he turned

in his last years to a new mystical Pan-Slavism which
under the influence of Hegel abandoned the humanitarianism of the Enlightenment and the restraint of
Kantian criticism. The two books which he wrote in
the last year of his life anticipate much of the turgid
thought and style of the later Russian Pan-Slav literature. They were no longer written in Slovak. The
one which was published during Štúr's life was written in Czech, "On the National Songs and Tales of
the Slav Tribes" (*O národních písních a pověstech
plemen slovanských*, Prague, 1853) and was dedicated to Prince Michael Obrenović of Serbia. It
compared in a rather familiar way the "characters"
of the successive world historical nations and civilizations. The Hindus expressed themselves in architec-
ture, the Greeks in sculpture, the Romans in painting, the Germans in music, and the Slavs (he accepted the derivation of the word Slovan from *Slovo*,
the word, the logos) in the word, which is the highest and most human form of expression. In their folk
poetry and the folk tales the Slavs achieved the
harmony of man and nature, of spirit and matter,
and thereby pointed the way to the solution of mankind's problems.

He went further in his last book on "The Slavs
and the World of the Future," which he wrote in
German but which was published only fourteen years
after his death in a Russian translation.[n] There he
proclaimed the superiority of the Slavs over the other
nations, for they were young, vigorous, uncorrupted,
and full of the spirit of fraternity. They had protected the Occident against the eastern barbarians
and had saved European civilization in times of
danger. At present they were endangered from many
sides but the future was theirs, as soon as they would
unite and, as true Christians, put the common good
above individual interests. A great burden was laid
by history on the Slavs. Western civilization was dis-
integrating. The Occident was corrupt and lacked

faith. Its democracy led by necessity to communism
and chaos. In the service of base interests the arts
and sciences there were decaying. He criticized one
after the other of the Occidental peoples and found
everywhere spiritual stagnation, vain strife, and
egoistic ambition. As against this dying world the
Slavs alone could raise the banner of salvation by
their living faith and their unity. Only in Russia the
ruler and the nation, the church and the people, were
one body and one soul. For the future of the Slavs
he saw three possibilities: a Slav federation, which
he believed out of the question because the ruler of
Russia could not submit to equality with the other
members of the federation; Austro-Slavism, which
he rejected because he believed Austria doomed;
and finally the union of all Slavs with Russia, their
acceptance of the Greek Orthodox faith and of the
Russian language. Though he knew little of Russia,
where he had never been, and though he condemned
serfdom in Russia, he saw that country as the only
beacon in the darkness of Slav life.

In the difficult days for the Slovak nation under
the drive of Magyarization in the later part of the
nineteenth century, some Slovaks understandably
turned their hopes to a romantic Pan-Slavism. Svetozar Hurban-Vajanský (1847–1916), who lived
through these dark times, brought to his fellow-
Slovaks the comfort of Slav messianism.

I am proud, proud of being a Slav.
My beloved fatherland
Counts one hundred million inhabitants.
It commands half of the globe.
With the Slav language
You can travel in the four quarters of the Universe.
One of our brothers cultivates the palm tree,
Another contemplates the eternal ice,
The third ploughs the seas.
I am proud, proud of being a Slav.

From this Kollár-inspired phantasy of one great Slav nation and one Slav language,[n] some Slovaks, feeling abandoned in Hungary and their national existence threatened, may have drawn strength and faith in the indestructibility of the Slovak people and language.

In the year 1836 in which Kollár's "Slav Solidarity" and Šafařík's "Slav Antiquities" were prepared for publication, another epoch-making work began to appear, the History of Bohemia (*Geschichte von Böhmen*) by František Palacký (1798–1876). Palacký was born of a Protestant family on the border of Moravia and Slovakia: he studied, like Kollár, at the Lyceum of Pressburg, and wrote his first book together with Šafařík. In 1823 he settled in Prague where he devoted his life to scholarly research and to the education of his people. "From my early youth," he wrote in the preface to his History of Bohemia, "I have known no higher and more burning desire than to be of service to my beloved people with a faithful picture of its past, in which it should recognize itself as in a mirror and remember what it is in need of."[n] In his work, which covered only the period to 1526, the year of the union of Bohemia with Austria under the Habsburgs, Palacký found in the Czech Reformation the culmination and the meaning of Czech history, the decisive period beginning with Hus and rising to its most sublime flowering in the Bohemian Brethren.

For the early history of the Slavs, Palacký uncritically accepted Herder's point of view and construed Czech history as a struggle between the peace-loving, naturally democratic Slavs and the bellicose and aristocratic Germans. This legend was common to the Russian Slavophiles, the Polish messianists, and the Czechoslovak writers. The famous Königinhofer and Grünberger manuscripts produced by Hanka seemed to furnish historical proof for this welcome and complimentary picture of early Slav

civilization. But Palacký aimed at more than did the
other Slav historians. His lifework, different in that
respect from Kollár's and Šafařík's, was entirely centered upon the Czechs alone. He did not look back
to pre-history or the dawn of Slavdom. He dated the
Czech contribution to mankind from the late Middle
Ages, which he interpreted in the light of modern
movements and concepts. He underestimated the
medieval character of the Hussite movement and
had no understanding of the theological disputes
involved. He saw in it the beginning of modern
Europe, the first blow against the spiritual authoritarianism and the feudal structure of the Middle
Ages. According to him the Hussite Czechs pio-
neered the freedom of conscience and the equality
of men in Europe. Their struggle carried the germs
of the future growth of rationalism and liberalism
in the reformations and revolutions of Western
Europe. The Czechs were then in closest touch with
all the intellectual movements of Europe, their
level of education was higher than that in the surrounding countries, and serfdom had not yet been
fully established among them. Unfortunately, at
the end of the fifteenth century, serfdom was introduced in Bohemia and Hussitism itself tended to
turn into an oppressive orthodoxy. Whereas Bohemia
thus retrogressed, the seeds of the new humanism
which the Hussites had sown began to bear fruit in
the progress of the Occident. The Czechs had undertaken the great task of the liberation of the human
spirit too early. It was left for the Occident to carry
it on. Palacký's historical conception did not look to
Russia; it tried to integrate the Czechs and their
national awakening into the liberal tradition of
Western Europe, into the progressive movement
which had started with the Reformation and the
English Revolutions. He linked the question of
Czech freedom and Czech national development
with the progress of European liberalism. He inter-

preted their struggle against the Germans for national self-preservation as a fight for a liberal world and for a more humane relationship among peoples.

Palacký was neither a radical nor a democrat in the modern sense of the word. He possessed the sense of realistic moderation and responsibility, so rare at that time among the Slav leaders with their lack of middle-class tradition and political experience. In the middle of the last century he was convinced that the time of small states had passed and that mankind was being driven toward the creation of very large political and economic units. Therefore federalism became, besides liberalism, a dominant political idea of his life. A small people like the Czechs could exist only in union with others, not by power but on the strength of its intellectual and moral achievements. "Whenever we were victorious," he used to remind the Czechs, "it was always more the result of spiritual forces than of physical might, and whenever we succumbed, there was always the insufficiency of our spiritual activity and of our moral courage responsible for it." He did not see in political independence a panacea. The Czechs had had political independence and had lost it.[n] Even in his last years, when he had been deeply disappointed by the Austrian policy and by aggressive German chauvinism against the Czechs, Palacký wrote in an article, "The Russians and the Czechs," on June 2, 1873, to Franz Schuselka, the editor of the Viennese weekly *Reform*, that he could not differentiate between "the fortunately not numerous" Pan-Slav party in Russia and the German and Magyar fanatics: "for they all equally seek to absorb and to destroy our nationality. Should we, however, be forced no longer to be Czechs, then it will make no great difference to us whether we shall become Germans, Italians, Magyars or Russians." Palacký's son-in-law, František Ladislav Rieger (1818–1903), summed up in a speech in the Austrian Reichsrat in 1861 the historical conception of his father-in-law: "We Czechs have always been a people of individual liberty from the oldest times to the present. We can pride ourselves that our ancestors were the first to resist manfully the whole of Europe in a war for the freedom of conscience. Our ancestors started the Thirty Years War for the liberty of conscience and of the individual and for the defense of the constitution. . . . We know it best that our nationality and liberty are inseparable." [n]

Palacký, by temperament an aristocrat and scholar, entered the political life of his nation at the same time as Karel Havlíček (1821–56), who from his native place Borov on the Bohemian-Moravian border received his second name of Borovský. By temperament the younger man was a democrat and a journalist. But both men saw their task in the serious education of their people and both shared the same attitude of a warm patriotism and critical liberalism, an aversion to revolutionary phrases, to violence and to illusionist dreams. Havlíček was a Catholic and as a young man he studied for the priesthood. On March 15, 1849, he wrote to his mother: "I can become nothing else but a priest, I feel badly disposed and averse toward everything else (*vor allem anderen habe ich fast ein Unbehagen und Abscheu*)." But soon he left the seminary as a disappointed man and a Voltairian free-thinker. He intended to translate Robert de Lamennais' *Paroles d'un croyant* into Czech, but later on he made Church and priest the object of his satire.

Under Kollár's influence he grew enthusiastic about Slav solidarity and began to study the languages and literatures of the various Slav nations. But he was the only one of the Pan-Slav Czechs who was not satisfied with programs and proclamations. He wished to see for himself what Poland and Russia were like. Šafařík procured him a position as a tutor in the house of the famous Moscow Slavophile,

Michael Pogodin. When he came to Moscow, he found the position instead in the house of Professor Shevyrov, another Pan-Slav whose home was the center of the national literary movement in Russia. Havlíček had a better opportunity to study Russia and Poland than any other Czech writer of his generation. After his return he wrote a series of descriptive articles, "Pictures from Russia." He did not see in Russia a country which can and must spread its light abroad. On the contrary, he became convinced that Russia needs the light from abroad. This opinion shocked the then widespread sentimental Russophilism among the Czech intellectuals, as did the literary criticism with which Havlíček, and Belinsky in the same decade in Russia, subjected the well-meant but tasteless and sentimental writing of the period to serious critical standards for the first time.

He was hardly twenty-six when he became, at the beginning of 1846, editor of the official Czech newspaper, *Pražské Noviny* (Prague Newspaper), and of its literary supplement *Česká Včela* (The Czech Bee). Within two years he increased the number of its subscribers from 240 to 860, figures which testify to his journalistic talent—he was in many ways the greatest journalist not only of the Czechs but of 19th century Austria—as well as to the political and social picture of the last years before March, 1848. He was a relentless foe of all romantic phraseology, in politics and in literature. In Palacký and Havlíček the Czechs probably had at their disposal in the 1840's a leadership with a greater sense for reality, for sober facts and truthful restraint than that of any other continental people.

In a famous article "Slav and Czech" he dared to write ironically about the "sacred cause" of Slav solidarity. But he, and he alone, spoke out of experience. "I learned to know Poland and I did not like it. With a feeling of hostility and pride I left the Sarmatian country, and in the worst cold I

arrived in Moscow, being warmed mostly by the
Slav feeling in my heart. The freezing temperature in
Russia and other Russian aspects extinguished the
last spark of Pan-Slav love in me. So I returned to
Prague as a simple Czech, even with some secret
sour feeling against the name Slav which a sufficient
knowledge of Russia and Poland has made suspect
to me. Above all, I express my firm conviction that
the Slavs, that means the Russians, the Poles, the
Czechs, the Illyrians, etc., are not one nation. The
name Slav is and should forever remain a purely geographical and scientific name. Nationality is not only
determined by language, but also by customs, religion, form of government, state of education, sympathies, etc." With great political clearsightedness
he saw the obstacle to Pan-Slavism in the relationship between Russians, Ukrainians, and Poles.

Pan-Slavism among the Russians and Poles he
found to be merely a desire on the part of these
two nations to use the other Slavs for their own purposes. "I admit that I prefer the Magyars, who are
open enemies of the Czechs and Illyrians, to the
Russians who approach us with the Judas embrace—
to put us into their pockets. We are Czechs and we
wish to remain Czechs forever, and we do not wish
to become either Germans or Magyars or Russians,
and therefore we shall be cool to the Russians, if we
do not wish to be hostile to them." He called the
Czechs to sober work and self-reliance. Only between
them and the Illyrians could there develop a tie of
sympathy without becoming dangerous to one or the
other. Havlíček propounded the theory of Austro-
Slavism which was to become the official line of the
responsible Czech statesmen for the coming decade.
"The Austrian monarchy is the best guarantee for
the preservation of our and the Illyrian nationality,
and the greater the power of the Austrian Empire
will grow, the more secure will our nationalities
be." [n]

To these principles Havlíček remained faithful even after the events of March 1848 had swept away the censorship. In an editorial of March 19, 1848, he demanded the separation of Austria from Germany and its transformation into a federation within which the Czechs would enjoy administrative and linguistic autonomy. Soon he resigned from his position on the official paper and at the beginning of April he founded his own paper, the first modern Czech newspaper which he called *Narodní Noviny* (National Newspaper). But the stormy times did not allow him to devote himself entirely to his editorial task. With Palacký he had led the Czechs from the romantic sentimentalism of the beginning of their national rebirth to a realism which abhorred rash adventures and grandiose hopes.[n] It was due to their leadership that the Czechs remained, on the whole, free from those messianic dreams and claims which characterized some of the noblest and most prominent Poles and Russians and which gave to their Pan-Slavism a mystical fervor and the strength of a rapturous vision devoid of any support in the drab and mournful reality of their peoples.[n]

2

Romanticism and
Messianism
Among the Poles

THE RISE of the Czech nation from its first awakening in the period of the Enlightenment to 1848, and even beyond, has been slow and steady, progressing by measured steps and continuous effort. Its foremost moulders, men like Palacký and Havlíček, were humanists and realists who saw their task in educating and not in exciting the people. Even in the years preceding 1848, which everywhere on the Continent were filled with ecstatic visions and expectations, they kept a sense of perspective and did not exaggerate the role of their nation unduly. In the tradition of the Bohemian Brethren they understood the value of tolerance and the moral dangers inherent in the glorification of force and revolution. The French Revolution and the Napoleonic Wars hardly exercized any direct influence upon the Czech development. The case of the Poles was entirely different. For them the century from the Enlightenment to 1863 was full of dramatic events, of sudden turns, of fantastic hopes and of bitter disappointments. In the eighteenth century, Poland, and her disorder and backwardness, with her great airs and pretensions, had been an object of derision and pity for the West; the Constitution of May 3, 1791, the heroic struggle of Tadeusz Kościuszko, the ensuing catastrophe and the action of the Russian army under Count Alexander Vasilievich Suvarov with its accompanying horrors, aroused everywhere a deep sympathy for the Polish people and the Polish cause. They became, rather uncritically, the favorite of the progressive parties throughout Europe. In German and French as well as in other languages many poems celebrated the struggles and hopes of the unfortunate nation."

At the beginning of the nineteenth century Europe hardly paid any attention to the Czechs. The Poles, on the other hand, occupied an eminent place in the period of the French Revolution and the Napoleonic Wars. Polish volunteer legions, a forerunner of similar legions which were to play a great role in the nationalist movements in Poland and elsewhere, appeared first on the scene fighting with the French revolutionary armies. There, among exiles seeking their way home, the Polish national anthem was written, their Marseillaise, "Jeszcze Polska nie zginęła" which proclaimed that as long as we live and fight, Poland has not yet perished; though lost at home, it lived on in the *émigrés'* camps, in their hopes and dreams. For a while Napoleon seemed to build a firmer and more real existence for Poland. The re-establishment of a Polish state occupied a prominent place in his plans though it was always subordinated to the changing needs and moods of his policy and was not motivated by a sincere support of Poland's cause. The Duchy of Warsaw, which he created and on the throne of which he placed the King of Saxony, formed in continuation of the Confederation of the Rhine the eastward outpost of the French empire; its Illyrian provinces formed, in continuation of the Kingdom of Italy, its southeast outpost. Both were directed against Russia, the imperial competitor. The decisive campaign of Napoleon, the Emperor of the West, against Alexander I, the Emperor of the East, was fought for the control of the two bastions of Poland and Constantinople. During those years most Poles fervently supported Napoleon. France and Poland were then regarded, and again in the years from 1830 to 1870, as the two bulwarks of the Roman West, linked in the brotherhood of knightly nations fighting for liberty and civilization. Victor Hugo's words in the French Chamber of Lords on March 19, 1846, when the fate of the Republic of Cracow was discussed, expressed a widespread feeling: "Two nations among all others have for four centuries played a disinterested role in European civilization: these two nations are France and Poland: France dispelled darkness, Poland repelled barbarism; France spread ideas, Poland covered frontiers. The French people has been civilization's missionary in Europe; the Polish people, its knight." [n] In many Polish ears of that time, the French romantic poet understated the Polish case. For the Poles regarded themselves by then as much more than Europe's knights.

Though the Congress of Vienna in 1815 recognized the principle of Polish nationality and the justice of its demands and created the autonomous Kingdom of Poland with a liberal constitution in loose union with Russia and the Republic of Cracow, [n] the disappointment in Napoleon came as a great shock to the Poles. Among many of them it aroused the consciousness of their Slavdom. Disillusioned by the West, they turned to the new gospel of Slav affinity and reciprocity. Many Poles of that period were willing to accept a Pan-Slav confederation under Russian leadership. The teachings of Herder, the influence of romanticism and the new philology, [n] the need for security and the lure of great aspirations, promoted the expectation that Poland and Russia, as the two principal Slav nations, could by united strength inaugurate the new Slav period of universal civilization. But other Poles, and their number grew rapidly with the stiffening of the Russian policy toward Poland after 1825, saw the Catholic Poles as the leaders of the Western Slavs against Russia—often regarded as a non-European and even a non-Slav power—or extolled Poland as the true Slav people and at the same time the true Christian people, the savior of Europe and civilization.

This Polish Slav mission became more pronounced as Poland's situation worsened and seemed to grow desperate. The formerly great power which originated in the union of the culturally more advanced Poland with the mighty Lithuanian and Ruthenian land under the Lithuanian dynasty of Jagiello as a pre-nationalist aristocratic commonwealth began in the eighteenth century to face grave threats to its existence. Without any natural frontiers, it found itself in the way of the expansionist drives of two rising and relatively modernized great powers, Russia and Prussia. In the nineteenth century, when nationalism and democracy destroyed the foundations of the old Polish commonwealth, when the Lithuanian and Ruthenian peasants awakened, like the Poles themselves, to national consciousness, the Poles, similar therein to the German nationalists, continued to regard themselves as mandated by history with a civilizing mission in the vast expanses of the East. They insisted on the restoration of the historical boundaries of the pre-nationalist commonwealth as a Polish national state in the age of nationalism. This romantic nationalism based on the veneration of a past without foundation in the present, and the consciousness of grave threats by power pressure from without and centrifugal forces from within, prepared the soil for the Polish messianic Slavism with its metaphysical dreamlands, its poetical grandiloquence, and its noble delusions. In their attitude the Polish messianists resembled most closely the Russian Slav-

ophiles of the same period. Men of great gifts and
high purpose, they burned with a similar religious
fervor put into the service of nationalist exaltation.
They read into history a universal mission mystically
and gloriously centered in their own nationality.[21]
This messianic Slav poetry and theurgy did not
sound strange in the Europe of the 1830's and 1840's,
the Europe of Schelling and Baader, Enfantin and
Lamennais, Michelet and Mazzini.[22]

After the collapse of the hopes of a Poland restored by Napoleon I, one of the greatest men of
the generation of the Enlightenment in Poland,
Stanisław Staszic (1775–1826), turned to the Slavs
and to Russia. An eighteenth-century Catholic priest
whose concern for social reform and scientific progress made him an outstanding civilizing influence in
Poland, he became the leader of the newly founded
Warsaw Society of Friends of Science (*Towarzystwo
przyjaciół nauk*). There he read in August 1815 a
paper, "Thoughts on the Political Equilibrium in
Europe" (*Myśli o rownowadze politycznei w Eu-
ropie*). He greeted Alexander I and pleaded for a
union of the Slavs in the great Russian empire on a
footing of brotherly equality. Such a union of the
Slavs would lead by necessity to a federation of
Europe, make wars there impossible and thus assure
the permanent peace of the continent. Federation
and union were, according to Staszic, a law of
nature; the Romance or Germanic peoples did not
feel sufficiently close to each other to point the road
to federation. Only the Slavs, especially the Poles
and the Russians, were able to fulfill the task,
though the Germans, whom Staszic always dis-
trusted, would try to hinder them. The Romance
nations were undermined by the struggle which
originated in the separation of the state from the
church; the Germans were demoralized by their
sectarianism and their "indomitable spirit of conquest and lust for cruelty," only the Slav nations

under Russia's political leadership—based upon the inexhaustible power shown by Russia in the "Slavic war of 1812"—and, as Staszic hoped, under Polish cultural guidance, could bring about the new age in history. Abandoned by the West whose ally Poland had wished to be, Poland, adapting itself to the reality of the situation, was willing to share with Russia the Slav leadership of Europe. Staszic and the other writers of the period proclaimed "a peculiar imperialism, the moral imperialism of a defeated nation which abdicated nothing. It prepared itself for new conquests, but in the cultural field. It believed that it could realize them thanks to the alliance with the Slavic Russia of Alexander." [n]

This faith in Russian-Polish leadership of Europe was also shared by a man who, twenty years younger than Staszic, had come under the influence of German idealist philosophy. Josef Marie Hoene-Wroński (1778–1853), a philosopher and mathematician who lived most of his mature life in Paris, wished to place all human knowledge on infallible foundations. He called his own system messianism or the absolute and, therefore, final reform of human knowledge. He was not a mystic but a disciple of Kant and of the post-Kantian German philosophy. "You, noble Germans," he wrote, "were the first to see the dawn of our rebirth; therefore we expect above all from you who can be at present the most enlightened judges, the evaluation of those truths which we have found following the way which you have opened up. Only don't depart from the road of reason on which you have set out and which has led you to your present superiority: reason alone and not blood can assure the triumph of the human race." Like Staszic, Hoene believed in a federation or league of nations and in the realization of this idea through the Slavs under Russian leadership. While France represented the rights of men, the revolution, Russia was the bulwark of divine right. Europe was in a critical stage of disintegration and would be helped by the Slavs who had saved mankind from two great enemies of civilization, Islam and Jacobinism. France had realized only the ideals of state and had thus arrived at the autocracy of the people; Germany had realized only the ideals of church and had arrived at the infallibility of reason. The Slavs would by their action realize the absolute philosophy, expressed by a Slav (Hoene himself), and would by the union of state and church, of reason and faith, also solve the social antinomy. Hoene was not a Pan-Slav in the revolutionary-universalist sense. He was as much opposed to the "anarchy" of revolution as to the despotism of a "universal monarchy." In 1848 he called upon the Slavs not to overthrow their governments. He warned the Poles against an insurrection: "Do you believe that even if all nations would unite against Russia, it could be defeated? Never: it would resist as it resisted Napoleon who carried the whole of Europe with him." [n]

Like Hoene, other Polish philosophers and historians of that time put their thought and scholarship at the service of the Polish and the Slav cause. Count August Cieszkowski (1814–94), a disciple of Hegel, corrected Hegel's philosophy of history by combining it with the teaching of Herder and of Saint-Simon. He could not regard the Prussian monarchy of Hegel's time which coincided with a partitioned and enslaved Poland as the fulfilment of history. What Hegel regarded as the last rational stage of history, Cieszkowski saw only as the second stage. The first stage was antiquity, the age of affirmation and sensuality; the second stage was the present, the age of Christianity, of negation and spirituality. The third period in the future would bring the harmony of the sensual and the spiritual life, the age of the Paraclete, the Comforter or Holy Spirit. The idea of the opposition between the ancient world of joy and the senses and the Christian world of the mortification of the flesh and of pure spirituality was common in the nineteenth century. Saint-Simon, Heine, and Ibsen expressed it, and Ibsen's "The Emperor and the Galilean" predicted a third epoch of synthesis. All of them go back to the prophetic vision of the Italian mystic Joachim of Floris who at the end of the twelfth century in his *Expositio in Apocalypsin* divided the history of mankind into the past age of the Father, the present age of the Son, and the future age of the Holy Spirit. But Cieszkowski identified this third age, and Kingdom of God on earth, with the reign of the Slavs who are called upon to transform Christian love of the individual into a political reality. "The fraternity of the peoples will become the law of the future, as the fraternity of men was the law of Christianity which led to liberty and equality." The Slavs are called to this creation of a Christian brotherhood of nations, the true realization of liberty, because they are fundamentally peace-loving and freedom-loving. Among the nations they represent the lowest group, the proletariat as it were, and by their rise therefore a new era of social justice will dawn."

This messianic conception was shared by the third great Polish philosopher of the period, Bronislaw Trentowski (1808–69). After having fought in the uprising of 1831, he studied and taught philosophy at the University of Freiburg i.B. and later settled in the then Prussian city of Posen. His Pan-Slavism was also based on Poland's co-operation with Russia but with a liberal and revolutionary Russia. In a series of lectures which he delivered in Cracow in 1848, published as *Przedburza Polityczna* and which are typical of the mood of that year, he expressed the wish to be in the Tsar's place: "If I were Tsar today, then I would form a free and happy Pan-Slav empire. I would first renew an independent Poland and by showing the most sincere justice to it as my conscience and God order, I would win the hearts of the Czechs, the Serbs, the Illyrians, all the southern Slavs. As they hate the Tsar, so they would love me. . . . I would kindle in them an enthusiasm as it has never been seen on earth before; I would subject them without having used military force or money for that purpose. . . . Everywhere I would plant the banner of liberty. I would destroy without effort the Turkish and the Austrian empires, for the Slavs would upon my call rush into battle in greatest numbers, inflamed by patriotic enthusiasm, and would fight like lions. I would drive the Turks back deep into Asia whence they once came, and I would write with bloody letters on the heads of the Germans where their frontiers are. All this I would have to do as a Slav, and also out of consideration for the political and immediate inevitability that France would become the great liberator of the Slavs from the German-Turkish yoke if Russia does not act."

Mankind, Trentowski proclaimed, was entering a new age in 1848. The Congress of the Monarchs which divided the spoils of Europe and founded the Holy Alliance, would be replaced by the Congress of the Peoples. He called upon the Poles to regard their patriotism in the new light of democracy, of a universal liberty and equality of the peoples. The new principles will bring to the Poles a free fatherland, though not along the old historical frontiers. "Our judgment tells us that we should rather follow a new principle and should seek our rebirth with its help than that we should cling stubbornly to the past." For the Slavs are called to help build the future. "Your history," he told the Slavs, "will start simultaneously with the third era of world history." Ancient history was determined by the Romans; the Middle Ages, which are now coming to their end, were determined by the Germans; the Slavs will determine the future."

A similar democratic note was sounded by the

greatest Polish historian of the period, Joachim
Lelewel (1786–1861), who had been professor at
Wilna and Warsaw and after 1831 lived in exile for
many years in Brussels. In his *Considération sur l'état
politique de l'ancienne Pologne et sur l'histoire de
son peuple* (Lille, 1844), he found under the influence of Rousseau and Herder in the early past of
the Slav village commune of Poland the ideal of
true liberty and equality. Poland began to decay
when alien ideas and social injustices were introduced by the feudal aristocracy and the Catholic
hierarchy. They undermined the true Slav character
of Poland which the reforms of the late eighteenth
century tried to re-establish but which can come into
its own only in a peasant democracy. Such a new
order would place Poland at the head of the Slav
nations. In his harking back to the illusionary idyll of
early Slavdom and in his rejection of feudalism and
serfdom, in his moralistic earnestness and in his
devotion to the national cause, Lelewel resembled
Palacký. But though Lelewel and his generation had
a great faith in the Western peoples, in the collaboration of free peoples for the liberation of
Poland, he did not integrate the history and the
future of Poland with the liberalism of the West as
Palacký did.

Lelewel's teachings were highly influential among
the Polish democrats in exile. In an appeal sent out
in 1832 to the Russian people for a common revolutionary action it was said that "the voice of enslaved
Slavdom which groans under the yoke also calls you
Russians. The German sovereigns and your autocrat
have united to subdue the Slavs. The Pole willingly
stretches his brotherly hand to the other Slavs and
with all his heart helps other Slavs to regain liberty."
The Polish Democratic Society fused at its foundation in 1832 the nationalist faith in the people with
the social message of land for the peasant. But
though it stressed the necessity of breaking with the

past, it insisted on the historical frontiers of Poland, one of the most debatable legacies of the aristocratic past. It rejected equally the Polish frontiers established by modern diplomacy and those set by ethnography, by the national will and the language of the awakening peasant peoples. It demanded that Poland be restored from sea to sea, from the Baltic to the Black Sea. Yet these democrats were convinced that once monarchs and cabinets were removed from the scene, national disputes formerly instigated by these evil forces, would disappear without leaving a trace and would be replaced by the sincere fraternization and collaboration of the nations. "Renascent Poland must propagate the democratic idea among the Slavs and must give the signal for the general emancipation of the European peoples. . . . Poland has preserved all the simplicity of its primitive virtues, it possesses rectitude and devotion; through them and through its religious sentiments, Poland is superior to Western Europe." Such a lack of realism and self-criticism animated the famous manifesto of 1839 of the Polish Democratic Society."

In November, 1830, the youth in Warsaw, students and young officers, under the influence of the example set by France and Belgium, raised the banner of revolt with the slogan "For your liberty and ours," words attributed to Joachim Lelewel. In spite of individual heroism, the revolt, badly led and unsupported by the people, collapsed. The vicissitudes of the struggle were followed with greatest sympathy all over Europe, especially in France. The Poles seemed to fight for the liberty of Europe against the self-appointed gendarme of reaction. In its defeat Poland was represented as a sacrificial victim for the cause of revolution: the Poles in 1794 had saved by their struggle and partition the French Revolution from the concerted action of the monarchs; now

they had again prevented Nicholas I from marching
against Belgium and suppressing the Revolution.
The French Catholic revolutionary newspaper
L'Avenir, the organ of Lamennais and Montalembert, wrote on June 9, 1831: "[The Polish] blood
flows for France, it flows for Christ and for Liberty.
. . . Poland has risen entirely alone, she has been
victorious entirely alone; God has proven to her
against all hope that she has received a mission from
Him."

After the fall of Warsaw, Lamennais wrote in the
issue of September 17, 1831: "Heroic people, people
of our love, rest in peace in the tomb which the
crime of some and the cowardice of others have dug
for you. But don't forget: that tomb is not void of
hope, it is surmounted by a cross, a prophetic cross
which announces: you will be reborn." [n] Some of
the most determined fighters for Poland's liberty
went into exile to France, where a preceding generation had once before formed legions for Poland's
liberation and where the fire of revolution seemed
to burn brightest. On their way from Poland to
Paris the exiles were greeted everywhere with sympathy. But soon the tragedy of their position became
apparent. The hope of returning to a reborn fatherland vanished fast. The political and intellectual life
in Poland came to a standstill. The nation lost not
only its constitution; no visible symbol of national
life and unity, no living center of loyalty existed to
serve as the basis of patriotism. In these difficult
times it was the exalted lyricism of three great
poets living in exile far away from Poland and
without any expectation of seeing it again, in whom
the national life and hope took refuge.

In the last months of the uprising of 1831, in an
address for the anniversary of the Constitution of
May 3, given before the Warsaw Society of Friends
of Science, Kazimierz Brodziński (1791–1835), a
mediocre poet and professor of Polish literature,

defined the essence of Polish nationality:[n] "A nation is an inborn idea which those whom it unites strive to realize. It is a family which has its own events and its mission. Is it not also like a man whom his desires, his imagination, his sentiment drive on? The setbacks of its destiny form its character. God wished to have the nations as separate individualties, like human beings, in order that they might be his instruments to influence the whole of mankind and to establish the necessary harmony of the world. . . . The difference between a nation and a man lies in the fact that man can die for the nation but the nation cannot die for mankind as long as it preserves its consciousness and feels itself a nation. Moreover, in a mature nation every man will be ready to sacrifice his life in order that his nation live for mankind. . . . Formerly each nation regarded itself as the goal and center of everything in the same way as the earth was regarded as the center of the universe. . . . Copernicus discovered the system of the material universe; the Polish nation alone (I say it boldly and with a patriotic pride) could have a foreboding of the true movement of the moral universe. It has recognized that every nation is a fragment of the whole and must roll on its orbit and around the center like the planets around theirs. Each one among them constitutes a coherent and necessary core and equilibrium of forces; only a blind egoism refuses to see it. The Polish nation, I declare, is through an inspiration from Heaven the philosopher, the Copernicus of the moral world. Misunderstood, persecuted, the Polish nation will continue its existence, it will find men who will profess its faith, and its crown of thorns will be changed into a crown of victory and national glory. . . . The idea of the Polish nation has been to develop under the sun of religion the tree of liberty and fraternity; to measure the rights of throne and people in the scales of a balance the beam of which stood fast in heaven itself; to grow in itself, according to the favorable hours which time brought, to become able to collaborate in the work of mankind. Its mission has been to stand guard in the midst of storms on the frontier which divides barbarism and civilization. Its miraculous predestination is to rise from its tomb to proclaim the attempt perpetrated against the liberty of the peoples, to serve them as a warning by testifying to the crime accomplished against it."

Brodziński presented Poland as Christ's most faithful disciple. After the national catastrophe, Adam Mickiewicz (1789–1855) in an effort to justify the nation's fate saw Poland crucified as the "Christ of the nations." It is noteworthy that the sublime flowering of Polish poetry occurred among exiles, at a time when the political existence of the nation seemed extinguished. Mickiewicz himself, the greatest poet of Poland and undoubtedly one of the outstanding poetical talents of all times, was born in Lithuania as a member of the Polonized lesser nobility. He spent his first twenty-five years there, and never lived in Poland, never saw Warsaw or Cracow. His two great epic poems "Grażyna" and "Konrad Wallenrod" present patriotic scenes and events from the Lithuanian, not the Polish, past. His greatest masterpiece "Pan Tadeusz" glorifies the Lithuanian landscape and the Byelorussian people. It begins "Lithuania, my fatherland, (Litwo, ojczyzno moja!) you are like health . . ." As a student at the University of Wilna which, then under the patronage of Prince Adam Czartoryski, numbered many prominent teachers, he participated in the secret patriotic and literary youth movements of the period. In 1824 some of the leading members of these conspiratorial societies were, not without justification, arrested by the Russian government. The sentences meted out to them were relatively lenient. Mickiewicz himself was expelled to Russia where he was treated kindly and graciously and lived until 1829. A few years later

he likened the persecution of the Wilna students by
Alexander I to Herod's massacre of innocents,
though with all its lawlessness and brutality the
Tsarist policy hardly lived up to this description.[n]
When he left Russia, in his thirtieth year, he was
already famous as a poet.

The next two years he spent in Italy where his
Catholic faith underwent a fervent revival. He did
not participate in the uprising of 1831. His friend
Stefan Garczyński (1805–33), who fought valiantly
during the struggle, wrote while Warsaw was bom-
barded: "O my nation! As the Saviour's head for
ever impressed its bloody image upon a veil, so
wilt thou, my nation, stamp the bloody image of
thy fate upon the whole of this generation. Thou
wilt throw this generation into the face of Europe
as if it were Veronica's veil, and the history of thy
suffering will be read on it. The time will come, O
nations of Europe, when your eyes and thoughts will
be fixed as by enchantment on the bloody image of
the crucified nation." The author of these pathetic
words joined Mickiewicz in Dresden in 1832. There
under the impress of the fate of the martyred nation and of his own hesitation to rush to its help
while the fighting was still going on, Mickiewicz
composed the grandiose dramatic poem which he
called *Dziady* (Forefathers' Eve, Part III). He based
it on his own personal experiences in Wilna and his
exile to Russia but he treated this theme "with such
unique power that he made his poem the finest expression in literature of the agelong antipathy between Russia and Poland and of the agony of
Poland's martyrdom." It did not reflect the realistic
truth about his own experiences; it was the result of
a patriotic transformation, of a deep shock suffered
by the poet. It is a poem "that boils and seethes with
hatred for Russia. He holds up to scorn the Russian
national character, and at the close of the poem
states that while in Russia, 'crawling like a snake,'

he 'duped the despot.' In this work he gives the most powerful literary expression that exists of the loathing felt by the Poles for their Russian oppressors." [n]

In the supreme scene of Forefathers' Eve, Part III, Father Peter in his cell has a mystic vision, seeing the Polish nation upon the cross:

The cross has arms that shadow all of Europe
Made of three withered peoples, like dead trees.
Now is my nation on the Martyr's throne.

On a less exalted level, Poland stood for self-sacrifice on behalf of universal liberty and equality. Opposed to it was Russia which stood not only for passive despotism but for "Tsarism," a new, active, propagandizing force. The theme of Poland's martyrdom and mission was taken up by Mickiewicz after he had moved to Paris, in a pseudobiblical prose work, showing the influence of the Hebrew prophets, of apocalyptic literature and of modern mystics like Jacob Böhme and Saint Martin, "The Books of the Polish Nation and of the Polish Pilgrims" (*Księgi Narodu polskiego i pielgrzymstwa polskiego*). In it Mickiewicz presented a brief picture of Polish history in the setting of a treacherous and idolatrous world. Poland was murdered because it was wholly devoted to the liberty and brotherhood of all peoples, an ideal which the other nations could not stand. But martyred Poland will rise again. "And as after the resurrection of Christ blood sacrifices ceased in all the world, so after the resurrection of the Polish nation wars shall cease in all Christendom. . . . Meanwhile, the Pole is called a pilgrim; and since he hath made a vow to journey to the holy land, the free country, he has vowed to journey until he shall find it."

In 1834, when he was only thirty-five years old and had twenty more years ahead, the greatest poet of the Polish language ceased writing poetry. The same mysticism which had inspired his last poems (with the exception of *Pan Tadeusz*, his greatest work) characterized his later activities. Teacher, journalist, organizer and devotee of a new cult, Mickiewicz was in all these activities an indefatigable propagandist of the one cause to which he dedicated his life. In 1840 he was appointed to the Collège de France as the first occupant of the newly created chair for Slav literature. At the end of the same year Andrzej Towiański (1799–1878), a man only a few days younger than Mickiewicz, arrived in Paris from Lithuania. It was the time when Napoleon's body was brought home from St. Helena to be put at rest in the beautiful tomb of the Invalides in order to satisfy the craving of the generation for legendary greatness. Towiański regarded Napoleon as God's envoy sent to establish social justice on earth and himself as his successor. Thanks to Napoleon, the hero of the Revolution, the French had become the second Israel and carried on the mission of world leadership along the road traced by God. The Slavs, however, were to fulfil the mission and thus to become the third Israel. Mickiewicz was quickly converted into a faithful follower of Towiański, of his mystical Christianity and of his Napoleonic enthusiasm. He accepted his fantastic religious dogma built upon the three-fold foundation of Catholic mysticism, Polish messianism, and Napoleonic revolutionism. In Towiański he saw the redeemer and comforter whose coming he had announced in the vision of *Forefathers' Eve*. (At the time when he wrote the scene he in all probability referred to himself as the coming man; it shows Mickiewicz' true devotion that he willingly subordinated himself to the new claimant). In 1849, when Mickiewicz edited the short-lived newspaper *La Tribune des Peuples*, in which he upheld the principles of the 1848 Revolution and his faith in Louis Napoleon— a faith to which he clung even after the coup of 1851—he wrote: "The political welfare of France as well as that of her sister nations, depends on the union of the Napoleonic idea with the socialist idea. . . . The Napoleonic idea must be understood as the personification of the French principle in its conflict with the Russian principle: both principles tend to spread throughout Europe."

In his lectures at the Collège de France, Mickiewicz expressed many views closely resembling those of the Russian Slavophiles. Alexander Herzen wrote of him on February 12, 1844: "Mickiewicz is a Slavophile, like Khomyakov and Co., with the sole difference that he is a Pole and not a Russian, that he lives in Europe and not in Moscow, that he talks not about Russia alone but also about Czechs, Illyrians, etc." [n] According to Mickiewicz the Slavs were not materialistic as Europe then appeared to him to be. Deriving the word "Slav" from "Slovo," the word, the Slavs were apparently for this etymological reason endowed with a special inspiration, with the gift of the tongue. "The whole of the Slav race has hardly any earthly possessions; it rests all its hopes in God, and this is the reason why it is chosen to receive the new revelation first." Among the Slavs, the Poles were superior to the Russians for historical causes: the Russian under attack from Asia had to sacrifice everything to a centralized and despotic power while Poland could develop liberty for the individual. Both, however, being Slav were capable of self-sacrifice and devotion to the spiritual world. "We have said," Mickiewicz lectured on February 21, 1843, "that the fundamental dogma upon which rested Slavic nationality in general and Polish nationality in particular was the belief in the uninterrupted influence of the invisible world upon the visible world; and . . . we have been careful to test our opinion against historical evidence, and to show the progress of this idea as it demonstrates itself also in Slavic poetry and philosophy." After quoting a passage from Emerson's lecture on "Man the Re-

former," in which the New England philosopher
told his fellow-Americans "that our life, as we lead
it, is common and mean," that the Americans are no
longer open to divine illumination or walk elevated
by intercourse with the spiritual world, Mickiewicz
went on contrasting the Slavs with the West: "If
that is the manner in which the American people
are addressed, people whom Emerson himself ac-
cuses of lacking the two necessary virtues, hope and
charity, what should be the language of politicians
and philosophers who address themselves to the
Slavic people, to whom no one will dare deny these
virtues, charity and hope? . . . What a responsibility
would it not be to speak to this people which has
preserved intact its faith, its great national traditions,
and a feeling of humanity so pure and so exquisite,
while avoiding mention of God, religion, and
charity?"

In his lecture of March 14, 1843, Mickiewicz rejected in the typical Slavophile way, the Westernization of the Slavs. "All those who have written about
the reform of the Slavic peoples express the wish to
Europeanize them. They wish first of all to civilize
them, that is, to make them merchants, shopkeepers,
industrialists, to make them English, German, or
French, to strip them of their Slavic characteristics."
Such an attempt appeared to Mickiewicz as a sac-
rilege. From this point of view it is understandable
that Mickiewicz criticized the Czechs. He rejected
the Russian orientation among them as much as
the Austro-Slavic. He advised them to follow the
romantic slogan, "Measure your strength according
to your intentions, not your intentions according to
your strength," to emancipate themselves from their
intellectual dependence on material forces, to lean
toward the emotional view of revolution held by
the Poles, and to fight their way toward a completely
national school of thought, entirely free of foreign
influences.[n] When Mickiewicz on March 19, 1848,

met his fellow poet Zygmunt Krasiński, he shocked the anti-revolutionary and pro-Western aristocrat by declaring himself for an anti-Western and anti-Latin federation of the Slav peasant peoples.[n]

In 1844 Mickiewicz who had turned his lectures more and more into propaganda for Towiański's messianism was removed from his chair. In his last lecture he called upon Napoleon's spirit: "Holy Master! Thou art present at this our last supper. Accept our solemn promise that we shall do our utmost to be faithful to thy inspiration." The French government, facing an impossible situation, acted with the greatest consideration. The new occupant of the chair, Cyprien Robert, was a friend of the Polish cause and of the Slavs in general. Mickiewicz continued to draw half of his salary. Family troubles caused his temporary withdrawal from public life, but two great events in Slav history which coincided with general European crises rekindled his energy. In 1848, when the Polish cause after the defeat of the uprising in Posen and Cracow two years before seemed hopeless, Mickiewicz organized a Polish legion in Italy to fight at the side of the Italians against the Habsburgs and the Russians. Margaret Fuller, who was then in Italy, reported from Rome in a Letter of April 19, 1848, to the *New York Daily Tribune*, a speech by Mickiewicz, the "Dante of Poland," to the people of Florence: "The glory of Poland, its only glory truly Christian, is to have suffered more than all the nations. . . . Conquered Poland, abandoned by the governments and the nations, lay in agony on her solitary Golgotha. She was believed slain, dead, buried. . . . There came a moment in which the world doubted of the mercy and justice of the Omnipotent . . . But God is just . . . Very soon will be heard the voice of Poland. Poland will rise again. Poland will call to life all the Slavonic races—the Croats, the Dalmatians, the Bohemians, the Moravians, the Illyrians. These will form the bulwark against the tyrant of the North. They will close forever the way against the barbarians of the North—destroyers of liberty and civilization. Poland is called to do more yet: Poland, as a crucified nation, is risen again, and called to serve her sister nations. The will of God is that Christianity should become in Poland, and through Poland elsewhere, no more a dead letter of the law, but the living law of states and civil associations; that Christianity should be manifested by acts, the sacrifices of generosity and liberality." [n]

In these words Mickiewicz summed up the essence of his messianism which, couched in the enthusiastic verbiage of the period, expressed a deeply ethical attitude. The concrete Slav program proclaimed by him in 1848, the unity of the Western Slavs against Russia, corresponded to the views of many of his French and Italian friends. It differed fundamentally from the Austro-Slavism of the Czech leaders Palacký and Havlíček. They started from the existing reality, and wished without destroying it, to transform Austria into a bulwark against Russian and German expansion, without, however, any intent of destroying these states either. Mickiewicz and his friends dreamt of a Slav federation which could be achieved only through the destruction, or at the expense, of Austria, Russia, and Germany. The Poles thought of such a co-operation of the Slavs under Polish leadership, and primarily for the sake of Poland's restoration. The French and Italian liberals envisaged it under Western leadership, fearing that otherwise Russia would unite the Slavs. Mazzini addressing the Slavs demanded that Italy take the initiative: "We who have ourselves arisen in the name of our national right, believe in your right, and offer to help you to win it. But the purpose of our mission is the permanent and peaceful organization of Europe. We cannot allow Russian Tsarism—a perennial menace to Europe—to step into the place now oc-

cupied by your masters, and no partial movement
executed by a simple element amongst you can be
victorious; nor, even were victory possible, could it
constitute a strong barrier against the avidity of the
Tsar: it would simply further his plans of aggrandizement. Unite, therefore; forget past rancor, and unite
in one confederation; let Constantinople be your
amphictyonic city, the center of your federative
power, free to all and servant to none." [n]

There is, with all due regard to fundamental difference, a great similarity between these two fervent
religious patriots living in exile and trusting in the
moral forces of their nation for its rebirth. Mazzini's
famous slogans, "God and the People" and
"Thought and Action," could have been expressed as
well by Mickiewicz. Of the two, the Pole was by far
the greater poet and writer; his religious faith had a
depth inaccessible to Mazzini; his nation was suffering infinitely more than the Italians. But both
shared the uncritical devotion to the nationalist
myth of the people, Mazzini to the workers of Italy,
Mickiewicz to the Slav peasants of Poland. Both
lived remote from the reality of their countries and
both were ready to stir them through revolutionary
action. When the Crimean War seemed to inaugurate the great battle between the free West and
Russia, Mickiewicz hurried to Constantinople to
organize there a Polish legion to fight side by side
with the Turks. Before he had to face failure on that
occasion as he had seven years before, he died of
cholera in 1855 in the city which played such a great
role in Slav thought.

In the age of nationalism, beginning with the 17th
century English Puritans, many writers and poets
have transferred the messianic hopes of the ancient
Hebrews to their own people and their own time. [n]
Mazzini himself was not free of it in his glorification
of "Rome of the People." Nowhere, however, has
this messianic expectation been raised to such a

fundamental system as with the Russian Slavophiles
and the Polish messianists. The faith in the trans-
figuration of history, in the approach of an age of
love and justice, through the Slavs as the God-bear-
ing people of the new era of mankind, was common to both. The Russians based it on the Greek
Orthodox Church and the superiority of Byzantium,
the Poles on the Catholic Church and the Roman
tradition. Mickiewicz himself, whose mother was
probably and whose wife was certainly of Jewish
descent, was the only one who tied the Slav messianism with Israel. Poland within her historical
frontiers counted many more Jews than any other
land. "It is not without reason," he declared in his
lectures, "that the people of Israel has chosen Poland
as its fatherland. The most spiritual people on earth,
capable of understanding what is most sublime in
mankind, but arrested in its development, powerless
to accomplish its destiny, a degraded people, it has
nevertheless not ceased to hope for the coming of
the Messiah: this expectation was probably not without influence on the character of Polish messianism.
These two questions are tied together." [n]

However, Mickiewicz was a Christian: for him
the Messiah had come but not yet the messianic
age because the Gospel received by individuals had
not yet entered the life of nations. The Christian
revelation in the new age must reveal itself in these
new instruments of the historical period. Saint Joan
was a forerunner of this new order, a servant of God
and a servant of the nation. "One begins today to
feel generally that after the individuals who have
revealed great truths in the world, the nations are
called to receive them and to use all their strength
to realize them, that the nations must act now as
the individuals did in former times. You understand
which are the nations upon which we can base our
philosophic hopes: these are the nations who act
and suffer for the truth. . . . You will also recog-

nize why the Polish nation is nearer to the truth
than any other Slav people, because the revelation
of Jesus Christ will be always the measure of all
those who follow him, because there is only one way
to truth: it will always be the way of the cross. You
know which is the nation that for a long time now
has walked this *via dolorosa*. . . . I said that the
spirit of Christianity preferentially works through
certain peoples of Europe, that it has entered their
historical life, has fused with their folk spirit and
has become really the national spirit. Such a nation
is France, such a nation is Poland and several other
Slav peoples. Each progress of Christianity involves
national progress." [n] "The Slav nationality has received a special mission; through it, it exercises a
magic influence on the souls and draws them toward
truth and toward God." The Slav race—Mickiewicz
uses the words "nationality" and "race" indiscrimi-
nately—leads mankind toward the universal goal of
realizing Christianity in the life of the nations.[n]

Most of the time when Mickiewicz spoke of the
Slavs, he really meant the Poles. His expectations
were shared by the two other great Polish poets of
the period, Juljusz Słowacki (1809–49) and Zygmunt
Krasiński (1812–59), men different in background
and in character. Słowacki grew up in Wilna where
his father, Euzebjusz Słowacki, who died when the
son was only five years old, was professor at the
University. After 1831 he lived in exile and joined
there for a short time the enthusiastic followers of
Towiański. Krasiński, the scion of two of the leading
families of Polish nobility, was more conservative in
his religion and a lover of the aristocratic traditions.
His father, Wincenty Count Krasiński, originally
a general in Napoleon's army, later became a loyal
officer in the Tsar's service and caused a tragic conflict in his son who was torn between love for his
father and his own ardent Polish and anti-Russian
patriotism. Thus he left early for a voluntary exile;

with his family name a reproach to many Poles, he
signed his works "the anonymous poet of Poland."
Krasiński's hopes for the realization of Christianity
as the law of nations were similar to those of Mickiewicz; both saw Poland as the nation to bring about
this transformation. In his "On the Position of
Poland in the View of God and Man" (*O stano-
wisku Polski z Bożych i ludzkich względow*, 1841)
Krasiński showed that Poland's past predestined her
to be the Messiah nation which would lead mankind
to a higher ethical life. The Poles alone combined
"a great love for a celestial religion with love for
terrestrial freedom"; they were a chivalrous nation
which defended the oppressed and increased its land
not by conquest but by agreement. Poland's suffering, her sojourn, as it were, in purgatory, qualified
her to rise to a more perfect, more Christian life.
While the Latin nations were too much interested
in outward matters, in society and in politics, the
Germans concentrated on the inward man, the
individual and philosophy; the Slavs alone combined
the outer and inner life, a dedication to the freedom
of the individual with devotion to the common good.
These thoughts were in no way new. Krasiński
shared them with Staszic and Hoene, with Mickiewicz and the Russian Slavophiles, but Krasiński regarded the Russians as the embodiment of the evil
principle. Moscow "learned its attitude toward God
from Byzantine cant, its attitude toward man from
Mongol bestiality." "In Russian history the passive
mother was Byzantine conservatism: the father who
fertilized her was the Tartar invasion; their offspring
which grew to gigantic proportions was the government of Russia." This government wished to combat
Europe and God, to deceive all Slavs and to conquer
the human race. To this end it used any and every
means, assimilated the methods of Prussian militarism and of French Jacobinism.

Krasiński pointed out in a letter to Montalembert

the danger that Russia might very well overpower
the Slav nations and as their leader conquer Europe
which would fall through internal disunity; as the
alternative he saw Poland leading the Slavs on the
road to Western civilization and thus serving mankind, as the bulwark of Christianity as she had already done in history. In a memorandum submitted
to Napoleon III during the Crimean War Krasiński
stressed the fact that Russia was appealing on the
one hand to the European conservatives who wrongly
regarded her as a rock of order and at the same time
was supporting with gold and propaganda all the
secret societies and revolutionary forces. Russia "is
the arisen revolution, organized, disciplined, armed
with a million bayonets knocking at the door of the
world. If one is not on guard, if she is not stopped
in time, she will sooner or later reach her aims. . . .
She proclaims the coming of a new society, religion
as the slave of the temporal power, the destruction
of every aristocracy, the obliteration of the individual
from the book of life, the realization of absolute
equality, it is true at the cost of the most execrable
of tyrannies." Far beyond the national framework in
which Polish poetry then moved Krasiński foresaw in
a work of universal significance, his *Nieboska
Komedja* (The Un-Divine Comedy), a truly astonishing dramatic poem which he wrote at the age of
21, the crucial human and historical problems of
the coming revolution of the totalitarian mass-age.
Despairing of the old societies which he loved but
which he saw undermined by egotism, distrustful of
the new society, born in violence and embodying the
terrible oversimplification of the quest for happiness
and power, Krasiński found his refuge in Christ.
Mickiewicz in discussing *The Un-Divine Comedy*
blamed the author for having believed it possible
that the Slav peasant could ever be won for the camp
of the materialist revolution. "Not on behalf of a
destructive theory," Mickiewicz maintained "could

one arouse this people and drive it to action, not by
promising them land and blood could one arm
them." But Krasiński saw the reality and the future
with deeper insight than Mickiewicz. The justice of
his vision can be better understood today than 120
years ago when he wrote this poetic drama of modern
civilization and modern man.

Krasiński strikes us also as a man of our own time
by his insistence on the sterility of hatred and vengeance. His beautiful "Psalm dobrej woli" (Psalm
of Good Will)—"To us first You vouchsafed to in-
corporate Your son into the lay history of the world,
to make of Poland the one country in the future,
from whose breast should flow love and not ban-
ditry"—never became as popular as the flamboyant
drama *Konrad Wallenrod* which Mickiewicz wrote
in 1828 while he was in Russia. There in a way recalling Heinrich von Kleist's *Hermannsschlacht,*
Mickiewicz glorified treason and violence in the "liberation" struggle of the Lithuanians against the Teutonic Knights. He referred in the motto of the play
to Machiavelli's teachings. But the singer of violence
among the three great poets of Poland was Słowacki.
Turning against Krasiński, the "Author of the Three
Psalms," he reminded him that "God's thought does
not only come with the angels; at times He gives it
birth in blood, at times projects it through the Mongol." [n] With an unsurpassed mastery of the language
he planned to write in an unfinished sequence of
rhapsodies a history of Poland, the King-Spirit (*Król-
Duch*); in the first rhapsody the hero, Popiel, the
founder of the nation, the embodiment of the national genius and in a strange way of the poet too,
impresses the reader as an anticipation and glorification of a Chinjiz Khan or Ivan the Terrible. This
demon of violence, this personified pride and folly,
a superman of devilish dimension, with unspeakable
cruelty hammers the dwellers of the land into the
Polish nation. When his death approaches, he tells

them in justifying his deeds: "You are no longer the blind instruments of my fury. You are warriors retempered in slaughter. I have redeemed this nation at the price of its own blood; I have shed this blood in rivers; but above these rivers soars the spirit which despises death. More than one villager will delight his long evenings with singing my heinous crimes, and his soul will become strong in thinking of his ancestors who marched boldly to their death upon the order of their king." This first incarnation of Poland's genius makes the reader think of the character which Krasiński and many other Poles attributed to Mongol Russia. No doubt, if Słowacki could have finished his poem, the later incarnations of the Polish spirit throughout history would have shown characters of love and light, but did not the Russian Slavophiles too find love and light incarnated in the "Mongol" Russian people? Some Slav dreams in the romantic period showed a closer affinity than Russian and Polish spokesmen would concede."

3

The Illyrian Movement

THE SOUTHERN SLAV peoples were at the beginning
of the nineteenth century in an infinitely more difficult position than the other Slavs from whom they
were separated by a belt of German, Magyar and
Rumanian settlement. Bohemia and Poland had
played a prominent role in central European history
as late as the seventeenth century. Long before then
the southern Slavs had lost their political independence. The Slovenes, the most western branch of the
southern Slavs, had never formed a state of their
own. Croatia became a part of the Kingdom of
Hungary in 1102, and Bulgaria, Serbia and Bosnia
fell under Turkish domination in the fourteenth and
fifteenth centuries. At the beginning of the nineteenth century the southern Slavs had neither national consciousness nor a literary language. They
were ethnographic raw material, without any clear
distinction separating the various groups and dialects.
The western and Roman Catholic branches shared
to a certain extent in the higher Austrian and Italian
civilizations; the eastern and Orthodox branches
lived in incredibly backward conditions in the Ottoman empire and in religious and cultural subordination to the Greek clergy of the Patriarch of Constan-

tinople. Of higher learning there were hardly any traces. While universities were founded in Prague in 1348 and in Cracow in 1364, the University of Agram dates from 1874 and the universities in Belgrade, Sofia, Lyublyana were founded at the beginning of the twentieth century. Only in the inaccessible fast-nesses of Montenegro had Serb highlanders preserved since 1697 a precarious independence under the rule of their prince-bishop.

The eighteenth century brought outside influences to bear upon future developments. The disintegra-tion of Ottoman power made the advance of Austria into the Balkans possible. From 1718 to 1739 Aus-trians occupied and administered Serbia from Bel-grade to Nish. Many Serbs left the Turkish territory and settled as an autonomous religious group in the neighboring Habsburg provinces. There a number of them acquired wealth, became merchants, got into touch with Western civilization and formed the nucleus of a middle class from which Serbia could later call its first educators and modern administra-tors. The Austrian advance was soon followed by successful Russian wars against Turkey. The Treaty of Kuchuk Kainarji (1774), near the mouth of the Danube, gave to the Russians an opportunity of regarding themselves as protectors of the Orthodox Church in the Ottoman empire. Catherine's famous "Greek Scheme" to divide the Balkans with the Austrians and to restore the Byzantine empire with her grandson Constantine on the imperial throne of Constantinople came to nought, but in 1783 the Russians annexed the Crimea. Thus the Black Sea ceased to be a Turkish sea, and since then the Russians have striven to transform it into a Russian sea. In 1791 the land between the mouths of the Dnieper and Dniester rivers was ceded by the Turks to the Russians, who three years later built there a port which quickly grew into the important city of Odessa. There a number of Bulgarian merchants settled who were to play a decisive role in the national awakening of their co-religionists in the Balkan peninsula.

This Russian advance stimulated the dim but persistent Pan-Slav hopes of the isolated southern Slavs. These hopes were understandably strong in the hearts of the Orthodox Slavs, among whom during the Turkish domination the famous heroic folk songs centering around Kraljević Marko kept the spirit of resistance alive. Characteristically, the historical Marko, who died in battle at the end of the fourteenth century, fought in the service of the Sultan of Turkey against the Christians. Nevertheless, endowed with all the qualities of Balkan mythology, supernatural strength, and a mixture of primitive cruelty and benevolent generosity, he has become throughout the Balkans, from Istria to the gates of Constantinople, from Yanina to Varna, the most popular hero, claimed and celebrated by all the Christians oppressed by the Turks, Serbs, and Bulgars alike who make rival claims to him as the French and German each claim Charlemagne. But more vocal in their early Pan-Slavism were the Catholic Slavs of Dalmatia and Croatia. Their turning to the great Orthodox brother implied in no way a weakening of their Catholic faith. They envisaged Russia as the means for establishing Slav unity and the reunion of the churches. The best known forerunner of modern Pan-Slavism, the seventeenth century Croatian priest Križanić, during his long sojourn in Russia, was the first to subordinate religious missionary zeal to the emphasis on the need for political emancipation and progress of the Slavs. In the second half of the nineteenth century this Catholic Pan-Slavism aiming at a reunion of the churches under Rome and of the Slavs under Russia will be represented by another Croat priest, Bishop Strossmayer.

But these hopes have so far proved vain; the ob-

stacles, not only to Pan-Slavism but even to a closer
union of the southern Slavs, revealed themselves in
their whole strength from the beginning: differences
of religion, of dialect, and above all of historical
memories. Serbs and Bulgars both claimed the Slav-
speaking populations of Macedonia as part of their
heritage; in a similar way Serbs and Croats both laid
claim to the Slavs of Bosnia and Herzegovina.
Though Pan-Slavism showed great strength in the
writings of many intellectuals and in the unsophisti-
cated feeling of the masses, it hardly determined
practical politics. Serbs and Bulgars at various times
in the last one hundred and fifty years were as willing to accept help and protection from Austria as
from Russia. The Croats looked as often to Vienna
for guidance and aid as to St. Petersburg. What these
people expected was national independence in the
exclusive sense of the word with only an emotional
aura of Pan-Slavism, but even in the twentieth
century this aura was not strong enough to bridge
the gulf between Belgrade and Zagreb in 1929 or
between Belgrade and Moscow twenty years later.

In the second half of the eighteenth century
powerful intellectual currents slowly penetrated from
abroad to some of the southern Slavs. Among the
Serbs who lived in southern Hungary, Dositej Obra-
dović (c. 1740–1811) came under the influence of
the Enlightenment, abandoned the dreams of his
youth of becoming an orthodox saint, traveled in
the Occident, wrote didactic literature, and became
deeply suspect as an "atheist" and "nationalist" to
the Serb clergy. "In Serbia, in Bosnia, in Dalmatia,
in Herzegovina, in Slavonia, the people have everywhere the same character; whatever the name by
which they are called, they form one family," he
wrote. "If there are frictions among them, they are
caused by the fact that some of them follow the
Latin rite, others the Greek rite; that is the reason
why they call each other insulting names. . . .

Serbia, Bosnia, Herzegovina will be able to shake off
the Turks, but the people must also shake off the
impious hatreds caused by difference of religion:
otherwise the people will become its own Turk and
torturer." [n] In the typical fashion of the rationalism
of the Enlightenment, this first Serbo-Croat nationalist underestimated the forces of tradition and
religion. But soon other and more powerful influences of the Enlightenment penetrated the Western fringes of the southern Slav world. In 1797, at
the conclusion of Bonaparte's victorious campaign in
Italy, Austria received the formerly Venetian territories of Istria and Dalmatia, and thus all Croats
and Slovenes found themselves for the first time
united under the same rule. The Dalmatian humanists had discovered in the sixteenth century the classical name of Illyrian for the Slav-speaking inhabitants
of these provinces. Even Kollár still regarded the
ancient Illyrians as Slavs. In the treaties of Pressburg in 1805 and of Schönbrunn in 1809 defeated
Austria ceded to France the former Venetian territories and all the lands beyond the Save River, from
Villach in Carinthia and Görz on the Isonzo to
Ragusa and Cattaro in Dalmatia. They were organized by Napoleon as the Illyrian provinces of
the French empire and were governed until 1810
by Marshal Auguste de Marmont who in 1808 was
made Duke of Ragusa. The French regarded Dalmatia as the basis for military operations across the
Balkans to Constantinople; the rivalry between
Russia and France for the control of the Adriatic
and the Balkans was acute in 1806.

In the few years from 1809 to 1814 the French
administration tried to introduce a number of reforms in the newly acquired provinces. Two reforms
alone were of lasting importance: the building of
military roads and the granting of full equality to
the Orthodox minority in Dalmatia. The attempts at
creating a Slav press and at introducing the Slav

language in the schools did not get far. One obstacle
was the indifference of the Slav population; they
were by far not ripe for nationalism by enlightened
reforms; they received the returning Austrians with
warm acclaim. The newspapers in Slavic could not
find any subscribers. But the greatest trouble was
caused by the fact that even the Slav intellectuals
could not agree on an "Illyrian" language. Marmont
favored the dialect of Ragusa which, however, turned
out to be unacceptable to the Slovenes who insisted
on their own dialect as much as the Croats of Karlo-
vac insisted on theirs. Yet the idea of a united Illyria
remained as a legacy of the French occupation. In
1811 the Slovene poet Valentin Vodnik (1758–
1819), who was director of public instruction in the
French administration, wrote an ode on the renaissance of Illyria in which he glorified Napoleon and
the national aspirations in the same way as the contemporary poets in the Confederation of the Rhine
and the Duchy of Warsaw did:

Napoleon said: "Wake up, Illyria."
She is waking up, she asks with a sigh:
"Who calls me back to the light?
O great hero, is it you?"
During fourteen centuries the moss has covered
*   Illyria.*
Today Napoleon calls upon her to shake off the dust
Napoleon's spirit penetrates to the Slovenes:
A whole generation rises from the soil . . .
Resting one hand upon Gaul
It gives its other hand to Greece.

Vodnik identified the Illyrians with his native
Slovenes. Ljudevit Gaj (1809–72), the real father of
Illyrism, identified the movement with his native
Croatia. Gaj studied in Graz and Budapest and
there came under the influence of Kollár. In 1830
he wrote a "Short Outline of Croat-Slovene Orthography" (*Kratka Osnova Hrvatsko-Slavenskoga Pra-*

vopisanja) in which he expressed the hope that "all the dialects of our great nation might come as near to each other as possible." Like Kollár he believed in the four main branches of the Slav nation and spoke of "our Slav brethren, the Czechs, Poles and Russians." His pamphlet rendered an immense service to the southern Slav cause because it solved the vexing question of a literary language in a way which made possible the modern Serbo-Croatian unified language."

The following year Gaj returned to Zagreb; his inspiring leadership made the Croatian capital the focus of a national movement appealing beyond the Croatian borders for southern Slav, or as it was then called, Illyrian, and Pan-Slav unity. In 1834 he founded the first Croatian newspaper which he called the "Croatian, Slovenian and Dalmatian Newspaper." There he introduced the new literary language and the new orthography. Through its literary supplement *Danica* (The Dawn) Gaj created a center for the new national poetical expression. He himself wrote the Croat anthem "Još Hrvatska nij propala" (Croatia has not yet fallen). In 1836 he renamed his paper *Narodne Ilirske Novine* (The National Illyrian Newspaper) and its supplement *Danica Ilirska*, thus making it clear that he aimed not only at the historical kingdom of Croatia, Slavonia, and Dalmatia but at all the southern Slavs and their cultural union. As Illyrians he claimed all the peoples living within the triangle formed by the three cities of Villach, Varna, and Skutari. The Bulgarians were included though little was known of them at that time. Gaj's agitation stirred Croatia deeply. He was supported by men like Count Janko Drašković (1770–1856), a scion of old nobility, who published two pamphlets in German, "Sollen wir Magyaren werden?" (Should we become Magyars?) in 1833 and "Ein Wort an Illyriens hochherzige Töchter über die älteste Geschichte und Regeneration ihres Vaterlandes" (A Word to Illyria's High-minded Daughters about the History and the Regeneration of their Fatherland) in 1838.

Gaj for a brief time succumbed to the lures of Pan-Slavism. In 1838 he sent a memorandum to Russia in which he spoke of the Russian mission as the Slavophiles did and of the Tsar as the leader of his peoples in the very same way in which Stalin was to be praised by his faithful a century later. He suggested to Russia the strategic value of controlling the Balkans through Croatian sympathies and spoke grandiloquently, without any foundation in fact, of his widespread conspiratorial preparations there.[n] But on the whole, Gaj like most Croatians, adhered to Austro-Slavism. Within this Western-centered movement, the southern Slavs occupied a position of their own in their fluctuating and yet persistent efforts to establish a unity of their own. The name of Illyrism fell completely into desuetude after having been forbidden in 1843 and was replaced by the new name of Yugoslav. In 1861 the Croat Sabor (Diet) accepted officially the name "Yugoslav" for the Croat-Serb language and in 1867 Bishop Josip Juraj Strossmayer (1815–1905) founded the Yugoslav Academy in Zagreb, of which his disciple and fellow priest Franko Rački became the first president. After 1848 Strossmayer, who became Bishop of Diakovar in 1850, succeeded Gaj as the leader of the Croat movement. His fervent Pan-Slavism was tempered by his loyalty to the Catholic Church and fanned by his hope for a reunion of the churches. "I am a Catholic," Strossmayer is reported to have said in 1876, "and the Servians are Orthodox, but it is only a difference of unimportant details, and I should be well content to be under the political administration of Servia." [n]

These Croatian aspirations were in no way accepted in good spirits by the Slovenes or the Serbs. Though

Stanko Vraz worked for Illyrism and for Slovene-
Croat unity of language and culture, the greatest
Slovene poet of the period, France Prešeren (1800–
49), the awakener and cultural and social organizer
of his people, fought for the maintenance of Slovene
individuality. He insisted on a separate literary language for the Slovenes for the same reason that Štúr
did among the Slovaks. A literary language that
deviated too much from the vernacular spoken by
the people would hardly have helped them in their
fight against Germanization. He found the support
of Dr. Janez Bleiweis (1808–81) who in 1843, in
Laibach, began to publish a weekly for the Slovene
peasants, and of Fran Levstik (1831–87), a gifted
satirical and critical prose writer. As a result of their
efforts the small Slovene people who, unlike the
Croats or the Serbs, composed no political autonomous body but were divided up among various
Austrian provinces became, culturally and socially,
the most advanced southern Slav people. Illiteracy
among their peasants disappeared at a time when it
was still very high among Croats and Serbs, the number of books and periodicals published grew rapidly,
and economic advance was secured by a highly developed system of co-operative organizations. The
Slovenes remained to the end loyal Austro-Slavs.[n]

But even more opposed to a merging of the various
southern Slav peoples than the Slovenes were the
Serbs. Among them Vuk Stefanović Karadžić (1787–
1864) laid the foundations for a modern Serb
literature by establishing a national language, reforming the alphabet, and collecting the folk literature.
He lived most of his life in Vienna and was supported in his work by the great Slovene and Catholic
scholar Bartholomew Kopitar (1780–1844), a relationship which made his reforms suspect to the
Orthodox Serbs. The new reforms were accepted
only after a bitter struggle. Through them and
through Gaj's language reform in Croatia the Serbs

and Croats enjoyed a common literary language and to some enthusiasts it seemed that they would form one nation "like the Germans of Roman and Lutheran doctrine." But even in Karadžić himself Serbian separatist feeling was much stronger than that for a new Illyrian or Yugoslav union in which the name and glory of Serbia would dissolve.

This feeling of Serbian pride was motivated by the fact that in their struggle for liberation from the Turks which started in 1804 under the leadership of George Petrović (1766–1817), called Karageorge (Turkish for Black George), and Miloš Obrenović (1780–1860) the Serbs were the only Balkan people who could claim for themselves the *farà da se*. Greeks, Rumanians, and Bulgarians owed their liberty to a large extent to outside intervention, to the active sympathies and the military and diplomatic support of some of the great powers. The Serbs owed everything to themselves, to the heroism and ferocity of their people and the daring of their leaders. They were men of patriarchal simplicity, much more backward than even the Turkish regime, and of primitive brutality, and the Croats, conscious of their own cultural and administrative superiority, looked down upon them. In fact, for many decades to come the intellectual center of the Serb awakening remained among the Serbs living in Habsburg territory where Novi Sad (Neusatz) was the Serbian Athens. From it came all the three leading Serb poets of the nineteenth century, Branko Radičević (1825–63), Djura Jakšić (1832–78) and Zmaj Jovan-Jovanović (1833–1904). Though these Serbs from the Vojvodina, a people of well-to-do farmers, merchants, and professional men, felt a strong Serb nationalism, they were often regarded by the Serbs south of the Save and Danube as "Germans." [n]

The Serbs in Serbia looked more and more only to themselves. In the second half of the nineteenth century they hardly expected political help or guid-

ance from Russia; for cultural direction the educated
class more and more looked to Paris. All attempts of
devising a common name for the southern Slavs
which, like the names "Helvetia" or "Belgium,"
would bridge differences of language and origin in a
common nationality, were resisted. The dominant
sentiment was well expressed by a young poet:[n]

> *My father is Serb, my mother is Serb.*
> *All my ancestors were Serb.*
> *The heaven is blue, Serbia's color.*
> *God who lives in heaven is Serb too.*

The dreams of a great Croatia were countered by
more ambitious and more aggressive dreams of a
Great Serbia. Serbia was regarded as the Piedmont
of a future Yugoslav unification for which organizations like the *Slovenski Jug* (The Slav South) and
Ujedinjenje ili smert (Union or Death) made propaganda. It was, however, forgotten that the unification
in Italy brought the absorption of Piedmont into
Italy and the transfer of the center of influence and
power from Turin to Florence and soon to Rome,
while the unification envisaged by the Serbs was to
bring added power to Belgrade and the Serbian leadership throughout Yugoslavia. Thus Serbia dreamt
rather of the role of Prussia, without the numerical
or administrative superiority of the latter, than of
the role of Piedmont.

The most acute disputes between Croats and
Serbs concerned Bosnia and Herzegovina. Their
inhabitants, divided by religion into Mohammedans,
Greek Orthodox and Roman Catholic Christians,
were with equally good historical and ethnographic
reasons claimed both as Croats and Serbs. The
Austrian administration after 1878 tried to resolve
this problem by promoting a local Bosnian patriotism, a solution to which many years later the
Federal People's Republic of Marshal Tito returned.
The same position which Bosnia occupied in the

struggle of the related yet hostile neighbors, the Croats and Serbs, Macedonia occupied in relation to the Serbs and Bulgars, neighborly people of the same faith and of an almost identical cultural background. Nevertheless, they too, since their national awakening in the middle of the nineteenth century, have in spite of their often repeated Pan-Slav affinity hardly ever seen eye to eye. Their hostility has gone so far that Serb writers have repeatedly doubted whether the Bulgars were Slavs (an attitude similar to that of some Poles with regard to the Russians), while Bulgar writers proudly proclaimed their affinity with the Turks and with the Magyars. Looking back to Bulgar and Serb expansion in the Middle Ages, each side drew maps of the Balkan peninsula in which it claimed almost three fourths of the peninsula as historically and ethnographically its own.

The Bulgarians owed their national awakening to the Pan-Slav enthusiasm of George Hutza, who was born in 1802 as the son of a priest in the Ukrainian counties of northern Hungary. As a young man he decided to dedicate himself to the study of the Slav world and to go to Russia. He changed his name to Yurij Ivanovich Venelin. In Moscow he studied the then very little known history of the Bulgars and published in 1829 his work, "The Ancient and the Present Bulgarians in their Political, Ethnographical, Historical and Religious Relationship to the Russians." He rejected the theory of the Tartar origin of the Bulgarians, defined them as a Slav people, and made many fantastic claims on behalf of their past glory and of their present virtue. He claimed Attila and the Huns as Volga Slavs, like the ancient Bulgars, and opposed the theory according to which the Varangians were Scandinavians. In 1830 he was sent by the Imperial Russian Academy to Rumania and Bulgaria to study the Bulgarian language and to collect all the available material which could throw light on the Slav past. Venelin,

who died in Moscow in 1839, was one of the first
to arouse in the small Bulgar merchant class living in
Odessa and Bucharest a love for the former glory of
the Bulgarians. Two years after his death the Bulgarian colony in Moscow erected a monument over his
tomb with the inscription: "He was the first who
reminded the world of the forgotten but once glorious and powerful Bulgarian people and who fervently desired its rebirth. Lord, fulfil the prayer of
Thy servant."

At that time the few educated Bulgars were entirely under the influence of Greek civilization. They
wrote and spoke Greek and participated in the Greek
war of independence. The Orthodox clergy in Bulgaria was under the control of the Greek Patriarch
in Constantinople and thus religious education and
literature, the only ones available, were Greek. All
that changed as a result of Venelin's work. Inspired
by him, a retired Bulgarian vodka merchant in
Odessa, Vasil Estafiyevich Aprilov (1789–1847), was
converted from a Grecophile to an ardent Bulgarian
Slav. At the beginning of 1835 he opened the first
Bulgarian school in his native town Gabrovo from
which he had emigrated at the age of eleven. This
school was soon followed by other Bulgarian schools,
and the next twenty years he spent in creating a
Bulgarian literary language out of the popular vernacular, in writing the first textbooks and in fighting
the influence of the Greek Church. In April 1844 the
first Bulgar periodical, a monthly called *Lyuboslovie*
(Philology), was founded in Smyrna but it lasted
less than three years. In spite of these late and slow
beginnings the struggle for the Bulgarian renaissance
was won within four decades. The 1870's brought
the ecclesiastical emancipation from the Greek
Church and, with Russian help, the beginning of
political independence. The short-lived peace treaty
of San Stefano in 1878 seemed to realize the dream
of Great Bulgaria. Most of Macedonia was promised

to Bulgarian rule. At this very moment when the
Bulgarian national aspirations, so recently aroused,
entered for the first time the realm of reality, they
clashed with Serbia's similar aspirations. In the
seventy years from 1880 to 1950 this antagonism led
to four bitter wars and even today has lost little of
its intensity. It affected Bulgarian policy much more
than any feeling of gratitude for Venelin's Pan-Slav
devotion or Russia's military assistance to Bulgaria's
liberation.[n]

Few Bulgars or Serbs were able to rise above narrow nationalism. Svetozar Marković (1846–75), who
in his brief life published a number of Serb periodicals, *Radnik* (The Worker), *Javnost* (Public Opinion) and *Oslobodjenje* (Liberation), fought for a
Westernization of Serbia, a true and free parliamentary life, for religious peace and tolerance, and
for a federation of the south Slavs after the model
of Switzerland. His Bulgar contemporary Christo
Botev (1847–76), a poet who died in the uprising
against the Turks, turned like Marković against
all national romanticism. About Yugoslav unity he
wrote: "This thought appeared recently among the
southern Slavs, but with our people so far it has
developed little, because it was presented without
sincerity and to the diminution of its dignity. The
unification of Germany with its despotic Prussia and
the unity of Italy with its Piedmont and its Victor
Emanuel are examples which frighten our people,
because to them Russia is not Prussia and Serbia is
not Piedmont. A Yugoslav federation should be
built on other liberal foundations so that no nationality may be wronged. The Prussian is a German, the
Piedmontese is an Italian, but a Bulgar is not a Serb
and a Serb is not a Russian."

4

The Prague Congress of 1848

THE SLOWLY MATURING harvest of the seeds sown by the French Revolution and by German philosophy and scholarship among the Slavs ripened quickly in the stormy spring of 1848. The new currents stirred even the numerically insignificant Lusatian Sorbs, an enclave in central Germany, and the numerous peoples of the Ukrainians until then lost in the Russian sea. After the example of the other Slav peoples, the Sorbs organized in 1847 in Bautzen (Saxony) a Macica serbska which published its own scholarly journal; in Andreas Seiler (Handrij Zejler, 1804–72) they found their first poet, in Johann Ernst Schmaler (Smoler, 1816–84) their first national organizer. Johann Peter Jordan, a Slavic scholar at the University of Leipzig, published there from 1843 to 1848 his important *Jahrbücher für Slawische Literatur, Kunst und Wissenschaft* and from 1846 onward, also a Slav Bibliography. With his help the Slav bookselling house of Ernst Keil & Co. was established in Leipzig. Thus for a few years some of Kollár's suggestions were realized through the initiative of a member of the smallest Slav people.

Among the Ukrainians Ivan Kotlyarevsky (1769–1838) laid the foundations of modern literature in his *Eneida*, a travesty of the *Aeneid* describing Aeneas and his companions as Ukrainian Kozaks wandering around Europe in search of a new home. In outlook and art he was still an eighteenth-century figure untouched by the new romanticism and populism of the following age. These influences also shaped the life and work of the greatest Ukrainian poet, Taras Shevchenko (1814–61), who was born a serf, was arrested in 1847 as a leading member of the Society of St. Cyril and St. Methodius, spent thereupon ten years in the army in remote parts of Russia and died soon after his release. This Society, founded in Kiev by Shevchenko and his friends, among whom the poet and scholar Pantaleimon Kulish (1818–97) and the historian Nicholas Kosto-mariv (1817–85) were the most prominent, not only wished to awaken Ukrainian national consciousness and literary life but also to propagate a Pan-Slav peoples on the basis of full equality. Each Slavic nation was to form a republic of its own, the head of the federation was to be elected and all Slav nations were to send their representatives to a congress to solve common problems. Shevchenko was the first not only to proclaim his opposition to autoc-racy and serfdom, but to demand a complete separa-tion of the Ukraine as a nation from Russia.

While the year 1847 marked the temporary end of the Ukrainian movement in the Russian Empire it brought encouragement to the Ukrainians living in Austrian Galicia. There a large group, the Old Ruthenians, clung to the traditional ecclesiastical language, supplementing it later with Great Russian words and syntax and leaning toward union with Russia. Younger writers, on the other hand, like Markian Shashkevich (1811–43), who published in 1837 the almanac *Rusalka Dnistrovaya* (The Nymph of the Dniestr) and Jakov Holovatsky who became professor of Ukrainian literature at the University of Lemberg, developed the language on the lines

laid down by Kotlyarevsky. Franz Seraph Count
Stadion (1806–53), who was Austrian Governor of
Galicia from 1846 to 1848, supported the Ukrainian
national movement; with his encouragement a
Ukrainian General Council (Holovna Rada) was
organized and published the first Ukrainian newspaper *Zorya Halitska* (The Galician Star). This
wave of awakening spread in 1848 even to the
Ukrainians in the Austrian Bukovina and on the
southern slopes of the Carpathian Mountains in
northern Hungary. Among the latter Adolph Do-
briansky, a man of energy and ability, seized the
opportunity offered by the Russian expedition into
Hungary to establish Carpatho-Ukrainian autonomy;
his Russophile attitude weakened for many years the
rise of a Ukrainian nationalism south of the Carpathian Mountains.[n]

The Polish uprisings in Galicia, Cracow, and
Posen in 1846, the national agitation in Italy at the
accession of Cardinal Mastai-Ferretti to the Papal
throne in the same year, the order summoning the
United Landtag in Prussia, and the elections to the
Hungarian Diet in the following year, all these made
a deep impression on the Austrian Slav intellectuals.
The masses stirred responsively when in the beginning of March the effects of the February revolution
in Paris spread east of the Rhine. As had happened
sixty years before, the often contradictory and
strangely intermingled slogans of liberty and nationality came again as a message from France; were they
to remain confined this time to rhetorical enthusiasm
or would they be supported again as in 1793 by the
mighty arms of an aroused nation? Counsels of pru-
dence prevailed: Lamartine, the foreign minister of
the young republic, warned in a circular letter to
the diplomatic agents of France: "The proclamation
of the French Republic is not an act of aggression
against any form of government. The French Republic proclaims itself the intellectual and cordial

ally of all the rights and of every progress. . . . It will not start any secret incendiary propaganda among its neighbors. It knows that there are no enduring liberties but those which grow spontaneously from their own soil. The world and we will march toward fraternity and peace." [n]

This medley of lyric utopianism and practical common sense appealed to the Austrian Slavs. 1789 had found them unprepared and unreceptive. Since then they had learned to think of fraternity and peace as Slav qualities. Now they were to come into their own in co-operation with France and with the liberal *Zeitgeist* represented by the rapid succession of miraculous events: the Heidelberg meeting of March 6, calling a preliminary German parliament to Frankfurt on the Main for the end of the month; the fall of Metternich on March 13; two days later the abolition of censorship and the promise of a constitutional assembly in Austria; and the adoption of the March Laws by the Hungarian Table of Deputies. 1848 was the birth-year of nationalism in Central Europe as 1789 had been in France; it was the year of the national awakening of the Slav peoples in the Austrian monarchy, though not yet of those in the Russian and Ottoman empires whither the liberating West wind did not penetrate. 1848 was the great year of the Austrian Slavs, of their Pan-Slavism and their Western liberal orientation. It ended in defeat for them as it did for the other Central European peoples. Yet the masses in the Habsburg monarchy did not return to their pre-March attitudes: their national consciousness remained and was strengthened by the two lasting achievements of the 1848 turmoil in Austria: the full emancipation of the peasants and a thorough modernization of the administrative and economic life of the monarchy.

From the beginning the two trends of the revolution conflicted: the liberal trend which wished to strengthen and secure the rights and liberties of the individual against authority, and the nationalist trend which stressed the power and growth of the national collectivity by endowing it with governmental authority. This conflict doomed the revolution; when it was resumed more than a decade later, the nationalist trend triumphed by absorbing the liberal trend. But in the dawn of the revolutionary year liberalism seemed to prevail. In Prague fifty-two intellectuals adopted on March 21, 1848, a resolution proposed by Palacký: "The Prague authors, those using the German language as well as those using the Czech language, elated in their hearts by the feeling of liberty and harmony manifested these days among the German and Czech inhabitants of our fatherland, have decided unanimously to proclaim publicly that they wish to do everything in their power to see to it that this happy agreement be not disturbed but preserved firmly and permanently, and this on the basis of full equality in a way which would give an advantage neither to the Germans over the Czechs nor to the Czechs over the Germans. For that reason efforts of the Czechs to make such an equality a reality in every respect should not be regarded as a disturbance of the harmony. Furthermore they attest that they wish to defend in writing and speaking as powerfully as possible the connection of the Czech crown with the Austrian empire through the tie of a constitutional monarchy." [n] In this resolution the pre-nationalist territorial patriotism of the Kingdom of Bohemia, which Czech and German-speaking inhabitants shared, found its last expression. It marked the end of an epoch.

Bohemia and Moravia, which formed part of the Holy Roman Empire, belonged also to the German Confederation as constituted in 1815. Neither the medieval empire nor the Metternichian Confederation was a national state. Their underlying conception was partly universal and partly dynastic. The same can be said of the lands of the Crown of St.

Stephen, inhabited by men of great ethnographic and linguistic diversity and using Latin as the official language of the Hungarian kingdom. Its founder St. Stephen had instructed his son, St. Emeric, to value high the multi-national character of the realm. "Nam unius linguae uniusque moris regnum imbecille et fragile est." [n] The nationalists of 1848 were easily induced to equate the supra-national dynastic, no-bilitarian or religious state of former times with the modern nation-state which they wished to create. Germans and Magyars claimed as their national heritage the territories and peoples which had his-torically formed part of the Holy Roman Empire, of the German Confederation, or of the lands of the Crown of St. Stephen. The simultaneous national awakening of the Slav and other peoples in central Europe made these claims unacceptable at the very moment when they were raised. The Czechs could form part of a dynastic German Confederation but not of a German nation-state. The Slovaks could accept Latin as the official language of the Hun-garian Kingdom; they could not accept Magyar without claiming the same position for Slovak. Nor was this identification of pre-nationalist historical frontiers with modern nationalist claims confined to Germans and Magyars: all Slav peoples with tradi-tions of statehood succumbed to the temptation of appealing simultaneously to historical rights of past ages and to the rights of ethnographic nationality regarded as "natural rights" in the age of nationalism, depending on which appeal promised greater expan-sion or prestige. In discussing Pan-Slavism, it should be noted that the Slav peoples used this dual appeal not only against Germans or Magyars but as lustily against their Slav neighbours. All the peoples of Europe east of the Rhine and the Alps shared a common fate: they entered the age of nationalism at a time when the nation-state solution of the West was no longer applicable. The great historical dy-

nastic states of Central and Eastern Europe were
bound to undergo a thorough process of liberal and
administrative reforms. In that respect the revolution
against the spirit of the Holy Alliance was justified
and inevitable. But it was a misfortune from which
Europe east of the Rhine and Alps—the peoples who
inhabit the former Germanies, the Italian peninsula,
the Danubian basin, the Balkans, and the immense
plains from the Vistula to the Urals—has not yet
recovered that this liberal revolution was harnessed
to the service of the nation-state. In 1848 the roads
to a supra-national federal solution were still wide
open. They were blocked by Bismarck's victory in the
German civil war of 1866 which deepened the difference in outlook and structure between the West
and the illegitimate heirs of the Holy Alliance.[n]

The invitation addressed to Palacký to join the
German National Assembly at Frankfurt gave him
an opportunity to express in a famous letter[n] the essence of the liberal Pan-Slavism of 1848: "I am a
Czech of Slav descent and with all the little I own
and possess I have devoted myself wholly and forever to the service of my nation. That nation is
small, it is true, but from time immemorial it has
been an independent nation with its own character;
its rulers have participated since old times in the
federation of German princes, but the nation never
regarded itself nor was it regarded by others throughout all the centuries, as part of the German nation.
The whole union of the Czech lands first with the
Holy German Empire and then with the German
Confederation was always a purely dynastic one of
which the Czech nation, the Czech Estates, hardly
wished to know and which they hardly noticed. . . .
If anyone asks that the Czech nation should now
unite with the German nation, beyond this hereto-
fore existing federation between princes, this is then
a new demand which has no historical legal basis,

a demand to which I personally do not feel justified in acceding until I receive an express and valid mandate for it. The second reason which prevents me from participating in your deliberations is the fact that from all that has been so far publicly announced of your aims and purposes you irrevocably are, and will be, aiming to undermine Austria forever as an independent empire and to make its existence impossible—an empire whose preservation, integrity and consolidation is, and must be, a great and important matter not only for my own nation but for the whole of Europe, indeed for mankind and civilization itself. Allow me kindly to explain myself briefly on this point.

"You know, gentlemen, what power it is that holds the great eastern part of our continent; you know that this power, which now already has grown to vast dimensions, increases and expends by its own strength every decade to a far greater extent than is possible in the Western countries; that being inaccessible at its own center to almost every attack, it has become, and has for a long time been, a threat to its neighbours; and that, although it has an open access to the north, it is nevertheless always seeking, led by natural instinct, to expand southwards and will continue to do it; that every further step which it will take forward on this path threatens at an ever accelerated pace to produce and found a *universal monarchy*, that is to say an infinite and inexpressible evil, a misfortune without measure or bound which I, though heart and soul a Slav, would nonetheless deeply regret for the good of mankind even though that monarchy proclaimed itself a Slav one. Many people in Russia call and regard me as an enemy of the Russians, with as little justice as those who among the Germans regard me as an enemy of the Germans. I proclaim loudly and publicly that I am in no way an enemy of the Russians: on the contrary, I observe with joyful sympathy every step by which this great nation within its natural borders progresses along the road of civilization: but with all my ardent love of my nation I always esteem more highly the good of mankind and of learning than the good of the nation; for this reason the bare possibility of a Russian universal monarchy has no more determined opponent or adversary than myself, not because that monarchy would be Russian but because it would be universal.

"You know that in south-east Europe, along the frontiers of the Russian empire, there live many nations widely different in origin, language, history, and habits—Slavs, Rumanians, Magyars, and Germans, not to speak of Greeks, Turks, and Albanians —none of whom is strong enough by itself to be able to resist successfully for all time the superior neighbour to the east; they could do it only if a close and firm tie bound them all together. The vital artery of this necessary union of nations is the Danube; the focus of its power must never be removed from this river, if the union is to be effective at all and to remain so. Certainly, if the Austrian state had not existed for ages, we would be obliged in the interests of Europe and even of mankind to endeavor to create it as fast as possible.

"But why have we seen this state, which by nature and history is destined to be the bulwark and guardian of Europe against Asiatic elements of every kind—why have we seen it in a critical moment helpless and almost unadvised in the face of the advancing storm? It is because in an unhappy blindness which has lasted for very long, Austria has not recognized the real legal and moral foundation of its existence and has denied it; the fundamental rule that all the nationalities united under its scepter should enjoy complete equality of rights and respect. The right of nations is truly a natural right; no nation on earth has the right to demand that its neighbour should sacrifice itself for its benefit, no

nation obliged to deny or sacrifice itself for the good
of its neighbour. Nature knows neither ruling nor
subservient nations. If the union which unites several
different nations is to be firm and lasting, no nation
must have cause to fear that by that union it will
lose any of the goods which it holds most dear; on
the contrary each must have the certain hope that it
will find in the central authority defense and protection against possible violations of equality by neighbours; then every nation will do its best to
strengthen that central authority so that it can successfully provide the aforesaid defense. I am convinced that even now it is not too late for the
Austrian empire to proclaim openly and sincerely
this fundamental rule of justice, the *sacra ancora*
for a ship in danger of floundering, and to carry it
out energetically in common and in every respect:
but every moment is precious; for God's sake do not
let us delay another hour with this! . . .

"When I look behind the Bohemian frontiers,
then natural and historical reasons make me turn not
to Frankfurt but to Vienna to seek there the center
which is fitted and destined to ensure and defend
the peace, the liberty, and the right of my nation.
Your efforts, gentlemen, seem to me now to be
directed as I have already stated, not only toward
ruinously undermining, but even utterly destroying
that center from whose might and strength I expect
the salvation not only of the Czech land. Or do you
think that the Austrian state will continue to exist
when you forbid it to maintain an army in its own
hereditary lands, independent of Frankfurt as the
joint head? Do you think that the Austrian emperor
or any succeeding sovereign will be able to maintain
his position if you impose upon him the duty of accepting all the more important laws from your committee, and thus make the institutions of the imperial Austrian parliament and the historical Diets
of the united Kingdoms mere shadows without sub-

stance and power? And if then Hungary, following
its instincts, severs its connections with the state or,
what would amount almost to the same, concentrates
within itself—will then Hungary, which does not
wish to hear of national equality within its borders,
be able to maintain itself free and strong in the
future? Only the just is truly free and strong. A
voluntary union of the Danubian Slavs and Rumanians, or even of the Poles themselves, with such a
state which declares that a man must first be a Magyar before he can be a human being is entirely out
of the question; and even less thinkable would be a
compulsory union of this kind. For the sake of
Europe, Vienna must not sink to the role of a provincial town. If there are in Vienna itself such people
who demand to have your Frankfurt as their capital,
then we must cry: Lord, forgive them, for they know
not what they ask!

"Finally, there is a third reason for which I must
decline to take part in your councils: I regard all
the attempts made so far to give to the German
empire a new constitution based on the will of the
people as impossible of achievement and as unstable
for the future, unless you decide upon a real life-or-
death operation; by this I mean the proclamation of
a German Republic. . . . I must, however, reject
in advance energetically and emphatically every
idea of a republic within the frontiers of the Austrian empire. Think of the Austrian empire divided
up into a number of republics and dwarf republics—
what a delightful basis for a universal Russian monarchy.

"In conclusion, to end these lengthy but rapidly
drawn-up remarks, I must briefly express my conviction that those who ask that Austria (and with it
Bohemia) should unite on national lines with the
German empire, demand its suicide, which is morally
and politically meaningless; on the contrary it would
be much more meaningful to demand that Germany

should unite with the Austrian empire, that is, that it should accede to the Austrian state under the conditions above mentioned. As that, however, does not accord with German national sentiment and opinion, nothing remains for the two powers, the Austrian and German empires, but to organize themselves side by side on a footing of equality, to convert the existing ties into a permanent alliance of defense and defiance, and should it be advantageous to both sides perhaps to create also a customs union. I am ready at every moment gladly to give a helping hand in all activities which do not endanger the independence, integrity, and growth in power of the Austrian empire."

With an unusual perspicacity Palacký proposed and defended here the need of a federal solution for Central Europe against the creation of nation-states. To the *Grossdeutsch* solution he opposed a great Austrian solution, a federation of equal nationalities, united militarily and economically for the assurance of their unhindered cultural and social development. What he feared, happened almost a century later. The disintegration of the Austrian monarchy, due largely as he foresaw to Magyar arrogance and intransigence, and the ensuing multiplicity of jealous and conflicting republics, made German and Russian expansion beyond the frontiers of 1815 possible. The catastrophe started when Vienna was reduced in 1938 to a provincial town for the *Grossdeutsches Reich* of Hitler carried not even that federal element which the *Grossdeutsch* solution of 1848 still preserved: it was nothing more than a daring extension of the Prussian *kleindeutsch* solution which made Berlin the capital of an ever-expanding and ever more centralized German empire. Seven years later the annexation of the former Habsburg lands to the Soviet empire created the basis for that universal Russian monarchy which Palacký

regarded as a misfortune without measure or bound
for mankind and for civilization.

Against the three dangers, an expansive Germany
then represented by Frankfurt, a domineering Magyar nationalism, and a Russian universal state,
Palacký sought to strengthen the bulwark of Austria
by transforming it into a federation of equal nationalities. This task fell according to him upon the Austrian Slavs who, if they would unite their strength,
could realize a program in accordance with the
peaceful and democratic inclinations which Herder
and Palacký attributed to them, and with the general trends of freedom and fraternization of nationalities voiced in 1848 in Western Europe. The idea of
a Pan-Slav action was in the air. Kollár's influence
had been preparing it for the last ten years. One of
Kollár's Croatian disciples, Ivan Kukuljević-Sakčinski
(1816–89), wrote on April 20, 1848, nine days after
Palacký had composed his letter to Frankfurt: "The
Slavs are, like the Germans, divided up among many
states and live under many rulers. Like the Germans
they must fear for their nationality and then for
their liberty in the spirit of our epoch. Like the Germans, the Slavs represent certain human liberal
ideas before the community of nations. Therefore
Slavs and Germans must follow the same policy
toward their nation and toward human liberty."
After the model of Frankfurt, he proposed to call a
Pan-Slav congress to Prague, then the cultural capital
of the Slav world. His article was published ten days
later in a Czech translation in Prague. It expressed
loyalty to the dynasty and the hope that it would
as soon as possible bring together under one rule
all the lands which "by history and law or by blood
and descent belong to our state or to the Yugoslav
nation." The historical rights of the Croatian state
and the "natural" rights of the Yugoslav nation were
both invoked as if they were identical. That they

might conflict or be differently interpreted by Croatians and Serbs, Bosnians and Slovenes, Dalmatians and Macedonians, was apparently not envisaged in the simplifying enthusiasm of 1848.

This voice from Croatia was echoed by the Czech writers who met at the end of April in Prague and whom Štúr asked to assume the leadership: "You Czech brothers, you were in the Middle Ages by your scholarship, your university, your heroism, the 'northern lights' shining above Europe. Be now, by your Slav intentions and actions, the 'northern lights' shining above the Slav world." The Czech leaders Palacký and Šafařík took the initiative for calling a Slav congress which convened in Prague on June 2. Three hundred forty-one delegates attended, in their overwhelming majority Austrian Slavs, but there were a few delegates from Prussian Poland and two Russians one of which was Mikhail Bakunin (1814–76). They set out to discuss four problems: the importance of the Slavs in Austria and their mutual relationship: their relations with the non-Slav Austrians; their relations with the non-Austrian Slavs; and finally their relation with the non-Slav peoples of Europe. Thus the program was firmly based on an Austro-Slav attitude but it broadened out to include the general Slav and European horizon. Great hopes were raised by this first gathering of Slavs, the representation of these largely unknown and long overlooked populations who for the first time presented themselves in a feverish fermentation before a Europe equally stirred in the search for new forms of self-expression. A joyous expectation filled the streets of Prague. The new Slav tricolor blue, white, and red—was everywhere seen; shouts of "Slava" replaced the usual "Heil" or "Vivat"; people appeared in fanciful and colorful national costumes; the young Czech artist, Joseph Manes (1820–71), designed decorations in a national style; the Slovak song "Hej Slovane," written in 1834 by the Rev. Samuel Tomasik, became a demonstrative assertion of Slav national vitality and eternity; the lime tree which Kollár had accepted in opposition to the German oak tree, the *Slovanská Lípa*, was chosen as a Slav symbol.

In his opening address Palacký emphasized his synthesis of the original Slav character in Herder's interpretation with the new spirit of liberty coming from the West: "The freedom which we are now seeking is not a newly arrived stranger among us; it is not a scion brought to us from abroad; it is a tree which has grown of its own on our domestic soil, it is the native and first born heritage of our ancestors." Other speakers expressed the hope that this congress would establish the Slavs definitely as the third main branch of mankind, side by side with the Latins and Germans. Previously the Slavs had cultivated Slav co-operation only in the literary and cultural field; now they were extending it to the political field with nationality and liberty based on Slav unity and love as their guiding stars. Not unexpectedly a Slav mission was claimed, a mission to expand and strengthen liberty and enlightenment. The Slovak M. M. Hodža wisely warned against hostile feelings toward the non-Slav neighbors. "Let us accept from other nations everything that is good and human. Let us not recoil from German culture for it is ours too. We too have helped to work on it, and never can a nation be so completely separated from another nation as not to undergo its strong influence." On the other hand the usually cautious Šafařík in his concluding address indulged in a fervent emotional appeal, calling for complete dedication to the Slav cause. "Even the cosmic forces do not equal the strength of a great nation which has risen to its moral consciousness and in a just struggle defends its existence. . . . We are all concerned with actions and deeds. No road leads from slavery to freedom without struggle—either victory and national liberty, or an honorable death and after death, glory."

This rhetorical stage was quickly passed when the next day the delegates met in three sections to discuss their concrete problems. In the first section the Czechs, Moravians, Silesians, and Slovaks were represented; in the second, Poles and Ukrainians from Galicia; in the third, Slovenes, Croats, Serbs, and Dalmatians, all of them from within the Habsburg monarchy. Many Galician Ukrainians, or Ruthenians as they were called, who could not come asked the Congress for help against their oppression by the Poles and warned of Polish ambitions. Polish *émigrés* expressed the hope that the congress would take a strong stand against the Tsar, "the enemy of all Slavs." While the southern Slavs saw in the Magyars the principal adversary, the Poles regarded the Magyars as their closest friends and did not wish to sacrifice a Polish program to the needs and demands of other Slavs. The Czechs, Slovaks, and Slovenes confined themselves to Austria, according to their national situation and the proclaimed aim of the congress, but the Serbs and Croats were interested in the Serbs and Croats in the Ottoman Empire and the Poles cared above all for the restoration of Poland to its historical frontiers. Unity was achieved only in the realm of pious hopes, expressed in the three declarations drawn up upon the suggestion of Karol Libelt (1808–75), one of the Polish delegates from Posen who had participated in the Polish revolutions of 1831 and 1846 and who later became a member of the Frankfurt National Assembly and of the Prussian Chamber of Deputies. He belonged with Bakunin to the small radical opposition to the loyalist Austro-Slavism of Palacký.

The three declarations—a petition to the Austrian Emperor, a manifesto to the Slav world, and an appeal to the nations of Europe—were never officially accepted. The congress could not agree whether to ask the Emperor for a federation based upon the historical frontiers of the various kingdoms and provinces or on the linguistic and ethnographic character of the population. The manifesto to the nations of Europe began with the statement that for the first time in history the widely scattered members of a great family of peoples had come together to deliberate as brothers on their common affairs. "We have understood one another not only through the beautiful tongue spoken by eighty millions"—Kollár's supposition of a common Slav language of mutual understanding which did not exist—"but also through our hearts beating in union and through the identity of spiritual interest." Then followed the by now well-known Herderian and Slavophile position: "The Latin and Germanic nations, formerly famous in Europe as powerful conquerors, have for centuries established their independence by the strength of the sword and have known how to satisfy their need for domination. Their constitutions, based mainly upon the idea of force, guaranteed liberty only to the upper classes which dominated, thanks to their privileges, while they imposed only duties upon the people. Only today, owing to the strength of public opinion, which like the spirit of God has suddenly spread throughout all lands, the people have succeeded in breaking the fetters of feudalism and in returning to the individuals the inalienable rights of man and mankind. Now, the Slav, long rejected, again raises his head. . . . Strong in numbers and even stronger in his will and in his newly acquired brotherly union, he remains nevertheless faithful to his natural character and to the principles of his ancestors: he demands neither domination nor conquest, he claims liberty for himself and for all, he asks that it be generally recognized without exception as the most sacred right of man. Therefore we Slavs reject and abhor all dominion by mere force . . . *liberty, equality* and *frater-*

nity for all who live in the state is our watchword
today, as it was a thousand years ago."

No less sacred than individual rights, according to
the manifesto and the spirit of 1848, were the rights
of nationality. Bitter words were directed against the
Germans and the Magyars for the oppression of the
Slavs. No mention was made of Russian conquests
and their oppression of Poles and Ukrainians nor of
the conflict between Poles and Ukrainians. Finally,
the manifesto called for a general European Congress
of Nations to discuss all international problems in
the conviction "that free nations will more easily
reach agreement than paid diplomats." Yet the Slav
Congress itself, where no paid diplomats met but
peoples "united in kinship and brotherly love," could
not agree upon a solution of the Slav Ruthenian
problem in Slavic Galicia or the disposal of the small
Duchy of Teschen between the two Slav neighbours,
the Czechs and Poles. 1848 started the age of nationalism in central Europe: the trouble existing then
still exists today. All the problems which were to
divide the Slavs (as well as all the other nationality
problems which were to plague Central Europe) for
the ensuing one hundred years were discussed in
1848. They were not solved then and have not been
solved since, for they cannot be solved on the basis
of nationalism.

The proclamation to the Slav peoples proposed
that the Slav Congress should become a continuous
institution, meeting every year in the month of May
always in a different Slav city. A central Slav committee should be in touch with national committees
for the discussion of political affairs. A similar net-
work of central and national committees for cultural
affairs should realize Kollár's proposals for publishing
a Slav periodical and establishing a Slav academy
and a Slav library. On June 14 the last meeting of
the Congress was to have been held to accept these

various proclamations. But the Whitsun uprising of radical students and workers in Prague on June 12 closed the Congress. The foreign delegates left; the Congress was adjourned indefinitely never to meet again.

Austro-Slavism remained for two more decades the goal of Palacký and his friends. The distrust of Russia which Palacký expressed in 1848 was shared by many Austrian Slavs. In 1843 an article appeared in the *Revue österreichischer Zustände* by an anonymous writer who objected to the general German opinion that Pan-Slavism meant that all Slavs felt tied to Russia ("dass alle Slawen russisch gesinnt sind"). The Germans know little, the writer insisted, about the western or southern Slavs, and Russia finds nowhere less sympathy than with the western Slavs. The writer of the article foresaw the coming conflict between Austria and Russia in the Balkans. Faced with the decision of taking a side between the two empires, the author wished the Slav peoples to stand with Austria, provided that Austria would treat her Slavs better.

"By distrusting her Slavs, by treating them stepmotherly as compared with her Germans and Magyars, Austria will perhaps in the future force them, which God forbid, to that kind of Pan-Slavism which Austria and Germany so prematurely and imprudently already now assume as existing. . . . There is only one way for Austria, which she will have to go sooner or later, to forestall the penetration of Russian influence among the western and southern Slavs—she must put herself at the head of the Slavs and must promote their national development. In this case she will gain the full sympathy of this numerous and intelligent (*geistreichen*) people and will occupy the place which Russia wishes to conquer. At one stroke she will thus destroy all illusions of a Russian Pan-Slavism and will find among her own peoples, who would no longer regard her as an alien ruler, a firm and unshakeable support. . . .

"The growth of Prussian influence in Germany will force Austria to follow that policy, if she wishes to restore and to maintain her position as a leading power in Central Europe. Austria could become for the western Slavs what Prussia is for Germany. Then she will face Russia and Germany with the compact power of a nationality which, equipped with all the qualities of a great people, would show in addition a dedicated loyalty to its sovereign. Then the pernicious discord between Slavs and Magyars would disappear, for the Magyar does not hate the Slav as such but as the secret ally of Russia. If Austria would promote her Slavs . . . she would have to make some concessions to liberalism. Such a step would be the heaviest blow wh.ch Austria could administer to Russia, should the latter have at any time intentions against the West. All Slavs, including the Poles, would then join Austria or would rise independently, for they would prefer always Austro-Slavism to Russian Slavism. Nor could then Germany allow herself any encroachments." [n]

The anonymous author, who perhaps was Johann Peter Jordan, a friend of Palacký, thus regarded Austro-Slavism as a desirable goal for the Austrian Slavs, for Austria herself, and for the peace in Central Europe. There can be little doubt that this Austro-Slavism and not a revolutionary Pan-Slavism predominated at the Prague Congress. Nevertheless, the German democrats in Vienna regarded the moderate Slav demands as a provocation. They believed that the Czechs should have welcomed Germanization under the banner of liberalism and progress. When the Prague movement was suppressed by Prince Alfred Windischgrätz (1787–1862), an extremely reactionary general, the Viennese radical *Volksfreund* hailed the victory of the military. "The prospects have become great since his victory," it wrote on June 24, "that Windischgrätz may even become a popular and much loved man. . . . A victory for German concerns in Bohemia and in the monarchy can never be a misfortune, for the Germans bring humanity and freedom to the conquered. A small, defeated party like the Czechs, over against whom there will always be forty million Germans, can be well satisfied with paying this price." Only four months later the same Prince Windischgrätz suppressed the freedom movement of the Viennese Germans and put an end there to the hopes of democracy and liberty.[n]

The Austro-Slav Congress of 1848 was as strongly rejected by Karl Marx as by the Viennese democrats. In 1852 the former wrote that in Bohemia "everywhere capital, trade, industry, and mental culture were in the hands of the Germans. The chief champion of the Czech nationality, Professor Palacký, is himself nothing but a learned German nomad, who even now cannot speak the Czech language correctly. . . ." Friedrich Engels was convinced that only Germans, Poles, and Magyars were bearers of progress and that the other national groups like the Czechs, Croats, and Ukrainians "have first of all the mission to perish in the revolutionary world tempest." [n] In the interest of Germans and Magyars whom he identified with the revolution, Engels thundered against the Slavs. In a rather typical misreading of history and of political reality, Engels wrote in January 1849: "With the first victorious rising of the French proletariat, which Louis Napoleon with all his might wants to bring about, the Austrian Germans and Magyars will be liberated and take their bloody vengeance on the Slav barbarians." The espousal by Marx and Engels of German (and Magyar) nationalism, of the right of big nations, and of violence and iron recklessness as midwives of history was directed not only against the

Slavs but also against Bakunin. Among the delegates at the Prague Congress this lonely Russian was the only revolutionary. His revolution did not stress the historical right and mission of great powers but the union of all peoples on the basis of equality and fraternity. He regarded the Slavs as the vanguard of human liberty, and in this position he was much nearer to eighteenth-century Herder than to the mid-nineteenth-century German radicals.

Bakunin had been for a few years a student of Hegel: disappointed by his sojourn in Germany, he turned to the more congenial a-historical faith of Rousseau and to a vague mythic belief in the revolutionary creative forces of primitive Slavdom. While Marx and Engels were the foremost exponents of the Hegelian doctrine of history as the unifying and driving force of all social life and development, Ludwig Feuerbach sharply attacked this historicism. "If mankind wishes to start a new epoch it must ruthlessly break with the past; it must assume that everything that has been so far is nothing. Only by this assumption will it gain the force and lust for new creations. All ties to the past would paralyze the *élan* of its will power. It must therefore from time to time cast away the good with the bad; it must learn to be unjust and prejudiced. Justice is a critical act, but critical insight follows upon the deed, it does not lead to it." [n] Bakunin followed Feuerbach in rejecting history: he could not identify himself with any of the historical states, neither with Austria which he hated as a part of Germany nor with his native Russia. He believed in the revolutionary *élan* of the peoples, above all those without a great civilized past who were the most oppressed. His Slav messianism which at times sounded almost like Slavophile prophecy, lacked the Slavophile glorification of the past; it was rooted in his belief that the Slavs were the most oppressed and least civilized people. In his "Appeal to the Slav peoples of a Russian patriot," which he wrote in French, at the end of 1848, and which soon reappeared in a German translation, he pointed out that though he was a Russian and a Slav he did not believe in the historical Russia but in a new revolutionary Russia which by its fire of blood would illuminate the whole of Europe. "It is in Moscow that the slavery of the peoples subjugated by the Russian scepter will be broken together with the slavery of all Slav peoples; there the whole European slavery will be buried among its own ruins. Out of an ocean of blood and fire there will rise in Moscow high in the sky the star of the revolution to become the guide of liberated mankind." [n]

In his "Appeal" Bakunin used the general slogans of the radical populists of 1848. But he added a new note rarely heard from "a Russian patriot" and practically silenced at the Prague Congress. He demanded "the dissolution of the Russian empire where, without mentioning other small peoples which lose themselves in its immensity like drops of water in the ocean, three great Slav nations, the Great Russians, the Ukrainians, and the Polish nation, of very different origin, with their own history, equally equipped with all the elements of a separate national existence, groan today under the scepter of the most horrible despot." He had expressed the same thought a year before in Paris in a meeting on November 29, 1847, in celebration of the 17th anniversary of the Polish revolution.[n] "Everywhere the name of Russian appears as the synonym of brutal oppression and shameful slavery. In the opinion of Europe, a Russian is nothing else but a vile instrument of conquest in the hands of the most hateful and most dangerous despotism." He called the Poles to an alliance with the Russians, a people equally oppressed by a foreign despot, a ruler of German origin "who will never understand the needs or the character of the Russian people." In 1848 Bakunin demanded also the independence of the Ukrainians, whom he regarded as more genuinely Slavic than the Russians ("beaucoup plus slave, moins mêlé avec l'élément finnois que le peuple Grand-Russe"), and of the Baltic nationalities. He warned the Prague Congress: "At the present time there is no place for you in the Russian empire: you ask for life, and there is only the silence of death; you demand independence and movement, and in Russia there is only mechanical obedience; you aspire toward resurrection, uplift, light and liberty, and there are only death, darkness and slave labor. If you entered the Russia of Emperor Nicholas you would descend into the tomb of all national life and of all liberty." [n]

While the western Slavs in 1848 looked to the West and to liberalism for guidance, Bakunin demanded a great Slavic federation of equals under the leadership of Russia, of a free Russia liberated by the federation of the free Slavs. His fanatic and contradictory plans—the Slav peoples without a strong Russia were much too weak to accomplish any great revolution; on the other hand, a strong Russia would not regard the small Slav peoples as equals—were foredoomed to failure. Arrested in Dresden and later extradited to Russia, Bakunin was imprisoned until 1857 in the Peter and Paul fortress and later in Schlüsselburg; then he was exiled to Siberia, whence he escaped in 1861. While a prisoner he wrote in 1851 a "confession" to the Tsar, a document of personal and national psychological interest, published only in 1919. His faith in the mystic power of revolution and of Slavdom grew here into a hope that the Tsar himself would become a true Slav and put himself at the head of the anti-German, anti-European Pan-Slav revolution. "In spite of my democratic convictions, I have worshipped you deeply in the last years, as it were against my will. Not I alone but many others, Poles and Europeans in general, have understood, like myself, that you are the only one among the ruling heads of the time who has preserved his faith in his imperial calling." He explained his activities of 1848 in a Pan-Slav and anti-European sense. He had left Paris in the spring of 1848 for Breslau. "Neither in Paris nor in France was my mission; my place was on the Russian border. There went also the Polish emigration which prepared a war against Russia; I had to be there too to influence Russians and Poles and to prevent the war in preparation from turning to a war of Europe against Russia in order that this barbarian people be driven back into the steppes of Asia, as it was then said. I made an effort not to allow it to become a war of the Germanized Poles against the Russian people, but to make it a Slav war, a war of the free Slav against the Russian dictator." Did he wish to fight this dictator any longer? After Bakunin's disappointment in the European revolution and in the Western Slavs assembled in Prague, a convinced autocrat compared favorably with the feeble liberals of Europe and became apparently acceptable to him.

"I wished for a republic (in Russia)," he wrote in his Confession. "But what kind of a republic? Certainly not a parliamentary republic. A parliamentary government, a constitutional form, a parliamentary aristocracy and the so-called balance of powers in which all forces are so cleverly arranged that none can singly become efficient—briefly this whole narrow cleverly interwoven and vapid political catechism of the Western liberals has never been an object of my idolization, nor of my sincere love, not even of my respect. On the contrary, I began to despise them even more strongly when I saw the fruit of the parliamentary forms in France, in Germany, even in the Slav Congress, especially in the Polish section where the Poles played parliament as the Germans played revolution. Moreover, a Russian

Parliament would be composed, like the Polish Parliament, only of members of the nobility—perhaps merchants would also enter the Russian Parliament —but the great mass of the people, the real nation, the shield and strength of Russia, in which its life and all its future dwells—this nation would not be represented and would be oppressed and offended by the same nobility which oppresses it now. I believe that in Russia more than anywhere else a strong dictatorial power is needed which would concern itself exclusively with the elevation and enlightenment of the masses, a power which is free in tendency and spirit but without parliamentary forms, a power which prints books of a free content without introducing the freedom of the press, a power which is surrounded, advised, and supported by the free co-operation of like-minded men but which is not limited by anybody or anything." Such a dictatorship must aim at its own final withering away after having educated and raised the masses.

There is no doubt that Bakunin spoke his innermost thoughts in the Confession to the Tsar. In it fundamental traits of the Russian revolutionary character, the generous impulses of the libertarian fighter, and a calculated understanding of the nature of Russian autocracy and of the reigning autocrat, are interwoven to form a unique document of individual and national significance. Bakunin wrote in the mood, as he expressed it, of a repentant child before his father-confessor, but he wrote without any concession to truth. "The driving force in Russia is fear, and fear destroys all life, all intelligence, every noble movement of the soul; it is hard and painful to live in Russia for anyone who loves truth; for anybody who loves his fellowmen, for anyone who respects the dignity and independence of the immortal soul equally in all men." While he summoned the Tsar to raise the Pan-Slav banner in Western Europe to frighten the Germans and all oppressors and enemies of the Slavs, he warned at the same time that the new union must be a federation of free Slavs. Otherwise Russia would become oppressive to its fellow-Slavs. "It would bring to the enslaved peoples neither liberty nor enlightenment nor prosperity of the masses but only its own nationality reduced to slavery . . . Russia would become hated by all the other Slavs as it is now hated by the Poles." With an uncanny understanding Bakunin foresaw the Pan-Slavism of a revolutionary Russian autocrat sitting in Moscow and the dangers involved in such a system if it were oppressive and not libertarian, maintaining itself by fear and terror and not by free consent.

The sincerity of the Confession is proved by the famous long letter which Bakunin wrote at the end of his Siberian exile from Irkutsk to Alexander Herzen in London on November 17, 1860. He spoke there of his admiration for Count Nikolai Nikolayevich Muravyev-Amursky (1810–81), a relative of his mother. Muravyev was Governor-General of eastern Siberia from 1848 to 1862. Under his direction this vast region was opened up and colonized by Russian settlers. In 1858 he forced China to cede to Russia northern Manchuria on the left bank of the Amur River and the Maritime province east of the Ussuri River where Vladivostok was founded. He established the first Russian settlement on the island of Sakhalin in 1857 and in 1859 with a number of warships he visited Yeddo, Japan's capital, to receive from that country, in addition to other concessions, the recognition of Russian ownership of the larger northern part of Sakhalin. This great imperial proconsul was a man according to Bakunin's heart. "He is unquestionably one of us and Russia may expect her salvation from him," he wrote to Herzen. The Governor-General and the exiled anarchist showed the same haughty Russian contempt for Western parliamentary constitutions and liberal intellectuals.

They hated the Germanized court, the aristocracy and bureaucracy of St. Petersburg, which they regarded as alienated from the Russian people. Their ideal was a truly nationalist and socialist dictatorship supported by the masses. They placed their trust in the peasants to advance Russia from her present state of inarticulate backwardness into a realm of social justice and national power without having to pass through the liberal bourgeois institutions of the West. "The peasants' axe will set St. Petersburg right and will make possible there that national dictatorship which alone can save Russia. This dictatorship is also necessary to establish Russia's power in Europe and to turn that power to the liberation of the Slavs from Austria and Turkey."

Muravyev and Bakunin (whose dream of the free Slavs freeing Russia had apparently evaporated in Siberia) would have gladly followed a Romanov if he were ready and determined to change from a St. Petersburg Emperor into a national Tsar. Alexander II in the year after the liberation of the serfs seemed a better candidate for this role than Nicholas I. Under the leadership of such a revolutionary ruler of the masses, Bakunin saw a Pan-Slav federation emerging which would also include, for geographical and historical reasons, a number of non-Slav peoples, Magyars, Rumanians, Greeks, and Constantinople. This libertarian anarchist in 1862 and the Pan-Slav nationalist Danilevsky in 1869 defined the frontiers of Pan-Slavia in almost identical terms. Bakunin dreamt of the Russian Tsar as a Napoleon of world revolution, the head of the universal monarchy dreaded by Palacký, a portentous dream indeed. In 1917 the Germanized court of St. Petersburg collapsed and the peasants' axe ruled almost unchecked over vast parts of the empire. In 1941 the invasion of the hated Germans—few Slavs ever found words of greater bitterness against the Germans than Bakunin —fanned the Russian and Pan-Slav patriotism of the masses to a realization of the Slav empire in the frontiers envisaged by Bakunin and Danilevsky, the libertarian pamphleteer and the conservative scientist, as the basis for a potential universal monarchy.

Bakunin at that time shared with the Slavophiles the distrust and fear of Europe and the faith in the Slav mission to renew the decadent West. He expressed it publicly and unmistakably in 1862 in his pamphlet "The People's Cause: Romanov, Pugachev or Pestel?" [n] Who should be the leader of the Russian people on the road to freedom—the Romanov Tsar (Alexander II); the intellectual officer Pavel Ivanovich Pestel (1792–1825), the leader of the Decembrists who in Bakunin's opinion stood for Western liberalism and constitutional ideas; or Yemelyan Ivanovich Pugachev, a Don Kozak who, claiming to be Tsar Peter III, led a mighty peasant uprising and was executed in 1775? "We will speak the truth," wrote the Russian revolutionary. "We should most gladly follow Romanov, if Romanov could and would transfer himself from a Petersburg Emperor into a national Tsar . . . because his strength is concentrated, ready to act and might become an irresistible strength if only he would give it a popular baptism." He asked Alexander II to free himself from the Germans and the German state of Peter the Great, to reconcile and liberate Poland, to become a popular Tsar and to carry through the real revolution: all soil to become the property of the people; the abolition of the bureaucracy; independence for the Poles, Ukrainians, Lithuanians, Latvians, Finns, and the peoples of the Caucasus and an alliance with them; the liberation of all Slavs; and finally close ties with Italy, Hungary, Rumania, and Greece. "We are neither friends nor enemies of the Tsar. We are friends of the cause of the Russian and Slav peoples. If the Tsar will be for it, we shall follow him. He must decide whether he wishes to serve Germans or Slavs." By 1870 Bakunin abandoned his hope in the Romanov. "L'heure de la lutte dernière entre les Romanoff-Holstein-Gottorp et le peuple russe approche, la lutte entre le joug tartaro-allemand et la large liberté slave." He now called upon a Pugachev and not upon Romanov, upon a "collective Stenka Razin," another primitive peasant Kozak whose revolt had preceded that of Pugachev by a century.[n] The one always excluded from his approval was Pestel, the liberal who looked to the West. Whatever the common Slav sympathies and devotion between the Austro-Slavs at Prague and Bakunin, whatever their common emphasis on freedom and democracy as a Slav inheritance and a human goal, no understanding was possible between them. Prague looked to the West, to patient constitutional labor, to safeguards for the rights of the individual, to the preservation of the European balance and of Austria as its indispensable foundation: Bakunin looked to Moscow, to the revolutionary and elemental *élan* of the Russian peasant masses, to a Slav utopia of perfect freedom and peace, to the destruction of the European balance and of Austria in favor of a universal monarchy which would eventually be transformed into a fraternal association of mankind.[n] Thus in 1848 two different concepts of Pan-Slavism faced each other. In that respect, too, the year 1848 set the pattern for the problems of the following century.

Though the Pan-Slav Congress of Prague had no practical results and did in no way fulfill the expectations of those who had called it together, it strengthened Slav self-confidence.[n] With typical exaggeration and self-praise a Czech member of the Congress, Jan Erazim Vocel (1803–71), wrote of the proclamation of the Congress to the nations of Europe: "Every unprejudiced man must acknowledge that the ennoblement of humanity would be markedly advanced by the realization of these principles; for liberty and equality of rights, which after millennial struggles among uncultured nations, have at last in our day been won for the individual, have been extended by the demand of the Slavonic Congress to whole nations. Thereby the Slavs have first of all nations given proof of their high moral ideal as well as of their sympathy and of their genuine, God-pleasing, brotherly love of all mankind. Wherefore we firmly believe that this first Slavonic Congress, baptized as it has been with blood, cannot but be fruitful of great moral and political achievement, and that in the pages of impartial history it will obtain a notable and glorious place." To the Slavs, Hegel's question as to whether or not that race had a world historical future seemed affirmatively answered after 1848. "We find moreover," Hegel had written, "in the East of Europe the great Slavonic nation, whose settlements extended east of the Elbe to the Don. . . . Yet this entire body of peoples remains excluded from our consideration because hitherto it has not appeared as an independent element in the series of phases that Reason has assumed in the World. Whether it will do so hereafter, is a question that does not concern us here; for in History we have to do with the Past."[n] The Slavs in 1848 looked to the future. Many of them were convinced that "as the third great European race the united Slavs must undertake and accomplish more for true humanity than the Romance or Germanic race has done hitherto."

This expectation was not shared by Marx and Engels. In their *Neue Rheinische Zeitung* they attacked the Prague Congress, the Austrian Slavs, and Bakunin's Pan-Slavism. Their wrath was partly motivated by the support which the Austrian Slavs in their fears of German or Magyar domination gave to the Habsburg monarchy, but contempt for the Slavs contributed most to a hostility which went so far as to threaten genocide. "We know now," said the *Neue Rheinische Zeitung* on the last day of 1848, "where the enemies of the revolution are: in Russia and in the Slav provinces of Austria. No phrases, no affirmation regarding the democratic future of these countries will hinder us from regarding them as our enemies. . . . Implacable struggle, war to death against the Slavs, traitors to the revolution, extermination, terrorism without consideration —not in the interest of Germany, but in that of the revolution." In typical Marxist fashion it was predicted that "the future world war will wipe from the face of the earth not only reactionary classes and dynasties but whole reactionary peoples. That too is part of progress." [n] The balance sheet of failure of the Prague Pan-Slav Congress was drawn up triumphantly by Marx and Engels in an article in the *New York Daily Tribune* on April 24, 1852:

"Thus ended for the present and perhaps forever the attempts of the Slavonians of Germany to recover an independent national existence. Scattered remnants of numerous nations whose national and political vitality had long been extinguished, and who in consequence had been obliged for almost a thousand years to follow in the wake of a mightier nation, their conqueror . . . these dying nationalities . . . had tried to profit by the universal confusion of 1848 in order to restore their political status quo of A.D. 800. The history of a thousand years ought to have shown them that such a retrogression was impossible, that if all the territory east of the Elbe and Saale had at one time been occupied by kindred Slavonians, this fact merely proved the historical tendency and at the same time the physical and intellectual power of the German nation to subdue, absorb, and assimilate its ancient eastern neighbours, and this tendency of absorption on the part of the Germans had always been, and still was, one of the mightiest means by which the civilization of Western Europe had been spread in the East of that continent. . . . How can they (the Pan-Slav dreamers) expect that history would retrograde a thousand years in order to please a few physical bodies of men, who in every part of the territory they occupy are interspread with, and surrounded by, Germans, who from time almost immemorial have had for all purposes of civilization no language but German, and who lack the very first condition of national existence, numbers and compactness of territory?" And on March 5, 1852, Marx predicted in the New York paper that "the dying Tschechian nationality made in 1848 a last effort to regain its former vitality—an effort whose failure, independent of all revolutionary considerations, was to prove that Bohemia could only exist henceforth as a portion of Germany, although part of its inhabitants might yet, for some centuries, continue to speak a non-German language." Little did Marx foresee that the restoration of the political *status quo* of A.D. 800, which he regarded as entirely impossible and which the "universal confusion of 1848" did not promote, would be brought about a century later under Marxist banners and in a "universal confusion" caused at least partly by Marxist thought.

Marx and Engels and many Western liberals shared with Palacký the fear of a Russian universal monarchy. Like Palacký, these Liberals regarded a federation of the Western Slavs in collaboration with the liberal West as a bulwark against Russia's expansion. Palacký wished to build the federation around the historic Habsburg monarchy; many Western liberals looked to the Poles as the initiators of this federation. Common to them both was their concern with Pan-Slavism and the Russian danger, a dominant intellectual and political preoccupation of Europe in the 1850's, which has been revived with infinitely greater urgency in the 1950's.[n]

5

Europe, Pan-Slavism, and the Russian Danger

THE TWO NATIONS on the fringes of Europe which remained practically untouched by the unrest of 1848 were Britain and Russia. Both appeared before the world as at the peak of their strength. Russia had emerged from the Napoleonic wars as the greatest land power and in 1849 her armies helped to re-establish order in Central Europe. Britain held after 1815 the undisputed mastery of the sea, and the exhibition of 1851 confirmed its global economic and technological leadership. Of the three territories involved in the ultimate clash between Napoleon and the two powers on the flanks of Europe—the Iberian peninsula, Poland, and the Straits of Constantinople—the third remained, after Napoleon's defeat, an open issue between Russia and Britain. It embittered their relationship for a whole century. Nevertheless, British statesmanship managed to keep the antagonism within reasonable bounds and, except for the Crimean War, to maintain peace; at times England and Russia even became allies as in the 1840's against France and seventy years later against Germany. Part of English public opinion was less moderate than the government; the leader of this outspoken fraction was David Urquhart (1805–77), who had had experience as a British diplomat in the Near East and who as a publicist—a contributor to the *Free Press* which he founded in 1855 was Karl Marx—violently denounced Russia. But though voices were raised against any "appeasement" of Russia, the government remained, on the whole, guided by a combination of firmness and cool-headed restraint. On May 22, 1853, during the strain of the Crimean War period, Lord Palmerston wrote to Lord Clarendon, then foreign secretary, that the policy and practice of the Russian government had always been "to put forward its encroachments as fast and as far as the apathy or want of firmness of other governments would allow it to go, but always to stop and retire when it was met with decided resistance, and then to wait for the next favorable opportunity to make another spring on its intended victim." [n]

The general fear of Russia was, however, not conditioned by any concrete clash of interests as in the case of the British-Russian rivalry in the Near East. In 1762 Oliver Goldsmith could not avoid "beholding the Russian Empire as the natural enemy of the more western parts of Europe; as an enemy already possessed of great strength, and, from the nature of the government, every day threatening to become more powerful. This extensive empire, which, both in Europe and Asia, occupies almost a third of the whole world, was, about two centuries ago, divided into separate kingdoms and dukedoms . . . (Today the united) kingdom thus enjoying peace internally, possessed of an unbounded extent of dominion, and learning the military art at the expense of others abroad, must every day grow more powerful; and it is probable we shall hear Russia, in future times, as formerly, called the *officina gentium*. It was long the wish of Peter, their great monarch, to have a fort in some of the western parts of Europe; many of his schemes and treaties were directed to this end, but happily for Europe he failed in them all. A fort in the power of this people would be like the possession of a floodgate; and whenever ambition, interest, or necessity prompted, they might then be able to deluge the whole western world with a barbarous inundation." [n] Fifty years later Europe was startled by the publication of an alleged testament of Peter projecting the course of conquest which Russia had followed after Peter's death.[n] The fear of Russia was not a product of the propaganda of the European foreign offices, and it often ran counter to their official policy. It was caused less by any act of Russian aggression than by Russia's separateness and inaccessibility and by her domestic policy. A London newspaper summed it up very well in 1914, at a time when the Conservative *Morning Post* deduced the greatness of Russian Tsarist civilization from the magnificence of the Russian Imperial ballet: "There is always in Europe an atmosphere favorable to anti-Russian agitation, and that atmosphere, in spite of the combination of the Chancelleries, tends every year to become more sensitive. It is due in part to the aggressive tendencies of Russian foreign policy, and in even greater measure to a detestable internal policy which not only outrages great masses of European public opinion, but is forever exporting legions of victims, who in the freer communities of the West become permanent and effective agents of Russophobia." [n]

This Russophobia was, in the middle of the last century, more pronounced among intellectuals on the European continent than in Britain. It was not confined to liberal or socialist circles. Clear-sighted monarchists of the Right were no less concerned about the dangers of the Russian autocracy and its implications. The Spanish diplomat and political thinker, Donoso Cortés (1809–53), in his speech of January 30, 1850, before the Spanish Parliament, pointed out that Russia was not strong enough to threaten a consolidated and patriotic Europe. How-

ever, should Europe be weakened by social conflict
and lack of patriotism, then the hour for Russia's
world domination might come; before it would
come, "the national idea of Pan-Slavism must have
been realized in the East, i.e., the Slav peoples
must have put themselves under Russian protection
and must have united with the Tsar's empire into
a great Slav confederation. Gentlemen, I must ask
you urgently, not to underrate this. For the Slav
peoples count together not less than 80 million inhabitants." He warned that the Slav conquerors
would not regenerate Europe as the German barbarians did who destroyed the Roman Empire. For
the dangerous sickness from which Europe suffered,
according to Cortés, had already begun to undermine
the Slavs and had made them into half-baked
Europeans."[n]

Cortés knew only Western Europe: the French
anti-revolutionary social philosopher, Joseph de
Maistre (1754–1821), who was Sardinian minister
plenipotentiary in St. Petersburg from 1802 to 1815,
saw more deeply. A devoted Roman Catholic, he
found religion to be non-existent in Russia as a conservative force. "Religion there has some power over
the human mind but none at all over the heart where
all the desires and all the crimes originate." He
looked with apprehension to the future, in which the
emancipated serfs would be exposed to the influence
of teachers who were more than suspect, and priests
who were neither strong nor respected. "Thus they
would pass suddenly and entirely unprepared from
superstition to atheism and from a passive obedience
to unbridled activity. On all these minds liberty will
exercise the influence of a strong wine on a man
who is in no way accustomed to it. . . . If in such a
moral and mental climate some intellectual Pugachev
(Pougatcheff d'Université) appears . . . then the
whole state will in all probability completely break
down." [n]

Half a century later another Western observer
shared the pessimism of De Maistre. Friedrich Boden
stedt (1819–92), a fertile German writer, poet, and
translator, lived as a tutor in Moscow, then became
the head of a school in Tiflis and returned in 185.
to Germany as professor of Slav languages in Munich
As a constitutional liberal he wished a Western
development for Russia, but he feared Russian ex
tremism. Many progressive intelligent men in Russia
seemed to agree with Emperor Nicholas, Bodenstedt
wrote, that for Russia only monarchist autocracy
or a revolutionary republic was a valid solution
Alexander II might still be able to steer the ship of
state toward a sound middle-of-the-road development
and to avert the revolution if he would grant quickly
and freely what he could not refuse in the long run
a liberal Russian constitution on a national basis and
the restoration of the Polish constitution. Thereby
he would crown the great work of the emancipation
of the serfs. Should he, however, try to dam the
movement by force instead of directing it into proper
channels, then he would call forth a revolution
"which would easily shake old Europe more violently
than the French Revolution has done. For nothing is
more terrible than the uprising of a people which has
never lived in an order based upon law but has
always been accustomed only to bow before crude
force and which now suddenly sees this power in its
hands." [n]

Those who warned most persistently against the
Russian Pan-Slav danger were socialists and liberals
The *New York Daily Tribune* of April 12, 1853
printed an article by Karl Marx in which he attacked
British public opinion for its lack of vigor in pursuing
an anti-Russian policy. He strongly stressed the strategic importance of the Straits of Constantinople.
For Russia could not stop at the Bosphorus. "But
having come thus far on the way to universal empire,
is it probable that this gigantic and swollen Power

will pause in its career? Circumstances, if not her own will, forbid it. With the annexation of Turkey and Greece she has excellent seaports, while the Greeks furnish skilful sailors for her navy. With Constantinople, she stands at the threshold of the Mediterranean; with Durazzo and the Albanian coast . . . she is in the very center of the Adriatic. . . . The broken and undulating western frontier of the Empire, ill-defined in respect of natural boundaries, would call for rectification; and it would appear that the natural frontier of Russia runs from Dantzic, or perhaps Stettin, to Trieste. And as sure as conquest follows conquest, and annexation follows annexation, so would the conquest of Turkey by Russia certainly be only the prelude to the annexation of Hungary, Prussia, Galicia, and to the ultimate realization of the Slavonic Empire which certain fanatical Pan-Slavistic philosophers dreamed of."

A week later in the same publication Marx painted a lurid picture of the Pan-Orthodox and Pan-Slav dealings of Russian agents in the Balkans. "Hundreds of Russian agents perambulated Turkey," he wrote, "pointing out to the Greek Christians the Orthodox Emperor as the head, the natural protector, and the ultimate liberator of the oppressed Eastern Church, and to the South Slavonians especially, pointing out that same Emperor as the almighty Czar, who was sooner or later to unite all the branches of the great Slave race under one scepter, and to make them the ruling race of Europe." Marx apparently took the most rabid Pan-Slav declarations of some Russian or Slovak intellectuals at their face value. When he continued in the same issue to describe the "vast conspiracy," his words again sound familiar a century later "The Servian insurrection of 1809, the Greek rising in 1821, were more or less directly urged on by Russian gold and Russian influence; and wherever among the Turkish pashas the standard of revolt was raised against the Central

Government, Russian intrigues and Russian funds were never wanting; and when thus internal Turkish questions had entirely perplexed the understanding of Western diplomatists, who knew no more about the real subject than about the man in the moon, then war was declared, Russian armies marched toward the Balkans, and portion by portion the Ottoman Empire was dismembered." With mordant irony Marx attacked the Russians for carrying on their conquests under the pretext of peaceful intentions and of protecting the interests of their victims. In a letter which he sent from London on May 31 and which the *New York Daily Tribune* published on June 14, 1853, he derided Russia's claim to protect the peoples of Turkey and her assurance of harboring a deep antipathy against aggrandizement and conquest. In the last sixty years, he claimed, Russia had acquired territories equal in extent and importance to the whole Empire she had held in Europe before that time.

Marx's hostility to Russia was partly based upon Russia's reactionary regime, but much of it was due to his identification of Russia with "Pan-Slavism." That was the title of an article based upon "reports" from Russia, which he published, after the accession of Alexander II to the Russian throne, in the *New York Daily Tribune* of May 5, 1855: ". . . The moment Austria shall irrevocably ally herself to the West, it (the report) says, or commit any overt act of hostility against Russia, Alexander II *will place himself at the head of the Pan-Slavist movement*, and change his title of Emperor of all the Russians into that of *Emperor of all the Slavonians*. . . . (The question would then arise) who is to command all Europe? The Slavonic race long divided by internal contests; repelled toward the East by Germans; subjugated, in part, by Turks, Germans, Hungarians; quickly reuniting its branches, after 1815, by the gradual rise of Pan-Slavism, would then for the first time assert its unity, and, in doing so, declare war to the knife against the Romano-Celtic and Germanic races which have hitherto ruled the Continent. Pan-Slavism is not a movement which strives after national independence; it is a movement which, thus acting upon Europe, would tend to undo what a thousand years of history have created; which could not realize itself without sweeping from the map Hungary, Turkey, and a large part of Germany. Moreover, it must subjugate Europe in order to secure the stability of these results, if they are ever obtained. Pan-Slavism is now, from a creed, turned into a political programme, or rather a vast political menace, with 800,000 bayonets to support it." [n]

More penetrating were the observations of the French republican historian Jules Michelet. In 1851, discussing democracy in northern Europe, he wrote: "I am, Prussia said, the civilization. And I, Russia said (or at least her friends said it for her), I am a power which is a friend of progress and, under an absolutist form, I am a revolutionary power." He believed that the Russian danger did not stem primarily from a threat of aggression, from the 800,000 bayonets of which Marx wrote four years later, but from Russian propaganda which disseminated doubt and confusion in Europe by using and perverting Western concepts of help to the oppressed and concern for liberty. Russia invaded Poland allegedly to protect the peasants against the nobility and invaded Turkey claiming to establish political and religious freedom. Russian propaganda aimed at paralyzing the intellectual and moral understanding of the potential victims. "Cette force dissolvante, ce froid poison, qu'elle fait circuler peu à peu, qui détend le nerf de la vie, démoralise ses futures victimes, les livre sans défense," is of an infinite variety. "Yesterday it (Russian propaganda) told us: I am Christianity; tomorrow it will tell us: I am socialism."

This empire, Michelet wrote, was built on a blind barbarous faith, without any regard or pity even for oneself, a faith which ultimately destroyed individual personality and spiritual life. This Russian Empire was firmly established, Michelet believed, foreseeing the strange confessions of Stalin's communist victims, on the day when the Muscovite aristocrat who was impaled by order of Ivan the Terrible shouted during the two days of his frightful agony: "My God, save the Czar." Only the rise of a skeptical individualism and of searching criticism after the Western model could weaken the empire. To prevent this, the Russian government, this "petrification of the Terror," maintained, according to Michelet, an absolute separation between the people of Russia and the rest of the world. "It in no way hinders the people from losing its ancient moral ideal but it hinders them from receiving the Western ideal which could replace the old idea on a new basis. It keeps the people morally empty, without defense against the suggestions of the evil spirit and the temptations of the desert. . . . La Russie n'admet rien de nous que le mal. Elle absorbe, attire à elle tout le poison de l'Europe. Elle le rend augmenté et plus dangereux."

Michelet saw Russia a century ago as a country where, under a cover of extreme rigidity, complete insecurity prevailed. "One has often spoken of the martyrs of Siberia. But why single them out? Any line of separation would be entirely fictitious. Except for an aggravation of the cold, Siberia is everywhere in Russia. It starts at the Vistula. One speaks of convicts. But every Russian is a convict. In a country where the law is only a mockery . . . all are convicts. One cannot distinguish between suffering and punishment. The general punishment is not some material evil. It is the heartbreak, the moral anxiety of a soul broken in advance by the eventuality of an infinity of misfortune. In this world which is so hard, where everything seems to be rigidly fixed like ice, nothing is fixed. In reality, everything is full of hazard and doubt." One hundred years ago, Michelet wrote in 1851, Russia abolished capital punishment. "Our philosophers, hearing about it, shed tears of joy . . . Happy humane Russia which alone on earth knows how to respect the living creation of God, while death is still enthroned in the impious legislations of the barbarous West. . . . They do not kill—they only send into exile. Only it can happen there that a man who is too delicate and is sent too far north, dies of cold and misery. What can one do about it?" Though the death penalty was abolished by the Russian Tsars, Michelet regarded the existing punishments as so severe that people did not escape alive."

Twenty years later, in his "La France devant l'Europe," which he wrote in February 1871, he looked beyond Germany farther east. The German invasion of France and the German arrogance following their easy triumph deeply shook Michelet, a life-long admirer of German life and scholarship. He warned the victors to transcend their narrow views, not to regard themselves as a young race and not to despise the French as old and decaying. The Germans should visualize the West as a whole, for on their eastern borders the Russians were clamoring: "We are young, the Germans are old. The Latins and the Germans are finished. Forward, Slav race! It is your turn, Moscovy!" Russia represented the religion of autocracy, of dedicated faith in, and blind obedience to, one ruler. "What a monstrous impiety to adore a living man." The then ruling Tsar, Alexander II, was widely acclaimed as social reformer and liberator. Many Russians pointed out with pride that Russia had received more actual liberty through the recent reforms than capitalist England or America with their relentless exploitation enjoyed, and, according to Michelet, many people in the West believed it. Michelet, on the other hand, saw in the emancipation of the serfs and in the administrative modernization of Russia only a means of strengthening autocracy. It made possible the emergence of a "socialist tyrant," of a Tsar who would become a "Messiah of the serfs, a barbarous Messiah, terrible to Europe." Against this danger he called upon all the Western nations to unite for common defense. "I call here to a European congress . . . the English, the French, the Belgians, the Dutch, the Swiss, I call the Germans. I call here the two worlds. I solemnly call upon young America. Let her justify our hope, let her be deaf to all petty interests, free of all petty rancours, devoted to the great general interest of human progress, closely associated with the civilized West with the cause of liberty which she has supported so recently and which she has made so gloriously victorious." [n]

Michelet was undoubtedly influenced by his old friendship for the Poles.[n] Many French and Polish writers of the period went so far as to declare the Great Russians to be not Slavs or Europeans but Turanians and Asiatics. Franciszek Duchiński (1817–93) quoted many authors in support of the thesis which he expounded in a book with the characteristic title *Peuples aryâs et tourans agriculteurs et nomades. Nécessité des reformes dans l'exposition des peuples aryâs-européens & tourans, particulièrement des Slaves et des Moscovites.* The same point of view was upheld by the French historian Henri Martin (1810–83) in a book *La Russie et l'Europe* which he published two years later and which carried the motto "l'Europe aux Européens." Like Michelet four years later, he called for a European federation, founded on individual liberty, individual property and respect for family, against Russia, which he regarded as a Turanian power by race and civilization. There the state, "l'association moscovite, . . . rests on a community personified in one man who can arbitrarily dispose of all liberties, all property and all the families." If Europe does not federate, it will be conquered by Russia, and then "America, our daughter, must alone preserve all the higher elements of human civilization. . . . Then there will be only two powers left on earth which will divide it up as between the light and the darkness. All moral life will then take its refuge in the other (Western) hemisphere." Should Europe unite, however, there would emerge three powers, the United States of America, the European federation, and the tsardom of Moscovy in the extreme east of Europe and the north of Asia, which would no longer be Europe's enemy."

Less extreme in his demands was Cyprien Robert who occupied the chair of Slavonic studies at the Collège de France after Mickiewicz. He, too, was full of anxiety in looking toward the future and surveying the moral ruins left by 1848. "Where do we go?" he asked in 1852." "Is it winter of one thousand years which soon will throw its snows and icy darkness upon us? Or does somewhere a new sun rise whose vernal warmth will restore the freshness of our blood? No prophet can answer this question. But all farsighted men look with anxiety upon the Slavs." A Western liberal, Robert welcomed the Slavs as mediators between East and West. He accepted, on the whole, the program of the Austro-Slavs for a federal Austria, a Western Pan-Slavism in an enlightened cosmopolitan spirit and the detachment of the Slavs from the hold and the ancient struggles of the Churches. Polish spokesmen were less definitely committed to the West. Count Valerian Krasiński (1780–1855) who, on the whole, supported the policy of the Prague Congress, pleaded in the same year for the restoration of Poland as a barrier between Europe and Russia. It alone would prevent Russian armies from occupying Breslau and rich Silesia. He favored a Pan-Slav movement of the Western Slavs, founded on liberal ideas, and opposed to Russia. Should the Germans, however, wish to keep the Prussian Polish provinces and not support the Poles, then the Poles might unite with the Russians on the basis of Slav equality, a true Pan-Slavism which would not Russify the Poles but equally Slavonize Poles and Russians. Seven years later, during the Crimean War, the author returned to the Polish question. He warned the West against sacrificing the Poles or trying to make use of them for the sole purpose of frightening Russia. "If such a conviction becomes prevalent among the Poles, and there can be no doubt that it is rapidly spreading, what will then remain to them except cordially to unite with the Russians, and to become, from a barrier between Russia and the rest of Europe, the vanguard of the Slavonic race against Western Europe and Germany in particular?" [n]

Though Polish disapproval of Russia's ways had, in the middle of the last century, a great influence on European public opinion,[n] the fear of Russia would have been widespread without the Poles. But there were even at that period some isolated thinkers who daringly anticipated twentieth-century developments. Ernest Coeurderoy (1825-62) participated actively in the rising of 1848 and spent his later life in exile, refusing to accept the amnesty. By profession a physician, he shared the positivist and scientific outlook imparted by that training. But in this style he was a typical enthusiast of the period, full of exuberant passion and of messianic vision. An anarchist influenced by Proudhon,[n] he aroused much opposition by his "scandalous" conviction that the triumph of liberty in Europe depended on a Slav hegemony which he thought inevitable. In his *De la Révolution dans l'homme et dans la société* (1852) he drew up the sum of his experiences of 1848. The only road to a solution, according to him, led through violence, war, and catastrophe of civilization —the Flood of the North would bring them about by inundating Europe. "Vive l'universelle Guerre! Et vive les Cosaques qui nous apportent l'une et qui forceront l'autre!" To clarify his position, Coeurderoy published in 1854 a book *Hurrah ! ! ! ou la Révolution par les Cosaques.*[11] It appeared during the siege of Sevastopol which many Pan-Slavs in Moscow regarded as the beginning of the decisive East-West struggle. Like them, Coeurderoy hoped for a Russian victory but for different reasons. Everything in the world he knew seemed to him ripe for total destruction, Western civilization having frozen into immobility, no longer able to support man's mind and body. Revolution was everything that was not immobilized in the past, all that was not civilized, all that strove to be born. The West was an immense cemetery of peoples and religions; the East, the great workshop of new forces. To those who like himself suffocated in old Europe he declared: "there is no life for you except in the universal ruin. And as you are not numerous enough in Western Europe for your despair to cause a breach, seek outside Western Europe. Seek and you will find in the North a people who are totally disinherited, totally homogeneous, totally strong, totally pitiless, a people of soldiers. You will find the Russians."[12]

The total war ending in Russian victory promised to bring the total revolution, which could come only through Russia. The Western peoples had too much to lose to be able to accomplish it, the Russians had hardly anything to lose by it, Coeurderoy argued. The citizen in the West faced many contradictory authorities and interests; the Russians faced only one despotism. This brutal, avowed, concentrated despotism was preferable to the hypocritical, divided and changing tyrannies of the West. Sixty million peasants would master the handful of Russian aristocrats with infinitely greater ease than the few thousand revolutionaries in the West could overcome the great number of property owners. "While the Slav world becomes more and more unified through despotism, the Germano-Latin world dissolves more and more through anarchy. While every Russian is a soldier who obediently takes his place in the army of conquest, every civilized Westerner is a property owner who wishes to preserve his parcel of land or a socialist philosopher who proudly claims his own part in the work of destruction." The West is satiated and desires rest; the Russians are driven on by their very privations. The West thinks that it has ideas and yet "we have only memories which hinder us from thinking courageously." The Slavs who have no ideas are therefore more open to ideas. "We are the female races full of grace, delicacy and voluptuous sensuality. They are the male races who hunt the female races, rape them and fertilize them." [n]

Coeurderoy was convinced that Russia would unite all Slav peoples, not in a free and equal federation, but in a huge centralized state under the despotism of one will possessed of a clear consciousness of his peoples' mission and thereby able to conquer Europe and regenerate civilization. This despot would appeal to some in the name of liberty, others he would win over by his agents, by gold, and by treason. He would know how to profit from all the divisions which he would favor. Through his policy he would add ever new protectorates to his realm.[n] The Slavs would accept his despotism as the only means for achieving victory. But they would overthrow it later on. Neither the despotism in the immediate future nor the revolution later on would be half-way measures with the Slavs. Coeurderoy did not doubt that Russian despotism with its great and united force would defeat Europe. The newly acquired subjects would love it as they loved Napoleon, as they love all successful masters. They would sing the praise of the Russian despotism which would despise them and make all privileges disappear under the leveling iron of its authority.

Like Marx, Coeurderoy expected the revolution in the almost immediate future. He proved an unreliable prophet. While the Western powers besieged Sevastopol, he wrote that the fall of Constantinople to the Russians would occur before the end of 1855. "Oh, Constantinople! The sun of thy glory will rise over the universe! Then the map of the world will be redrawn! The Revolution must be accomplished! The Russians thirst for blood." [n] He described what would happen after the fall of the second Rome to the third Rome. Britain and Turkey would be forced out of the war, while in France corruption and appeasement would assure Russian victory. Then France with Belgium and the former Confederation of the Rhine would be placed under the rule of a Russian archduke, the Slavs would mingle with the Latin races, the result would be a rapid increase of population and a rise in the standard of living which in turn would force the real revolution, ushering in the new age of true liberty.

It may not be without interest to note the future predicted by Coeurderoy for the United States. He praised its federal system which he regarded as a guarantee of liberty. But the United States would be unable to influence decisively the events in the Old World. There for the time being the leadership would fall to Russia. "The next revolution in Europe will be accomplished by Violence, by Centralization, by Russia; the other revolution, by Liberty, by Federation, by America will come only much later when the consequences of the first revolution will be exhausted." The United States and Russia will settle the borders of the two spheres by agreement, the sphere of individual liberty under the leadership of the Anglo-Americans and the sphere of human solidarity represented by the Slavs. [n] Britain will evacuate India, and this evacuation will be a signal for the invasion of Asia by Russia and by America. Endless revolutions will stir and shake the whole

East, especially China, and the two great invading opponents will try to influence the outcome of these revolutions.

With this political vision Coeurderoy concluded his book. He promised to write a sequel. At the moment he could do no more than to give a breathtaking description of the social destruction, of the audacious Negation which, however, by necessity must lead to social reconstruction, to a glorious Affirmation. "The socialist Revolution, that is the Individual, that is Happiness! What could such a revolution do with the present men as they are, regimented men who deny the surpassing excellence of Self-interest, of Well-being, of Pride and of Individual Liberty?" He hoped for years of health to allow him to write his positive gospel. "Then I shall predict all the future events according to their hour. And with ardent word I shall force them into reality as the Spring rays of the sun awaken the anemones! Then I shall break the seal which suffering forces me to put on the terrible Book of the Future. From the depth of my exile calm as in the night of the grave, I shall write on each of my terrifying pages the menaces and the promises of the eternal revolution." [n] Thirty years before Nietzsche, this other solitary man and homeless wanderer in old Europe, overshadowed by his approaching personal end, impatient with the pettiness of man and of society in the face of expected catastrophes, aspired to write the tables of the new law.

Like the Russian Slavophiles, Coeurderoy believed in the distinctive character and the mission of the Russians. But his evaluation was different from theirs. The Slavophiles regarded the Russians as the embodiment of eighteenth-century nature, seen through the eyes of Rousseau and Herder, carrying the message of peace and love, of concord and humility, the constructive builders of the Kingdom of God in liberty and harmony. To Coeurderoy the Russians represented the entirely different nineteenth-century interpretation of nature, barbaric and Dionysian, a pitiless force of ever-recurrent destruction and rebirth, best realized by despotism and innocent of civilization. He welcomed the barbarians out of his despair of old Europe. More clearly did Astolphe Marquis de Custine (1790–1857) recognize that the Russians were not the primitive barbarians whom Coeurderoy assumed them to be; at the same time he had a higher opinion of modern Europe. In his pessimism he wrote: "Lorsque . . . les nations, soi-disant les plus civilisées de la terre, auront achevé de s'énerver dans leurs débauches politiques, et que de chute en chute elles seront tombées dans le sommeil au dédans et dans le mépris au dehors . . . les écluses du nord se lèveront de nouveau sur nous: alors nous subirons une dernière invasion, non plus de barbares ignorants, mais de maîtres rusés, éclairés, plus éclairés que nous, car ils auront appris de nos propres excès, comment l'on peut et l'on doit gouverner." But he did not long for this future. He knew that "the present order, with all its shortcomings, is yet a happier order for all than the century will be which it announces for us and from which I try in vain to turn my thoughts away." [n] Custine found the Russians eager for submission and obedience ("Tandis que d'autres nations ont supporté l'oppression, la nation russe l'a aimée; elle l'aime encore; et l'on peut dire des Russes qu'ils sont ivres d'esclavage") and at the same time inspired by a great national ambition which makes them accept the absence of liberty. "An immense and boundless ambition, one of these ambitions which can spring up only in the soul of the oppressed and draw their nourishment from the misfortune of a whole nation, was seething in the heart of the Russian people. This essentially conquering nation, greedy as a result of its hardships, atones in advance for the hope of exercising tyranny abroad by a degrading submission at home; the glory and the wealth which the Russian nation expects distract it from the shame which it suffers at home; in order to clean itself of the ungodly sacrifice of all its public and personal liberties, the kneeling slave nation dreams of the domination of the world." Custine thought to find a new Roman Empire smouldering in Russia under the embers of the Byzantine Empire. "The Russians see in Europe a prize which will fall to them sooner or later through our dissensions; it foments anarchy in our ranks in the hope to profit by a corruption which it favors . . . it is the history of Poland restarted on a grand scale." [n]

The most remarkable representative of liberal Russia in the middle of the last century, Alexander Herzen, read Custine's book in October 1843, and judged it to be one of the most intelligent of those written by a foreigner. On the 26th he noted in his diary: "The impression which this book makes upon a Russian is extremely painful. . . . One feels the terrible truth." [n] A decade later, after having lived in Europe during the revolutionary crisis of 1848, though he remained throughout his life dedicated to individual liberty as the cornerstone of all social life, Herzen became aware of the complexity of European-Russian relations. Yet at times he could reduce this complexity to an apparent simplicity which from the other side recalled some of the fears and prophecies of Michelet, Coeurderoy and Custine: "Since the thick fog which enveloped the February Revolution has disappeared, one begins to see more and more clearly. A decisive simplicity replaces the complexity: there are the only two real problems: the social problem and the Russian problem. Essentially they are one and the same. The Russian problem, that is the accidental side, the negative test; it is the new appearance of the barbarians smelling of agony, shouting their *memento mori* to the old world, and offering it a murderer if it does not wish to commit suicide. In fact, if revolutionary socialism does not succeed in putting an end to decaying society, Russia will do it. I do not say that this is necessary, but it is possible. . . . The future is never unalterably predetermined. . . . The general tendencies of the future which are only vaguely expressed become modified according to the circumstances. They determine the how, and the floating possibility becomes the accomplished fact. Russia can as well invade Europe to the Atlantic as she can be invaded to the Ural Mountains. The first case presupposes a Europe deeply divided. The second case demands a Europe firmly united. Is it united?" [n]

Like Herzen many Russians in the 19th century felt that the destiny of Europe and civilization would be decided by Russia. They emphasized the Slav character and traditions of Russia and regarded a Slav union as the necessary basis for the exercise of Russian influence. In the first half of the 19th century most educated Russians looked to the West for inspiration and guidance. German philosophy and French socialism formed their minds and hopes. The prevailing optimistic liberalism of the generations of July 1830 and February 1848 penetrated into Russia. All that changed in the 1860's. The unification of Germany by Prussia, the strongest and easternmost of the German states, seemed to set a precedent for the Slav world; the methods and the triumph of Bismarck scorned and apparently defeated the humanitarianism and individualism of the Western middle classes; the events of 1866 and 1867 doomed the hopes of the Austro-Slavs. In the new age which the Iron Chancellor inaugurated, were not the Slavs bound to unite, to shift from Prague to Moscow, from the West to the East? Yet no simple decision was reached, no unity established. The second half of the 19th century was filled with a growing debate about the meaning and mission of the Slav peoples, about the possibility or necessity of Pan-Slavism. But the center of the debate was no longer among the Western Slavs. It became a debate among Russians who presumed to speak for their "Slav brothers." The astonishing growth of Russian cultural life, the flowering of a Russian literature of world-wide significance, which set in when the reform era of the early 1860's brought the promise of European liberty under law to Russia and allowed closer contact with the West, heightened Russian self-confidence. The Russians were conscious of their rapid progress in surpassing the civilization of Poles, Czechs, and Illyrians. Pan-Slavism in the first half of the nineteenth century was a movement of the Western Slavs born out of their cultural awakening and their political weakness. In the second half of the century it became a predominantly Russian movement, rooted in a feeling of spiritual and material grandeur and in a consciousness of historical destiny.

PART II

Pan-Slavism and Russian Messianism

1860-1905

No, a thousand times no. It is not thus that we loved our country in our youth. We wished its welfare, we desired good institutions for it, we even sometimes went so far as to wish for it, if that could be, more liberty; we knew that it was great and powerful, full of a future; but we did not think either that it was the most powerful nor the most fortunate country in the world. We were far from imagining that Russia represented some kind of abstract principle comprising the definite solution of the social problem, that she by herself constituted a whole world apart, which was the direct and legitimate heir of the glorious Eastern empire, its titles and wishes, that she had a special mission of absorbing all the Slav peoples in her bosom, and thereby achieving the regeneration of mankind.

Above all, we did not think that Europe was on the point of falling back into barbarism and that we were called to save civilization with those few rags of that same civilization which had formerly served to save us from our ancient torpor. We treated Europe with civility, nay, even with respect, for we knew that she had taught us many things, and among others, our own history. . . . Then one fine day we reached Paris (1814) and they gave us the welcome you know of, forgetting for the moment that we were really only young upstarts and that we had put nothing into the common stock of nations, not even a poor little solar system like the Poles, our subjects, not even some miserable algebra like the Arabs, those infidels whose absurd and barbarous religion we are now fighting. They treated us well because they found that we had the manners of decently brought up people, because we were polite and modest, as befits newcomers without any other title to public esteem but the advantages of their stature.

You have changed all that; so be it! But let me, I beg you, love my country in the way of Peter the Great, of Catherine and Alexander. The time is not far off, I hope, when we shall perhaps find this patriotism well worth any other.

                                                              Chaadayev (1854)

1

The Slavophiles and Russia's Mission

IN 1814 Russian troops entered Paris, the capital of the West. Their ruler, Alexander I, stood at the pinnacle of prestige, backed by an immense army and by Russia's fame as "Europe's savior" from Napoleon. The West feared the potentialities of the new situation. But for the next one hundred years the peace, on the whole, was kept. Alexander I, educated in the spirit of the Enlightenment and later swayed by the European current of romantic mysticism, regarded the war against Napoleon as a common European enterprise for the independence of its princes and the peace of Christendom. The Holy Alliance represented a European conception; under the influence of Franz Xavier von Baader (1765–1841), the Bavarian speculative mystic, leading Russian Orthodox thinkers looked forward to the unity of the Christian churches.[n] Under Alexander's successors, the Court remained conscious of its European position and responsibility. The Russian autocrats of the period did not regard themselves as world conquerors or world saviors; they were mediocre personalities and not men of steel; they were related to the European dynasties by ties of family and interest; the dominant language in St. Petersburg was French; many of the influential members of the high society were of German origin; the leading statesmen were conservative.

Count Charles Robert de Nesselrode (1780–1862), whose father, a scion of Rhenish nobility, served as Russian minister in Lisbon, entered the Russian diplomatic service at the age of twenty-two and was from 1816 to 1856 Russian Foreign Minister and later Chancellor. A devoted servant of Russian interests and Russian dignity, he was at the same time sincerely attached to the cause of peace and moderation.[n] Nesselrode, like Metternich an eighteenth-century aristocrat, had no sympathy for nationalism or Pan-Slavism.[n] Russian public opinion welcomed the appointment of Prince Alexander Mikhailovich Gorchakov (1793–1883), a descendant of the oldest Russian nobility, as his successor. Foreign Minister and later Chancellor from 1856 to 1882, he understood how to respond in his declarations to the nationalist and Pan-Slav mood of Russian society; in his policy, however, he remained, on the whole, faithful to the school of Nesselrode in which he had grown up. Pan-Slavism and nationalism did not draw their strength in nineteenth-century Russia from the Court and government; the source of their inspiration was, as similar movements a century later in Asia, the small educated class which found itself suddenly face to face with Europe, a situation for which Russian history had not prepared it.

For Russia, which in her Kiev period had formed the eastern border of Europe, had later been separated from it for many centuries. The intellectual and social revolutions which shaped modern Europe, the reception of Aristotelian philosophy and of Roman law, the Renaissance and the Reformation, the rise of the middle class and of scientific thought, did not reach and fertilize Russia. In the sixteenth century the fragile roots of lawful life and traditional freedom which had existed in Russia before the Mongol invasion withered away. The new capital, Moscow, grew up, like the German cities founded east of the Elbe, far from the old cultural centers of the west, on recently colonized land. Though its church kept the communion of faith with Byzantium, the ties grew weaker. It became purely Russian; its Slavonic liturgy cut it off from Byzantium as well as from ancient civilization. This national church which dominated Russian life was at the same time deeply conscious of its universal mission. For Moscow felt itself more and more the center of the true faith.

It was this adherence to the faith which preserved the Russians from absorption by the Mongols whose political order and outward civilization they readily accepted. Soon the Russians became convinced that Moscow alone lived the faith in undefiled purity. They hated any deviation which would endanger the unity of the faith that assured salvation. After the fall of Constantinople Moscow stood forth as the guardian of the faith. The fall of the city which had been the capital of the universal empire and of the true church for eleven centuries appeared to the Russians as God's punishment upon the Byzantine church for having been ready, at the Council of Florence, to accept union with Rome and to bow before the Latin infidels. Moscow remained uncompromisingly hostile to the West. God had clearly rejected the Rome of Augustus and the new Rome of Constantine as unworthy of the task to bring peace and justice to the world and to guide it to the true faith. "A new and third Rome has sprung up in the North, illuminating the whole universe like a sun," wrote the monk Philotheus. "The third Rome will stand to the end of history, for it is the last Rome. Moscow had no successor; a fourth Rome is inconceivable." Russia became the holy

land, Moscow the successor to the imperial mission
of Rome.

At the end of the seventeenth century Peter had
attempted to Westernize and secularize Holy Russia,
had led her into a "Babylonian captivity." To the
dismay of the Russians, Moscow was replaced as the
capital by an entirely new city, St. Petersburg, consciously and intentionally turned toward Europe.[n]
But Peter tried to introduce Western administrative
methods and technology only, and did not care for
the European spirit of liberty. A ruthless despotism
and regimentation were to overcome the inertia
and backwardness of the Russian people. They were
educated neither for liberty nor law but reared, to
quote the words of a great Russian historian, in "an
atmosphere of arbitrary rule, general contempt for
legality and the person, and to a blunted sense of
morality." The nation was in no way prepared for
the sudden shift.

Only in the nineteenth century, after the Napoleonic wars, did European ideas begin to penetrate
more deeply into the consciousness of the small
educated class. With an astonishing eagerness the
thought of free Europe was received, foreign literatures were translated, science and knowledge popularized. This Europeanization of a small elite split
the nation, and the unity of faith in which it had
gloried waned. The peasants and tradesmen looked
upon European ways as the work of the devil. Some
educated Russians became fully integrated into
Europe and accepted the critical approach of the
West. Leading Russian historians, far from idealizing the national past, as so many Prussian historians
did, exposed the backwardness, ruthlessness, and brutality of the Russian state and society. But most
Russians were bewildered. The victory over Napoleon
made them conscious of Russia's might and power
as never before. Did not the imperial greatness of
Russia dwarf that of Rome? Karamzin expressed a

widespread feeling when he wrote that "looking on the immensity of the Russian monarchy, which is unique in the world, our mind feels overwhelmed. Never did Rome equal it in greatness." [n] Nowhere were Russians subject to foreign domination; as masters they ruled many peoples in West and East. The Empire's fast-growing population and its vastness guaranteed its future.

Yet mighty Russia suffered because of her backward and primitive civilization; she suspected Europe of looking down on her with contempt or condescension. When in 1831 all liberal Europe sympathized with the Poles in their struggle for independence from Russia, Russia's greatest poet, Pushkin, turned violently against Poland's friends with a fierce warning to the Europeans that they had nothing to seek in a strife among Slavs. He saw in Europe's sympathy not the desire to help an oppressed nationality to liberty but ungrateful hatred of Russia, of that very Russia which had not bowed to the insolent will of Napoleon and had with its blood redeemed Europe's freedom, honor, and peace. Let the Western liberals heed the warning; any enemy of Russia would be destroyed, like Napoleon, by her innumerable warriors who, from the cold cliffs of Finland to the flaming Colchis, were ever ready to meet again Russia's foes, not with words but with deeds. [n] Above all Pushkin emphasized that the quarrels of Russia with other Slavs were an internal Russian affair. Russia was the mother of the Slavs or, better, the great sea into which all Slav rivers were flowing.

The anomalous situation was resented even more because many Russians admired the civilization of the West and had become convinced in the first decade of Alexander's reign of its rapid progress in Russia. In the *Vestnik Evropy* which he edited in 1802 and 1803, Karamzin was enthusiastic about European enlightenment and its spread in Russia thanks to Alexander's benevolence. "The philanthropist and patriot sees with joy how the light of reason more and more narrows in Russia the dark realm of ignorance, how noble and truly humane ideas work more and more in the minds, how reason affirms its rights and how the spirit of the Russians grows." Regarding the new plan for popular education, Karamzin wrote: "Let us anticipate the voice of posterity, the judgment of the historian and of Europe which looks now with greatest curiosity upon Russia, and let us say that all our new laws are wise and humane, but that this law on public education is the strongest proof for the divine kindness of the monarch." True, the law was only on paper, but according to Karamzin that was sufficient, for nothing more was needed but the correct implementation of the law: "Is it permissible to doubt that what the monarch of Russia orders his Russians to do will be done?" In 1803 Karamzin, noting what Alexander did to implant science in Russia, blamed the Russians who "do not fulfill their patriotic duty and even act unreasonably, when they send young men into foreign lands in order that they should learn what is prescribed in our universities." And Pushkin in his "The Captain's Daughter," thinking back to Pugachev's rebellion half a century before, wrote: "When I recall that this happened in my lifetime and that I lived to see the gentle reign of the Emperor Alexander, I cannot but marvel at the rapid progress of enlightenment and the diffusion of humane principles." A generous hope filled many hearts. Pushkin expressed it in his poem, dedicated in 1818 to Chaadayev[n]

> In hope, in ferment, we are turning
> Toward freedom, waiting for her command . . .
> Russia will rouse from her long sleep
> And where Autocracy lies broken,
> Our names shall yet be graven deep.

These hopes inspired the youthful conspirators who staged the uprising of December 14, 1825, after the death of Alexander I, and who became known as the Decembrists. They were moved by a deep patriotism, and sometimes even by an extreme nationalism.[n] They wished to establish Russia's greatness on firmer foundations, some of them even envisaged a vast Pan-Slav empire. Executions and Siberia broke their dream. Though they were related to many leading Russian families, Russian society turned away from them and vied in loyalty to the new ruler, Nicholas I.[n] Russian traditional autocracy seemed more firmly established than ever; the short-lived, stray liberal impulses of the reign of Alexander receded into unreality. Tyutchev could proclaim in his poem "Vas razvratilo samovlastie" that the memory of the Decembrists was buried for posterity like a corpse in the earth. In the fire of their youth they had hoped to melt the eternal pole with their warm blood but the ageless mass of ice breathed and no traces of the self-sacrificial effort remained. The spring had not come; the torpor and terror of Nicholas's winter covered Russia like a shroud.

This dismal reality was the background against which small circles of young men debated the future of Russia. They met in Moscow, the city which remained the intellectual center.

> *Moscow: these syllables can start*
> *A tumult in the Russian heart,*

Pushkin wrote in "Eugene Onegin." The question of the relations of Russia and Europe was ever-present before their minds: was Russia to become a part of Europe following its lead and accepting its values and standards, or was Russia to remain conscious of and to cultivate her deep historical difference from Europe? Questions like these had already moved the preceding generation[n] which had been guided by the rational ideas of the European Enlightenment. Now, after 1820, German romantic philosophy, above all the transcendental idealism and the positive philosophy of Schelling, began to influence Russian intellectual thought. The all-consuming quest for the meaning of Russian history and of the peculiar Russian way received an added impetus from the fact that Russia entered Europe at a time when Europe herself was deeply stirred. Unfamiliar with the historical realities of the West and judging it purely in the realm of irresponsible thought, many Russians began to see Europe with a critical insight to which the weaknesses revealed themselves more easily than the intrinsic strength. Did not many Europeans, like De Maistre in France, Carlyle in England, and the German romantics, castigate the decadence and shallowness of modern Europe and look longingly to a romantically idealized past? Should Russia eagerly accept this modern civilization which was so far from perfection? Was she not better off for the very reason of her "backwardness" and separation? Were not Rousseau and Herder right in condemning civilization which alienated man from the true sources of existence? Were there not better conditions in Russia for the full integration of personality, for overcoming the dispersion and alienation of modern man, than in Europe? Was the Russian peasant not a superior type compared with the *bourgeoisie* of the West? The longings of romantic reactionaries and socialist messianists, both equally popular in the Europe of the 1820's to the 1850's, seemed destined to be realized in Russia where there was supposed to exist a living tradition of an organic community based upon mutual love and harmony, while Western society was held together, in competition and exploitation, by the coldness of law and the brutality of force.

Russian nationalists, without due acknowledgment, borrowed their concepts from Europe to idealize and mobilize Russia against Europe. The German romanticists emphasized German peculiarity and uniqueness against the West rather than the common development and future. They rejected the legalistic individualism and the middle-class capitalism of the West as unsuited to Germany, which had to find in her own past and in her own character her own solutions for her problems. Between the supposedly old West and the supposedly young Germany, a spiritual struggle was often visualized in almost apocalyptic imagery.[n] But this self-centered Germanophilism could be easily transferred. The German romantic rejection of the West was adopted and surpassed by the nationalist romantic "lovers of Russia," who called themselves Slavophiles, their Slavophilism being Russian-centered, their Pan-Slavism representing more a Pan-Russism. They borrowed their intellectual guns from the Germans and turned them not only against what the German considered the West but also against Germany herself. In spite of all their insistence on the uniqueness and originality of Russia, the *Eigenart* or *samobynost* of their *Urvolk* or folkish archetype, the Slavophiles depended in their struggle against the West upon concepts borrowed from the West. They saw Russian history in the perspective of Hegelian dialects as the development from the thesis of pre-Petrinian Russia to the synthesis of the Slavophile Russia of the future.

With a far greater remoteness from the common traditions and the social structure of Europe, and with an even greater readiness to go to extremes and to reject and despise the common sense of the middle road and of moderation—the Russian word *meshchanstvo* carries in Russian literature a pejorative and contemptuous implication alien to "middle class" or "Bürgertum"—the Russians went beyond the Germans in their rejection of the West and in their apocalyptic expectations. Aristocrats in a stagnant rural economy or litterateurs and Bohemians without productive employment, they had little use for bourgeois virtues and discipline. Kant's criticism and English thought found hardly any followers in early nineteenth-century Russia: their cautious approach, their sense of responsibility and of limits, did not appeal to a Russian extremism which was as violent in its affirmation of faith as in its denunciation.[n] The most various and daring European ideas, all the conflicting and turbulent currents of the first half of the nineteenth century, poured suddenly into the entirely different Russian society. Detached from their social background and intellectual tradition, they formed in Russia a tiny and floating superstructure without any foundation in the ancient and immobilized Russian reality. Neither the political nor the social conditions existed for any practical application of the new ideas, the discussion of which became ever more heated the more it moved in a vacuum. Everything seemed possible; the magic world of romanticism received its sanction in an over-generous misinterpretation of Russian history and of the Russian folk.[n] Yet this whole intense intellectual life of Russia between the uprising of the Decembrists and the Crimean War, these unreal discussions leading only to endless talk and a few significant essays—books and deeds were equally rare—illumined the face of Russia as she struggled to gain consciousness of herself through contact with the alien world of Europe.

In the intellectual circles of Moscow, in which Slavophilism originated, the German influences of Schelling and Hegel, of Fichte and Schlegel—extremist thinkers like the philosophical radical Max Stirner (1806–56) were more widely read in Russia than in Germany—were supplemented in the 1840's by a new wave of French thought. It was no longer the rationalism of the eighteenth century, but the

apocalyptic religiosity of a Lamennais and the socialism of Saint-Simon's disciples and of Charles Fourier
which helped to fan the great hopes of an approaching new age, of the fulfillment of history, in which
Russia would play the decisive role.[n] The young men
mostly in their twenties formed in their passionate
discussions a youth movement of unsurpassed intensity, animated by a consuming devotion to
ideas and ideals.[n] From the letters and documents of
the time, the reader will catch even today some of
the high excitement of the period. Though relatively
few people were involved, the number of remarkable
personalities was surprisingly great. Personal friend-
ships and ideological groupings were formed and
dissolved, for the dividing lines were not sharply
drawn in an air swarming with ideas, ill-defined and,
though referring mostly to history and politics, of a
rather metaphysical and poetic character. In spite
of the similarity of some extreme Slavophile ideas
to Stalin's concepts a century later, the atmosphere
was entirely different: even the Slavophiles were in
closest touch with the intellectual movements of
Europe and the newest books and periodicals arriv-
ing from the West were avidly read and discussed.
The oppressive censorship from above existed and
civic courage was rare, even with men like Chaadayev, but Russian society including the Slavophiles
was in opposition to the censorship and within its
own ranks the discussion was animated by a spirit of
freedom and exploration. Supported by the general
mood of the period, all these young men were in a
non-technical sense philosophers of history. But they
were removed from the universalism of the eighteenth century; none of them could rise above the
national problem which faced them like a sphinx
challenging and fascinating. Their thoughts centered
incessantly on the destinies of Russia and of humanity, which, to them, were one.

In December, 1832, Count Sergei Semenovich

Uvarov (1786–1855), a highly educated and originally liberal aristocrat who had grown up under
Alexander I and who became in the spring of 1833
minister of education, submitted to Emperor
Nicholas a report on the University of Moscow in
which he suggested that education should be based
upon the "truly Russian and conservative principles
of Orthodoxy, autocracy and *narodnost* . . . the last
anchor of our salvation and the most secure guarantee
of the strength and greatness of our fatherland."
Narodnost was a translation of the German word
Volkstum;[n] though never strictly defined, it means
apparently a concentration on the study of Russian
history and civilization, loyalty to the traditional institutions, a greater ability to resist "European
ideas" without, however, any thought of complete
separation.[n] In spite of its lack of clarity the new
concept corresponded to the general feeling of national pride based upon the idealization of a hardly
explored past, the overestimation of an insufficiently
analyzed present strength, and the hopeful glorification of an unknown future.

This exuberance was deeply shocked by the publication, in 1836, of the *Lettre philosophique écrite à
une dame* in the Moscow *Teleskop*. The author was
Peter Yakovlevich Chaadayev (1794–1856), a lonely
and gloomy wit of Moscow society who belonged to
an older generation and had participated in the
Napoleonic wars. On his mother's side he came from
one of the great families of Russian nobility, his
grandfather Prince Mikhail Mikhailovich Shcherba-
tov (1733–90), a cultured aristocrat of the old
school, was the author, among other books, of a
"History of Russia since the Oldest Times" in seven
volumes. Nor was the grandson a revolutionary or a
liberal; under the influence of De Maistre, he was a
deeply religious man and a convinced monarchist.
But he challenged the general conviction of the
primacy and superiority of Russia and of the Ortho-

dox Church. In a French of great distinction and classical purity, he described courageously the desert of the Russian past, the deadness of Russian life, and explained Russia's backwardness by her separation from Rome and her dependence on "decadent and corrupt" Byzantium. "Isolated from the world, we have given or taught nothing to the world; we have added no thoughts to the sum of human ideas; we have in no way collaborated in the progress of reason and we have disfigured everything that penetrated to us from this progress. . . . The history of other nations is a true story of their emancipation. Russian history is the development of serfdom and autocracy." He too foresaw a great future for Russia which, however, could not be built upon her past (*"sur un passé qui n'est rein que néant"*) nor upon uncritical self-glorification ("contemplation imbécile de ses perfections imaginaires"). Russia must first break her isolation, learn from Europe, vitalize her faith by contact with the Western church, join the common stream of European unity, for which the Catholic Middle Ages seemed to him to set a model. Naturally, he fully approved Peter's reforms. Before him Russia had been nothing. "He found only a clean slate. With his powerful hand he wrote on it the words: Europe and the West. Since then we have belonged to Europe and the West."

His "Letter" aroused a storm of indignation. Russian society was even more upset and outraged than the authorities who stopped the publication of the review and declared Chaadayev insane. He did not flinch. In his "Apologie d'un fou" he wrote: "Love of one's country is a very fine sentiment but there is something more beautiful, the love of truth. Patriotism produces heroes, the love of truth creates wise men, the benefactors of mankind. Love of the fatherland divides people, feeds national hatreds and from time to time dresses the earth in mourning; the love of truth extends the light of knowledge, produces the joys of the mind, brings man nearer to God. . . . Our fanatical Slavs may be able from time to time to exhume objects of curiosity for museums or libraries through their researches, but I doubt whether they would ever succeed in drawing from our historic soil anything to fill the void in our souls; anything to give more body to the fogginess of our minds. . . . Do not imagine that we have ever lived the life of historic nations: when buried in your immense tomb you have been only living the life of fossils." But though Russia had neither a significant nor a worthwhile present, though all the great creations of civilization had seen the light of history in the West, nevertheless Russia could have a future if she would learn humbly from Europe, make the Western heritage her own, and as a late comer avoid the mistakes which brought Europe to the "catastrophes" of 1830 and 1848, events which closed, in Chaadayev's opinion, the golden age of his beloved Europe."

His pitiless criticism of the Russian past, of the Orthodox faith, of the Slav folk, presented with a rare lucidity and incisiveness of language, with a deep sense of moral and human responsibility, shocked not only the Slavophiles but with the exception of Herzen even the liberals." The editor of *Teleskop*, Nikolai Ivanovich Nadezhdin (1804–56), a professor of the history of the arts at Moscow University, wrote an article to prove that Chaadayev was wrong: Paris, the capital of the so-called European civilization, could hardly compare with St. Petersburg, "the most grandiose and the most beautiful city not only of Europe but of the whole world," nor could the few French or German railroads compare with the gigantic Russian project to build a railroad from Petersburg to Moscow and Nizhny-Novgorod. "We do not march step by step with the European civilization, we are running a race with it and we shall soon surpass it if we have not already done so. . . . It is not our role to be the echo of a civilization which lies in ruins and agony and of which we see perhaps already the convulsions announcing its death but to produce ourselves a new, young, strong civilization, a genuine Russian civilization which will renew old Europe." [n] Nadezhdin was not a Slavophile; his attitude was representative of the complete isolation in which Chaadayev found himself. Even the Russian Westernizers did not support him; they belonged to a younger generation which did not share his religious attitude, least of all his preference for Catholicism, nor his monarchist conservatism. But his chief opponents were the Slavophiles with their anti-Western emphasis on the glories of the Russian past and the promise of a Pan-Slav mission.

The Slavophiles, a highly differentiated group, collaborated in the review *Moskvityanin* which was founded in 1841 under the patronage of Uvarov. Its editor in chief was Mikhail Petrovich Pogodin (1800–75), professor of history at the University of Moscow; another professor, Stepan Petrovich Shevyrev, was in charge of literary criticism; among the important members of the circle were Alexei Stepanovich Khomyakov (1804–60), Ivan Vasilevich Kireyevsky (1806–59) and his brother Peter (1808–56); to a somewhat later generation belonged Yurij Fedorovich Samarin (1819–76) and the two sons, Konstantin (1817–60) and Ivan (1823–86), of Sergei Timofeyevich Aksakov (1791–1859), who in his family chronicles so masterfully described the idyllic patriarchal life of provincial Russia at the end of the eighteenth century. Of these men Shevyrev, in whose house the Czech writer Havlíček had lived, was the most violent in his formulations. In a famous article, "A Russian Views European Civilization," in the very first issue of the new review, he opposed the West, "carrier of a terrible and contagious disease, surrounded by an air created by its dangerous breath" to "the true governmental and social health of Russia." He called the West rotting and on its way to become a putrifying corpse.

Three years later, in the same periodical, Shevyrev led an attack against Timofei Nikolayevich Granovsky (1813–55) who lectured at the University on European medieval history and whom he accused of lacking the "breadth of view and impartiality which is to be expected from a Russian scholar" by drawing a favorable picture of the Western development. Granovsky defended himself at the conclusion of his next lecture: "I am being accused of partiality for the West; I have undertaken to teach a part of its history and I do it with love; I do not see why I should do it with hatred. The West has forged its history in sweat and blood; we receive its results almost painlessly; why should we not love it?" It is important today to emphasize that the Slavophile and Pan-Slav movement was not a strong force in the Russia of that time. The student body of Moscow University answered Granovsky's declarations with long, enthusiastic ovation. The *Moskvityanin* had only 300 subscribers while the Westernizing *Otechestvenniya Zapiski* (The Annals of the Fatherland) which appeared in St. Petersburg under the editorship of Andrei Alexandrovich Krayevsky (1810–89) had ten times as many subscribers.

Among the Slavophiles, who at that time were generally called "Slavs" in Russia—Chaadayev spoke of "Slavons fanatiques"—Pogodin was by far the most active. Equally industrious as a historian, a publicist, and an organizer, he was inspired in his youth by Karamzin's *History*, though he recognized its scholarly weaknesses, and by the new wave of romanticism. From 1827 to 1830 he edited the short-lived *Moskovskij Vestnik*. In 1828 he noted in his diary the desire to write a work on the essential traits of Russian history;[n] in searching for the principles underlying Russian development he reached two conclusions: looking at the immensity of Russia at his time, the grandeur and might of the Russian state, how could one fail to see that it must have grown out of a long past of similar grandeur? And how could one doubt that in leading Russia along the glorious path of one thousand years to her present splendor, Providence had not some unique mission and an even greater future planned for her? Of all the early Slavophiles, Pogodin was also the most conscious political Pan-Slav. In 1835 he traveled to Europe to visit Prague and the other Slav cities and to get acquainted with the Austrian Slavs and their leaders. From 1839 to 1853, on four other occasions, he went West to strengthen his contacts with the Western Slavs. At the end of 1838, before he set out for his second voyage, he composed for the "education" of the heir to the throne, the Grand Duke Alexander Nikolayevich, the future Alexander II, then a young man of twenty, a Letter on Russian History. He gave it for transmission to Count Sergei Grigorovich Stroganov (1794–1882), then the director of education of the Moscow district. This letter is the earliest concise formulation of Russian Pan-Slavism; its climax was the stress on that "universal monarchy" of which Palacký ten years later warned Europe. It reads in part:

"Russia—what a wonderful phenomenon on the world stage. . . . Which country can compare with its magnitude? Which merely compares with half of its magnitude? . . . A population of 60 million people, aside from those who have not been counted, a population that increases by one million every year, and soon will amount to 100 million! . . . Let us add to this multitude 30 million more of our brothers and cousins, the Slavs, who are scattered over the whole of Europe from Constantinople to Venice, from the Morea to the Baltic and the North Sea, the Slavs in whose veins the same blood flows as in ours, who speak the same language as we do, and who, therefore, according to the law of nature, feel as we do, the Slavs who in spite of geographic and political separation form by origin and language a spiritual entity with us. Thus we may subtract their number from the population of neighbouring Austria and Turkey and from the rest of Europe, and add it to our numbers. What will then be left to them, what will be ours? I cannot think any longer, I am overwhelmed by this vision. . . .

"Russia is a country that contains all kinds of soil, all climates, . . . that abounds in all products . . . a world in itself, self-contained, independent. . . . What do we lack? What is it that we cannot obtain at home? What, that we could not furnish to others? . . . Where is the country more fit for the establishment of factories? . . . Only a short while ago did we start thinking of factories—and yet how well have they developed. . . . Wherein should Russia fear the rivalry of the English in spite of all their steamboats on the Euphrates and on the Nile and their railroads at Suez and Panama? True, much of what I mentioned is not yet in existence, but everything is within possible reach . . . and could be ordered tomorrow if necessary by supreme command. . . .

"As to spiritual resources, I wish to point out a peculiar trait of the Russian people, their *tolk* and their *udal*,[n] for which no words exist in any other European language, their good sense, vitality, patience, devotion, proficiency in time of emergency, this happy union of the qualities of northern and southern men. Education in Europe is a matter of caste, although allegedly open to everyone, and the lower classes—with few exceptions—are conspicuous for dullness of wit as the traveller quickly finds out. But what is the capacity of the Russian? . . . A muzhik with his heavy hands called for military service has just been taken from behind the plow, he cannot look straight on anything, he cannot make a step without bumping into something, the real Russian bear—he may be thirty, sometimes almost forty years old—but his hair will be cut and a year later one cannot recognize him: he marches in the first platoon of the guard, he carries his rifle . . . in a skillful, even elegant manner. A bugle or a fagot or flute is put into his hands, and he becomes a regimental musician and plays in such a way that foreign artists come to listen to him. When placed in the firing line, he will stand and not falter; when sent to death, he will go without thinking; he suffers everything possible: he would don a sheepskin in hot summer and go barefooted in icy winter, he would live off biscuit for weeks and in forced marches he is not inferior to a horse. Charles XII, Frederick the Great, and Napoleon, unbiased judges indeed, preferred him to all other soldiers and extended the palm of victory to him . . . How proficient in physics and chemistry are the Russian peasant children in technical and agricultural schools! How gifted are the youngsters in the Moscow Art School! How many remarkable inventions remained without consequences just because of the lack of communications and publicity! . . . What a spiritual strength in addition to the physical!

"All these physical and spiritual forces form a gigantic machine, constructed in a simply purposeful way, directed by the hand of one single man, . . . who can put it in action at any moment by one motion, who can give it any direction, any speed he wishes. And mind, that machine . . . is animated by one feeling, an ancient legacy from the ancestors: allegiance, limitless confidence and devotion for the Tsar, their God on earth.

"Who can compare with us? Whom will we not force into submission? Is not the political destiny of the world in our hands whenever we want to decide it one way or the other? The truth of my words will be even more manifest if we consider the conditions in other European countries. In contrast to Russia's strength, unity and harmony, we find there nothing but quarrel, division, and weakness, by which our greatness—as light by shadow—is still more enhanced."

Then Pogodin turned to a survey of the European countries. A discussion of conditions in Spain, Portugal, Austria, Turkey, Prussia, the German Confederation, France, and England, convinced him of the truth of his general observations. He did not deny the former strength of France and England but he arrived at the conclusion that they were on the decline and that the individual liberties existing there had politically weakened the states and impeded their power of decision and action. On the other hand, nothing appeared impossible for the Russian Emperor. Though Russia did not participate in the Crusades, she liberated Jerusalem by a mere article in a treaty.[n] Though she did not discover America, the fast-increasing output of Russian gold promised to become a counterpoison against the western poison.

"It is known that our present Emperor does not think of any conquest, but I cannot help, I dare not fail to remark as a historian, that the Russian ruler now, without such an intention, without any preparation, quietly seated in his office at Tsarskoye Selo, is nearer to the universal monarchy than Charles V and Napoleon ever were in their dreams. . . . Europe itself is well aware of it, though ashamed to admit it. The untiring attention with which Europe follows every step by us, the incessant suspicion of our slightest move, the muffled grumbling of jealousy, envy, and malice . . . are they not the most convincing proof of Russia's strength . . . ?"

Pogodin, however, knew—a wisdom repeated for the next 120 years by all Russian imperialists, Slavophile or Bolshevik—that Russia did not aspire to outward conquests or power. She sought her glory in the moral and social perfection of man and humanity. The European countries, in spite of their great merits in the past, had each one developed only one side of human nature and of social growth. Where has the ideal society been achieved? "It is the Golden Calf, the mammon, to which all Europe without exception pays homage. America on which our contemporaries had pinned their hopes for a time, has clearly revealed the vices of her illegitimate birth. She is not a state, rather a trading company. . . . To be sure, she has grown rich, but she will hardly ever produce anything great of national, even less of universal significance."

In his quest for the land which promises to bring forth man and society in their fulness, Pogodin found himself confirmed by Kollár, "the famous Slav poet of our time." Kollár, overwhelmed like Pogodin by the numbers and talents of the Slavs, was convinced that Providence destined them for great purposes in the arts. Pogodin did not wish to limit the Slav future to the arts. He did not, like Kollár, address powerless intellectuals of a small awakening people but the heirs of a mighty empire.

"It seems to me one can extend the meaning of Kollár's prophecy and say that the future altogether belongs to the Slavs. In history nations succeed each other: one after another steps forward . . . and renders its service to mankind. Until now the Slavs have been missing in this illustrious procession. Their time therefore has come to begin their noble work for mankind and to display their highest capacity. But which of the Slav tribes occupies the first rank today, which can by number, language, and qualities represent the entire Slav world? Which offers the best prospect for future greatness by its present state and past history? Which of all comes nearest to the noble goal? . . . My heart trembles with joy. Oh, Russia, oh, my fatherland! Is it not you? Oh, if it were only you! You are chosen to consummate, to crown the development of humanity, . . . to harmonize ancient and modern civilizations, to reconcile heart with reason, to establish real justice and peace, and to prove . . . that there is something higher than education, freedom and wealth— . . . the Divine Word which alone can impart earthly and heavenly happiness to man. . . ."

This letter written at the end of 1838 never reached its destination. Count Stroganov did not forward it. When it was later returned to Pogodin, he found on its last page a handwritten note by Stroganov which well expressed the then prevailing official attitude to the Slavophile dreams of Russia's universal mission and to Pan-Slavism: "Many words, only one new thought (Pan-Slavism) and that too is false." When Pogodin published the Letter thirty years later, in 1867, he referred disparagingly to the novel *Smoke* published in that year by the great Russian novelist and unrepentant Westerner, Ivan Sergeyevich Turgenev. "Turgenev once divided people into Hamlets and Don Quixotes," Pogodin wrote. "I always have preferred the latter category. I sincerely believe that one cannot elevate the national mind by 'Smoky' pictures, however artistic they may be, and that we need different ones, precisely at the present time." [n] It was the year when the second Pan-Slav Congress met in Moscow, in the preparation of which Pogodin took a leading part.

Pogodin was a publicist without deep philosophical or theological interests. The case of the two leading Slavophile thinkers Khomyakov and Ivan Kireyevsky was different. They did not see eye to eye with the government and found themselves exposed to its censorship and persecution. The official theory of the *narodnost* expressed a belief in a Russian civilization directed authoritatively by the government which regarded itself as more "enlightened" than the people. It was the glory of the Russian rulers, the official theory proclaimed, not to abandon the formation of the Russian mind and its growth to chance but to mold and guide it. Practically, this attitude resulted in *narodnost* being identified with loyalty and unlimited obedience to the autocracy. The Slavophile philosophers, on the other hand, believed in the creative originality and spontaneity of the Russian people. The government of St. Petersburg appeared to them, as to Bakunin in his Slavophile period, not Russian and not national enough. Khomyakov fought valiantly against the corruption in Russia, for a free spiritual development and for the emancipation of the serf with an allotment of land. What distinguished these thinkers from the populism of Bakunin was not only their rejection of violence but their profound Christian faith and their identification of Russia with Orthodoxy. Schelling's philosophy of mythology and revelation to which the West paid hardly any attention, justified to the Slavophiles their opposition of the positive Christianity of Russia to the negative rationalism of Europe which was accused of destroying the faith and thereby of destroying itself.[n]

In his youth Kireyevsky regarded Russia as the youngest member of the European family, enriched by, and the heir to, the civilization of the older countries. But Europe was old, and of the two young nations, the United States and Russia, the former one was too onesidedly English or Western in its formation, so that the whole hope of Europe had to turn to Russia. His voyage to Europe resulted in 1832 in the foundation of the review *Evropeyets* (The European) in which he published his famous article "The Nineteenth Century," as a result of which the review was suppressed.[n] There the future Slavophile came near to Chaadayev's Westernism. "A Chinese wall has separated Russia from Europe. Through it the air of the civilized West could pene-

trate to us only through a few cracks; that wall . . .
still stands today." At the moment the situation had
changed. Western civilization based upon the classical heritage had reached its climax before the nineteenth century; therefore a new stage of civilization
was beginning and Russia, which had lacked the tie
with classical civilization, could fully enter into it.

But soon Kireyevsky under the influence of
Khomyakov changed his views. The classical heritage
was now recognized to be of a two-fold character:
the West was the heir of Rome and perhaps of
Aristotle, of the rationalism in Roman law and
scholastic philosophy; Russia, through its Orthodox
Christianity, the heir of Greece and of the Platonic
Eros. Europe was the creation of Roman and Teuton
conquests; even Christianity had been introduced
there by the sword. Russia had accepted Christianity
peacefully; the Slavs had not been conquered by
their rulers but had invited them to come and rule.
Russia was thus an organic growth permeated by the
feeling of unity and not threatened by the internal
strife of class and race characteristic of the West.
Therefore Russia did not need the legal and formal-
istic safeguards of European constitutions: she
possessed a true democracy; its decisions were not
imposed by majorities but were the expression of a
highly moral unity. "Not private, wavering, and arbitrary conceptions, which by nature tend to dissen-
sion, were the foundation of opinion (in the Russian
tradition), but the ancient customs—the same for
all the Russians, and the divine law—the same for
all the Orthodox." Khomyakov's words could with
due alteration be applied to the "true" democracy
of Stalin's classless society of fraternal peoples.

Europe was doomed, according to the Slavophiles,
by lack of faith and of unity. The wishful expectation of the "Untergang des Abendlandes" so dear to
some modern German thinkers moved Russian hearts
even more strongly, sometimes to a feeling of tri-

umph, more often and more typically Russian, to deep pity. The European nations, it was maintained, suffered from the inescapable hostility between the people and a power imposed by conquest; their constitutions were only a compromise between two hostile camps, the basis of a continuous struggle for power. No real peace nor freedom could grow there. They existed only in Russia, at least potentially, where the whole people freely recognized authority and formed one great family, a patriarchal state where the children did not need any formal safeguards against fathers or brothers.[n] The Orthodox Church put its emphasis on *sobornost*, togetherness, the communion of all members in mutual love. Khomyakov found the spirit of the Orthodox faith expressed in the verse of the liturgy: "Let us love one another so that we confess with one common thought the Father, the Son, and the Holy Spirit." [n] In this spirit the Russian church alone realized the identity of liberty and unity and, thereby, true society. Catholicism sacrificed liberty to unity and led to despotism; Protestantism sacrificed unity to liberty and led to anarchy.

The Slavophiles misread reality under the spell of a noble utopianism. They regarded passivity as proof of unity and harmony and did not recognize that their emphasis upon the primacy of the social communal element over the individual political claims led to the absorption of the individual into the community; in the "true community" the state disregarded with greater ease, and encroached more and more upon, the sphere and rights of the individual. At the same time the Slavophiles hoped, under the same utopian impulsion as their illegitimate successors one century later, for the withering away of this all-powerful state. Fundamentally they were religious anarchists who deeply disliked the state and above all the bureaucracy, an element which they regarded as of Byzantine or

Germanic origin, and which interfered with the
organic life of the people's community. They saw in
Peter, whom Chaadayev and Pushkin had venerated,
and in his reforms a great misfortune; he had repudiated Moscow and the people and had built a
solitary city far away from the *narod*, the common
folk, whom the Slavophiles and many later Russian
revolutionaries adored. He had increased German
influence in Russia, and had despised Slav traditions.
In protest some Slavophiles went so far as to imitate
the Teutomania, the *Deutschtümelei*, of the German
nationalists, by masquerading in dresses and beards
supposedly genuine Slavic.[n]

A great poet who combined the religious Orthodoxy
of Khomyakov with the political Pan-Slavism of
Pogodin was Fyodor Ivanovich Tyutchev (1803–
75), perhaps Russia's greatest lyrical poet since Pushkin, who "discovered in the Russian language resources and finesses of expression none before him
had realized." He was as little a professional writer as
Chaadayev, whom he resembled in his upbringing
and in his masterful use of the French language
which he preferred for his correspondence and for
daily life. His whole œuvre consisted of little more
than two hundred poems written over almost half
a century, of which nearly one third were of a political content, a fervent Pan-Slav commentary upon
the events of his time. He left Russia as a young
man of 19 and did not return until more than twenty
years later after diplomatic service abroad. He married twice; both of his wives were Germans without
any knowledge of Russian.

But his poems and articles proclaimed and glorified the supposedly inevitable struggle between a
triumphant Slavdom led by Russia and a Western
conspiracy determined to crush Moscow. He saw
this struggle in almost supernatural apocalyptic
colors and in a wide world-historical perspective. Like

Dante, he believed in the need of a universal empire based upon a universal faith; such a world order could not center, as Dante had believed, in the capital of the old pagan Empire but only in Constantinople, where Constantine, after the fall of the four heathen Empires, the Assyrian, Persian, Macedonian, and Roman, predicted by Daniel, had established the fifth and definitely Christian Empire. As against this true Empire, there was the illegitimate Empire: the West beginning with Charlemagne had usurped the Empire with the help of the Pope, the leader of the schismatic revolt against the Universal Church. In the East, Empire and Church, growing out of the same soil of legitimate tradition, remained united; in the West the schismatic Pope and the usurping Emperor fought a bitter struggle which ended in the Reformation, the denial of the Church, and in the Revolution, the denial of the Empire. Napoleon had tried in vain to restore the unity of the West; his attempt was only an episode in the rapidly progressing collapse of faith and order in the West. The nineteenth century presented Russia with the mission and burden to restore the Empire and to reunite the churches on a Greco-Slavonic foundation. Tyutchev saw two convincing proofs for the approach of the new age: Austria, which had been saved only by Russian help, would be absorbed by her—which would lead in turn to "the indispensable fulfillment of Russia as the Slavonic Empire" and the submission of Germany and Italy to Russia's leadership—and the Pope's loss of temporal power would form the first step toward the reunion of the Church.[n]

To the Western Slavs the February Revolution of 1848 carried the promise of a liberal era for Europe and their full integration with it; the same event signified to Tyutchev the beginning of the very end of Europe and of liberalism. On April 12, 1848, he wrote a memorandum on "Russia and the Revolu-

tion," which appeared the following year in the
Revue des Deux Mondes. In it he interpreted the
meaning of the period as the revelation of two
powers facing each other, the Revolution and Russia,
a division of the world into two hostile camps.
"Neither treaty nor negotiations are possible between the two. One's life means the other's death.
The whole political and religious future of mankind
depends for centuries ahead on the outcome of the
struggle between the two, the greatest struggle which
the world has witnessed." The Revolution, though
it pretended to fulfill the promise of the Gospel,
was based on the rejection of Christianity, on the
substitution of the human ego for God. "Instead of
a fraternity preached and accepted in the name of
God, it (the Revolution) wishes to establish a fraternity imposed by the fear of the sovereign people."
Russia, on the other hand, is "above all the Christian
Empire; the Russian people is not only Christian
through the Orthodoxy of its beliefs but also by
something more intimate than belief. It is Christian
by that ability of renunciation and sacrifice which
forms the basis of its moral nature." In his poems
Tyutchev sang of this Christ-bearing people and its
land, Christian in its poverty and humility:

> These poor villages,
> this sterile nature,
> homeland of patience,
> land of the Russian people!
> The proud glance of the foreigner
> can neither see nor observe
> that which pierces through and shines hidden
> in its humble nakedness.
> The King of Heaven, under the guise of a serf,
> has traversed and blessed Thee,
> Thee my native land,
> bowed down by the weight of the cross.

Tyutchev found that the Revolution was at home not only in France; in the last eighteen years it had transformed Germany. "Germany was thought to be a country of order because it was tranquil, and one did not wish to see the terrifying anarchy which had penetrated there and undermined the intellect. Sixty years of a destructive philosophy have completely dissolved there all Christian belief and have developed, in this void of all faith, the revolutionary sentiment to its highest degree, the pride of the mind, so that at present this wound of the century is perhaps nowhere deeper and more poisonous than in Germany. Necessarily, the more Germany became revolutionary, the more it hated Russia." Germany, Tyutchev wrote, had enjoyed 33 years of peace because Austria and Prussia at the end of the Napoleonic wars had rallied around Russia, an alliance which without imposing any sacrifice protected Germany's national existence. The German revolutionaries wished to replace this solid foundation by making common cause with the French republicans in a war against Russia. But in reality they had by breaking or weakening the political order of the country, "awakened there the most terrifying complication, a question of life and death for its future—the racial question. They had forgotten that in the heart of Germany of whose unity they dreamt, there lived in the basin of Bohemia and in the surrounding Slav countries six to seven million men for whom the German has not ceased for one moment during all the centuries to be something worse than an alien, for whom the German is always a *nyemets*. . . ."

Tyutchev's memorandum was written almost on the very day on which Palacký sent his reply to the Frankfurt Assembly declining, on behalf of the Czechs, to participate in its deliberations. Tyutchev in his memorandum also referred to the Slavism of the Czechs. However, while Palacký saw in the

Hussite movement a forerunner of the Reformation and of the liberal revolutions, Tyutchev interpreted it in the opposite way: he regarded it as an expression of affinity with the Eastern Church, as a revival of the spirit of the Slav Apostles, St. Cyril and St. Methodius, who had come from Byzantium to convert the Western Slavs. "Everything that remains of true national life in Bohemia lies in its Hussite tradition," Tyutchev wrote, "in this ever alive protest of oppressed Slav national feeling against usurpation by the Roman Church and against German domination. This tie unites the Bohemian Czech with his whole past of struggle and glory, and this link could attach him one day to his brothers in the East. We cannot insist strongly enough on this point. For precisely these cherished recollections of the Church of the East, these returns to the old faith of which Hussitism in its own time was only an imperfect and disfigured expression, established a profound difference between Poland and Bohemia: between Bohemia which suffers against its will the yoke of the Occident, and the seditiously Catholic Poland, a fanatical partisan of the Occident and always a traitor to its own race." Understandably, therefore, the Poles were the one Slav people whom the Europeans loved. "Only our Judas is honored by their kiss," Tyutchev wrote in one of his poems.

Palacký wished to strengthen the Austrian Empire, Tyutchev expected its disintegration. During a visit to Prague in 1841, Tyutchev had been assured by the Czech nationalist Václav Hanka that Bohemia would not feel free until Russia would gain possession of Galicia. "Every Russian who has visited Prague during these last years can certify that the only complaint which he heard there against us was about the caution and lukewarmness with which we have received the national sympathies of the Czechs." A similar sympathy was found according to Tyutchev among the Southern Slavs in the Habsburg monarchy. "Among the whole Military Frontier, three-fourths of which consists of Orthodox Serbs, there is not one cottage (according even to Austrian travellers) where one would not find side by side with the portrait of the Austrian Emperor the portrait of another emperor whom these faithful races obstinately consider the only legitimate one." These Slavs in 1848 were seriously threatened by the Magyars, who as Tyutchev believed regarded themselves predestined to keep the Slavs and the Russians in check. "So far the moderating authority of Austria has kept this turbulence and this madness more or less under control; but now . . . the completely emancipated Magyarism will probably give full vent to all its eccentricities and run the most foolish risks." Tyutchev was convinced that the Orthodox Slavs outside and inside Russia were indissolubly bound together by a common danger which might lead at any moment to the great struggle to which he looked forward with supreme confidence.

"For all the various agitations at work, Catholic propaganda, Revolutionary propaganda, etc., all of them at cross-purposes among themselves but united in common hatred against Russia, will now start to work more fervently than ever. . . . Russia, the land of faith, will not be unfaithful in the supreme hour. It will not be frightened by the greatness of its destiny and will not retreat from its mission. And when has this mission been more indisputably evident? One can say that God writes it in flaming signs across the sky blackened with storm clouds. The Occident disappears, everything collapses, everything totters in a general conflagration, the Europe of Charlemagne and the Europe of the treaties of 1815; the papacy of Rome and all the kingdoms of the West; Catholicism and Protestantism; faith long lost and reason reduced to absurdity; order henceforth impossible, freedom henceforth impossible, and civilization commits suicide on top of all these ruins accumulated by it. . . . And when we see rising above this immense wreck this even more immense Empire like the Ark of the Covenant, who could doubt its mission? Should we, its children, show ourselves sceptic and pusillanimous?"

One year later the *Revue des Deux Mondes* published another article by Tyutchev, "La Papauté et la Question Romaine." [n] His attitude toward the Western church was as negative as Khomyakov's and Dostoyevsky's. By separating from the Orthodox tradition of the universal church, Rome had divided Christianity into two different worlds (". . . l'abîme qui s'est creusé non pas entre les deux Églises—puisque l'Église est Une et Universelle—mais entre les deux mondes, les deux humanités pour ainsi dire . . ."). While Protestantism suppressed the Church for the sake of the individual ego, Rome absorbed the Church into the Roman ego. Rome was not "a society of the faithful freely united in the spirit and the truth under the law of Christ. It was a political power, a state in the state." During the Middle Ages it was a Roman colony established in conquered lands. In that way it became a terrestrial and quasimortal institution, addicted to wars and politics. "The truly impious and sacrilegious duel (between the Papacy and the Empire) which lasted throughout the Middle Ages, dealt a mortal blow to the principle of authority in the Occident." Tyutchev did not mention, and probably even did not consider, the fact that this very same struggle, unknown in the East, promoted in the West the growth of the principle of liberty.

The champion of the Orthodox Church regarded the Reformation as justified in its struggle against Rome, but wished it had appealed to the true tribunal of the Orthodox Church instead of making itself judge in its own cause and appealing to the individual conscience. By destroying further the principle of authority, the Reformation prepared the

way for the French Revolution with its theory of
popular and national sovereignty. As a result, Italian
nationalism created the "Roman question" in its
contemporary form, the incompatibility of the
priestly office of the Pope with territorial rule in an
Italian nation-state. Italian nationalists of the neo-
Guelph school like Gioberti dreamt even of a Third
Rome, an Italian world leadership under the Pope.[n]
Soon, however, the Revolution went farther and over-
threw the Pope; in an attempt to suppress the past
of Italy it proclaimed, by way of pure abstraction,
its link to the long extinct ancient Rome. Tyutchev
rightly castigated Mazzini's fantastic visions of a
Third Rome;[n] he seemed unaware of the similarly
fantastic abstraction which proclaimed Moscow the
Third Rome. On the contrary, he was convinced
that in view of the inability of the French intervention to solve the Roman question,[n] the only hope for
a solution of the Roman question lay not in Papal
resistance to the secularization of the State of the
Church—a resistance which would only strengthen
the anti-Christian attitude among the Italian nationalists—but in the Pope's turning away from the
centuries of terrestrial pre-occupations to the unity of
the true church.

But the fervent hopes and thoughts of Tyutchev
circled less around a reunited Rome than around a
reconquered Constantinople, the center of the new
Pan-Slav empire. In a poem "Russian Geography"
he wrote: "Moscow, Peter's city, and Constantine's
city—these are the sacred capitals of the Russian
Empire. But where are its limits? where its boundaries? . . . The future is destined to discover it.
Seven inland seas and seven great rivers. . . . From
the Nile to the Neva, from the Elbe to China, from
the Volga to the Euphrates, from the Ganges to the
Danube, Behold the Russian realm, and never will
it end, As the Spirit foresaw and Daniel foretold."
The fulfillment of Daniel's prophecy seemed at

hand, as another poem announced: "This is an ancient voice, the voice from above: The fourth age is already passing, drawing to its end—and the hour thunders. The ancient vaults of St. Sophia in newly reborn Byzantium shield anew the altar of Christ. Fall down before it, oh Tsar of Russia,—and rise as Tsar of all the Slavs." Yet though carried away by his visions of the grandiose future of the Pan-Slav empire, Tyutchev like Khomyakov was in no way blind to the shortcomings of the Russian government of his day. In a letter which he wrote (in French) in November 1857 to Prince M. D. Gorchakov, he protested against the prohibitive and deadening censorship in Russia and demanded instead a positive effort on the part of the government to create a live public opinion, a conscious directing of minds. Only through a closer union of government and people could Russia accomplish her mission. The more national the Russian autocracy grew, the more autocratic would the nation become. His faith in the ultimate destiny of Russia remained unshaken. In 1853, the year in which he predicted the capture of Constantinople, he wrote to Chaadayev with whom in spite of their ideological differences he was on the friendliest terms: "After many trials and vicissitudes, the last word will belong to Russia, I know . . . but it will be a Russia very different from what she is at present. She will have become herself, and yet, she will be associated with so many other elements which will complement and transform her that her very name will be changed. She will no longer be an empire but a world." [n] For like Khomyakov, Tyutchev was convinced that the Russian problem was in its essence neither political nor national but metaphysical and religious, and in that sense *the* problem of modern history, a problem of faith.

One cannot understand Russia by reason
And measure her by a common yardstick,

She has a peculiar nature,
One must simply believe in Russia.

So ran a short poem of his which he wrote in 1860. Fifteen years before, Khomyakov, referring to his discussion with the English theologian William Palmer on the union of the Anglican and Orthodox churches, wrote to Samarin: "I feel and I am deeply convinced that the religious dispute comprises the whole essence and the whole meaning of all the vital disputes which we have to face. The Russian question in all its aspects is without doubt the only truly universal question of our time." [n] This faith could not be shaken even when the Crimean War, instead of bringing the liberation of Constantinople and of the Orthodox Balkan peoples, revealed Russia's weakness. Events, however, seemed to favor Pan-Slav feeling. The unity of Europe in the defense of Turkey and the emancipation of the serfs by Alexander II gave to the Pan-Slav movement a wider backing than it had possessed in the time of Nicholas I.

Pogodin returning in 1853 from his last trip to Europe pointed out that Russia, faced by the hostility of the West, could rely only on her Slav brethren. His *Moskvityanin* regarded it "as its mission to spread in Russia the knowledge about the Slav peoples." When it ceased to appear in April 1856, it had acquainted the Russian public with the national movements of the Austrian Slavs, especially the Czechs. The long neglected "Slav brothers," who had hardly been considered worthy of any serious interest, began to loom up more importantly from the political point of view. The Holy Alliance and the treaties of 1835 had been upset by Napoleon III and were soon to be destroyed in their last vestiges by Bismarck. Russia felt alone. On June 26, 1864, Tyutchev wrote to his sister: "I of course am not one of those who in their gloomy patriotism would like to doom Russia to permanent isolation. I am willing to enter into agreements but only if they are of a temporary character and if their acceptance does not make us forget the axiomatic truth that there can be no alliance between Russia and the West, neither for the sake of interests nor for the sake of principles. There is not a single interest, not a single trend in the West which would not conspire against Russia, especially against its future, and would not try to harm us. Therefore the only natural policy of Russia toward the West must not be an alliance with one or the other of these powers, but their disunion and division, because only when they are divided among themselves, they are not hostile to us—never of course out of conviction but out of impotence. This severe truth will perhaps shock tender souls but it is the law of our existence as a race and as an empire, and if we would ignore it we would cease to be Russian." [n] It was under these conditions that the second Pan-Slav Congress was called to Moscow in 1867. It met no longer in the glow of the liberal hopes of 1848 but in the stern nationalist atmosphere of the 1860's.

2

The Moscow Congress of 1867

IN THE FIFTEEN YEARS after 1852 the moral and intellectual climate of Europe changed, and with it that of Russia. Chaadayev and the Slavophiles, in spite of their opposite evaluations of the fact, were at one in regarding Russia before the eighteenth century, thanks to her Byzantine origin, as separated from Europe. In the nineteenth century, however, Russia was becoming more and more integrated with the general trend of European development. European culture and political events determined Russian history. The Crimean War; Alexander II's emancipation of the serfs and liberal reforms at a period of general advancement of liberalism throughout Europe; the Polish uprising of 1863; Bismarck's wars against Denmark and against the German Confederation—the shift in European thought from idealism, religiosity, and metaphysical concern to materialism, realism, and interest in science and technology—shaped a new Russian attitude. The Slavophile movement changed its character. Khomyakov and the brothers Kireyevsky were dead by 1860; the new generation emptied the doctrine of its theological and humanitarian content and discovered in it a crude appeal to the nationalist and xenophobe instincts of the masses."

European culture was no longer as in the time of Alexander I a coveted prize, Europe was no longer "the land of holy miracles." By 1860 the educated Russian felt that European culture was part of his heritage, that Russian intellectual life was in its full development, that Russia was the leading country of Europe, and not merely in size and population." The Crimean War and the Polish uprising directed public attention to the Slav problems. The unification of the Italian and of the German states with its elimination of the Habsburgs from Italy and Germany and the reorganization of Central Europe on a racial-linguistic basis popularized for the first time the Pan-Slav idea among the Russian public. The Russian government, however, remained aloof; it was afraid to arouse popular forces. In 1847 Uvarov circularized among the curators of the Russian universities an official warning against Pan-Slavism stating that the other Slavs looked to Russia for their own purposes, not out of love, and that not Pan-Slavism was needed but Russian *narodnost*. Count Arseni Andreyevich Zakrevsky, Governor General of Moscow from 1848 to 1859, called the Slavophiles "communists," Samarin was arrested, his and his friends' writings were put under strictest censorship." Even as late as 1872 the government forced the closing of the last Slavophile review, the *Beseda*."

At the beginning of the Crimean War, Khomyakov wrote his famous poem "To Russia" in which he exhorted her in the manner of the Hebrew prophets to repent of her sins and iniquities in order to become worthy of being God's chosen people, called by God to carry arms across the Danube in defense of brotherly peoples: "Oh Thou, unworthy of being chosen, and yet the chosen people! Lave thyself quickly with the water of penitence so that the thunder of a twofold chastisement does not fall on thy head! . . . And then rise, faithful to thy mission, and throw thyself into the dust of bloody combats! Fight for thy brothers with strong-armed might, uphold the banner of God with a strong hand, strike with the sword—it is God's sword." Though no one in his senses could accuse Khomyakov of lack of patriotism or of pacifist opposition to the war, his poem by daring to speak of Russia's iniquities aroused much indignation and could not be printed. Before the beginning of the war in 1854, Khomyakov sent a letter "to a foreign friend" in which he pleaded for an understanding of Russia's position in her struggle against Turkey. "The Russian people is bound by ties of blood to the Slav peoples and by ties of faith to the Greeks." While Europe was satisfied to push back the dreaded force of the Ottomans, Russia had revived the Christian Balkan peoples forgotten by the rest of the world. In their interest Russia demanded guarantees from Turkey, while England and France, without concern for the duties of humanity, supported Turkey. "As a result our duty has become more difficult to fulfill; it has also become more urgent, and it will be fulfilled."

Khomyakov was at pains to emphasize that Russia was not arming for conquest. "Here is not the proud armament of England nor the bellicose fervor of France; it is the calm and considerate movement of a man who has . . . listened to his conscience, consulted his duty and takes up arms because he would think himself guilty if he did not. . . . The Russian people does not think of conquest: conquest had never anything appealing for it. It does not think of glory: that is a sentiment which has never moved its heart. It thinks of its duty, it thinks of a holy war. . . . God has not given us the task to conquer far off lands however precious they may be to our religious feelings, but he imposes upon us the task of saving brothers who are blood of our blood and heart of our heart. . . . Thus Russia understands the struggle which she is entering; that is why she arms with joy. . . ."

After blaming Christian nations and especially the Pope for shielding Turkey, Khomyakov proclaimed the war not only holy but providential for the ultimate triumph of the Slav and the Orthodox cause. "Whatever will happen, Providence has marked out our time to become a decisive era in the destiny of the world. From now on two great principles are on the rise: the first, the Russian or rather Slav principle, the principle of the real fraternity of blood and spirit; the second, much higher, the principle of the Church—under its protecting wings the first principle will preserve itself in the midst of a world of trouble and discord; only thanks to divine might it will rise from being the almost instinctive tendency of one race alone to the dignity of the moral law guiding the future steps of mankind. . . . Human blood is precious, war is horrible—but the designs of Providence are inscrutable, and a task must be fulfilled whatever its rigors. Wave, flags! Sound, trumpet of battle! Nations! forward into battle! God orders mankind to march on!" This Hegelian mood of the *Weltgeist* marching on in the advancing ranks of the nation fulfilling the destiny of mankind soon evaporated in the failures of the Crimean War. The Eagle of the northern Slavs, whom Khomyakov had called upon in an earlier poem to hurry to the liberation of the younger Slav brothers, revealed an astonishing lack of strength. Nor was the war, as Tyutchev had proclaimed, a "conspiracy of all hell" bent upon the destruction of Russia; neither the Russian peasants nor the Russian nobility were eager to fight in defense of the honor of the fatherland,[n] the peace which ended the war did not impose any heavy sacrifices upon Russia; it was settled in a spirit of moderation by the old school of diplomacy which had no understanding of apocalyptic visions.

Herzen, who represented at that period the conscience of Russia, had opposed the war. In his appeal of March 1854, "to the Russian Soldiers in Poland" he wrote: "At last the Tsar has managed to bring war upon Russia. No matter how his colleagues . . . tried to make concessions, he has succeeded in provoking a contest. . . . The whole world compassionates the Turks, not from sympathy with them, but because they are fighting for a just cause; they were attacked, and so they must defend themselves. . . . Orthodox Christians, the Tsar adds, are oppressed by the Turks. We have never heard that the Christians in Turkey are more oppressed than our peasants, especially those who are serfs in bondage by the Tsar's command. Would it not be better to begin by freeing the slaves at home? After all, they are Orthodox too, fellow believers, and Russians into the bargain." Herzen expressed the hope that as the 14th of December 1825 followed upon 1812 some great act of liberation would follow 1854. He knew that Polish exiles tried to use the Crimean War for the liberation of their homeland. With great courage he drew attention to the case of Poland "waiting for a chance to rise once more for her rights, her freedom." In ringing words he called upon the Russian soldiers in Poland not to allow themselves to be abused for the suppression of the Polish struggle for liberty. "What does Poland want? She wants to be a free state. She is willing for union with Russia but with a Russia that is also free. If she is to unite with Russia, she must first have complete freedom." Out of such a free union the beginning of "a free union of all Slavs" might come."

Herzen, imbued with all the literature of the Hegelian Left and of French socialist and messianic expectations, came to Europe in 1847 in the youthful anticipation of the "miracle" of Europe; he was thrown into the opposite extreme of disillusionment by the collapse of the Revolution of 1848 and the caution and narrowness of the Western middle class;

as a result he yearned sometimes like a Slavophile, sharing their hopes and illusions for the future without accepting in the slightest their misconstructions of the past. In reality, he remained an unprejudiced and open-minded critic of Russia, in spite of or perhaps because of his deep and all-consuming love for his homeland, which he was not to enter again. He was one of the few Russians who fully valued individual liberty and the freedom of the West; and the longer he lived there the more critical he grew of Russian extremism, authoritarianism, and impatience. At the time of the Crimean War he wrote to Michelet that the Slavs "are in need of the vigorous and virile thought of the West. . . . We do not aim at the famous *farà da se* without the solidarity and community of nations. . . . I tell the Russians, I repeat it in every possible way, that the social idea which has been elaborated by the West is the only means by which the social faculties and dispositions of the Slavs can be developed rationally." [n]

From July 1, 1857 on, Herzen published in London the *Kolokol* (The Bell), the first free Russian newspaper. In its second issue he wrote: "While France's history has taken a bloody course since 1789, look upon England where deep changes have been accomplished without bloody catastrophes because the leading statesmen have understood how to meet the demands of life wisely and in good time. . . . The artists of the revolution don't like this way but this is not our concern; we prefer decidedly this way to the bloody one." In the following year he wrote: "We have ceased to love terror, in whichever way it may be presented and whatever its goal." He had witnessed the June 1848 uprising in Paris, and he had come to the conclusion that bloody revolutions do not bear fruit. Herzen was the one Russian liberal who throughout respected and honored Chaadayev;[n] the pen portrait which he drew of Vissarion Grigoryevich Belinsky (1811–48), the friend of his youth and Russia's leading literary and social critic of the period, showed the same respect for intellectual independence: "He was one of the freest men, bound neither by beliefs nor by tradition. He did not depend upon public opinion and accepted no authority. He feared neither the ire of his friends nor the shock of the good souls. He was always ready to denounce everything that he believed vile. How could he have left in peace the Orthodox and ultra-patriotic Slavophiles, he who saw heavy chains in everything which the Slavophiles accepted as the most sacred ties? . . . Belinsky and his friends have not opposed an exclusive doctrine or system to that of the Slavophiles, but a lively sympathy for everything which was agitating their contemporaries, a limitless love for liberty of thought and an equally strong hatred for everything which curtailed that liberty: authority, force, or faith. . . . It seemed to them that one of the most serious causes of the slavery in which Russia found herself was the lack of personal independence. Thence came the complete absence of respect for the individual, the cynicism of the government and the long patience of the people. Russia's future will present great danger for Europe and great misfortune for Russia herself, if no emancipating ferments will secure individual rights. One more century of the present despotism, and all the good qualities of the Russian people will be destroyed. . . . A long servitude cannot be accidental, it corresponds to some element in the national character. This element can be absorbed and defeated by other elements, but it can also remain victorious. . . . If Russia continues the period of St. Petersburg or returns to the period of Moscow, she will have no other vocation but to throw herself upon Europe, like a semi-barbarian and semi-corrupted horde, to devastate the civilized countries and to perish in the midst of the general destruction. Was it not therefore necessary to call upon the

Russian people by all means to become conscious
of its tragic position? . . . Instead, the Slavophiles
preached submission, . . . the formation of the
Muscovite Tsardom; they preached the contempt
of the West which alone could enlighten the abyss
of Russian life; they glorified the past, which on the
contrary it was necessary to get rid of in favor of a
future which should be in common to the East and
to the West." [n]

Immediately after the Revolution of 1848, Herzen
wrote in "*Vom anderen Ufer*": "Individual liberty is
the greatest of all things; the real will of the people
can be formed only on its basis. . . . to subordinate
the individual to society, to the people, to humanity,
to an idea, means the continuation of human sacrifices . . . the crucifixion of the innocent for the
guilty ones." [n] This fundamental liberalism and his
growing realism regarding the myth of revolution—
an attitude similar to that of the other great Slav
liberal T. G. Masaryk—brought him ten years later
into widening conflicts with the radicalism and
revolutionary messianism of the Russian and Polish
youth. At the end of 1858 he was attacked in an
anonymous Polish pamphlet, and in January 1859 in
an article in the *Sovremennik* (The Contemporary),
by Nikolai Gavrilovich Chernyshevsky (1828–89), at
that time its foremost contributor, and the revered
leader of the young generation. Herzen's replies in
the *Kolokol* threw light not only on his political
philosophy but also upon his attitude to the burning nationality problems of Poland and the Ukraine
with which Russia was then faced and which have
lost nothing in urgency today.

In his reply to the Polish pamphlet, Herzen first
developed his general philosophy: "There was a
time—how well I remember it—when the mere word
republic would set hearts a-beating; but now, after
1849, 1850, 1851, this word raises as many doubts
as hopes. Have we not seen for ourselves that a re-

public with governmental initiative, with despotic centralization, with a huge army, will do far less to promote free progress than does the English monarchy without initiative, without centralization? Have we not seen that the French 'democracy,' i.e., equality in slavery, is the form nearest to absolutism? . . . I know it is not consistent with the *religion of democracy* to speak anything but evil about crowned heads. . . . Democratic orthodoxy grants the mind as little freedom and hems it in no less than (any other orthodoxy). The man who does not consult it and his conscience to get his standard of behavior: *that man is not free.*" Herzen's political realism, acquired by years of thought and experience, had carried him far from his 1848 utopianism and the ensuing bitter disappointment with reality, and from the extremism of his fellow Russians. He had grown too conscious of human misery and human weaknesses to wish to add deliberately to them. To Chernyshevsky's question, what would happen if the people, feeling itself deceived by the Tsarist government, would take to the axe, Herzen replied: "That would be a great misfortune but one which could happen. Then it will no longer be possible to reason. Everybody will have to act as his conscience and his love will order him. But even then, I state definitely, the appeal to take the axe will not come from London. We shall use all our strength to avoid it." [n]

In treating of the even more difficult and over-emotionalized national question, Herzen showed a similar penetrating liberalism, free from any Russian chauvinism. In the second part of his answer to the Polish pamphlet, which appeared in the *Kolokol* on January 15, 1859, he wrote: "Poland possesses . . . the full and imprescriptible right to have a political existence independent from Russia. It is another question whether we desire the separation of a free Poland from a free Russia. We do not desire it. Could it be possible to desire it at a time when exclusive nationalism and hatred between peoples represent one of the principal obstacles to the development of universal liberty? I hate deeply all centralization, but I am convinced that federal unions between peoples of the same race offer an undoubtedly larger political milieu than the division of one race into different parts. But a federal union must be voluntary. Russia has no right over Poland. She must merit what she has taken by force. And if Poland does not wish this alliance, we can be chagrined by it, but we could not refuse her complete liberty without denying our fundamental convictions. . . . And if the Ukraine wishes to be neither Polish nor Russian? The solution seems to me simple. We have then to recognize the Ukraine as a free and independent nation. Among us who are living in exile . . . there should not even arise the question to whom this or that inhabited land should *belong*. In the Ukraine there live people whom serfdom has crushed but whom the government and the landowners have not broken to the point of making them lose their sentiment of nationality. . . . Set free their hands, set free their tongue, that their words become entirely free and let them express their will." [n] Few Russian or Polish liberals had then the courage to see the Ukrainian question in the light of liberty. Both sides appealed to historical rights or to other "superior" considerations.[n] None wished to renounce what had historically "belonged" to them. On each side, reactionaries and liberals, monarchists and republicans, were alike willing and eager to oppress other Slavs. Herzen stood almost alone. His organ, formerly so influential, the voice and conscience of free Russia, dropped rapidly in circulation and soon ceased publication.[n]

Herzen tried in 1863 to dissuade the Poles from armed insurrection. He was afraid of the useless bloodshed, the innumerable victims, and the bloody reaction which would follow. He tried to bring about

a close co-operation of the Polish and Russian movements for freedom and was convinced that their success depended upon their solidarity. But when the
Polish Central Committee on January 22, 1863, proclaimed the uprising, Herzen printed in the *Kolokol*
on February 1 an article entitled "Resurrexit," and
two weeks later he castigated the Russian "Crimes
in Poland." [n] He showed the same courage as the
many Englishmen who fought for Irish home rule or
who opposed the Boer War. But these Englishmen
in spite of all passionate discussions remained respected and the majority of their countrymen supported them a short time later. The Russian liberals,
on the other hand, never forgave Herzen for his
pro-Polish attitude. Nor were the Poles much better.
They began their insurrection by committing atroc-
ities, massacring the Russian soldiers surprised in
their barracks. Though they promised personal
freedom to all citizens and the rights of the peasants
to the soil which they tilled, they claimed the independence of Poland within the "historical" frontiers
of 1771. Their democratic wing was as nationalistic
as the Russian liberals. Herzen was one of the few
free minds who in his deep love for the Russian and
Polish people and in his devotion to truth could rise
above the conflict.

The popularity which Herzen lost in Russia was
gained by Mikhail Nikiforovich Katkov (1818–87),
a gifted editor and journalist who turned at the beginning of the 1860's from a moderate liberal into a
fervent Russian nationalist and Pan-Slav propagandist.[n] Pan-Slavism received new slogans and goals
when the Crimean War and the antagonism to the
Catholic Poles directed the Russian Slav sympathies
to the Orthodox Serbs. In the 1840's Prague and the
Czechs held the center of Pan-Slav interests; Pogodin
had been inspired by them, and Khomyakov on his
way to England in 1847 was deeply impressed by his

brief sojourn in Prague and his meeting with Hanka.
But the events of 1848 convinced him, as they did
Tyutchev, that hope resided only in Orthodox Slavdom. Like Tyutchev, though entirely independent of
him, he predicted in 1848 the end of Austria and of
the last remnants of Charlemagne's Empire, and
the disappearance of papal power "in the archives of
history, followed by Protestantism and by Catholicism. . . . Now it is the turn of Orthodoxy, the
turn of the Slav races to enter the stage of the world;
a solemn moment which we have felt coming but
for which we did not prepare. Shall we know how to
profit from it? . . . It is sad, but we must admit
that we should harbor as many fears as hopes. The
greater part of the Slavs (Bohemia and Poland) has
been corrupted to the marrow of the bone by
Germano-Roman influence. . . . The races which
remained most pure and least exposed to Western
influence in all respects and especially in respect to
religion (the Serbs) will probably succumb to the
two-fold temptation of political organization and
material civilization which has carried away ourselves
since the days of Peter the Great." [n] A young scholar
in the field of Slav ethnography, Alexander Fyodoro-
vich Hilferding (1831–72), published in 1854 and
1857 his "Pisma ob istorii Serbov i Bolgar" (Letters
on the History of the Serbs and Bulgars).

When Khomyakov in the last year of his life
decided to sum up his message, he wrote it in the
form of a "Letter from Moscow to the Serbs," and
asked all leading Slavophiles to sign it and thus to
make it into the testament of the Slavophile movement. He warned the Serbs against the spiritual
pride of the Greeks and the intellectual pride of the
Western nations, against pride of race, against social
inequalities and an aristocracy by birth. He asked
them to preserve above all their Orthodox faith
which alone can form the foundation of a true society. "It is not without reason that true communal

life, the sanctity of the judgment of the *mir,* and the full submission of every individual to the unanimous decision of his brothers have been maintained only in the Orthodox lands. . . . Only the Orthodox preserves his liberty while humbly aware of his weakness, submits to the unanimous decision of the conscience of the assembly. . . . A Slav cannot be therefore truly Slav outside Orthodoxy." In an Orthodox country like Serbia everybody should have the same rights in private life, but only those of the Orthodox faith should have political rights and occupy public offices. The letter exhorted the Serbs to follow the highest moral and Christian ideals, to form an ideal community, and not to forget that only that country could be great and truly strong "Where there is no misery among the poor and no luxury among the rich, where everything is simple and unostentatious except God's temple." In its conclusion, the Letter cited the Czechs and the Poles as an example of the danger caused to the Slavs by too close a contact with Europe.

The Letter was directed as much to the Russians as to the Serbs.[n] Its noble contents, its Rousseauic idyl, interpreted as typically and uniquely Orthodox and Slav, aroused hardly any attention. It sounded like the forlorn echo of a time long past. What remained for the new generation was the identification of Slavdom with Orthodoxy, and soon even of Slavdom with Russia. When seven years later the second Pan-Slav Congress met in Moscow, the visiting Slavs were told that Slav unity demanded unity of faith, of alphabet and of language, the acceptance by all the Slavs of Orthodoxy, of the Cyrillic alphabet and of the Russian language. To a part of Russian public opinion this Pan-Slavism appealed as a vehicle of Russian imperialism against the West. It did not achieve much because it was rejected by the Western Slavs and was not supported by the Russian government.

One of the best French observers of Russia under
Alexander II wrote in 1868: "The Crimean War
detached Russia from the traditions of 1815; the
insurrection of Poland hastened the transformation
by completing the confusion of the European diplomacy and by infiltrating into the Russian policy all
the nationalist and even revolutionary passions. . . .
The new Russia has become an agitator and even
a revolutionary. She has come to understand that
public opinion is a power and she has addressed
herself to public opinion. One has used propaganda
against her, and now she has released all kinds of
propaganda against the others. One has threatened
her with the right of the peoples, with this new
principle of nationality, and now she has begun herself to use this weapon which she handles with
Byzantine dexterity united to the whole pride of
force." [n]

In another article, a few months before, the same
author had used a language which seemed to confirm
the attitude of the Slavophiles and to inspire that of
men like Danilevsky: "One of the most characteristic
and most dangerous signs of our time is definitely the
ambiguous and manifold antagonism between Russian and Western Europe. In whatever way we may
judge it, it exists, and in a strange way one could
even say that in spite of the spread of general civilization, instead of calming down and growing less, it
increases and gets more and more irritated. . . . It
is no longer the accidental clash of contrary interests
of rival ambitions, as happens much too often in
Europe, among powers which collide with each other
for a moment but which belong definitely to the
same civilization and are destined to live in peace
and to find themselves in agreement again sooner or
later. It is rather the struggle of two spiritual entities
(deux génies), of two worlds which feel themselves
radical enemies, which do not know in which higher
harmony they could find conciliation, for they pro-

ceed from different principles and they represent morally and politically entirely separate or opposite trends." [n]

These conclusions of Charles de Mazade may be countered by opposite observations: the Europeanization of all branches of Russian life and the modernization of Russian economy in the last part of the nineteenth century; the rise of new classes; the ever closer intellectual and artistic contact with Europe; the sincere efforts of the Russian government to arrive at an alliance with Bismarckian Germany; the close *rapprochement* later on with France and even with Britain. All these factors diminished the historical antagonism between Russia and Europe and made Russia more and more, even in its contrary interests of rival ambitions, one of the European powers belonging to the same civilization and destined to find themselves sooner or later in agreement. But Charles de Mazade was understandably fascinated by that vocal influential part of Russian public opinion which organized the Pan-Slav Congress of 1867; he accepted their evaluation of Russia as a world by itself, alien and superior to Europe and at the same time suffering from Europe's hostility and arrogance, an interpretation then not shared by the Russian government and repudiated by important sections of Russian society, which triumphed only after 1917 when it was officially imposed upon Russia.

But half a century before, in 1867, the Moscow Pan-Slav Congress was not initiated by the government. It was organized by the Slav Committee which was formed in Moscow in 1857 for the support of the southern Slavs and of which in 1861 Pogodin became chairman, while Ivan Aksakov was secretary and treasurer. In 1863 a Society of the Friends of Natural Science was founded at Moscow University. These organizations evolved the plan of arranging in 1867 a Slav ethnographic exhibition in

Moscow and of inviting Slavs from outside Russia to participate. All in all eighty-four non-Russian Slavs attended. Qualitatively and quantitatively the Czechs formed the most important delegation; without them there would have been no congress. Among them were Palacký, his son-in-law Dr. Rieger, and Dr. František August Brauner (1810–80). The Slav "pilgrims" went first to St. Petersburg where they were received in audience by Alexander II, but though this reception aroused great expectations among Czechs and southern Slavs, the Emperor confined himself to friendly banalities and carefully avoided any political implication. At a banquet given in St. Petersburg in honor of the Slav delegates, the only official spokesman, Count Dmitri Andreyevich Tolstoy (1823–89), then minister of education and a fanatical Russian nationalist and Orthodox reactionary, spoke vaguely of the importance of the Slavs and concretely of the study of the various Slav languages for a better understanding of their grammar.

The unofficial speakers were much less restrained. Tyutchev read a long poem of welcome "To the Slavs": "Not in vain did Russia call you to this festival of peace and love. You must know, beloved guests, you are not guests here, you are at home. You are more at home here than in your native lands . . . here where people and rulers speak but one tongue and where it is not judged a crime to be born a Slav. Although we were separated by harsh fate, we have remained a single nation, the sons of one mother. . . . This is what the world cannot forgive us." He went on to assert that the world, which has injured and insulted the Slavs for such a long time, dreads now the thought of the new Slav unity and self-awareness which looms over them like heaven's wrath and has not forgotten all the ancient wrongs which are still unavenged. In spite of all the sacrifices which it will demand, the Slavs will always believe in Divine justice. For He is still mighty and the Tsar-Liberator will be hailed some day beyond Russia's frontiers."

On behalf of the Slav delegates from outside Russia, Rieger and the Austrian Serb Mihajle Polit spoke. Both stressed the brotherhood uniting the Slavs with their powerful kinsmen in Russia. "The creative task of Russia lies not only in Asia, but on what may be called the threshold of her house—the European East," Polit exclaimed. "Russia is no longer Russia; it is Slavonia, nay Pan-Slavonia." But as soon as the real meeting started at the end of May in Moscow, the divergence between the Russians and their Western guests, whose spokesman was Rieger, became apparent. It is true that Vladimir Ivanovich Lamansky (1833–1914) had pointed out that the invitation to the Slavs—which he called a great historical event —came in the framework of an ethnographic exhibition, thus proving that Russia did not wish to deprive the various Slav peoples of their ethnographically different characters but recognized "magnanimously" the historical rights of the weaker Slav brothers, thereby acquiring a position of strong moral leadership among them. But in the same speech he demanded that Russian should become the official language of all Slavs and these words of his were greeted by his Russian audience with thunderous applause. The Slav guests got more and more the impression that by Pan-Slavism their Russian hosts understood a Pan-Russianism, the acceptance of the Russian language and of the Orthodox faith by all other Slavs, a Russification of the Austro-Hungarian and Balkan Slavs similar to the process which then operated within the Russian borders in the Russification of the Ukrainians and the Poles.

The Ukrainian question was hardly discussed, but the Polish question loomed over the whole meeting. No Ukrainian from Russia, where the huge majority of the Ukrainian nation lived, participated; only

from Austrian Galicia and from northern Hungary
a few Russophile Ukrainian delegates attended.[n] The
Poles, the second most important Slav nation, ostentatiously remained away. Rieger made himself the
spokesman of the Polish cause. Before starting on
the "pilgrimage" to Moscow, he and Palacký had
gone to Paris to see French and Polish leaders there.
They wished to assure their bridges to the West to
avoid the impression of an anti-Polish attitude.
Count Andrzej Zamoyski (1800–74), a liberal Polish
aristocrat who had done much for the economic
improvement and the modernization of agriculture
in Poland, warned the Czechs that their going to
Moscow was an act of treason to Europe. Rieger
courageously insisted in Moscow that no Slav people
should lord it over another Slav people; if the Poles
recognized the rights of the Little Russians (Ukrainians), then Russia should meet them in brotherly
love and respect their nationality. Rieger's words
provoked a storm of indignation among the Russians.
Prince Vladimir Cherkassky declared that Russia
alone had created Poland in 1815 and that the Poles,
ungrateful for this beneficial generosity, had lost irrevocably by their uprisings the liberty granted to
them.

There existed no power on earth which could
change the Russian position in Poland. A Russian-
Polish reconciliation would be possible only when
the "several Vistula governments" would completely
renounce thought of a distinct political existence
and when the Poles would return voluntarily under
the common roof of the family like the prodigal son
of the Gospel with a contrite heart and humbly do
penance. "Then we shall open our arms wide and
there will be no calf fat enough in our herd which
we would not like to slaughter for this joyful feast."
Katkov expressed the same point of view clearly in
the *Moskovskie Vedomosti* leaving out the pious
Slavophile reference to the Gospel: no Polish nation

existed any longer, the sword had decided against the Poles.

While Rieger alone spoke up for the Poles, though in a form which did not satisfy the latter, the Serb delegates supported him strongly in opposing the Russian demand for the Russification of all Slavs. They stressed autonomy and diversity in mutual harmony, but not in subordination, as the principle of Pan-Slavism. Even to their most ardent Pan-Slav guests the Russians seemed too outspoken. Katkov called upon Russia to unite the Slavs as Prussia had united the Germans. "This task is noble, for it is devoid of egoism; it is beneficial, for it will complete the triumph of the principle of nationality and will provide a solid foundation for the modern equilibrium of Europe; it is worthy of Russia and her greatness, and we are firmly convinced that Russia will fulfill it." [n] The rector of the University of Moscow went even further. He called the Slavs one nation and he found it like all modern nations irresistibly drawn toward centralized unity. Modern international law had recognized this new right of national unity. "Clearly under such circumstances our efforts for unity are perfectly legitimate and must be recognized as such in Europe. . . . Strongly tied together by all the ties of blood and mind, what could the Slavs not achieve in a common effort! Mountains will be moved when we shall attack them together! . . . Let us unite as Italy and Germany have been united in one whole, and the name of the great united nation will be: Giant!" [n]

Naturally, national unity demanded unity of language. "God alone knows," the orator continued, "where He leads the great Slav race; but to march together toward the goal to which He leads us, we must understand each other. The unity of language is the strongest of all unities." Again appealing to the example of Western Europe, where in modern nations a number of local idioms were preserved but one literary language was established, another Russian delegate exhorted the Slav brothers to follow this example. "Let every idiom develop in its own way, but let all of them bring their local differences and their particular genius as a contribution to the common treasure of a Pan-Slav language! May one literary language alone cover all the lands from the Adriatic Sea and Prague to Arkhangelsk and the Pacific Ocean, and may every Slav nation without regard for its religion adopt this language as its means of communication with the others!"

It is easily understandable that the conference discussing these typical dreams of intellectuals showed no practical results. Some proposed the foundation of a pan-Slav university in Warsaw, of all cities; others suggested the division of the Slav world into three parts, one exclusively Russian which would consist of all the territories east of the Vistula; a West Slav empire with Prague as Capital; and a South Slav realm with Belgrade as its center. The establishment of publishing houses, literary magazines, and economic institutions was again discussed. The enthusiasm at the final meeting at the beginning of June was great. After his farewell speech Palacký was approached by a Russian officer, Mikhail Terentyev, a soldier with many decorations for his services in the Caucasus and in Asia, who made a fiery speech and at the end drew his sword, exclaiming: "Tu me defendas calamo, ego te defendam gladio." Palacký embraced and kissed him to the applause of the audience. But though it was decided to call Pan-Slav congresses from now on to meet every two years in the month of August, the next time in Belgrade, no Pan-Slav congress was to meet for more than forty years, and when it met it was in an atmosphere of much greater sobriety though with no greater efficacy.

The ten years following the Congress of Moscow were devoted to an elaboration of the Pan-Slav theory by Russian writers and military men. This stage of Pan-Slav thought was confronted by a new situation: Prussia and Germany, which in the first half of the century had been Russia's friends and clients, seemed now, after the unification by Bismarck, which had been made possible by Russia's benevolent attitude, to present a heightened danger to the Slav world and its aspirations. The union of the Germans had to be answered by the union of the Slavs. In typically Slavophile fashion Tyutchev in a poem "Two Nations" (1870) stressed that the Slav union would be different from that which Bismarck created "with blood and iron."

From a cup overflowing with the wrath of God
Blood pours o'er the land and the West drowns in
    it—
Blood drenches you too, oh our friends and brothers!
Slavonic world, shut tighter still! . . .

'Union' the oracle of our day proclaimed,
'Is to be welded by iron and blood.'
But we shall try to forge it out of love—
And then we shall see which union will endure
    longer.

3

Pan-Slavism and the Unification of Germany

FOR HALF A CENTURY after the Napoleonic wars, peace was the prevailing mood of Europe. The Crimean War revealed the military unpreparedness and the lack of a bellicose spirit in all the nations involved. Italy's unification was not achieved by Italian arms; even Napoleon's armed intervention was brief and half-hearted; the unification was the result of diplomatic adroitness, middle-class agitation and French and British benevolence. Its success encouraged and inspired Poles and Germans. Under the mistaken impression that Italian unification had been the result of Italian daring alone, of an Italy *farà da se*, acting out of its own strength, the Poles started the uprising of 1863 which ended in complete failure. Though in the unification of Germany diplomatic adroitness and middle-class agitation also played a role, the decisive factor there was the intervention of the Prussian army which in 1866 destroyed the German Confederation and the peace treaties of 1815.

The war of 1866 was the divide of nineteenth century European history, occupying therein a similar position to that of the nearly contemporary Civil

War in American history. But the long-lasting and sanguinary conflict in the United States resulted in strengthening the country's peace and unity; the short war of 1866 opened an era of growing national apprehensions and armaments in Europe. The misfortunes of Europe for the last ninety years originated in the year 1866. Fateful consequences were clearly foreseen by most contemporary observers. The German historian Georg Gottfried Gervinus (1805–71) wrote shortly before his death: "Prussia has been reproached with having by its war and its methods transformed the whole of Europe into one armed camp; it would be impossible to consider as a malevolent phrase in the mouth of an enemy what can be simply proved by facts. It is not wise to disregard out of patriotism the fact that the events of 1866 have revived for the whole continent and for the whole epoch the dangers of a system which was generally held to be vanishing, and to have immeasurably magnified them. After the hopes and strivings of half a century to outgrow the military systems of former times, there has here been created a permanent military power of such tremendous superiority as the world has not known even in the iron age of the Napoleonic wars." [n]

Like Gervinus, a much younger German writer, Julius Eckardt (1836–1908), writing in 1870, recognized the importance of the events of 1866: "Das Jahr 1866 hat unseren Weltteil in ein Kriegslager verwandelt, wie es seit Jahrhunderten kein zweites gegeben hat." (The year 1866 has transformed our continent into an armed camp the like of which has been unknown for centuries). Typically, however, Eckardt wished to assure the world of German peacefulness and characterized Bismarck and Moltke as imbued with the ideas of the Society of Friends. "Die wachsende industrielle Bedeutung unserer Nation ist ein natürlicher Hebel der angeborenen deutschen Friedfertigkeit, und unsere grossen Staats-

und Kriegsmänner, dieselben, die die Welt zum zweiten Mal durch unvergleichliche Taten in Erstaunen und Bewunderung versetzt haben,—sie hassen den Krieg, wie die Quäker." (The growing industrial importance of our nation is a natural lever of the innate German love of peace, and our great statesmen and warriors, the same men who by their incomparable deeds have aroused the astonishment and admiration of the world for the second time (in 1866 and 1870)—they hate war as the Quakers do).

Eckardt seemed amazed that the Slavs were not equally convinced of the pacifism of German industrialists and Prussian generals. He himself, born in Latvia, was a Baltic German who knew Russia well. After journalistic work in Riga, he collaborated from 1867 to 1870 with Gustav Freytag as editor of the famous German liberal nationalist weekly *Grenzboten*. He was a prolific writer on Baltic and Russian conditions: in 1870 he translated into German the articles on the reorganization of Russia's military forces which General Rotislav Andreyevich Fadeyev (1826–84) published in 1867 in Katkov's *Russky Vestnik*.[n] Intelligent and progressive in his proposals for a reform of Russia's army, Fadeyev in his introductory general remarks showed himself entirely under the influence of the Pan-Slav myth: "This hostility (of Western Europe) has its cause not in this or that political system of Russian government, but in the distrust against a new, alien, all too numerous nation which has suddenly emerged on the borders of Europe, an immense empire with traditions different from those of the West, where so many fundamental social questions are differently handled, where the whole mass of people possesses land, and where a religion is professed which is one hundred times more dangerous to papacy than even Protestantism, a religion which rejects both. In addition it has been shown, that this unexpected enigmatic empire is surrounded by Slav and orthodox kindred elements, which Western Europe would have . . . subjected and assimilated . . . , if their dormant consciousness had not been suddenly awakened by the surprising appearance of the Orthodox Slav Empire. Whatever we shall do, . . . we shall never destroy Europe's fear of us, for the simple reason that we are growing more powerful every day; we do not yet know ourselves how we shall feel in a few years about Slavism and Orthodoxy, for we cannot speak for ourselves, and even less for our children." Fadeyev was convinced that Europe wished to Germanize the non-Russian Slavs and convert the non-Russian Orthodox Christians to Catholicism. Russia's strength was imperilling these alleged plans. Like Bismarck and the German nationalists of his day, Fadeyev felt only scorn for the Holy Alliance which according to him sacrificed Russia's national interests to European peace. In both cases the conviction was expressed that in this new age of the self-awareness of their historical individuality the Germans and the Russians had to be materially strong and spiritually aroused to protect themselves and to maintain peace.

The events of 1870 clarified Fadeyev's foreign policy. He no longer regarded Western Europe as Russia's chief enemy. The new threat was Germany whose expected expansion to the east and southeast would doom the Czechs and the other non-Russian Slavs. He demanded open and strong official Russian support for the Slav cause; in such a case, the Slavs of Austria and Turkey would rally to the Russian arms, and the road to Constantinople, leading through Vienna, would lie open. The first step in that direction would be the reincorporation into the Russian empire of Austrian Galicia ("Carpathian Russia") and of the parts of Bessarabia lost in 1856. The Slavs, trusting Russia, would then form a federation with her, within which national individualities would be respected. Poland having only the choice between becoming a German subject people or accepting the position of Russia's younger brother, should within her ethnographic frontiers be included in the federation. Constantinople and the Straits should not be annexed to Russia but, cleared of the Turks, should become a free city of the whole confederation. Fadeyev took a broader and more "liberal" view than most Russian Pan-Slavs. He regarded the Czechs as the vanguard of the Slavs and Bohemia as a most valuable strategic bastion; he did not wish Russia to become an Asiatic empire; to avoid this danger it had to transform itself into a Slav state; it was therefore Russia's mission to save the Slavs in order to secure her own future, for her own non-Asiatic and truly Slav character depended on the non-Russian Slavs. To help in the coming struggle against the Germans, Fadeyev suggested an alliance with France. Official Russia, in 1870, was, however, so far removed from any Pan-Slav or anti-German policy that General Fadeyev was retired from active service for his outspoken advocacy of his views.

But even more than the Russians, the Czechs were deeply stirred by the Prussian victory of 1866 and the ensuing precipitate "compromise" of the Habsburg monarchy with the demands of the Hungarian nationalists. The new dual form of the monarchy resulting from the settlement of 1867 abandoned the non-Magyar populations of Hungary, the Slavs and the Rumanians, to the ruthless rule of a Magyar oligarchy which soon ceased even to pay lip-service to the national rights of these peoples. Palacký saw in this dualism the end of his hopes for a federal solution acceptable to the Austrian Slavs, and a return to the dreaded dangers of 1848. "Did they not wish then," he asked in an article in *Národ* of November 9, 1864, "to tear Austria into two parts and to add the one to the new German state, of which it was then even unknown, whether it would be a

republic or a Prussian empire, and to form out of the
other part an independent kingdom of Hungary?
. . . Who did then fight sincerely and resolutely
for Austria's unity? Were not the Slavs the only
ones? . . . The introduction of dualism in Austria
must without doubt lead to tremendous convulsions.
. . . (which) with the existence of whole peoples at
stake would affect all of Europe; and at the same
time the existence of Austria itself would be at
stake. . . . We Czechs certainly desire sincerely the
preservation and unity of Austria; for as we cannot
hope to build by our own forces our own sovereign
state, we believe that our historical-political individuality, our peculiar nationality and civilization
and our autonomous life could nowhere and in no
other way be better guaranteed than in Austria—in
a free Austria built upon the principles of autonomy
and equality. We have no patriots outside Austria's
frontiers, nor any prospects there. If some one will
tell us that we are Austria's friends only out of self-
interest, we shall willingly agree: but politicians who
are not naive, will concede that such friends are generally the most faithful and reliable ones." One year
later, in his "The Idea of the Austrian State," he
wrote: "The day of the proclamation of the (Austro-
Hungarian) dualism will be with irresistible necessity
the birthday of Pan-Slavism in its least pleasant
form; its godfathers will be the leaders of dualism.
. . . We Slavs shall look forward to it with justified
grief but without fear. We existed before Austria,
we shall exist also after it." [n] In the Bohemian Diet
on December 6, 1866, Rieger repeated the warning.
Some countries and peoples, he said, find themselves
in Europe placed between the Russian and the
German colossi in such a way that they cannot exist
for themselves alone without falling victims to their
larger neighbors. Austria's historical task was the
unification of these lands for common defense and
mutual support. The Czech people did not demand

privileges, it asked only for equal rights with the Magyars.

These warnings remained unheeded. Francis Joseph and the Saxon minister Count Friedrich Ferdinand von Beust (1809–86) whom he made Austrian minister of foreign affairs and chancellor, dreamt of the restoration of a German confederation under Austrian leadership. They thought that they needed the support of the Magyars for undoing the defeat of 1866. They envisaged the Austrian problem in terms of its historical position in Germany, they had no understanding of the Slav problem, Beust least of all. In 1867 Hungary became a sovereign and independent Magyar state tied loosely to the rest of the Habsburg monarchy; the whole agreement, which was regarded by the Habsburgs as a final settlement, by the Magyars, however, as only a first concession, was conceived in such a way as to leave to the smaller and more backward Hungarian partner the advantage and initiative in the few common concerns of the monarchy. On the other hand, the Constitution promulgated for the remaining parts of Austria on December 21, 1867, stipulated in its Article 19 that "all nationalities have equal rights in the state and each nationality has an inviolable right to preserve and cultivate its nationality and language. The equality of all languages used in the country in schools, offices and public life is recognized by the state." The respect for this article and the growing liberalization of the administrative practice in Austria allowed the nationalities there after 1867 a rapid progress in popular education, economic strength and national consciousness.

Nothing similar existed in Hungary. Only the Croats in the historical kingdom of Croatia-Slavonia received in 1868 in an agreement with Hungary autonomous rights guaranteeing the use and development of their language.[n] Among them, however, there were two opposite schools of thought: Bishop

Strossmayer was a Pan-Slav who felt much more strongly for the unity of the Catholic Croats and Slovenes with the Orthodox Serbs and Bulgars than for Croatia. The Yugoslav Academy of the Sciences and Arts which he founded in Zagreb on July 28, 1867, was destined to serve the idea of a unification of the literatures, languages and political lives of the four southern Slav peoples. On the other hand, the Croatian nationalists, the Party of (Croatian) Right, under the leadership of Ante Starčević, adhered to the Great Croatian idea. It felt no kinship with the Orthodox Serbs and wished to include the Slovene provinces of Austria and Dalmatia as parts of the Croatian kingdom. Thus none of the Slav peoples was satisfied with the new dualism.

After the defeat of France in 1870 the reasons which had induced Francis Joseph and Beust to agree to the Magyar demands had lost even a semblance of validity. There could be no question any more of Austria's returning to a leading role in Germany. Francis Joseph even promised on September 12, 1871, to be crowned as King of Bohemia and to recognize the historical rights of the kingdom. But German and Magyar pressure forced him to abandon this concession to Czech demands; dualism became the accepted foundation of the Habsburg monarchy; its Magyar aristocracy and its German middle class welcomed the conclusion of the alliance of Austria-Hungary with Germany which Count Gyula Andrássy (1823–90), the first Hungarian prime minister in the era of dualism and Beust's successor as minister of foreign affairs, arranged. These events destroyed the hopes which Austro-Slavism had cherished in 1848. One consequence of this disillusionment was the pilgrimage of the Czech leaders to Moscow in 1867; more serious was the epitaph which Palacký in his "Political Testament" wrote to Austria: "I myself now regretfully abandon the hope for a permanent preservation of the Austrian state:

not because it would not be desirable or is in itself impossible, but because the Germans and the Magyars were allowed to seize power and to establish in the monarchy a one-sided racial domination which cannot exist long in a multi-national and constitutional state where it is political nonsense, *a contradictio in adjecto.*" [n] The Magyars, deluded by nationalist and class conceit, never realized that the complete separation from Austria which they desired doomed their own historical existence. Their arrogance devoid of any sense of reality destroyed not only Austria and the hope for a Central European federation. It paved the way for the realization, less than a century later, of the worst fears of Palacký and of the daring hopes of Danilevsky who in 1869 wrote the Pan-Slav reply to the unification of Germany.

Nikolai Yakovlevich Danilevsky (1822–85) had none of the religious interests of the older Slavophiles. By training and outlook he was a scientist. His book "Russia and Europe, an Inquiry into the Cultural and Political Relations of the Slav to the Germano-Latin World" was published in 1869 in ten issues of the monthly *Zarya* (The Dawn). [n] Dostoyevsky read the first articles while he was in Florence. On March 20, 1869, he wrote to his niece Sophia Alexandrovna Ivanova-Khmyrova: "This Danilevsky is an entirely unusual personality. Formerly he was a socialist, an adherent of Fourier; even twenty years ago when he was implicated in our affair, he impressed me as most remarkable; he returned from exile as a true Russian and nationalist. This article which I recommended to you especially is his first publication." Ten days later he wrote to Nikolai Strakhov: "Danilevsky's article seems to me more and more important and valuable. It will remain for a long time the daily reading of every Russian. . . . It coincides so much with my own opinions and convictions that I am sometimes amazed by the identity of our conclusions; . . . I had intended to write an article with a similar title and the same tendency and conclusions. How great was my joy and my astonishment when I found this plan which I hoped to realize in the future already realized, and this in such harmonious, logical and scholarly form as I could not achieve with the best intentions. I am looking forward with such expectation to the continuations of this article that I rush every day to the post office and always calculate the probability of the arrival of the next issue of *Zarya*. . . . I wish only to add that after all our miserable, affected, irritated, one-sided and sterile negations a periodical with such a strict, truly Russian, and invigorating direction which has a positive attitude to our state must be successful."

Strakhov who was editor of *Zarya* called Danilevsky's book, in his introduction to the fourth edition, "the most complete catechism of Slavophilism." It hardly revealed any new viewpoints beyond those professed by Pogodin and Tyutchev, but it was the first comprehensive treatise presenting the subject in the framework of a general history of civilization. In that regard his work though practically unknown abroad and even not very influential in Russia can be compared to that of Oswald Spengler half a century later: both started from the supposition that civilizations mature and decay in turn and both used this theory for a wishful interpretation of the present, according to which Western civilization, rationalist, individualist and capitalist, was in a state of senility and decline. Understandably Danilevsky counted Germany as part of the doomed West, while Spengler confined the area of irremediable disintegration to the democracies and looked to Germany for salvation. Danilevsky borrowed the general framework of his cyclic interpretation of the process of history, the theory of successive cultural-historical types, from the German historian Heinrich Rückert

(1823–75), professor at the University of Breslau and son of the well known German poet Friedrich Rückert. But, as in the case of Spengler, this "scientific" framework is of little importance except that it gives to these writers the feeling of clothing their social and cultural observations and their predictions of the future with the coat of objective necessity. In such cases it is useless to discuss the scholarly value or the historical accuracy of the "cyclic" theories; these writers offer not a picture of reality in its complex texture but a mirror of the emotions, fears and hopes animating certain peoples and civilizations at given times.

The background of the emotions dominating some Russians at that time was stated in Danilevsky's introductory chapter where he referred to the events of 1864 and 1866, and complained with bitterness that while in 1854 the whole of Europe helped Turkey, a non-Christian barbarian country, against Russia, a Christian nation protecting other Christians, in 1864 Europe abandoned Christian Denmark, a small liberal and civilized European country, to the kind graces of Germany. How to explain this different attitude? Danilevsky was convinced that it could not be explained by anything Russia was doing, Russia which fought for Europe in 1799, 1805, 1807 and 1813 and which was neither an aggressive power nor hostile to liberty. "The reason is that Europe does not recognize us as of its own kind. . . . Whether Schleswig and Holstein will belong to Denmark or to Germany, does not matter, because in either case they will remain European. . . . But how can one allow an alien, hostile, barbarian world to expand its influence, even if it expands over lands which according to all divine and human laws belong to it? Europe will not allow it—it will become a common concern for all who feel themselves European. In such a case even Turkey becomes acceptable as an ally. . . . Here nothing conscious is involved of which Europeans could give themselves an unprejudiced account. The cause lies much more deeply. It lies in historical instincts and these instincts hinder Europe from loving Russia." [n]

In the third chapter of his book Danilevsky, starting with a quotation from Kollár's *Slávy dcera*, asked whether Russia was part of Europe. "Europe," he answered, could be defined only as a cultural historical concept, not by geography; nor was it identical with the area of Greco-Roman civilization which centered around the Mediterranean and included southern Europe, Western Asia and northern Africa. Europe of modern times was synonymous with German-Romance civilization. "Does Russia in this sense belong to Europe? Regretfully or happily, for better or for worse—no, it does not belong. None of the intellectual forces which fertilized Europe nourished Russia. . . . Neither true modesty nor true pride allow Russia to appear as part of Europe. It does not merit this honor, and if it wishes to merit another honor, it should not long for one which does not come to it." [n] Not belonging to Europe by birthright, Russia should not make an effort to be adopted by Europe. A historical organism which nourished itself for so long from its own roots and soil, could not allow its own roots suddenly to dry up and become nourished from alien roots. Nor had Europe any tasks to offer to a Europeanized Russia. When Russia tried to carry and propagate European civilization to the Balkans and to the Near East, Europe always protested: "The noble German urge to the East progresses along the German Danube. The Germans have known well how to deal with the Slavs; they Europeanize them better than you could do." When the Russians wished to bring European civilization to Persia or China, they were met by similar objections from Europeans. Thus the only part of the East where the Russians were allowed to expand and to civilize, was Turkestan which was geographically too secluded and economically too backward, to attract the Europeans. With a feeling of deep hurt, Danilevsky exclaimed: "To build in the course of one thousand years with sweat and blood an empire of 80 million souls (of whom 60 millions are of the same race and descent, a unique case in the world outside China) only in order to carry European civilization to some five or six million primitive Central Asian and perhaps two or three million Mongol nomads, . . . that is the sublime world historical role reserved for Russia as the bearer of European civilization."

This humiliating predicament was brought about by the fact that the Russians accepted the assertion by the Europeans that their civilization was the final form of human civilization and therefore of universal validity. In reality European civilization was only a product of history, nothing final; it was as one-sided as other civilizations had been and like them subject to the law of growth and decay of civilizations. History should not be considered as a continuous progressive whole divided into antiquity, the Middle Ages and modern times and culminating in present-day European civilization. One must distinguish in history several different cultural historical types or original forms of civilization, each one of which develops independently a principle founded on its peculiar spiritual nature and its own conditions of life. Each cultural type has only a relatively short period in which at the height of its growth it bears fruit, then it begins to decline. There is no endless progress in one direction; once a civilization has started to decline, mankind sets out to follow new paths.

The Slavs represent one of the cultural-historical types of human history, and if they do not wish to become ethnographic material without any role in history, they must develop independently. European civilization reached its creative peak in the sixteenth and seventeenth centuries, since then it has been declining. Conscious of its own growing desiccation in spite of all continuing outside splendor, Europe feels an instinctive hostility toward the Slavs, its heirs. The cultural-historical type is in each given period the highest manifestation of history to which man's supreme loyalty here on earth belongs. "And thus for every Slav: Russian, Czech, Serb, Croat, Slovene, Slovak, Bulgar (I wish to add also Pole)— after God and His Holy Church—the idea of Slavdom (*slavyanstvo*) must be the highest idea, higher than any earthly good, for none of these is attainable to him without its existence, without an intellectually, nationally and politically independent Slavdom; and on the other side all these blessings will be the inescapable consequence of its independence and originality (*samobytnost*)." [n]

What will be the distinguishing trait of Slav civilization? Western civilization, according to Danilevsky, has been marked throughout by force and violence in all its great enterprises: the spread of Christianity; the discovery and colonization of new worlds; the struggle for emancipation and liberty; and finally the scramble for commercial profit. Slav civilization, on the other hand, Danilevsky maintained in one of the many repetitions of the Rousseau-Herder pattern, has known neither force nor intolerance as a dominant trait. The acceptance and spread of Christianity, the introduction of governmental organization and of a dynasty which ruled for centuries undisputed, the colonization and fertilization of vast tracts of land by the Russian plough, the emancipation of the serf and the introduction of great liberal reforms—all that happened without the struggle and conflicts which accompanied similar great movements in the West. Nor had the Slavs succumbed in modern times to the greed of capitalism and the idolization of commercial expansion. In the West, Christianity had been preached by knightly orders with the sword, and this tradition was still alive in secular disguise: the European revolutionists spread liberty, equality and fraternity by forcing them upon unwilling people and the trading middle class distributed the blessing of civilization to backward lands by a similar show of force. In all these cases the end was always justifying the means to produce desired changes. In Russia and among the Slavs the historical changes were produced peacefully, through an organic development, as if by unanimous consent. European history was propelled by the interests of conflicting parties; Russian history, by the growth of the people's moral consciousness. For that reason there was no need in Russia for the formation of parties, for the existence of an opposition. The attempt to introduce the social organization and the political methods of the West into Russia threatened to destroy the true foundations of Slav civilization: it caused the serious malady from which Russia was suffering in the nineteenth century and which only a newly regained consciousness of her Slavdom could heal.[n]

Having thus laid the general foundations, Danilevsky turned[n] to the discussion of the "Oriental question," for him the decisive world historical problem of the period. In a style anticipating that of Spengler, he wrote: "The oriental question is not one of those which are decided by diplomats. Events of minor importance are left by history to the chancelleries of diplomacy, but history itself proclaims its great decisions which impose their life-laws upon peoples for whole centuries without any intermediary, surrounded by thunder and lightning, like the Lord from the top of Sinai." It may strike the reader as strange how much the champions of supposedly peace-loving Slav Russia sound like the spokesmen of supposedly war-enthused Germany. With a contempt similar to Spengler's—for the bourgeois mentality of capitalist nations, Danilevsky condemned attempts at peaceful diplomatic settlement of vital historical problems as "a stock-exchange concept of politics." Ten years before the Congress of Berlin where Disraeli's diplomatic adroitness "settled" the Oriental question in such a way that it has not led so far to the apocalyptic struggle between East and West expected by Danilevsky and Dostoyevsky, Danilevsky denied the possibility of such a settlement for meta-political or meta-historical reasons. He saw the Oriental question as an expression of "an elemental" and therefore uncontrollable opposition between the interests of the Slav and of the Western worlds.

Like Spengler, Danilevsky was never in want of a daring and fascinating historical parallel supporting, according to him, the inevitable coming of his wishful prophecy. He regarded the Oriental question of the nineteenth century as the continuation of the struggle between the Roman and the Greek types of civilization of two thousand years before, with the Germans as the heirs of Rome and the Slavs as the heirs of Greece. Greek cultural life had found its fulfillment, Danilevsky taught, in the Byzantine Empire the heirs of which were the Slavs; Greek philosophy, in the dogma of the Orthodox Church; Greek art, in the Orthodox divine service. For a long time the struggle between the West and the Slavs had gone in favor of the former. Danilevsky regarded the Islamic domination of the Balkan peninsula as a Providential act which had protected the Slavs from falling victim to Western Christianity. "Even today the Slavs prefer the heavy yoke of the Mohammedans to the civilized domination of Austria." [n] But by the middle of the eighteenth century Islam and Turkey were no longer needed to shield the true faith of the Slavs because by then Russia, "the protector of Orthodoxy and Slavdom which had been called to this role from the beginning," had grown into manhood and had become able to oppose the West.

The reign of Catherine II ended the period of aggression of the Western world against the Slav heirs of Greece. World history entered into a new, the third stage of the Oriental question; in its course, the West tried to use Turkey as one of its points of support and bridgeheads against the Slavs—the others being Poland and the small but ambitious Magyar people. Napoleon I and Napoleon III had both tried to lead Europe to fight Russia using Turkey and Poland as pretexts and advance posts. In the manner of Tyutchev, Danilevsky called Poland "the old traitor to Slavdom, where the West has tried to establish the rule of the Polish nobility over millions of Russian and even of Polish people, without caring in the slightest for the principle of nationality which it itself had proclaimed, and in so doing, it has distorted indubitable facts, without any pangs of conscience. Of all Slav countries Poland alone has enjoyed the sympathy of Europe, because it forms the type and the example after which Europe would like to mold all the other Slavs in order to subject them completely—even granting them purely external political independence which the true Slavs have always valued less than the internal intellectual and national freedom."

But Turkey's support was more important than Poland's for Europe. Its fear of the rising, rival East "obscured so much every sentiment of truth and justice that Europe shut not only its eyes to the suffering of the Turkish Christians who had the misfortune of being Slavs and Orthodox but it even fell in love with the Turks and began to see in them the only element capable of bringing to the Orient the beginning of true European civilization. Europe, especially England, had now many Turkophiles instead of Philhellenes. All Europe began to discover that not Isalm and Turkey were the enemies of its civilization, but the Slavs and their representative, Russia." Ten years before the Russian-Turkish war of 1878, Danilevsky wrote that "from now on war between Russian and Turkey had become impossible and unnecessary; possible and thereby indispensable is now the struggle of Slavdom with Europe,—a struggle which cannot be decided in one year or one campaign but which will fill a whole historical period. The Crimean War terminated the third period of the Oriental question and began its fourth and last stage which will decide whether the Slavs are powerful only by their number and the vastness of their territory or whether they are powerful by their significance, whether they are an equal member in the family of Aryan nations, called to play the role of a world power like their older brothers and to form one of the original cultural types of world history— or whether they are destined to be only vassals, ethnographic material serving as nourishment to its proud rulers." Danilevsky's happy conviction to the contrary seemed to be borne out by his laws of historical development. "This forces us to use all our means and our whole energy for this decisive struggle which cannot be postponed much longer."

Russia had entered the European system with Suvorov's campaign in Italy. But what profit, Danilevsky asked, has Russia ever reaped out of its wars and services for Europe? When her own interests were at stake, did not her relationship to Europe develop into fetters on her actions? Did not Europe always exploit Russia without accepting her into true partnership? Danilevsky did not blame Europe for it: Russia represented by its vastness and its fast-growing population a disturbing anomaly in Europe. No European state alone could measure up to Russia; in the Crimean War four nations needed a whole year to capture one Russian fortress. Russia was too immense to be one of the European great

powers; it had played this role for the last seventy
years only because it had renounced the fulfillment
of its own historical destiny. But for this fulfillment
Russia alone was not sufficiently strong; it needed
the support of those forces on the enemy's side
which served there only against their will. "The
Pan-Slav union is the only firm foundation in which
can grow an original Slav civilization. It is the indispensable condition of this cultural development.
This is the general sense and the main conclusion of
our whole inquiry."

For this coming struggle, Russia, supported by the
Slavs, found herself in a much happier situation
than any of the competing powers and civilizations.
They, the representatives of violence, had to subject or to enslave other peoples and to numb their
cultural growth; Russia had only to liberate kindred
peoples and help them to fulfill their destiny. "In
this divine and perhaps unique coincidence of moral
motives and obligations with political advantage and
necessity, we must see a guarantee for the fulfillment
of Russia's great task. Otherwise our world would be
only a miserable chain of accidents and not the reflection of supreme reason, right and goodness."
Danilevsky worked out in detail the composition and
frontiers of this Pan-Slav union. It would consist of
the Russian Empire in its frontiers of 1869 (that
means including Poland) with the addition of
Austrian Galicia and northern Bukovina and of
Hungarian Carpatho-Ukraine; the kingdom of Bohemia, Moravia and Slovakia; the kingdom of the
Serbs, Croats and Slovenes which would include
also Montenegro, Bosnia-Herzegovina and northern
Albania from Turkey, the Voivodina and the Banat
from Hungary, Dalmatia, Istria, Trieste, Görz and
Gradisca, Carniola, two thirds of Carinthia and one
fifth of Styria from Austria; the kingdom of Bulgaria with the greater part of Macedonia; the kingdom of Rumania with parts of Austrian Bukovina

and half of Hungarian Transylvania; the kingdom of Greece with Thessaly, Epirus, southwest Macedonia, Crete, Rhodes, Cyprus and the Anatolian coast of the Aegean Sea; the kingdom of Hungary shorn of these parts which were ceded to Russia, Bohemia, Serbia and Rumania; and finally Constantinople and its environment.[n]

The reader will note two remarkable facts about Danilevsky's Pan-Slav union. The frontiers which he suggested were, on the whole, realized in 1945 except for the fact that Stalin went one step further and also annexed Königsberg. (That Greece and Constantinople were not included in 1945 in Stalin's acquisitions, was not his fault.) Poland "which had lost its Slav soul" was not admitted by Danilevsky into his Pan-Slav union, but he left the future open in case that Poland should turn away from Europe and renounce its claim to its Eastern territories. These two conditions were apparently fulfilled in 1945 and thus Poland has been admitted as a member, a happy turn which Danilevsky did not foresee. He offered several justifications for the inclusion of the non-Slavic Greeks, Rumanians and Magyars into the Slav union: besides geographic and strategic reasons, he found the Rumanians and Greeks strongly intermixed with Slav elements and, through their Orthodox faith, spiritually related to the Slavs. These peoples had never formed part of Europe and had been only abused for the purposes of European imperialism; on the other hand, they would profit from their bond with Russia and their territories would be enlarged. The Magyars formed the only exception in this picture of happiness, but even they would be saved from the fate of the other Finnish-Ugrian populations in the Russian Empire who had become ethnographic material.

To his regret Danilevsky found many Slavs, distrusting Russia's intentions under Polish and European influence, terrified by the thought of Russian domination. To counter these apprehensions, he tried to prove that Russia had never been an oppressive ruler, that it respected the inner autonomy of allied peoples and did not try to Russify Finland, the Baltic Provinces, or even Poland before the latter's attempt to annex Western Russia. Danilevsky could not foresee that Russia would inaugurate a few years later a ruthless policy of Russification; only Lenin returned to Danilevsky's "respect" for the autonomy of the non-Russian peoples, trying to prove as Danilevsky had done that Russia was neither imperialist nor an oppressor. The non-Russian Slavs who read Danilevsky were, however, hardly convinced of the benevolent nature of his proposed federation. In his opinion, the neighborhood of a powerful and hostile Europe forced the Slavs to accept a close union under the leadership of Russia. He anticipated that the continuous struggle with Europe would have a beneficial effect on all the Slavs; it would alienate them from Western influences and produce in them an ever-increasing love for everything Slav and Russian. Should such an attitude result in even temporary full separation from Europe and in a patriotic fanaticism, it would be welcome after such a long period of Slav subservience to the West. The result would be a close cultural and linguistic unity among the Slavs, but Danilevsky stressed that such a cultural Pan-Slavism was in no way enough. The Western Slavs were unprepared for a political union; Russia could not trust to educational propaganda and diplomatic wiles.

The historic destiny of peace-loving Russia could be fulfilled only through war, which would arouse the powerful sympathies slumbering in the depth of the souls of the Slav peoples. "The war with the West is the only way of salvation to heal our Russian cultural disease and to develop Pan-Slav sympathies." Already the mere preparations for the war would arouse a true national spirit and put an end to the

most dangerous illness of the Slav mind, the imitation of, and the toadying before, the West. With
Spenglerian vision he predicted "a series of events
the like of which the world has not seen since the
fall of the western Roman Empire and the great
migration of peoples." While all great events of
Western history had been only manifestations of the
inner development of one and the same type of
civilization, "the Oriental question is a struggle between two different types, the probable outcome of
which will give the historical life of mankind an
entirely new content." Danilevsky did not sound different from modern Russian "Marxism" when he
wrote: "It is as impossible to fight the historical
course of events as it is impossible to fight superior
violence. From these general considerations we gain
the certitude that the Russian and Slav sacred cause,
which is in truth the universal and Pan-human cause,
cannot be lost."

Danilevsky admonished Russia to be guided in her
relation with Europe by the sole criterion of the
promotion of Slav interests. "We must have the
firm faith that our goal is sublime and sacred, that
only that which leads to it should concern us, that
we promote every good cause whatever its name—
humanity, freedom, civilization, etc.,—only if we
serve our goal and in no other way." Russia should
be indifferent to the various trends in Europe, to
revolution or monarchy, to Germans or French, to
Gladstone or Garibaldi—each one was of importance
only in so far as it could serve the achievement of
the Slav goal. Nor was European peace or unity in
Russia's interest; in a disunited Europe all parties
would try to win Russia to their side, which would
allow her to keep complete liberty of action. In the
course of an extremely interesting survey of the situation and prospects of the various European powers
of his time, Danilevsky came to the conclusion that
Russia's interest was compatible with that of Prussia

and that Prussia needed Russia much more than the other way around.

But whatever the European powers might do, Russia was infinitely superior to them because she had a unity and a cause lacking in the West. The emancipation of the serfs had immensely increased Russia's strength and provided her with a social and moral superiority. True, Russia was financially weak, but in a struggle of life and death gold counted much less than enthusiasm and moral force. Western society—herein Danilevsky again anticipated Spengler and the latter-day German prophets—was an atomized mass civilization, incapable of action as a result of parliamentary strife, a soulless mechanism in which relationships were determined by the abstract and anonymous power of money. On the other hand, "the moral peculiarity of the Russian constitution was founded on the fact that the Russian people represented a close organic unity held together not through a more or less artificial political mechanism but through the deep-rooted popular confidence in the Tsar, the living realization of the political self-consciousness and will of the people. . . . This was the meaning and importance of the Russian autocracy, which was not a 'form' of government, something outward which could be easily changed but something which could not be separated from the substance to which it belonged. . . . The Russian people could be brought into a state of disciplined enthusiasm, through the will of the Tsar. . . . Such a people is a force the like of which the world has not seen for a very long time or perhaps never."

Danilevsky favored Russia's full acceptance of European technology and science. These he considered as transferrable achievements, the cumulative product of successive civilizations, which could be put into the service of different intellectual and social attitudes. The Slavs thought and felt differently from the West and though they had to make use of Western science and to develop and expand it themselves, nothing would be more dangerous than to imitate Europe as the "so-called educated classes" of Russian society had done. There was no reason for this undignified self-abasement and this nihilistic lack of faith in oneself. Russia had a noble and appealing cause: she was fighting for the liberation of oppressed peoples and, having realized social justice for all her citizens she carried the promise of land for the disinherited peasant masses. Danilevsky was convinced that the Russians were possessed of a unique gift for social and economic activity; for the first time in history they would realize justice not as an abstract and legalistic conception but as a concrete and real force in communal life. No other people could bear a similar measure of liberty without abusing it.

Greece, Rome and Britain had expanded by creating colonies; the Russians showed their feeling for social harmony and their lack of love for power by expanding without succumbing to the curse of colonialism or of exploiting other peoples. If Russia remained faithful to her own civilization, she would not need a political revolution, that is, a revolution which aims at the limitation of the power of the government. Russia was secure because her peasant masses owned land and because her social structure was not founded on the misery and insecurity of the urban proletariat of Europe with its glaring discrepancy between political democratic ideals and economic enslavement. True, in the field of culture and art the Russians had so far produced much less than the Greeks or the Europeans, but this was due only to the fact that the Slavs had not yet established their spiritual and political independence. Yet even under the present adverse circumstances, the Russians had shown in their novels and poetry that they were equal to Europe. What great promise did the future hold in store for them who only now were setting out to liberate the other Slavs and to grow in this struggle to a full consciousness and creativeness of the Slav type! "

The various types of civilization, which had flourished so far, had each developed one aspect of cultural life: the Hebrews the religious aspect; the Greeks the artistic one; the Romans the political one; the Europeans the economic one. European civilization could not arrive at a synthesis of these four aspects, because the violence inherent in it had produced a threefold crisis—the religious crisis expressing itself in Protestantism; the philosophical crisis leading to capitalistic materialism; the social crisis manifested in the contrast of political democracy and economic feudalism—which threatened a dissolution of civilization into moral and social anarchy. Only Russia offered the hope of a harmonious synthesis of all aspects of civilization. The Russian people were as thirsty for the absolute truth of religion as the Hebrews had been. They were the third embodiment, after Israel and Byzantium, of the religious ideal, the people chosen by God. Their character, alien to all violence, corresponded to true Christianity. They had shown a unique gift for a non-violent political order embracing many peoples, for a concrete and real solution of the social economic problem. They carried the promise of great artistic achievement. Thus the world could expect from them that their new historical cultural type which would begin to flower after the solution of the Oriental question, would for the first time achieve the synthesis of the highest achievements in religion (the heritage of Israel), in culture and arts (the heritage of Greece), in political world order (the heritage of Rome) and finally in social and economic progress (the transformed legacy of Europe) and would become an entirely new type, the culmination and consummation of world history.

"Its main stream started with two sources on the

shores of the Old Nile. One, the celestial and divine, has flowed over Jerusalem and Constantinople and has reached in perfect purity Kiev and Moscow; the other, the terrestrial and human, divided itself again into two rivers, that of culture and that of politics, and has flowed through Athens, Alexandria and Rome into Europe, sometimes desiccated, then again enriched with new and ever fuller waters. On the soil of Russia a new and fourth river originates, a social economic system which satisfies the masses in a just way. These four rivers will unite on the wide plains of Slavdom into a mighty sea." These concluding words sound like the announcement of the coming Kingdom of Heaven on earth through the development of Slavdom, (which Marx expected at the same time through the development of the proletariat), of a society of perfect justice which would fulfill and terminate history. This faith was in apparent contradiction to Danilevsky's own "scientific" promises in other parts of his book where he regarded the Slav type of civilization as the coming one but not as the final and universal one, and envisaged the peaceful co-existence of the Slav and other civilizations. He proclaimed that the Slav union once achieved would threaten nobody and would not try to expand and to conquer the world. Its task was rather to oppose the European tendency to world domination. It was the mistake of the West to regard its type of civilization as of universal validity; Danilevsky was certain that the Slavs would not repeat that mistake, though the Slavophiles had dreamt of it. Danilevsky's "realistic" and "scientific" Pan-Slavism rejected the Slavophile religious utopianism. "Slavophilism believed that the Slavs were destined to solve a universal task; but there is no such task." Yet he himself succumbed to the lure of Slavophile eschatology; to the promise of a "perfect" social order. Pan-Slavism could logically pursue limited goals; Pan-Orthodoxism (the faith in true

Christianity as the only source of salvation) and
Pan-Communism (the faith in the true social doctrine as the only source of salvation) must by
necessity strive to include the whole of mankind.
Danilevsky oscillated between these two positions
and the Russian government in the 1940's followed
in his way.

Danilevsky's Pan-Slavism was much more than an
answer to the problem which the rise of a powerful
centralized German state in the heart of Europe
presented to Russia and the Slavs; it was also a challenge to European civilization, based upon an interpretation of history and social and cultural
growth which claimed the validity of a universal law.
In the world of political reality of the nineteenth
century Danilevsky's Pan-Slavism remained as much
an empty dream as the simultaneous Pan-Germanism
of some German intellectuals. Like Pan-Germanism
for which few sympathies existed among the Swiss,
Dutch or Scandinavians, Pan-Slavism as a political
union of the Slavs was rejected by the smaller Slav
nationalities. A few years after the publication of
Danilevsky's book, in connection with the uprisings
of the Orthodox Balkan Christians against the
Ottoman government, Pan-Slavism became a force
supported by public opinion in Russia. "Never have
there been as many Slavophiles in Russia as now,"
wrote Koshelev in his diary in the winter of 1876–7.
Ivan Aksakov became for a short while a leading and
representative figure. Though the government yielded
to public pressure and declared war on Turkey in
support of the Balkan Slavs, it did not succumb to
Pan-Slavism; it banished Aksakov from Moscow and
ordered the dissolution of the Slav Committee."

But in the 1870's Pan-Slavism received the mighty
and passionate support of Russia's greatest writer,
Fyodor Mikhailovich Dostoyevsky (1821–81). One
of the most creative men of genius in the exploration of the human heart, he showed himself a

bigoted fanatic without any originality when he approached the problems, central and vital to him, of Russia's relationship to Europe. The ambivalence and ambiguity of all his thought as soon as he dealt with Russian nationalism was one of the great mysteries of the human mind, which he never explored. His attitude toward Russia and Europe, toward war and peace, toward human brotherhood and group-pride, had a mystical and exalted quality which defied reason. In him Russia, in self-centered arrogance and as a servant of world-salvation, challenged the West as she was not to do again for almost seventy years. For Dostoyevsky, the greatest prophet of Slavophilism, whose early youth coincided with its first flowering, was its last outstanding spokesman. By 1881 Koshelev, who was to die two years later, thought the role of Slavophilism terminated and himself abandoned it for a more Western type of liberalism.

4

Russia and Europe

WHILE STILL IN SIBERIA, where he had been sent for unpatriotic and "radical" leanings, Dostoyevsky wrote from Semipalatinsk on January 18, 1856, to Apollon Maikov who had reported to him on the astonishing change of the last decade, the new Slavophile patriotism then captivating Russia: "I have read your letter but I did not understand . . . what you say so enthusiastically about patriotism, the Russian idea, the sentiment of duty, national honor, etc. But my friend, have you ever felt otherwise? I too have been animated always by the same feelings and convictions. . . . I have always been through and through a Russian, and I say it in all sincerity. What is new in the movement around you, of which you write as of a new trend? I tell you openly, that I do not understand you. I read your poems and I found them beautiful; I share entirely your patriotic sentiment, your longing for a moral liberation of the Slavs. That is the task of Russia, of our great and noble Russia, of our saintly mother. . . . I entirely share your idea, that Europe and its mission will be consummated by Russia." For the remaining twenty-five years of his life all of Dostoyevsky's thought was more and more obsessed

by the one idea, Russia's Pan-Slav mission for the
leadership and salvation of mankind. On May 27,
1869, he wrote from Florence to Maikov that he
planned writing a great national epic "with love
for Russia streaming forth as from a living spring."
It would present Russian history from the moment
when Ivan III of Moscow by marrying the imperial heiress of Constantinople "laid the first stone
for the future hegemony of the East, . . . not only
of a great state but of a whole new world, destined
to renew Christianity by Pan-Slavism and Pan-
Orthodoxy and to introduce a new idea to mankind."
Dostoyevsky was convinced that the nineteenth
century with "the defiled humanity in the West"
would prepare the final vision of a twentieth century
in which a triumphant Russia would face Europe
and its civilization eclipsed, lacerated, and brutalized.
"Here I would not stop at any imagination." But no
epic poem could contain his vision. Though his
ideas emerged from time to time in his novels, they
were most often expressed in his letters and in his
prolific journalistic articles.[n]

Dostoyevsky, a master in the creation of complex
human characters and situations in his novels, over-
simplified in his political thinking after the well-
known pattern of Slavophile and Pan-Slav Russian
nationalism. Everything in the West seemed to him
vile and mean, and in contrast everything Russian
seemed infinitely noble. He ascribed Russia's claim
to world leadership to her humility and love of peace;
yet in his glorification of Russia there was no trace
of humility and in his judgment of foreign nations
and religions there was no indication of peace. He
scented the danger which Western liberalism harbored for the traditional ways of Russia; to heighten
the faith in Russia, he compared the realities of the
West, with a heavy stress on their imperfection and
sordid side, to an ideal Russia as it existed in lofty
programs and daring anticipations. He saw nothing

but force and violence in the West; he did not notice that there were few states in history as warlike and oppressive as the Russian autocracy. He glorified war, when it was Russia's, in glowing terms; war by other nations seemed to him acts of imperialism which he bitterly condemned; he never applied the same yardstick to Russia. He found harsh words for the poverty and exploitation encountered in capitalistic Europe; he never seemed to notice the incomparably greater oppression and misery of the masses in Russia. The two entirely different worlds were not held together by any common moral standards; Dostoyevsky called black white and white black, depending upon the circumstances of the "inevitable" struggle between the Russian and the alien faiths.

During the Crimean War, Dostoyevsky was in Siberia. Then Khomyakov was the Pan-Slav spokesman. Twenty years later, in the Balkan crisis which originated in the uprisings of the Orthodox Slavs, Bulgars and Serbs, against the Turks, Dostoyevsky, infinitely more famous than Khomyakov had been, voiced the Pan-Slav hopes. He did it in his journal, *The Diary of a Writer*, with a shrillness unthinkable in the more noble and restrained language of Khomyakov. In the January, 1877, issue he expressed the expectation that with the settlement of the Oriental question a new element would enter and transform mankind, the third world idea—the Slav idea—which now "really begins to kindle and shine with unprecedented and never-heard-of light." The April issue jubilantly welcomed Russia's declaration of war against Turkey. "It was a wonderful time; the spirit and the heart of the whole Russia rose and the people marched out voluntarily, to fight for those who are our brethren by religion and by blood." But it was not only a war for other Slavs: "We need the war for ourselves; we are rising not only for our Slav brothers tortured by the Turks, but for our own salvation. War will clear the air which we breathe, the air in which we stifle. . . . With war and victories the new world will come and the new life will begin."

To the objections of a pacifist Dostoyevsky answered that pacifism could not at present be applied to Russia: "In the present historical period Russia represents an exception," though Europe, judging Russia after its own image, did not yet realize it. Russia would emerge from the war immensely strengthened; by this very fact she would spread love and brotherhood and would assure peace, because a strong Russia would finally be able to set the example of true peace, international harmony and disinterestedness. Russia's war was not a selfish war; it wished to promote the liberty and brotherly union of all nations; it was a war for a sacred idea, the first step in the realization of eternal peace. "So much that is new and progressive will begin in human relations that it would be useless to mourn and to hesitate on the eve of the last great struggle, which will bring about the great regeneration of all Europe." [n]

In the issue of November 1877 Dostoyevsky discussed the coming peace settlement in the Near East. He rejected Danilevsky's suggestion that Constantinople should belong to all the Eastern Orthodox peoples, that Russia should share it on equal terms with the other Slavs. To Dostoyevsky such a proposal seemed strange. How could one compare the Russians and the Slavs, how could Russia share on an equal basis when she was in every respect so unequal to the other Slavs—to every Slav people separately and even to all of them combined? "Constantinople must be ours . . . and remain ours for ever." He was certain that Russia would take possession of Constantinople and the Straits and there maintain her troops and fortifications. In this expectation Dostoyevsky launched into some of the wildest "predictions" which perhaps any writer of repute ever made: the end of the universal Catholic conspiracy—"and the monster begotten by it, socialism"—the immediate doom of France, Germany's need for an eternal political alliance with Russia. All those prospects created according to him the opportune moment for Russia to solve once and for all the Oriental question.

Dostoyevsky was badly mistaken. The following year brought the election of Leo XIII to the papal throne; the stabilization of the French Republic; and the Congress of Berlin, which under Bismarck's leadership deprived the Russians of the coveted goal. The Oriental question was not solved by Russia but was settled in the compromise of a European conference. The great expectations aroused among the Pan-Slavs, when Alexander II spoke in November, 1876, of defending the Slav cause, were sadly disappointed. "The historical conscience of all Russia," Ivan Aksakov had declared, "spoke from the lips of the Tsar; on that memorable day he spoke as the descendant of Ivan III, who received from the Palaeologi the Byzantine arms and combined them with the arms of Moscow, as the descendant of Peter and Catherine. . . . From these words there can be no drawing back, they shine through the darkness as a star to encourage and guide us. These words and the unanimous, spontaneous, popular expression of fraternal love for the oppressed Slavs form such historical landmarks, that if we only let ourselves be guided by them, we cannot lose our way and cannot fail to fulfill our mission, whatever obstacles we may have to encounter. The slumbering East is now awakened, and not only the Slavs of the Balkans but the whole Slavonic world, awaits its regeneration."

As in the sixties, the Slavophile writers were joined in their agitation by Slavophile generals. Mikhail Grigorievich Cherniayev (1828–89) who had led the Russian army which in 1864 captured

Tashkent in Central Asia, was dismissed from the
army on account of his violent Pan-Slavism; he became in 1876 the Commander-in-Chief of the Serb
army in the unsuccessful war against Turkey. His
younger colleague, Mikhail Dimitrievich Skobelev
(1843–82), gained wide fame by his exploits in
Turkestan in 1874 and distinguished himself in the
battles for Plevna in the Russian-Turkish War of
1877. After the war he returned to Turkestan for
further military victories which culminated in the
capture of the Turkoman fortress of Geok-Tepe in
December, 1880. But he too incurred the disfavor
of the Russian authorities by his violent Pan-Slav
agitation and by his advocacy of a Russian alliance
with France against Germany.[n]

However, after the brief war against Turkey, not
only the government looked with disfavor upon Pan-
Slavism; the great majority of Russian society rejected the nationalist philosophy of Slavophilism
and its anti-Western attitude. When after the assassination of Alexander II Ivan Aksakov addressed the
St. Petersburg Benevolent Slav Committee in March,
1881, he pleaded for a lost cause: "Is it (the assassination) not the product of our moral treason of
which almost all the so-called liberal press is guilty?
Can it be anything else but the logical outcome of
that Westernism which since Peter the Great has
demoralized both our government and our society?
. . . In their servile imitation of foreign teaching
and alien ideals, they only borrow from Western
Europe what can there be easily explained, if not
excused, by historical and social conditions, as a
protest caused by the unequal division of land, the
unjust reign of the bourgeoisie over the proletariat—
a protest against the present constitutional forms."

Aksakov was convinced that in Russia this injustice of bourgeois society did not exist and that
therefore a constitution after the Western model was
unwanted. "But that injustice is exactly what we do

not possess. Thank God, and thanks to the martyr Emperor so brutally murdered, our 'proletariat,' our peasantry, forming almost eighty percent of the whole nation, now own land and dispose of the most complete self-government. . . . Is it not monstrous that at present, when everywhere in the West violent protests are heard against constitutionalism and parliamentarism, the so-called intelligentsia should be craving in Russia for the constitutional rags that Europe will charitably throw to its valets! Who accepts a constitution according to the Western model has also to bear the ultimate consequence of Western political life, social revolution with all its manifestations." [n] Aksakov who wished to preserve Russia from the Western "curse" of factionalism and political party strife, from parliamentary bribery and capitalistic corruption, showed no perception of the fact that it might have been the very introduction of Western constitutional life which might have saved Russia from "social revolution with all its manifestations." [n]

A few weeks before the assassination of the Emperor, Dostoyevsky died. Three days later the last issue of his *Diary of a Writer* appeared. Celebrating Skobelev's victory at Geok-Tepe, Dostoyevsky demanded that the name of the Russian autocrat be raised in the mind of all Asians high above that of all the princes of the East, including the Caliph of all the Mohammedans, for "our hopes lie perhaps more in Asia than in Europe: in our future Asia will be our salvation." Dostoyevsky reiterated his usual complaint that Europe despised the Russians as Asiatics and would never treat them as equals. But in Asia the Russians would come not as imitators but as civilizers. Dostoyevsky regretted that the Russians in 1812 had not stopped at Russia's frontiers, after having driven out Napoleon, and had not left the West, at least temporarily, to him. If they divided the world with him and turned to the conquest of Asia, Napoleon's dynasty might have been overthrown in the West in any case, but the Orient would have remained Russian, Dostoyevsky believed, "and we would at present have controlled the oceans and could have opposed England at sea as well as on land." For the march across Asia was to Dostoyevsky only a detour on the way to dominate the West. He had a truly prophetic vision of Asia becoming Russia's America, where the Russians would produce immense wealth and, with the help of science, exploit the resources, increase the population, build mighty industries, and by so doing acquire a new sense of power, dignity and creative joy. A new Russia would grow up in Asia which would regenerate old Russia and make her masses understand their destiny. With the productive power and the population of her Asiatic empire, Russia would become materially and morally strong enough to fulfill her world mission. Then Russia's hour would strike. Shortly before his death he wrote: "The future genuine Russian idea has not yet appeared among us, but the earth is portentously pregnant with it and is making ready to deliver it amid agonizing pain."

In his last article on "What is Asia to us?" Dostoyevsky was even willing to abandon, at least for the foreseeable future, the Pan-Slav aims. In sharpest contrast to what he had written less than four years before, he declared that at present no political mind would consider it common sense "that Constantinople must be ours, save in some remote, enigmatic future." If Russia would make it appear that she did not intend to meddle with European affairs, the European powers, Dostoyevsky was convinced, would quarrel among themselves and thus afford Russia new opportunity later. Meanwhile Russia would find new strength and a new field of activity in Asia. Dostoyevsky expressed a general feeling of disappointment with Pan-Slavism and with the westward trend of Russian expansionism and intellectual life. The 1880's marked a period of withdrawal, of concentration on Russia and her self-sufficiency. Former generations, liberals as well as Slavophiles, had been stirred and fascinated by the cultural effervescence of an older Germany; the new Germany seemed cold and unattractive.[n] The new Emperor, Alexander III, was the first Russian nationalist on the throne. In his reign the court, until then in language and habit much more French and German than Russian, became thoroughly "nationalized."[n]

But Alexander III after 1880 was as little a Pan-Slav as his teacher and mentor, Konstantin Petrovich Pobedonostsev (1827–1907).[n] They did not believe in the Slavs but in the Russian state and the Orthodox Church. The Bulgar attitude in 1885 was a deep disappointment to the Russians. Though Pobedonostsev wished to base the power of the Tsar "on the unity of consciousness between the people and the state, on the national faith," he had no trace of the Slavophile idolization of the Russian masses. "He told an English journalist that neither the spiritual instinct nor the moral restraints of the Russian people were adequate to subdue 'the ferocious passions that lie dormant in their breasts' without the aid of physical sanctions. He was convinced that the Russian man was inferior to all others and once described Russia beyond the imperial palaces as 'an icy desert and an abode of the Bad Man.'"[n] To his cold bureaucratic nature the enthusiastic utopianism of a Third Rome or of Russia's universal mission seemed alien. He wished to subject the Russian Empire to an integral Russian nationalism based upon the Orthodox Church. Under the reign of Alexander III began the policy of a ruthless Russification of all the peoples of the Empire, including the Slav peoples, the Poles, the Ukrainians and the Byelorussians. Naturally enough, such a policy could arouse little sympathy among the Western Slavs.

The penetration of capitalism into Russia in the 1880's and the beginning industrialization of the country were hardly favorable to Slavophile romanticism. Even Dostoyevsky was fascinated by the machine and its implication for Russian power. "My heart stopped overcome with joy," he wrote to Maikov from Geneva on October 21, 1867, "when I read that the railroad to Kursk will be opened. May it only happen faster: and long live Russia!" Sergei Yulievich Count Witte (1849–1915) who started his public career as a railway functionary and later became minister of finance, a post which he retained for eleven years—in the crisis of 1905 he was for a short time prime minister and promulgated the October manifesto proclaiming civil liberties and promising a constitution—published in 1889 a pamphlet *Po povodu natsionalizma* (Concerning Nationalism) in which he pleaded for a national system of political economy based upon Friedrich List, the German-American economic nationalist and proponent of industrialization of the first half of the nineteenth century.[n]

Witte took Germany as his model; he believed in the benevolent autocracy of an enlightened bureaucracy and, in the backward conditions of Russia, in the concentration of economic power and direction in the hands of the state. Witte, like Dostoyevsky, was convinced that Asia offered an outlet for Russia's creative expansion. He secured the rights to the Chinese Eastern Railway across northern Manchuria providing a shortcut from Eastern Siberia to Vladivostok. He sincerely wished a "peaceful colonization." "In contrast with the Western European powers, which aim at economic and frequently even political subjugation of the peoples of the East, Russia's mission in the East must be a protective and educational mission," he wrote. "It is Russia's natural task to guard her neighboring Eastern lands which lie in her sphere of influence, against the excessive political and colonial claims of the other powers." But Russian imperialism frustrated his peaceful intentions. The war with Japan in 1904 was the consequence of Russia's aggressive expansionism in the Far East.

The future Emperor Nicholas II who ruled as last Russian Tsar from 1894 to 1917, visited Asia as a crown prince in 1890-1. The young man, then 23 years old, was accompanied by his younger brother George (who was to die in 1899) and by a numerous suite. One of them, Prince Esper Ukhtomsky, developed in his description of the voyage a new theory of Russian Pan-Asiatism. "At all times," he wrote, "we Russians were part of Asia. . . . Our geographic situation has destined us to head the still undeveloped peoples of the East. . . . It is high time that the Russians should recognize this heritage bequeathed to them by Genghis Khan and Tamerlan." The voyage apparently made a deep impression upon Nicholas. He is reported to have declared in 1896 to Emperor William II: "I do not concern myself with Constantinople, my eyes are directed towards China." In 1887 the governor-general of Irkutsk suggested the building of a railroad across Eastern Siberia. Witte carried the project through. In 1892 Crown Prince Nicholas proclaimed solemnly in Vladivostok the beginning of the building of the railroad. At the end of that year Witte wrote: "The Trans-Siberian Railroad opens up a new road and new horizons for world commerce; in this respect its building ranks among the events of universal importance which signify the beginning of a new era in the history of the nations and frequently bring about radical changes in the economic relations among states."

This expectation was not fulfilled. The railroad was to serve military and not commercial purposes.

In 1900 Russia occupied Manchuria, after having secured in an agreement with Japan in 1898 the southern part of the Liao-Tung peninsula. From 1902 on provocative Russian schemes in Korea led against Witte's protest to a growing tension in relations with Japan. The Russian nationalist newspaper *Novoe Vremya* (New Times), since 1876 under the editorship of Alexei Sergeyevich Suvorin (1834–1912), wrote that Japan would not dare to start a war against Russia because such a war would mean suicide for Japan. Japan was ready for a compromise with Russia, abandoning Manchuria to her, if Russia would renounce the control of Korea. But the war party in Russia forced the decision by arms. Russia's defeat had two consequences: it brought about a half-hearted attempt at the reform and liberalization of the Russian regime—in that sense the defeat of 1905 was as salutary for Russia as the defeat of 1855 —and it turned Russia's attention back from the Far East to the Balkans, where Russia had followed in the last decade a policy of loyal recognition of the *status quo*. The agreement of Mürzsteg in Styria of October 9, 1903, seemed to consecrate the reconciliation between Austria-Hungary and Russia in the Balkans. These hopes were shattered when Russia after 1905 renewed a Pan-Slav policy with the goal of Constantinople again in sight.

But before Russia entered on this dangerous path which was the principal element in unleashing the war of 1914, Slavophilism reached its spiritual sublimation in the work of Vladimir Sergeyevich Solovyev (1853–1900), the son of Sergey Mikhailovich Solovyev (1820–79), whose *Istoriya Rossii s drevneishikh vremen* (History of Russia since the Oldest Times, 29 vols., St. Petersburg, 1851–79) accepted, on the whole, the point of view of the Westernizers. The son, Russia's foremost philosopher who led a life of saintly nobility, as a young man came under the influence of the older Slavophile writers and of Dostoyevsky who is reported to have used him as his model for Alyosha Karamazov. In this period Solovyev wrote that the Christian or messianic idea of the Kingdom of God revealed itself progressively in the life of mankind and represented the meaning of history. The Russian people and its civilization would realize the final unity of mankind and of its faith. The Russians would not add to the three elements of the historical tradition—science which was the fruit of reason; the political and social life, the fruit of the will; and art, the fruit of the creative force—but integrate them in the new age and the new complete human being.

Dostoyevsky in the beginning of the May-June issue of the *Dnevnik pisatela* of 1877 quoted from a rare book, the *Prognosticatio* by Johannes Lichtenberger (1528), found probably by Solovyev in the Royal Library in London, a prediction that after the appearance of *Aquila Grandis* (which he interpreted as Napoleon I) another great eagle would arise in the Orient which "ignem fovebit in gremio sponsae Christi" (who shall kindle a fire in the bosom of Christ's bride). "Et amore charitatis inflammabit Deus aquilam orientalem volando ad ardua alis duabus fulgens in mentibus Christianitatis" (And God will kindle the Oriental eagle with love of mercy so that he will fly on his two wings to accomplish the difficult task, flashing upon the peaks of Christianity). Dostoyevsky saw in it a prediction concerning the Russian-Turkish war of 1877 and Solovyev hoped too that the war would arouse in the Russian people a positive consciousness of their lofty mission.

His expectations were not fulfilled. After the assassination of Alexander II, Solovyev pleaded in vain for the pardon of the plotters. Their execution proved to him that Russia was not the ideal Christian empire which could sanctify the world by a free theocracy. He found the deeper cause for Russia's spiritual weakness in the religious schism and became from that moment on the prophet of the unity of Western and Eastern Europe and of the Universal Church. His recognition of the role of Rome separated Solovyev from the Slavophiles. He accused them of working not *ad majorem Dei* but *ad majorem Russiae gloriam*. Russia's true mission was the union of Europe and of the churches through an act of sacrificial renunciation. "Caetorum censeo: primum et ante omnia Ecclesiae unitas instauranda, ignis fovendus in gremio sponsae Christi," he wrote. (Again and again I think that the unity of the Church must be established first and before everything else which will kindle a fire in the bosom of Christ's bride.) The messianic force of the West having exhausted itself in the two attempts of Constantine and Charlemagne to establish God's Kingdom on earth, Russia might succeed in uniting the first two Romes in a synthesis of Social Christianity, if she would renounce her self-sufficiency and her fundamentally pagan nationalism. Twice she had done so, according to Solovyev: when she called Varangians to rule Russia, and again when Peter the Great opened the gates wide to the influx of Western civilization. The Slavophiles, on the other hand, had accepted in theory the principle of a universal church, but according to Solovyev had denied it in fact and had reduced Christian universality to a particular church which was far removed from corresponding to the ideal which they professed to see in it. Solovyev believed in Russia's great future but he based his belief on a severe criticism of the realities of Russian life and history and he demanded above all the sacrifice of the Orthodox nationalism.

In a series of articles which were later published under the title, "The National Problem in Russia," Solovyev produced the most penetrating criticism of

the Slavophile theory, especially of Danilevsky and
of Strakhov who had been Dostoyevsky's faithful
friend and with whom until then Solovyev himself
had been on intimate terms. He denied that Russia
and the Slavs represented an independent type of
historical civilization; neither in philosophy or science, nor in literature or social life, had the Russians
created anything fundamentally original. "Whenever Russia affirmed herself in her national egoism
and separated herself from the Christian world, she
always found herself impotent to produce something
great or important. Only in close communion, ex-
ternally and internally, with Europe has Russian
life produced truly great events (the reform of Peter
the Great, the poetry of Pushkin)." Solovyev found
that Slavophilism had rapidly and steadily declined,
until in his own day the Pan-Slavs preached a
"fatalistic Islam" of the state, a resignation in face
of the state, the incarnation of the people's strength.
He pictured the successive stages of this ideological
descent—which resembled in Germany that from
Fichte through Treitschke to the National Socialists
—in the famous saying: "The worshipping of one's
own people as the chosen vessel of the universal
truth; then the worshipping of one's own people as
an elemental force, independent of its relationship to
the universal truth; finally the worshipping of the
historical anomalies and the national particularism
which separates one's people from civilized mankind,
i.e., the worshipping of one's own people on the
basis of a denial of the universal truth; these are the
three stages of our nationalism, successively represented by the Slavophiles, by Danilevsky, and by
Katkov and the modern obscurantists."

Solovyev praised Peter the Great who "mercilessly
broke down the hard crust of nationalistic exclusiveness which contained the seed of original Russian
culture and boldly threw this seed into the soil of

universal European history." Thus Peter contributed much more to Russia's and Europe's future than the Slavophiles. In them Solovyev found a "fatal internal contradiction between the demands of true patriotism which wanted Russia to become as perfect as possible and the false claim of nationalism which asserted that she already was better than any other nation in the world." He feared for Russia's future. "When one ascribes to any nation a monopoly of the absolute truth, then nationality becomes an idol the worshipping of which is based on a falsehood and leads first to a moral, and then to a material catastrophe. . . . For a true and farsighted patriotism, the most essential, even the only essential question, is not the question of Russia's might but that of Russia's sins." [n]

In his last years Solovyev abandoned all hope of a messianic task for the Russian people. In a lecture on Belinsky and in an article on Chernyshevsky he showed admiration for the practical humanitarianism of these non-Christian positivists and called them "wise and just men." His last book, however, "Three Conversations on War, Progress, and the End of World History, including a Short Story of the Anti-Christ," which appeared in 1900, the year of his death, testified to his eschatological pessimism, his abandonment of the idea of establishing the Kingdom of God on earth, especially in or through Russia. He now regarded the establishment of a universal monarchy, even one dedicated to peace and social justice, as the work of an impostor and usurper. He was haunted by the danger of Pan-Mongolism, the vision of an invasion of Europe in the twentieth century by the masses of China organized under Japanese leadership, and he was afraid that the division of Europe and its moral and spiritual stagnation would facilitate the conquest of Europe. In one of his poems he wrote:

> *Pan-Mongolism! A savage name*
> *But it pleases my ear immensely,*
> *As if it were full of forebodings*
> *Of the great destiny appointed by God.*

Solovyev hoped against this danger for the unity
and revitalization of Europe into which he wished
to integrate Russia. His disciple, the great symbolist
poet, Alexander Alexandrovich Blok (1880–1921),
took up the theme of Pan-Mongolism in "The
Scythians," the last poem which he wrote, on January 30, 1918. He prefaced it with the first two lines
of Solovyev's poem quoted above. But Blok, at the
moment captivated for a short time by the elemental
force and the nationalist missionary appeal of Lenin's
revolution, turned Solovyev's position into the
opposite: he threatened a Russian-Mongol alliance
against Europe:

> *You are millions, we are an immense multitude.*
> *Try to fight with us!*
> *Yes, we are Scythians! Yes, we are Asians—*
> *With slanted and greedy eyes! . . .*
> *Like obedient serfs*
> *We held the shield between two hostile races—*
> *The Mongols and Europe . . .*
> *Oh, old world! While you are still alive, . . .*
> *Halt here, oh wise as Oedipus*
> *Before the Sphinx with its ancient riddle!*
> *Russia is a sphinx exulting and grieving, . . .*
> *She looks and looks and looks at you*
> *With hate and with love! . . .*
> *Come unto us! From the horrors of war*
> *Come to our peaceful embraces!*
> *Before it is too late—sheathe the old sword,*
> *Comrades! Let us become brothers!*
> *If not, we have nothing to lose.*
> *But we ourselves, from now on, will not be your*
>   *shield . . .*
> *We shall not move when the bestial Hun . . .*

Burns your towns and herds his cattle in your
      churches,
And the flesh of the white brothers is roasting!
For the last time—mind this, old world!
The barbarous lyre is calling
To a brotherly feast of work and peace,
For the last time—to a bright fraternal feast.

In this poem the former disciple of Solovyev, in the midst of the strangely intermingling war-cries and peace-promises of the Bolshevik Revolution, sounded like the heir of Dostoyevsky and Leontev. The problem of Russia and Europe had apparently not been solved when the twentieth century began.

PART III

Pan-Slavism and the World Wars

1905-1950

The Russian who has a sane intelligence and a living heart has been unable until today and is unable to be anything but a patriot in the sense of Peter the Great, i.e., a collaborator in the great work of enlightening the Russian people. All other interests—pure science if he is a scholar; pure art if he is a painter; even the idea of a universal human law, if he is a jurist—must be subordinated by the Russian scholar, artist, jurist to the great idea of working for the good of his own fatherland.

NIKOLAI GAVRILEVICH CHERNYSCHEVSKY

Great Power chauvinism is growing in our country daily and hourly—Great Power chauvinism, the rankest kind of nationalism, which strives to obliterate all that is not Russian, to gather together all the threads of administration into the hands of Russians and to crush everything that is not Russian.

STALIN, "Report on National Factors in Party and State" (1923)

Naturally our literature, which reflects a system much higher than any bourgeois democratic system, a culture many times higher than any bourgeois culture, has the right to teach others a new universal morality. Where can you find such a people or such a country as ours?

ANDREI ALEXANDREVICH ZHDANOV, Pravda, September 21, 1946

1

The Neo-Pan-Slavism
Before World War I

THE IMMEDIATE CAUSE of World War I which ended a century of relative peace in Europe was a crisis in the Slav Balkans. Its repercussions threatened the foundations of the Habsburg monarchy, which suffered grievously from lack of leadership.[n] Nothing was done to make the Austrians themselves realize "the idea of the Austrian state," to use Palacký's words. Austria languished and finally perished from ideological anemia. The years during which Pan-Slavism played hardly any role in Russian society and policy—thus offering an opportunity for the solution of Austria's nationality problems—were in Austria filled with growing tensions and mounting bitterness which was most pronounced in the struggle between the Czechs and the Germans. Again, as in the beginning of the Pan-Slav movement, the initiative to new Pan-Slav development came from the Czechs. No other Slav people equalled their economic, social and cultural progress in the 19th century. At its beginning it was doubtful that the language of the peasant people would survive at all and that it would not succumb, in the natural course of events and without any governmental enforcement, to complete Germanization.

By the end of the century, however, the Czech peasantry had become prosperous and progressive and a fast-growing Czech middle class held commanding positions in industry, finance and trade. In the Austrian bureaucracy the Czechs were well represented. In poetry and the novel, in painting and in sculpture, their creative level was high; in the field of music they achieved through Bedřich Smetana (1824–84) and Antonin Dvořák (1841–1904) an international reputation. From 1866, when his opera "The Bartered Bride" was first performed, to 1874, Smetana was conductor of the Czech National Theatre in Prague, one of the most potent centers of the Czech cultural renaissance. Smetana was particularly famous for his operas—one of them "Libuša" written in honor of a legendary Czech queen, the founder of Prague, opened, in 1883, the new theatre built after the old one had burned down —but he also wrote some vast orchestral canvases on scenes of Bohemian landscape and history which were included under the common title "Má Vlast" (My Fatherland). All this the Czechs achieved by systematic and disciplined work, through their own strength. The new building of their National Theatre carried the proud inscription "Národ Sobě" (natio sibi ipsa). Yet this progress was made possible by the tolerant and encouraging Austrian policy after 1860.

The greatest inspiration to the Czech national movement came from the university and from the gymnastic organization known under the name Sokol (The Falcon). The Sokol was organized by Jindřich Fügner (1822–65) and Dr. Mirslav Tyrš (1832–84) in 1862 under the influence of the German gymnastic movement, founded by Jahn, to animate the nation with the ideals of equality and brotherhood (the Sokols called each other "brother" and addressed each other with "thou"), mental vigor and physical fitness. Similar organizations were later

founded among other Slav peoples, especially the
southern Slavs, and the great Sokol congresses in
Prague of which the first was held in 1882 and the
sixth and last before World War I in 1912, became
manifestations of Slav solidarity. Tyrš was a student
of classical antiquity and of the history and theory of
the arts: from the beginning he tried to make the
Sokol an educational movement on a broad cultural
basis. Rieger, then the recognized political leader
of his people, began in 1859 the publication of a
scholarly Encyclopedia (Slovník naučný) in eleven
volumes, and on January 1, 1861, he founded, together with Dr. Julius Grégr (1831–96), a great representative daily newspaper, *Narodní Listy*. In the
Prague University, after 1848, lectures were given in
German or Czech, and Czech professors were appointed. A decree of April 10, 1881, established two
universities, a German and a Czech, after a Czech
Institute of Technology with the rank of a university had existed in Prague since 1869. In the Slav
philologist Jan Gebauer (1838–1907), in the historian Jaroslav Goll (1846–1929), and in the philosopher Thomas Garrigue Masaryk (1850–1937), the
Czech University had from the beginning three
prominent educators.[n]

The Czech national leaders at the beginning of
the 20th century, Masaryk, Dr. Karl Kramář (1860–
1937) and Josef Kaizl (1854–1901), showed, on the
whole, a realistic moderation. In 1895 Masaryk
wrote in his most important programmatic book
"The Czech Question": "As regards the relation of
the Czech lands to the Austrian state, I regard
(Palacký's) idea of the Austrian state, in spite of all
constitutional changes, as a still reliable guide: it is
regrettable, that Palacký . . . himself abandoned to
a certain degree his idea and recommended a more
Slav national program; thereby he has unwittingly
strengthened the political phantasts . . . I act according to this program when I express my political

experiences in the words, that our policy cannot be successful if it is not supported by a true and strong interest in the fate of Austria, . . . the cultural and political effort to work in harmony with the needs of our people for the advancement of the whole of Austria and its political administration." [n] Kramář was undoubtedly sincere when he declared at his trial before a military court in Vienna at the end of 1915 that "I have seen the future of my people in the framework of the (Austrian) monarchy and I was convinced that we would approach slowly but steadily the goal of making the monarchy a just guardian of the political freedom and autonomy of all its nationalities. . . . I stood for a moderate policy out of innermost conviction . . . It is unthinkable that a politician who has worked so diligently and so sincerely for Austria's future could have envisaged at the same time the destruction of the monarchy."

In the *Narodní Listy* of January 1, 1913, Kramář published an editorial under the title "Slavdom," in which on behalf of the Czechs he fervently greeted the Serb and Bulgarian victory over the Turks. He claimed that to express such an attitude was a natural right of the Austrian Slavs and added: "We never intended in our Slav policy to oppose the true interests of Austria and all its nationalities; in the same way as we desire within the monarchy an equal justice for all, we believe that the only rational and absolutely safe foreign policy for Austria is a sincere benevolence for the neighboring nations, especially in the Balkans. We believe that every Austrian policy of territorial expansion presents a danger for its future and its existence, and because we really wish the existence and flowering and strength of an Austria just to all its peoples, we cannot understand why Austria should not be able to live in the greatest friendship with the Slav nations and why it could not support their endeavors, as far as they do not conflict with the vital interests of the monarchy, its real interests and not the prejudices of some Viennese circles."

The moderation of the leaders was not shared by large parts of the people.[n] A young nationalism easily inclines to declamatory radicalism and to self-intoxication with the justice of its own case. Unfortunately the academic youth often inclined to an intolerant radicalism: it played in the central and eastern European national movements—as later in Asia—an excessive and harmful part, regarding violence as proof of heroic devotion. Such an emotionalism took equal hold on the Czechs and the Germans in Bohemia and made a rational settlement impossible. Many Germans dreamt of incorporating Bohemia into Germany and appealed to the past for justification; many Czechs unearthed a so-called "Bohemian state right" of the "Crown of St. Wenceslav," imitating the Hungarian "sacred" symbol of the Crown of St. Stephen, and expected a Bohemia from which the German "intruders" would be excluded, the ancestors of whom had settled there in the later Middle Ages upon the invitation of the Bohemian kings. Nowhere did the Austrian Pan-Germans receive as vigorous support as among the Bohemian Germans. The Pan-German leader Georg von Schönerer (1842–1921) wished to destroy Austria and to unite the Austrian Germans with the Bismarckian German Empire. He combined racial anti-Semitism with a violent anti-Catholicism and a bitter hostility to the Habsburgs.[n]

Among the Czechs an extreme radical party, mainly composed of youth and the lower middle class, was formed in 1898 under the name of the National Socialist Party, thus combining the mass appeal of nationalism and socialism as Schönerer did in his agitation for racialism and against capitalism and the "plutocracy" of Viennese liberalism. The German nationalist scholar and writer Felix Dahn

(1834–1912) whose historical novels were most popular in the Bismarckian empire, dedicated to the Bohemian Germans a poem which they inscribed in the townhall of Eger:

> Das höchste Gut des Mannes ist sein Volk,
> Das höchste Gut des Volkes ist sein Staat,
> Des Volkes Seele lebt in seiner Sprache:
> Dem Volk, dem Staat und unserer Sprache treu
> Fand uns der Tag, wird jeder Tag uns finden.

Both peoples accepted this idolatry of nationality and language: "The nation is man's supreme good, its own state is the nation's supreme good, the nation's soul lives in its language: the day found us faithful to our nation, our state and language and every future day will find us equally faithful." They did not recognize any moral obligation to values transcending the national group or the national language nor the national wisdom of a multi-national Danubian state as a guardian of peace and social economic development. Many Austrians looked beyond the frontiers:[n] the Germans to Germany, the Czechs, after the conclusion of the Franco-Russian alliance, to Russia and to France. In 1891 during the Prague fair the nationalist song "Hej Slovane" received an additional verse:

> Žije, žije, duch slovanský, na vzdor roste, kvete!
> Rus je s námi; kdo proti nám, toho Francouz smete!
> It lives, it lives, the Slav spirit, defiantly it grows and
>   flowers!
> The Russian is with us; the Frenchman will sweep
>   away whoever is against us.

Under these circumstances it was not astonishing that many observers regarded the Habsburg monarchy as obsolete and doomed. It seemed to contradict the contemporary dogma of the self-contained nation-state. Yet the necessity for the survival of the multi-national Empire on a federal basis was

recognized and stressed by many writers besides the
Czech leaders. The Austrian Social Democratic Party
came out in September, 1899, at its party convention
in Brünn, Moravia, for a program of federalization,
and the introduction of the principle of autonomy
and federal structure within some of the Austrian
provinces (Moravia, Bukovina, Dalmatia) secured
there a peaceful and orderly development. Prominent
Austrians like the Viennese liberal Adolf Fischhof
(1816–93) who had played a leading part in the
Revolution of 1848, the Transylvanian Rumanian
Aurel C. Popovici (1863–1917) and the highly respected jurist Heinrich Lammasch (1853–1922), a
Catholic conservative, proposed various schemes of
federalization.

The most interesting personality among them,
from the point of view of Pan-Slavism, was Franz
Schuselka (1811–86), a Bohemian German,[*] who as
a young man emigrated to Germany and there wrote
many articles in favor of German unity against
Austrian absolutism.[*] In the Frankfurt National
Assembly he was one of the spokesmen for Jewish
emancipation and for the Polish cause. Later he
entered the Austrian Parliament as a member of the
Left. From that time on he favored a strong and
free Austria and suggested its expansion along the
Danube.[*] The political convictions he then held
were best expressed in a widely discussed book "German or Russian? Austria's Life and Death Question."
He was then still a German nationalist and a liberal.
Writing at the very moment when the leading circles
in Austria felt hostile to Prussia and Germany and
were relying on Russia in the war against Hungary,
he proposed a German-Austrian alliance. He affirmed
his faith in Austria. "I have never wished the disintegration of Austria. I was enthusiastically for
the idea of a great cultural state Austria even at
the time when I was expelled from Austria and had
abandoned hope ever to see it again. In the interest

of liberty and culture not in the interest of the
dynasty I wish a powerful Austria."

In the interest of liberty and culture he wished
Austria to guard the European frontier against Russia. "A conciliation between Germany and Russia
is impossible; the genius of these nations and the
interests of these states are at conflict. Austria must
decide for one or the other; a vacillating policy can
neither last nor can it be useful or honorable.
Europe's fate unmistakably points to a great struggle
of the West against the East. Austria cannot remain
neutral in this struggle, if it does not wish to become
the prize of the contest between the two nations."
He judged Russia's aspirations in the same way as
Palacký and Marx did. He found her animated by a
two-fold enthusiasm, "the pious religious idea of a
renewal of the Greek Empire and the nationalist
fantasy of uniting all Slav nations into a great world
empire. Russia, however, is not satisfied with theo-
retical enthusiasm. She works with confident faith
and therefore with unbreakable perseverance for the
practical realization of her enthusiasms." Russia
neither could keep pace with European civilization
nor was she willing to withdraw modestly. Therefore
she tried to influence Europe and to work there
against the Western liberal tradition. Under Metternich, Austria had supported Russia and had
thereby harmed Austria and the cause of liberty. A
free Austria would stand up to Russia on behalf
of European liberty. "Whether rightly or partly
wrongly, the whole civilized world looks upon Russia
with dislike, fear and resentment. Whether that be
the case because Russia threatens European liberty,
or whether it simply expresses the awe felt before
the immense mass of the Russian despotism with its
Asiatic forms; the name of Russia terrifies the whole
of Europe." Russia could not tolerate along her
borders a political system of liberty, especially among
peoples akin to hers. She would be afraid that even

an "iron curtain" (sechsfache Kosakenkordone) could not hinder a model of political freedom from shining into the Russian darkness. "Russia does not wish to change her system, she even maintains that she cannot change it. To a certain extent she is right. Military autocracy is the sole form of union possible for her measureless empire."

Austrian resistance against Russia backed by Germany, was not only in the interest of Europe, Schuselka believed, but also in that of the Austrian Slavs who desired above all to enjoy Western liberty. He thought Pan-Slavism as impossible of realization as Pan-Germanism, a union of all the Germanic nations, the Germans, the Scandinavians, the Dutch and the English. "Yet the consideration of Pan-Slavism is not entirely in vain. While nobody thinks of Pan-Germanism, Pan-Slavism occupies the minds of many people and there are some who work for its realization. An attempt to realize it would seriously threaten Austria's existence." Beyond such an attempt, Schuselka visualized "the most daring thought of Russian policy—the establishment of a world empire. . . . Everywhere people tremble at this thought. I permit myself to doubt its possibility. I do not think Russia so powerful. I share the opinion of those who regard her as a colossus with feet of clay." [n]

Soon Schuselka outgrew this narrow anti-Russian point of view and arrived at a positive program for Austria. "Every thoughtful man will realize," he wrote in 1850, "that Austria can be preserved only by a happy and original combination of the federal and of the centralized system." He asked the Austrian Germans to sacrifice their natural fatherland, Germany, to their political fatherland, Austria—a sacrifice which would in the long run be useful to Germany—and appealed to all Austrians to work together for liberty. "The frustration of the highest interests of liberty and humanity by infantile disputes about the rights and rank of the various languages," he warned, "will be justly cursed by history. Peoples of Austria, unanimously demand a parliament, and you will get it. Don't worry whether the elections will bring a majority to this or that nationality. Vote in such a way that the party of liberty will have the majority. Then the liberty of each nationality will be secured in the liberty of all." [n]

Schuselka's next pamphlet, a "contribution to the reconciliation of Austria's nationalities," [n] carried as a motto Herder's words: "Kein Vorwurf ist drückender als der, fremden Nationen unrecht getan zu haben." (No reproach is more crushing than that of having been unjust to other nations.) In the age of nationalism, Schuselka had the magnanimous courage to follow the precept of 18th century humanitarianism. "As one of the fighters for German nationality," he wrote in the preface to the new book, "I have said some hard words which were unjust and painful to the other nationalities. They have paid me back amply. Yet the contemplation of our common misfortune has taught me to avoid the former and to forget the latter. I wish fervently that all my adversaries, that all Austrian peoples and their spokesmen would change as I have done." After 1860 he began to fight the centralizing tendencies of the Austrian Germans, became more and more friendly to the cause of the Slavs, and implored Austria to satisfy equally all her nationalities. [n]

In 1852 he founded the weekly *Die Reform* which he edited until 1879, a lonely fighter for a federal Austria. "In Austria no people should rule over another and least of all over all other peoples. All peoples must enjoy equal rights, which will result in their voluntary fulfillment of common duties. Austria must be conceived as a multi-national state (ein Völkerreich), it must be so constituted that it does not absorb any nationality but preserves all. To that end Austria was created; in this end lies the justification of its continued existence." [n] His fight for federalism brought him into a growing conflict with the liberals in Vienna; he became more and more conservative, regarding the secular nationalist liberalism of the Kultur-kampf-period as almost as despotic as he had formerly regarded the monarchical absolutism. He rejoined the Catholic Church which he had left as a young man to become a Protestant. But the number of men like Fischhof or Schuselka was small among the Austrian Germans, and among the Czechs the tumultuous crowd did not follow Palacký or Masaryk.

At the time of the Prague fair of 1891, Alois Lexa von Aehrenthal (1854–1912)—he was then councillor of the Austrian embassy to St. Petersburg, where he later became (1899) ambassador remaining such until his appointment as foreign minister in the fall of 1906—wrote on September 24, 1891, to the Austro-Hungarian foreign minister Count Gustav Siegmund Kalnoky (1832–98) who held that office from 1881 to 1895 and followed on the whole a policy of great friendliness toward Russia: "The first conclusion (from my observation) is the lack of interest—which could be perhaps more correctly called apathy—which prevails at present in Russian society for everything Slav. . . . My second conclusion is that the focus for a more energetic and faster development of the Pan-Slav idea must be sought within and not without the Austro-Hungarian monarchy. . . . In my opinion the driving force of the Slav question must always be sought in the highly developed western and southern Slavs."

The initiative to a new Slav movement came, as Aehrenthal had predicted, from Prague and Belgrade, not from Moscow or St. Petersburg. In the 1880's isolated Pan-Slav sentiments were expressed among the various branches of western Slavdom. The popular poet Svatopluk Čech (1846–1908) published in

1884, under the influence of Kollár and Dostoyevsky, a long Czech poem "Slavie." It expressed his fervent expectation that only a united Slav world under Russia's leadership would be able to save Europe from an impending catastrophe. His "Písně otroka" (Songs of the Slave, 1895) bitterly attacked Austrian domination, vastly exaggerating the difficulties of Czech national development in the later stages of Austrian rule. His journeys to Poland, to the Ukraine, and to Constantinople brought him into touch with other Slav centers.

In June 1898 the centenary of the birth of Palacký and the fiftieth anniversary of the Pan-Slav congress of 1848 were celebrated in Prague with the laying of the cornerstone for a monument to Palacký. At the great banquet which was held in Sophie Island, which has been renamed Slavonic Island, a Russian officer who appeared in the uniform of a Serb general and who was the editor of the Pan-Slav Petersburg newspaper *Svyet* assured the Czechs and the Slavs of Russia's complete solidarity in their common struggle against German encroachment. He recalled the battle at Tannenberg where in 1410 the Lithuanians and the Poles—or, as he said, the united Czechs, Poles, and Russians—had defeated the Teutonic Knights and put an end to German aggression. After a new decisive victory over the German enemy, the speaker concluded, the Slav peoples will more easily settle the differences which still separate them. Colonel Komarov did not speak on behalf of the Russian government. In fact, in the following year, when he was elected chairman of the Slav Benevolent Society in Russia, the government refused to confirm him in this position.

As a result of this Slav gathering a new and ably edited periodical *Slovanský přehled* (Slav Survey) was founded to stress Slav mutuality.[n] Only five years later Prague was followed by Belgrade: for it should not be forgotten that for twenty years Russian policy had hardly any following among the Slavs in the Balkans, where from 1885 on, Austrian influence predominated in Bulgaria and in Serbia. The assassination on June 11, 1903, of King Alexander I (1889–1903) of Serbia and his wife put an end to the house of Obrenović and its Austrophile orientation; the regicides belonged to a secret society of officers, the Black Hand (*Crna ruka*), later called Union or Death (*Uyedinyenye ili smert*), led by the mysterious Col. Dragutin Dimitrievic, known as "Aspis" who inspired Gavrilo Princip, the assassin of Archduke Francis Ferdinand. The conspirators put Peter I (1903–21) of the house of Karageorgević into power. Austria-Hungary recognized him immediately and was willing to continue the good neighborly relationship. Émile Haumant, the French scholar whose whole work showed his lively sympathy for the Serbs and their cause, stressed that it depended only upon the new rulers in Serbia to enter into a friendly association with Austria, for which there existed many good economic and political reasons.[n]

But the new rulers, the officers of the conspiracy and the Radical party under Nikola Pašić (1846–1926), were determined to turn toward Russia, and expected the dissolution of Austria-Hungary (as well as of Turkey). In any case they worked hard to this end. Organizations like the Slovensky yug (The Slav South) and the Narodna odbrana (The National Defense) spread the conviction that Serbia was destined to become the Piedmont for the unification of all the southern Slavs. A great self-confidence and an aggressive nationalism pushed the ruling circles of Serbia to challenge the "ramshackle" Empires of Turkey and of Austria-Hungary. Not only out of Slav sympathy but also because they knew that the two Empires were supported by Germany, the Serbs turned eagerly to Russia and to France. Their hearts were beating for Russia; their cannons came from France. More dangerous was the spirit of violence which developed fast among the Serbian youth, and a brutalization of public life and the celebration as heroes of terrorist "martyrs," beginning with Bogdan Žerajić, a Serb from Herzegovina who on June 10, 1910, shot General Varešanin at the opening of the Bosnian Sabor (Diet) and then committed suicide. This aggressive overflow of misguided energy expressed itself later also in Serb policy toward other Slavs, Croatians and Macedonians. It produced in the south a military "heroic" mood which was absent among the Czechs of that period.

In the tense European atmosphere after the Morocco crisis of 1905 and the Anglo-Russian entente of 1907, the suggestion for closer Slav contacts came from the Czechs. The year 1908 marked the sixtieth anniversary of the first Slav congress: the time seemed propitious for calling another Slav congress to Prague, oriented again towards the Western ideas of liberty and towards the equality of the Slav nations. The Russian constitution, the fruit of the revolution of 1905, had granted certain liberties to the oppressed Slav nationalities in Russia, the Poles, the Ukrainians and the Byelorussians; with the introduction of general suffrage in Austria in 1907 the position of the Slav nationalities there had still further improved; on the other hand (as in 1848) the fear of German expansion was growing and the situation of the Slav nationalities in Prussia and Hungary was deteriorating.[n]

The time for a new Slav movement seemed propitious, because even among the Poles the thought of Slav solidarity had made some progress. In 1901 a "Slavonic Club" was founded in Cracow; it published a monthly *Swiat Słowiański* (The Slav World). Its inspirer was a professor of literature, Maryan Sdziechowski, who believed in a close affinity of the Polish messianism of the 1830's and the Russian Slavophilism of Khomyakov. Of much greater political importance, however, was the change in the ideology of Roman Dmowski (1864–1939), the representative leader of extreme Polish nationalism before World War I. As a student he participated in anti-Russian demonstrations in Warsaw, and as a result he had to take refuge in Austrian Lemberg. There he founded the *Przegląd Wszechpolski* (The All-Polish Review) with Jan Popławski in 1895. Their party, called *National Democracy*, propagated the creation of a great Poland at the expense of Austria, Prussia, and Russia, claiming wide lands for the future Polish state. But by 1903 Dmowski's ideas, expressed in his *Myśli nowoczesnego Polaka* (1903), had undergone a drastic change. He was fascinated by the extreme Pan-German nationalism and wished to outdo Prussian power politics. Prussia's success seemed to prove that only a ruthless policy, which did not recognize justice or injustice but only strength and weakness, can prosper. Dmowski rejected all liberalism and humanitarianism and demanded the pitiless struggle against the Ukrainians, Lithuanians, and Jews. It was the policy of an unlimited *sacro egoism*, as it was also propagated by his friend Zygmunt Balicki, a former Polish socialist, whose *Egoism narodowy wobec etyki* (1892, new ed. 1903) proclaimed national egotism as the foundation of all ethical life, rejecting the emphasis on individual rights as much as that on humanitarian universalism.

A few years later Dmowski executed a complete change in his political orientation. He remained as extreme a nationalist as he had been, but he decided that in view of the anti-Polish policy in Prussia and of the approaching European conflict, in which Russia would fight on the side of France against Germany, the Poles had to come to an understanding with Russia. To that end he began to play a Pan-Slav policy.[*] In the period of the first two Dumas the Russian government had made certain concessions in its nationality policy which aroused the hope of a coming grant of autonomy for Poland. The Russian liberals supported such a policy. Some of them expressed the opinion that the coming conflict with Germany necessitated a more liberal policy not only in Russia but in Russia's relationship with the other Slavs. French informed circles supported this point of view. At the beginning of the century interest in the Slav peoples grew in Paris, where in 1906 the monthly *Revue slave* was founded, to stress the need for Slav unity.

The *rapprochement* between Russians and Poles seemed a necessary condition for a revival of Pan-Slavism. In Petersburg General Vladimir M. Volodimirov suggested the convocation of a Slav congress, which would abandon the reactionary character of the old Pan-Slav movement and would proclaim liberty, equality, and fraternity as the basis of Slav co-operation. In April 1908 liberal Russian circles founded a Society for Slav Culture in Moscow and a Society for Slav Scholarship in St. Petersburg. "We must convince the Slav peoples," one of the Russian liberal leaders, Prince Evgeny Nikolayevich Trubetskoy (1862–1920), wrote, "that we do in no way intend to interfere in the development characteristic of each Slav people, and that we are resolved, different therein from Slavophilism, to respect their spiritual and intellectual identity. In the Balkans Russia claimed the task of liberating the Slav brother-peoples. But at home Russia oppressed her Slav peoples. Thus the other Slavs feared the fate of Poland and became alienated from us. This is the principal reason for the deeply rooted distrust of us among the Austrian nationalities. We must overcome this distrust by all means. This is necessary for the security of our western borders." [n]

The leaders of the Austrian Slavs, Karl Kramář and Ivan Hribar (1851–1941), a Slovene member of the Austrian parliament and mayor of the Slovene capital Liubliana (Laibach), visited St. Petersburg in May 1908. They received from Dmowski, who was the leader of the Polish members in the Russian Duma, the assurance of Polish co-operation. As a result of the contacts between the Austrian and the Russian Slavs, it was decided to call a new Pan-Slav congress to meet in Prague from July 12 to July 17, 1908. To distinguish the movement from the old Pan-Slavism, which was rejected by the non-Russians for its subservience to Russian imperialism, autocracy, and Orthodoxy, a new word was coined: Neo-Slavism. The Congress was the best attended of all Slav congresses. It coincided with a great Sokol manifestation.[n] From Russia, among others, came Prince George Evgenevich Lvov (1861–1925), later the Prime Minister of the first Russian Provisional Government in 1917; from Croatia, Stjepan Radić (1871–1928), the leader of the Croatian Peasant Party; from Poland, Roman Dmowski. Only the Prussian Poles, the Austrian Ukrainians, the Slovaks, and the Lusatians were not represented. On behalf of the Ukrainians their great historian, Mykhailo Hrushevsky, wrote that "the basis of Neo-Slavism is a policy directed against the German people. This people has done no harm to the Ukrainians. Why should they who are oppressed by Russians and Poles act against the Germans? The anti-German Neo-Slavism is directed against Western civilization, which the Ukrainians will never abandon. Neo-Slavism is an instrument of reaction and we were and we always are on the side of progress."[n]

The discussions of the Neo-Slav Congress avoided political issues. The emphasis was placed throughout on economic and cultural collaboration. It was decided to arrange a Pan-Slav fair in Moscow and to establish a Pan-Slav bank, to promote tourism in the Slav countries, to establish Sokol organizations among all Slav peoples, and to improve and expand co-operation among Slav journalists, artists, scholars, and booksellers. The first Congress of Slav Journalists had been held in Prague in June 1898 at the time of the celebration of Palacký's centenary. But it had been restricted to journalists from the Austrian monarchy. Now it was to be expanded to include newspapermen from all Slav nationalities. Finally it was decided to establish a Slavic Telegraphic and News Agency as a news-service for the Slav and non-Slav press concerning matters of Slav interest.

As the leader of the Czech delegation, Dr. Kramář stressed Czech loyalty towards the monarchy. Originally the association of Czech writers "Maj" had even suggested that the Congress be confined to Austrian Slavs, in order to follow the example of the congress of 1848, and make it a demonstration of Austro-Slavism. Dr. Kramář had rejected this proposal, but in his opening address he sounded a note not fundamentally different from that of sixty years before: "I am deeply convinced that our congress will accomplish a great work if it will succeed in strengthening in the heart of all Slavs the consciousness that we Slavs shall fulfil our great mission in the history of mankind only through liberty, equality and fraternal solidarity of all our branches. We bring to the world peace and love; we don't wish to overthrow any throne or to destroy any empire or state. We wish only to feel ourselves one great whole held together by common cultural interests, lest we fall, in disunity and discord, one after the other, under the pressure of an overly-powerful organized and planned cultural and economic expansion. This consciousness that it is to the advantage of all of us to join together for cultural and economic work, brought us here, and the iron necessity of the common danger will oblige us, not to separate ourselves but to work with all our force for the strengthening of the fraternity and solidarity of the Slav peoples, free and equal among themselves."

In the concluding address Dmowski made even a more sensational declaration of Polish loyalty to the

Russian state: "In Austria . . . we were never persecuted. In the Russian state too, where we make a
supreme effort to achieve normal conditions of development, our people stands on the basis of being
part of that state and recognizes its general require-
ments. It is deeply convinced that a regenerated
Russia founded on the rights of all its peoples will
be a state not only needed for the Russian nation
but also for the Polish nation and for all of mankind." In the same year Dmowski published a book
Niemcy, Rosya i kwestiya polska (The Germans,
Russia and the Polish Question) in which he declared himself ready to abandon the Yagellonian concept of Polish history, with its emphasis on the Lithuanian, Byelorussian and Ukrainian lands, for the
older Piast conception which stressed the Western
marches lost in the 13th and 14th centuries to the
advancing Germans. He pleaded for the recognition
of the German danger and of Poland's importance
for Russia as a bulwark against German expansion.
"This present role of our nation must make the
Polish question in the near future one of the most
important European problems." After the war of
1870 he believed it to be also in the interest of
France that Poland should no longer form a bulwark
against the East but against the danger from the
West. Dmowski tried to find a platform for a
Polish-Russian reconciliation. "The collapse of the
uprising of 1863–4 was . . . the end of the armed
struggles for Polish independence. The Poles have
realized that the reconstruction of an independent
state represents in the existing international situation
an unobtainable goal and that all efforts in this
direction would mean only a useless squandering of
Polish strength." [n] Kramář and Dmowski shared the
Neo-Slav conception of a *rapprochement* between
Russia and Austria-Hungary against German expansion, if possible in collaboration with the West. Such
a Russian-Austrian entente might have preserved the

peace in the Balkans and perhaps the peace of Europe. For that very reason it ran counter to the nationalist aspirations of the Balkan Slavs whose ambitions demanded the destruction of the *status quo* and the expansion of their frontiers. It also presupposed the introduction by Russia of a liberal policy of respect for the rights of the non-Russian nationalities assembled under Moscow.

Hardly had the Prague Slav Congress dispersed, when two blows shattered its hopes. The Russian government, under the influence of mounting Russian chauvinism, started a strongly anti-Polish policy which went at least as far as the anti-Polish policy in Prussia at that time. There seemed to be no prospect of a liberal nationality policy in Russia. The second blow came from Vienna and Belgrade. On September 15, 1908, the Austro-Hungarian Minister Aehrenthal met with the Russian Foreign Minister Alexander Petrovich Isvolsky (1856–1919) in the castle of Buchlau in Moravia, the family seat of Count Leopold Berchtold (1863–1942), the Austro-Hungarian Ambassador in St. Petersburg (and after Aehrenthal's death in 1912 his successor as foreign minister). An agreement between Russia and Austro-Hungary seemed in the making, but the annexation of Bosnia-Herzegovina by the Habsburg Empire in the following month caused much bitterness between the two foreign ministers. Aehrenthal claimed, and Isvolsky denied, Russia's agreement to this step which aroused the violent opposition of the Serbs. It is noteworthy that the Slav deputies, including the Czechs and South Slavs, in the Austro-Hungarian Delegations voted in an overwhelming majority for the annexation of Bosnia-Herzegovina. They saw in it a strengthening of the Slav element in the Habsburg monarchy. Especially the Croats welcomed a measure which promised to make Croatia and not Serbia the center of Yugoslav unity. But the Austro-Hungarian government missed the opportunity of a positive Southern-Slav policy which would have united the Southern Slavs of Austria, Hungary and Bosnia-Herzegovina and would have transformed the Austro-Hungarian dualism into an Austro-Hungarian-Slav trialism. The Austrian heir to the throne, Archduke Francis Ferdinand was reported favorable to such plans and incurred thereby the hostility not only of the Magyars but of the Serbs from the Kingdom, whose dream of being the Southern-Slav Piedmont and of pushing the frontiers of the Balkans deep to the northwest would have been upset by such a policy.[n]

Writing after World War II, the Czech statesman, Dr. Edward Beneš (1884–1948), criticized the neo-Slav conception: "No real Slav policy was imaginable without thinking through the practical political consequences, and these could always be only one and the same for every consistent Slav policy: the destruction of the existing territorial status quo and the creation either of a great Pan-Slav empire under Russian leadership, or the abandonment of the existing frontiers and the creation of individual united Slav nation-States on a progressive and people's democratic basis. Another alternative Slav policy never existed."[n] This point of view which dominated Beneš's policy during and after World War II explains the events in Czechoslovakia during that time. For an illusionary Slavism had a strong hold on the Czech mind. These "Slavs" assumed that there was a basis for such a Slav policy comprising Russians, Poles, Czechs and other very diverse nations having in common only a similarity of languages, but they denied rightly, the desirability and feasibility of a similar pan-German policy uniting the Germans, the Dutch, the Scandinavians and the Anglo-Saxons, or a pan-Latin policy linking together French and Belgians, Italians and Rumanians, the people of Ibero-America and of Haiti.

That such a Slav policy might conflict with all

considerations of civilization, humanity and peace, apparently did not impress some. Yet they did not face sincerely even the equality of Czechs or Russians. On the contrary, they identified Pan-Slavism, but not Pan-Germanism or Pan-Latinism, with peace and human progress. There was little interest among the Russians, Poles, Czechs and Southern Slavs in the right of the Ukrainians or Byelorussians for national statehood. Nor did the Czechs acknowledge such rights to the Slovaks, nor the Serbs to the Croats. Thus there remained as the only possible consistent Slav policy the creation of a great Pan-Slav empire under Russian leadership, which actually emerged in the end. Among the Germans and Latins there were some dreamers and intellectuals who played with Pan-German or Pan-Latin ideas; only among the Slavs similar ideas were discussed seriously by responsible statesmen and politicians. By doing so they played unwittingly into the hands of Great Russian imperialism.

The Prague Slav Congress before dissolving had chosen a Slav committee which met in St. Petersburg in May, 1909, and in February, 1910, to prepare for a second congress which duly convened in July, 1910, in Sofia under the chairmanship of Professor Stefan Savov Bobchev (1853–1940). The Bulgarian government ostentatiously ignored the congress. The Ukrainians again did not participate; nor was there any mention of the Byelorussians.[n] But this time the Poles too were absent. Dr. Kramář, elected honorary chairman, proclaimed: "He is no Slav, who oppresses Slavs." According to this definition there would have been few Slavs in the world. Alexander Ivanovich Guchkov (1862–1936) a Russian nationalist who had volunteered for service against the British in the Boer War, and who was then Mayor of Moscow and President of the Third Duma, greeted the Congress on behalf of the Russian capital and expressed the wish that the Congress might unite all Slavs culturally and in mutual love as Moscow had gathered and united all the Russian principalities. In spite of similar enthusiastic speeches, the Congress revealed the growing disunity not only among the Slav peoples but also between the liberals and socialists on the one hand and the reactionary parties on the other hand within the various nations.

The practical results of the Sofia Slav Congress were nil. The same cultural and economic problems and tasks were discussed as two years before in Prague. None of them was brought nearer to solution. It was decided to hold the Pan-Slav fair in Prague in 1915, in case it should be impossible to hold it in Moscow or St. Petersburg. An association of all Slav libraries; a society for the translation of the classical writings of the Slav peoples into the other Slav languages; the exchange of professors and students among the various Slav universities; the publication of a popular Slav encyclopedia; the establishment of a Slav theatrical agency—these were some of the proposals discussed and unanimously approved. In the concluding speech on July 10, Professor Bobchev announced that the next Slav congress would meet soon in Belgrade. A conference of Slav journalists met there in July 1911, but the projected Slav Congress never met. The Prague Congress of 1908 had hoped to cement a Polish-Russian agreement. It had failed. The Sofia Congress had expected to cement the unity of the Balkan Slavs. But within three years Serbs and Bulgarians met at the battlefield as implacable enemies. For the next thirty-five years a co-operation among the Balkan Slavs and a Slav Congress in Belgrade were unthinkable. When it finally did meet in Belgrade in 1946, it happened under entirely different circumstances and in a spirit, diametrically opposed to that of Neo-Slavism.

The peace of Europe maintained in the west in

spite of colonial tensions, was ominously broken in the Balkans. The united aggression of the Slav and Orthodox Balkan peoples against Turkey in 1912 aroused great enthusiasm among the Pan-Slavs, especially among the Czechs. But the second Balkan war in 1913 revealed in the bitter struggle between the Serbs and Bulgars the deep and lasting antagonism even between Slav peoples of common faith and with a similar background of history and civilization. The Serb victory in both Balkan wars strengthened the Serb conviction of their mission as unifiers and leaders of all Southern Slavs. Serb aggressiveness, supported by Russian and Czech Pan-Slavism, facilitated by Austrian inertia and Magyar obstinacy, led to the crisis of July, 1914; the self-confident dynamism of the new Germany built upon the traditions of the Prussian power-state turned the crisis into a world war. The conflict which arose from the age-old border struggles of Germans and Slavs—in July, 1910, the 500th anniversary of the Battle of Tannenberg, in which a Lithuanian-Polish army defeated the Teutonic knights, was celebrated in Cracow with the unveiling of a monument for the victor Vladislav Jagiello—grew into a war for Germany's hegemony over Europe.[n] It opened thereby an entirely new era in the history not only of Europe but also and above all of the Slav nations.

2

The Triumphs of the West-Slavs After World War I

THE COURSE of great wars is difficult to foresee; their results are often surprising and unexpected. In 1915 most observers counted either upon the victory of Germany or upon the victory of Russia and her allies. In either case the Western Slavs seemed threatened with falling under great power domination, German or Russian. Victory of the Central Powers would have strengthened the German Magyar preponderance throughout central and southeastern Europe. The German Chancellor Theobald von Bethmann-Hollweg (1856–1921) in his speech of April 7, 1913, characterized the struggle as a conflict between the Germans and the Slavs. Such an attitude was hardly of the nature to arouse the enthusiasm of the Austro-Hungarian Slavs in a war against Russia and Serbia. It involved a dangerous shift from a war among states which could count upon the support of all their citizens to a war between races, appealing to racial loyalties. Bethmann-Hollweg thought perhaps to make the war more palatable to the German workers. The possibility of a Russian invasion, of the famous "steam-roller" approaching Berlin from the east, united the overwhelming majority of the

German Social Democratic Party behind the war
efforts of the government. On behalf of the party
Hugo Haase declared on August 4, 1914, in the
Reichstag: "The victory of Russian despotism sullied
with the blood of the best of its own people, would
endanger much, if not everything, for our people
and their future freedom. It is our duty to repel this
danger and to safeguard the culture and independence of our country. We reiterate what we have always emphasized: We shall not abandon our native
land in its hour of need. In this respect we feel ourselves in accord with the International, which has
always conceded the right of every people to national
independence and self-defense, even if we agree in
denouncing every war and conquest." [n]

The German socialists took the attitude of the
legitimate defense of national independence, but
this stand was made easier for them by identifying
the warring states with two opposite forms of political organization and civilization. Avoiding the pitfall
of a racial war, they came dangerously near to the
concept of an ideological war. Such a concept was
used later by the West against Germany. It can be
safely assumed that a German victory would have
brought to the Western Slavs neither greater political
nor national liberty. Nor did it hold much promise
for the Habsburg monarchy. In the long run it
would have aggravated its problem because it would
have enhanced Magyar pride and made a federal
solution more difficult.

Similarly a victory for Russia would have had
adverse effects on the Western Slavs and on Russia's
allies. The vast majority of the Poles expected no real
benefit from Moscow's increased strength. Though
the other Western Slavs might have gained formal
independence, they would have been placed under
Russian hegemony, hardly conducive to a growth of
Western liberty among them. A Russian victory
might have realized the Pan-Slav union as foreseen

by Danilevsky. The triumph of arms would have fortified the grip of the reactionary nationalists on the
Russian government and silenced, at least for some
time, the voices of liberal Russian public opinion.
It would have brought Russian arms and Russian
rule into central Europe and to the eastern Mediterranean. On March 18, 1915, Britain and France concluded an agreement with Russia, the so-called
"Constantinople" agreement, by which Russia was
to receive in case of victory "the town of Constantinople, the western coast of the Bosporus, the Sea
of Marmara and the Dardanelles; southern Thrace
as far as the Enos-Midia line; the coast of Asia
Minor between the Bosporus and the River Sakaria
and a point on the Gulf of Ismid to be defined later;
the islands in the Sea of Marmara and the islands
of Imbros and Tenedos,"—more or less the same
territory as claimed by Danilevsky. The Allies were
by that time determined upon the partition of
Turkey, but a Russian victory would have brought
her also large parts of the territory of Germany and
Austria-Hungary and would have established her as
a hegemonial power on the European continent, perhaps in a position as strong as the one in which she
found herself after victory in World War II.

Such a danger was dreaded by some Englishmen,
by all Turks, and by most of the Poles. At the end
of July, 1914, a group of Englishmen having formed
a Neutrality League warned that the war undertaken
to preserve the balance of power might destroy it
and create a Russian Europe: "If we are successful
in securing the victory of Russia in this war, we shall
upset that balance enormously by making her the
dominant military power of Europe possibly the
dictator both in this Continent and in Asia. . . . All
her history shows her to be impregnable by invasion.
. . . She is able to put nearly six million men into
the field, to draw upon vast resources of human military material, only partly civilized, governed by a

military autocracy largely hostile to Western ideas of political and religious freedom." [n] This manifesto was of little avail. The British who had fought the Russians in 1854 to preserve the balance of power in southeast Europe, in 1914 regarded the Germans as by far the greater threat. Their estimate was correct: the war itself revealed that the Russia of 1914 had neither the moral cohesion nor the material forces to establish herself as the hegemonial power of Europe and Asia. The Germans came very near to victory and establishment of an imperial basis reaching from the English Channel to the Black Sea and the Persian Gulf. Between 1916 and 1918 Germany, and not Russia, controlled directly or indirectly all Slav lands with the sole exception of the Great Russian homeland—the whole of Poland, most of the Ukraine, the Austro-Hungarian Slavs, Serbia, Montenegro and Bulgaria. What seemed to emerge as a possibility for a short while, was however, not an enlarged Austro-Slavism as intended in 1848, with the addition of Poland and the Balkan Slavs, but Austria-Hungary and all the non-Russian Slavs subservient to a German-dominated Mitteleuropa— one of the two dangers dreaded by Palacký. It was, however, as far from realization as the other danger, feared by him, a Pan-Slav union under Russian domination.

Unexpectedly, the war ended with the defeat both of Russia and of Germany. What the British did not foresee, however, was the impossibility of restoring the balance of power after the War. This balance of power rested in the 19th century on a generally recognized mentality, the very same foundation on which Britain's greatness and leadership since the Glorious Revolution were based: the acceptance of rational compromise, of humaine reasonableness, of fair play, of ethical practicability. This attitude was threatened by the upsurge over most of the European Continent since the beginning of the

twentieth century of a wave of nationalist and socialist passion, of world-saving expectations and men-
destroying hatreds. A romantic search for new values
led especially among Germans and Slavs to a
dangerous cult of heroism and to an identification
with old myths.[n] Elemental and primitive forces
were called up and like Goethe's sorcerer's apprentice
became difficult to control. This moral and intellectual crisis was one of the factors leading to war and
expressed itself in it. The war could not solve it; it
aggravated it. It unleashed all the passions of nationalism which as Lord Acton had foreseen,[n] proved
in central and eastern Europe, and a little later in
Asia, the greatest revolutionary force. They found
their justification in the wide-spread belief that the
fulfillment of national aspirations was the instrument
of human progress in the irresistible march of history,
which would redeem the unredeemed and establish
a reign of peace and justice for all. Mazzini might
dream thus in 1848[n]—seventy years later it could
be seen that all these national aspirations conflicted
with each other and that they certainly did not bring
peace and justice nearer to a mankind sorely tried
by them.

These passions had a contagious effect. Slav aggressiveness and nationalist mythology were part of
this new mentality in continental Europe; they
aroused a similar reaction among the Turks: Pan-
Slavism was the father of Pan-Turanism. While some
Slavs lived in the Ottoman Empire, many more
Turkish-speaking peoples were Russian subjects. By
1905 they longed as fervently for "liberation" from
the alien yoke as the Serbs and Bulgars had done half
a century before. These Turkish-speaking peoples
who lived in the Crimea and along the lower Volga,
in Azerbaijan and in the northern Caucasus,
throughout Turkestan and far into Eastern Siberia,
found themselves united by linguistic and religious
ties with the Turks who formed the ruling race in

the Ottoman Empire. They all supposedly came from one common homeland, Turan. Under the stimulus of this newly discovered Turanian kinship, the Turks after 1908 became aware of a pre-Islamic "original" culture, providing them with the myth of a glorious past holding out the prospect of a rich future. Deprived of their posessions in Europe, they could hope by the liberation of the kindred Turkish tribes to create a homogeneous state consolidated by unity of race and speech; should that prove to be an unrealizable dream, the program could still serve as a counter-weapon against Russian and Pan-Slav aggressive plans.

In 1878 Ismail Gasprinski (1841–1914), a Crimean Turk, started there the first newspaper in Turkish, *Tercüman*, which had for its motto "Unity in Language, Thought and Action." His brother-in-law Yussuf Aktshura Oghlu founded in Constantinople in 1911 a journal *Türk Yurdu* (The Turkish Homeland). After 1908 many young Turkish writers like Halide Edib in her novel *Yeni Turan* (New Turan) and Ziya Gökalp (1875–1924) began to develop a Turanian theory much akin to Slavophilism and to German romantic nationalism, glorifying the legendary past of the race and the unique character of its people, fighting against alien influences and drawing a strangely idealized picture of the past on the strength of doubtful history and anthropology. Turkish history proved to Gökalp the moral superiority of his race, which he regarded as the cradle of democracy; it confirmed his belief in the mission of the Turks "to realize the highest moral virtues and to prove that the sacrifices and heroic deed which are generally regarded as impossible are not beyond human strength." [n] Like other contemporary nationalists, these Turks erected nationalism into a supreme ideal, disregarding the old solidarity of Islam or the new rights of the individual. In a poem, published

early in 1915 during the war against Russia, Gökalp
wrote:

> *What is duty? A voice coming down from God's*
>   *throne,*
> *Which reverberates the consciousness of my nation.*
> *I am a soldier; it is my commander,*
> *I obey without question all its orders.*
> *With closed eyes I carry out my duty.*

National heroes of the far-away past were glorified
and homage was paid to them with great pride.
Gökalp wrote a poem in 1911: "The feelings pulsing
in my blood are the echo of my past. I do not read
of the glorious deeds of my ancestors in withered,
yellow, dusty pages of history, but in the blood flowing in my veins, in my heart. My Attila, my Jenghis,
heroic figures, the pride and glory of my race, are
no less in stature than Alexander and Caesar. Oghuz
Khan, a figure obscure and vague to the scholar, is
familiar and clearly known to my heart. In my blood
he lives in all his greatness and glory. He it is that
delights in my heart and inspires me to shout exult-
antly: the fatherland of the Turks is not Turkey, it
is not Turkestan, it is the far-flung and ever-lasting
land—Turan." The hero of Halide Edib's political
novel was "the type of an Attila or Jenghis Khan
evolved into a civilized man." [n]

Thus the exalted nationalism of Slavophiles and
Pan-Slavs aroused a similar counter-movement among
the Turks. It helped them to defeat the Russian and
later the Greek advance. After the successful defense
of Turkey the Pan-Turanian movement was shelved
by Atatürk's realism, which abandoned all imperialist dreams and insisted on Turkish withdrawal within
the national frontiers. This rejection of Pan-Turanism coincided with Lenin's abandonment of Pan-
Slavism. During World War II, when Stalin revived
Pan-Slavism, there was a renewed though slight in-

terest in Pan-Turanism among some Turks. Significantly the Soviet peoples which during the war went over to the German side—as the result of which after Stalin's victory their autonomous statehood was abolished and they were deported and dispersed—were mostly of "Turanian" origin.[n]

Such a mood of absolute devotion to one's nation and its aspirations, of a half-historical and half-mythical evocation of the racial past at the expense of critical realism, of an emotionally charged activist dynamism, and of impatience with mediation and caution, characterized many intellectual trends in the decades before 1914. Among the Czechs, the poetry of Svatopluk Čech and the national heroic novels by Alois Jirásek (1851–1930) gained widest popularity. A new Slavophilism took hold of some of the most subtle Russian writers: Vasily Vasilyevich Rozanov (1856–1919)[n] a biological mystic who in his teaching achieved the almost impossible synthesis of Dostoyevsky and Nietzsche; the great symbolist poet Valery Yakovlevich Bryusov (1873–1924) who though a-political, joined Lenin's revolution because he hated half-measures and regarded it as the realization of his esthetic ideal of an "Ocean of a people's wrath"; Maximilian Alexandrovich Voloshin (1877–1932) who was converted by the Bolshevik Revolution from a Westerner into a mystic worshipper of Holy Russia liberated by Lenin from its subservience to alien fetters;[n] André Byely (1880–1934), another symbolist poet who like Blok attempted a synthesis of Bolshevism and religious mysticism and believed that the new revolutionary culture would replace the obsolete civilization of Europe; Nicholas Klyuyev (1885–1937) who identified Bolshevism with the old forms of folk religion in Russia.

Though futurism with its glorification of violence and of the machine originated in 1912 in Italy, it made practically no impression anywhere but in Russia. The futurist leader Velemir Khlebnikov

(1885–1922) became the singer of a pagan Slavophilism, "a Slav who wished to get back to the soul
of his race before Christianity and Westernization
had imposed their patterns." [n] Recently a Soviet
author V. Shklovsky praised him for having pointed
out the need as far back as 1912 to learn from the
old Slavonic and Asiatic literature. "Khlebnikov said
that it was now necessary to study the songs of the
Adriatic Slavs and the Mongolian epics." [n] Futurism's most gifted poet, Vladimir Vladimirovich
Mayakovsky (1894–1930) turned the futurist ecstasy
of energy into a rhetorical poetry of the revolutionary world proletariat.[n] In 1918 he presented the
Russian peasant Ivan, the representative of the communist world revolution, wading through the Atlantic Ocean to fight and defeat Woodrow Wilson, the
representative of world capitalism.[n] Though the
muzhik was fighting the cause of the world proletariat and of the one proletarian world, in accordance with Lenin's doctrine, the emphasis in all this
poetry from the symbolists to the futurists, was on
the Russian people, the Russian land and a rising
Russian civilization, even though it were, as with
the older Slavophiles, of a world-embracing nature.
The national socialist element, with a heavy accent
on the national component part, was from the beginning represented in the October Revolution. The
Civil War brought it even more clearly to the fore.
Boris Pilnyak in *The Naked Year* (1922), the best
novel of the period, interpreted the Revolution as the
uprising of an elemental Russia against foreign
masters. Yet after 1917 in this "elemental" outburst
of Russian nationalism and messianic social imperialism there was no reference to Pan-Slavism.

There were some Pan-Slav sentiments expressed in
Russia at the outbreak of the war. The Emperor
alluded officially to them in his manifesto of August
8, 1914: "According to her historical traditions,
Russia united by faith and blood with the Slav

peoples, has never regarded their fate with indifference. The fraternal feelings of the Russian people for the Slavs were aroused in unanimous enthusiasm and with special force in these last days, in the moment, when Austria-Hungary put before Serbia conditions manifestly unacceptable to a sovereign state." But there was no mention in the manifesto of the Austrian Slavs, nor of their "liberation." It was clearly stated that Russia went to war to preserve her position as a great power. "Now it is not only the question of making common cause with an unjustly offended sister-nation, but to defend Russia's honor, dignity and integrity as well as her position among the great powers." On the same day the Russian minister for foreign affairs declared in the Duma: ". . . though it had to undergo severe trials, the union of the Orthodox Balkan peoples will, so God wills, one day be realized. You know the reason for the war. Torn by internal disorders, Austria tried to deal a blow which would at the same time prove its strength and humiliate us. For that purpose Serbia had to serve, that Serbia with which ties of history, of common descent and faith unite us. You know the circumstances under which the ultimatum was presented to Serbia. Had Serbia accepted these conditions, it would have become an Austrian vassal. An attitude of indifference on our part would have meant the abandonment of our centuries-old role as protector of the Balkan nations. Simultaneously we would have agreed that the will of Austria and of Germany which was supporting it would have become law for Europe; neither we nor France nor England could allow this to happen."

Bernard Pares, an English scholar and friend of Russia who was there at the beginning of the war, confirmed the impression, reported by the French Ambassador Maurice Paléologue, of "the people's frantic enthusiasm." [n] But there were warning voices, especially among the anti-revolutionary adherents of

the monarchy, which pointed to the essential domestic weakness of Russia, that is, to the lack of enthusiasm or conviction on the part of the people for
the Pan-Slav cause and of loyalty to the Russian
government. Many Russian statesmen were convinced, as one of them expressed it in November,
1913, "that Russia needed peace more than any other
country, if for no other reason than because of the
great results attained during the last six or seven
years of her economic development; deplorable indeed, would be any stop in this progress." [n] The
Siberian "monk" Rasputin—so influential then at
the imperial court—is reported to have emphasized
again and again that "the Balkans were not worth
fighting about." [n] Witte told the French ambassador
on September 10, 1941: "You probably allude to our
prestige in the Balkans, to our pious duty, to protect
our brothers by race, to our sacred historical mission
in the East? . . . But that is a romantic, old-
fashioned phantasy. Nobody here, no serious thinker,
is interested in these restless and vain Balkan peoples
who are not really Slavs but are nothing else than
badly baptized Turks. One should abandon the Serbs
to the castigation which they deserve. Besides, did
they worry about their Slavism at the time when
their King Milan made them Austria's vassals?" After
having questioned the desirability of Russian conquests in eastern Prussia or Galicia, Witte continued:
"What should we hope for? Constantinople, the
cross of Saint Sophia, the Bosporus, the Dardanelles?
That is so absurd that it is even not worthwhile to
consider." [n] And the Russian minister of the interior of the day, Nikolai Maklakov, said in July,
1914: "With us the war cannot be popular among
the masses; the revolutionary ideas are nearer to
them than in victory over Germany. But one can't
escape one's fate." [n]

These certainly not disinterested and undoubtedly
"reactionary" but realistic warnings went unheeded.

Too strong was the call of destiny, the heroic and activist mood which since 1900 had influenced thought in France and Italy, in Germany and in Russia, among the Serbs and also among the Poles."
In the second half of the 19th century a school of critical realism had developed among the Galician Poles. Franciszek Smolka (1810–99) defended an Austro-Slav point of view; the famous Cracow historian Józef Szujski (1835–83) regarded Poland's colonizing mission in Lithuania and the Ukraine as an ambitious enterprise which exceeded the strength of the nation; the Polish "Drang nach Osten" absorbed too many forces which should have been devoted to reforming the nation. His disciple Michał Bobrzyński (1849–1935), historian and statesman, in his "History of Poland in Outline" which appeared in 1879 explained the decline and loss of Poland's statehood in the 18th century by Polish shortcomings and not primarily by the greed of her neighbors."

This "pessimistic" school was, however, replaced at the beginning of the 20th century by an "optimistic" approach. Warsaw historians writing at the beginning of World War I were convinced that "Poland had produced a superior type of state (compared with the European West and the East), a morally superior historic type, preceding other countries in this field, and there lay the principal cause of her fall." " The romantic mind of the great messianic poets, of Mickiewicz, Krasiński and Słowacki, was rekindled with all its mystic exaltation of the Polish nation and of its unique place in history. In that spirit Krasiński had written to the French poet Lamartine, the historian of the Girondists protesting against a misrepresentation of Poland as an aristocratic republic: "To say that of the single, the only, the most magnificent democracy that ever existed in Europe—but really that is puerile. . . . Everything dreamt of by the (French)

Revolution whose efforts you are recounting was already realized in Poland, and that in the 15th century; but everything the Revolution accomplished in place of its dreams, that is to say, all the unspeakable crimes that have come to be put between it and its idea, never found a place in Poland." [n]

The idealizing mood of glorifying Polish history was spurred on by the popularity of the large-scale magnificent canvases of the painter Jan Matejko (1838–93) and of the novelist Henryk Sienkiewicz (1846–1916) whose romances may be compared to those of Walter Scott or Alexandre Dumas. These Western writers, however, wrote without political purpose, as Sienkiewicz himself did in his "*Quo Vadis?*" More famous in Poland became his huge nationalistic epic trilogy "Ogniem i mieczem" (With Fire and Sword, 1884), "Potop" (The Deluge, 1886) and "Pan Wołodyjowski" (1887–8), a sentimental eulogy of Polish chivalry in the wars of the 17th century. Political thinkers like Władysław Gizbert Studnicki foresaw that the 20th century would not be a period of peace but one of great wars and that it was necessary to prepare the people for it. He came out for the necessity of a national state and with a call to deeds and uprisings. At the Polish Congress held in Washington in May, 1909, he demanded that the Poles should fight in the coming war against Russia and, as he could not foresee the simultaneous collapse of Austria and Russia, he wished to fight on the side of Austria with the goal of an Austro-Hungarian-Polish trialism. Austria should not seek her expansion towards the Balkans but along the Vistula and thus create with the help of the Poles a true bulwark for the protection of Europe.

The greatest Polish poet and artist of the period, Stanisław Wyspiański (1869–1907), [n] fused in his own art and personality the Konrad of Mickiewicz (with its glorification of Machiavellian striving for national victory and greatness) and the King-Spirit

of Słowacki (the proud embodiment of national
fury). In mighty images rarely surpassed in world
literature, perhaps never equalled in their totality,
the artist, under the influence of antiquity, of Wagner and Nietzsche, re-created for his generation the
whole heroic history of Poland from the legendary
past of Cracow, his native place, to Mickiewicz'
Legion of 1848. In his plays he wished to shake the
soul of the people out of lethargy into heroism, into
the fullness of an inspired life of action and strength.
Unflinchingly he accepted even the certainty of renewed ruin, death and cruel sacrifice as the road
to a new birth of national freedom to the new
Polish state. His two greatest plays Wesele (The
Wedding, 1901) and Wyzwolenie (Deliverance,
1903) proclaimed the need of a new armed rising.
To his despair he found the Polish intellectuals and
leaders in the midst of irresolute resignation and
half-hearted shames not ripe for it.[n]

The Liga narodowa (National League) founded
in 1886 under the influence of the old revolutionary
Zygmunt Fortunat Miłkowski (1822–1914) who had
fought in 1848–63, took the lead for an active policy.
Out of this movement came Dmowski who in his
"Myśli nowoczesnego Polaka" (Thoughts of a Modern Pole, 1903) put up Prussia and Prussian methods
as the model to follow in public affairs. The founder
of the National Democratic Party preached a gospel
of national egoism. "Critics of National Democracy
were not slow to point out the similarity between
these basic principles and the hatred methods em-
ployed in the Prussian provinces against the Poles
themselves." [n] The Polish National Democrats in
fact used against the Ukrainians and the Jews in the
Polish state methods surpassing in rigor those used
by the Prussians against the Poles.

A different brand of a semi-realistic and semi
romantic subordination of all considerations to the
goal of the national state was represented by Józef

Piłsudski (1867–1935), who in 1893 helped found the Polish Socialist Party and became the first editor of its then secret organ *Robotnik* (The Worker). "He had schooled himself for years on Słowacki," the great singer of national violence and hatred. For twenty years he worked incessantly for a military uprising and a military organization of the Polish nation. He became the embodiment of a soldierly nationalism. In 1904 he went to Tokyo to offer to the Japanese a Polish uprising if they would help. The following year he became the leader of armed bands in Russian Poland, the last deed of which in 1908 was the robbery of a large amount of government money from a mail train—an action regarded by Piłsudski as a capture of war booty. Then he left for Cracow where he organized the cadres of a Polish army. At the head of his Legion of sharp-shooters, at the outbreak of the war in 1914, he crossed the Russian frontier together with the Austrian armies, to become Poland's "man of destiny." [n] As a typical "soldier hero" he despised parliamentary democracy and parties. His career and his success were part of the general picture which arose for central and eastern Europe in the wake of World War I. Nor was the moral and political mood for which he stood in any way peculiar to the Slavs: it was shared by Germans and Italians, by Magyars and Rumanians. It triumphed at a time when Pan-Slavism was at its nadir for the whole century of its existence. Piłsudski and the Poles of his generation were hostile to Pan-Slavism. The only people among whom Pan-Slavism showed any sign of vitality at all after 1918, the Czechs, were the very ones relatively untouched by the new climate of violence and enthusiasm.

"The further the World War progressed," wrote Count Ottokar Czernin (1872–1932), Austro-Hungarian foreign minister from the end of 1916 to April, 1918, "the more it lost the character of an enterprise which could be directed by individuals. It assumed the character of a cosmic event disengaging itself more and more from the influence of single men even of the most powerful." [n] At the beginning of the War, the peoples of Austria-Hungary, including the Croats and the Czechs, on the whole fought loyally for Austria-Hungary. The primary cause for the fall of the Russian regime was not the disloyalty of its subjects but the appalling inefficiency and corruption of the court and administration. In Austria-Hungary Emperor Charles who succeeded his great-uncle Francis Joseph in November, 1916, a weak and badly advised man, tried in vain to conclude a separate peace and to federalize the Empire. His attempts to follow the course suggested by Palacký in 1848 failed because of their half-heartedness and because of Magyar and German intransigence. The year 1918 witnessed the final break-down of the system of 1815. Then four dynasties, the Habsburgs, the Hohenzollern, the Romanovs and the Ottomans, controlled the whole of central and eastern Europe. Now all four were gone; in their stead arose new nation-states. Chief among them were the three western Slav states, Poland, Czechoslovakia, and the Kingdom of the Serbs, Croats and Slovenes, later called Yugoslavia. Their formation which represented to a certain extent the triumph of the intentions of the Prague Slav Congress of 1848, resulted from the (temporary) disappearance of that German and Russian menace which Palacký had dreaded; it brought with it liberal democratic constitutions after the Western model, and thereby the apparent victory of the ideas of 1848; and it established close ties between Warsaw, Prague, Belgrade and Zagreb on the one hand and Paris, the hope and capital of 1848, on the other hand. But in spite of outward similarities, the solution of 1918 had neither liberal depth nor national duration. Strengthened by nationalism and liberalism, the twin

forces which the Holy Alliance had tried to keep
out and which in 1848 were for a time defeated,
these new nation-states were supposed to form a
bulwark against a new expansion of German militarism or Russian revolutionism and thus to help protect peace and liberty. Unfortunately, their liberalism was much too weak and too much undermined
by nationalism; their nationalism was too closely
linked up with revolutionism and militarism, to
become a reliable support for peace and liberty.

The truth of Palacký's insistence of 1848 on the
need of Austria ("if there were no Austria, it would
be necessary to create it") was borne out a century
later. Masaryk himself on the eve of World War
I "did not despair of an evolution (of Austria) in a
federal direction—what was often called a monarchical Switzerland, in which all the many nationalities of Austria-Hungary would attain equal rights." [n]
When war broke out, Masaryk abandoned that expectation. "His realism, based upon prolonged and
intimate study of Russian psychology and political
thought, warned him that Russia alone would never
be able to solve the problem of the Western Slav
nations, much less to bring them liberty. But while
the ultra-Russophiles (all Czechs were Russophiles
up to a certain point) were depressed by the terrible
reverses which followed upon the first victories of the
Tsarist armies, Masaryk never lost his balance, and
soon realized that the fate of his nation was bound
up with that of the Western democracies and America." [n]

But even more it was bound up, as Masaryk, in
the heated atmosphere of the war, apparently did
not realize, with the survival of some kind of Austrian
federation. In a confidential memorandum on the
independence of Bohemia, which he wrote in April,
1915, he miscalculated the future. "Austria was
created as a confederation of smaller states in the
Middle Ages, against the fierce Turks and Huns,

against the oppressive spirit of the age in general. Since the military spirit and oppressive propensities of nations have grown relatively weaker, and as there is some good hope that the war will bring about a longer time of peace (1870 was followed by a 45 years' peace), Bohemia can, during that time, relatively easily be consolidated. The necessary protection against hostile neighbors free Bohemia can get from alliances with equally threatened neighbours or with friendly neighbours. Bohemia will be contiguous with Poland and Russia, and perhaps with Serbia." [n]

Rarely have so few sentences contained so many unwarranted predictions. The military spirit and oppressive propensities of nations grew stronger not weaker after 1914; "fierce Turks and Huns" reappeared in a modernized and more dangerous form; the war did not bring about a long time of peace, and Bohemia was given no time for consolidation. Nor were alliances with neighbours a substitute for federation. Though Bohemia was contiguous with Poland, a spirit of bitter hostility grew up between these two Slav nations as soon as they were independent. [n] The supposition that Russia would remain a friendly neighbour, did not take into account Palacký's fear of the Russian trend toward a universal monarchy. Palacký believed that in modern times, for economic and military reasons, the problems of the existence and security of small nations could be solved only through federation and integration. Masaryk proclaimed from 1915 on, that the construction or reconstruction of independent Bohemia, Poland and Serbo-Croatia was "the very aim of regenerating Europe. All these questions together form the European problem." In reality, the regeneration of Europe after the immense loss of material and spiritual values in the war could be achieved only by less independence and by a growing unity in a spirit of conciliation.

Though the Western Slavs emerged as the real

victors of World War I, to the detriment of the
Germans and Russians (and Magyars), their victory
was not built on solid foundations and was therefore of short duration. In the hour of triumph, it
was overlooked that victory was due to an unusual
combination of circumstances which might not last.
In Warsaw and in Belgrade, and to a lesser extent
in Prague too, pride and confidence dominated where
modesty and moderation would have been advisable.
In a similar misunderstanding of history and of the
forces at work, the great Atlantic nations turned to
isolationism after 1919 and thereby undid the victory so dearly bought in the War. With the small
succession states in central-eastern Europe such an
attitude was even more shortsighted. They had
destroyed the Habsburg monarchy; they did not
create anything to take its place. Instead, the stra-
tegically most important barrier zone between Germans and Russians was filled by a number of weak
states, often bitterly hostile to each other; new
frontiers impeded commerce and communications;
and in their domestic structure Poland, Yugoslavia
and Czechoslovakia faced the problem of fiercely
contending nationalities and dissatisfied minorities.
For they were not nation-states, not even to the extent that Hungary before 1918 had been a nation-
state; they were multi-national states like Austria
without acknowledging it, however. Each one claimed
to be based on the principle of nationality. Yet even
their wisest statesman, Masaryk, openly interpreted
the principle of nationality to fit political aims.
"Though we advocate the principle of nationality,"
he wrote in the confidential memorandum of April,
1915, "we wish to retain our German minority. It
seems to be a paradox, but it is on the principle of
nationality that we retain the German minority.
Bohemia is a quite unique example of a mixed country . . ." [n] Unfortunately so many nationalities
tended to regard their own case as unique and their

claims as specially justified sometimes even by Providence. Masaryk took a similar "interpretation" attitude of the principle of nationality toward the Slovaks. Without consulting them, he declared: "The Slovaks are Bohemians, in spite of their use of their dialect as their literary language." [n] Some German writers were inclined to dispose similarly of the Swiss and the Dutch; and Slav peoples like Byelorussians and Ukrainians, Croats and Macedonians, have been equally divested of the rights of separate statehood and nationality by interested Slav neighbors.

In all these uncertainties and struggles there was after 1918 little talk of Pan-Slavism or Slav solidarity, movements and sentiments so much emphasized before 1914. Was their goal achieved with the disintegration of the Ottoman and Habsburg Empires? In any case, there was no sign of any Slav collaboration after 1918. [n] Czechoslovakia and Yugoslavia were allied in the Little Entente, it is true, but non-Slav Rumania was a member of this alliance too and Rumania remained faithful to her obligations towards Czechoslovakia when Yugoslavia had long turned away to befriend Czechoslovakia's enemies. Outside this one doubtful case of Slav collaboration, much more deeply cherished by the Czech statesmen than by the Serbs, no instance of Slav solidarity can be found in the period between the two wars. Independent Ukraine fell a victim to merciless Russian and Polish expansion; Poland proudly participated in the partition of Czechoslovakia in the fall of 1938; Russia followed the example one year later without hesitation and on a larger scale in the partition of Poland. Both did it under pretense of reclaiming their "brothers by blood" from the domination by other Slavs. The Poles felt and professed greater friendship for the Magyars than for any Slav people. The hostility between Czechs and Slovaks, Serbs and Croats, grew more bitter after 1918 than it had ever been previously. In spite of some attempts at reconciliation, the gulf separating Serbs and Bulgars remained wide open. Czechoslovakia and Yugoslavia were among the last European nations to recognize the Soviet Union; Russian *émigré* monarchists found a refuge in Belgrade, while Russian and Ukrainian liberals were welcomed in Prague and there given the opportunity for studying and developing their traditional national cultures.

Among the Balkan Slavs and among the Czechs and Slovaks, much sympathy for the Russian people and for Slavdom remained alive; on the governmental level it was expressed only in Czechoslovakia. This fact is the more remarkable in view of the Western character of the Czechs and of their government headed by Masaryk. Among all the Slav peoples the Czechs are, in social structure and national attitudes, farthest removed from "Eurasia" and the "Balkans"—their land does not form part of the vast northeastern European plain which stretches from the Ural to the Elbe, and has never been subject to Russian or Turkish rule. Masaryk, though born on the border of Moravia and Slovakia and educated in German universities, was a Westerner through and through. "I overcame the Slav anarchy in myself," he told Karel Čapek, "by the help of the British philosophers Locke, Hume and other empiricists." His inaugural lecture at Prague University was on Hume and Skepticism. Of all German philosophers he honored Kant most highly because of his rigorous critical method, and his adverse attitude to the Russian mind was based on the fact that the Russians knew too little of Kant and too much of historical myths and utopian revolutionism. The name of the party which he founded in 1900, the "Realists"—a party of a small and unpopular minority of thoughtful individuals, represented at its strongest in the Austrian Reichsrat by two deputies, both professors of philosophy—he explained to Emil Ludwig as meaning "res contra historiam." [n] He knew Russia better than any other Western statesman and was from the beginning an astute critic and inflexible opponent of Bolshevism. In his *Sur le Bolshévisme* he wrote in 1921: "The Bolsheviks have accepted Marxism and pride themselves on being its only Orthodox adherents. They don't realize how much they owe to Bakunin, the adversary of Marx. From him they took over the mystic faith in the revolution, in the Russian people, in its unique socialist and communist ability . . . All the short-comings which characterized the Russian state, the Russian school, the Russian Church, etc., characterize also the Bolshevik state and regime because they come from the same people and have undergone the same formation." [n] In his message to the Czechoslovak people and parliament on the first anniversary of the proclamation of Czechoslovak independence, October 28, 1919, Masaryk pointed out that Lenin was a typical Russian and that the Bolshevik regime had not outgrown, but had continued, Tsarism and even the methods and spirit of Ivan the Terrible. This view is the more remarkable because at that time Bolshevism was regarded generally as a "Western," un-Russian ideology. In the Christmas issue of the *Lidové Noviny* of 1920 Masaryk stressed the fact, so often overlooked in the West, that Lenin's revolution was not undertaken in self-defense against an oppressive regime, since Russia had by then a regime of great liberty, but that it sprang from a lust for power. "I saw with my own eyes the horrible acts of the Bolshevik revolution. They revealed an almost barbarian cruelty, something almost bestial; I felt the greatest moral horror for the apparently superfluous sacrifices of human lives." [n] His friend and collaborator, Emanuel Rádl, could truly say of him: "In the history of Slav thought, Masaryk's philosophy represented a definite, decisive and triumphant turn to the West." [n]

Yet Masaryk always recognized the deep-rooted Slav feeling of the Czechs. "The Bohemians are, since the awakening of the national feeling, strongly Slavophile," he wrote in 1915. "The Bohemian people, it must be emphasized once more, are thoroughly Russophile," he wrote in the same memorandum destined for English and not for Russian politicians. "A Russian dynasty, in whatever form, would be most popular. At any rate, the Bohemian politicians wish the establishment of the Kingdom of Bohemia in full accordance with Russia. Russia's wishes and plans will be of determinating influence." [n] No Polish or Ukrainian, Serb or Croat statesman would or could have written about the political plans of his people in such a way. This ardent Russophilism went even so far, according to Masaryk in the same memorandum, that the Czechs while aspiring to national independence on behalf of the principle of nationality, hoped and wished "that Turkey would be wiped off the map" and would become part of Russia. These Pan-Slav sentiments continued in the entirely changed political situation after 1918 among some of the Western Slavs and especially among the Czechs. They found no opportunity of expressing themselves until the 1930's when a strengthened Germany threatened to resume its march eastwards. In his *Mein Kampf* Adolf Hitler expressed the German desire for smashing the European pattern established by the "dictated" peace of Versailles, the peace to which the Western Slav nations owed their new statehood. Beyond that, there lived in him the old contempt of the *Grenzdeutscher*, of the German who had grown up on the frontiers of the German-Slav struggle, for the Slavs, and the German romantic emphasis on the racial past and on the community of blood and folk tradition. It should be noted, however, that Hitlerism aroused no Pan-Slav or Slavophile sentiments among Poles or Slovaks, Croats or Bulgarians. It exercised its strongest influence surprisingly among that Slav people which under Lenin's leadership seemed to have abandoned for ever a Slav or Russo-centered attitude.

The Russian Revolution of March, 1917, was motivated as much by liberalism as by patriotism, as much by the desire for a free state, respecting the individual, as for an efficient state, able to assure the rank of the Russian nation among the great powers and the welfare of its citizens. The Revolution failed because the masses did not understand their stake in juridical liberalism and enlightened patriotism. Both were Western concepts, alien to the traditional thinking of the Russian people. When the liberal patriotic revolution, which tried to follow in the wake of 1776, 1789 and 1848, perished in the terror of Lenin's regime, apparently not only liberalism but also patriotism became its victim. Lenin assumed power as the disciple of the international proletarian socialism of Marx and Engels: this Western ideology caused many observers to overlook how many ancient Russian traditions and attitudes survived in the new regime. The new government transferred the capital from St. Petersburg back to Moscow and entrenched itself behind the ancient walls of the Kremlin. Many of its spokesmen regarded it as an entirely new beginning, as an order guided by reason and science alone. But Moscow and the Kremlin harbored tenacious memories of Tsarist rule, of Russian destiny, and of imperial greatness.[n] The Bolshevik leaders were faced by the task of imposing their ideology on the many peoples of the Russian Empire and with its help to train the masses for an active participation in the industrialization and modernization of the country. For assuring the continuous security of their positions of power and for the success of the ideology, they needed as mighty, as large and as efficient a basis as possible. They had to follow a twofold line—to win on the one hand the various nationalities for co-operation with the new rulers without diminishing on the other hand the extent of power of the Moscow-ruled state.

Though the Declaration of the Rights of the Peoples of Russia of November 15, 1917, proclaimed their right to full self-determination, including secession from Russia and setting up independent states, this "right" was always qualified by a superior "duty" —the power-considerations of the class war and the strengthening of the proletarian revolution. In his pamphlet on "Marxism and the National Question" Stalin had made this clear as far back as January, 1913. "The nation has the right of secession. But that does not mean that it must do this under all circumstances, that autonomy or separation will always and everywhere be advantageous to the nation, that is to its majority, that is to the working classes. . . . All these are questions of which the solution depends on the concrete historical conditions." The Petrograd City and all-Russian Conference of the Russian Social Democratic Workers' Party (Bolsheviki) adopted in April, 1917, a resolution on the national question, in which it was stated: "The question of the right of nations freely to secede is unjustifiably confused with the question of the expediency of the secession of one or another nation at one or another moment. This latter question must in each separate instance be determined entirely by a proletarian party from the point of view of the interests of the general development and of the proletarian class struggle for socialism." In 1917 and 1918 the Bolsheviks recognized national independence wherever they had to do it for the time being as in the case of the Poles, the Finns, and the Baltic Republics, countries lying near to Europe and European influence. In all other cases the Red Army re-established Moscow's unlimited control in spite of the wishes of the non-Russian peoples for national independence. These peoples were in their large majority not communists and therefore unable to "understand" the dialectic needs of history. The Ukrainians, the Georgians, the Mohammedans of Central Asia were quickly subjected by Moscow's armed forces in the interest, as it was said, of the proletariat and its vanguard, the communist party, which was strictly centralized and unified from Moscow throughout the vast empire.

On the other hand, Lenin recognized that the imposition of the new policy if it was not to be wrecked in advance on the violent mistrust of populations that had learned in the course of centuries to expect only evil from Moscow and from the Russians, had to be applied with some regard to the national feelings of these populations. He knew that his policy was endangered by "Pan-Russian chauvinism," as the official terminology of that time called the widespread attitude of many party members who wished to maintain the privileged position of the Russian element, language and culture within the Soviet Union. According to repeated warnings by Lenin and Stalin uttered in numerous speeches from 1918 to 1930, this spirit of Russian chauvinism showed itself to an ever-growing degree in the ranks of the communist party and of its representatives who had to carry out its policy among the non-Russian populations. Until the 1930's this pan-Russian nationalism was officially rejected and combatted as a "Tsarist" heritage. The Union of the Socialist Soviet Republics was constituted in 1923 as an international and supra-national federation. Part I of its constitution declared that "the very structure of Soviet power, international in its class essence, impels the toiling masses of the Soviet Republics to enter the path of union to form one socialist family. . . . The will of the peoples constituting the Soviet Republics which recently assembled in the congresses of their respective Soviets and there unanimously decided to form the Union of Socialist Soviet Republics, is a reliable guarantee that the Union is a voluntary association of peoples enjoying equal rights, that the right of each republic to secede from the Union is inviolable, that admission to the Union is open to all socialist Soviet Republics whether now existing or hereafter to come into being, that the new federal state . . . will mark a new and decisive step towards uniting the workers of the world into a World Socialist Soviet Republic."

Yet the Soviet Union was a strange federation from the beginning. The enormous numerical and historical preponderance of one partner in it, even without the acknowledged surviving pan-Russian chauvinism, made a true federation as it exists in Switzerland or the United States impossible. The Soviet Union in this respect resembled much more Bismarck's Germany with its undisputed preponderance of Prussia. There, however, true autonomy was given in varying degrees to the component parts and their dynasties; in the Soviet Union all power was centered, to a degree nowhere on earth equalled, in one city and in one man." Moscow, retained as the capital of a "supra-national" federation, inevitably represented old and hated memories to the non-Russian peoples and a symbol of national greatness and power to the Russians. Should the peoples of the Soviet Union ever voluntarily decide to form for mutual economic advantage and security a federation, the first condition of its success and the proof of its sincerity would be the transfer of the capital from Moscow and the Kremlin with their sinister connotations throughout Russian history to some nationally and historically neutral site. Of the whole area of the Soviet Union which in 1926 measured 21,355,520 sq. km., the Russian Republic, one of then six component republics, covered 19,758,000 sq. km., or almost nine tenths of the area, with more than two thirds of the whole population (100,-

800,000 in the Russian Republic out of a total of 146,943,000) living there.

But this Russian preponderance implied on the part of the Soviet governments no Pan-Slav or Slavophile policy, certainly no friendship or interest for the new Western Slav states After the attempt of the Red Army to regain control of Poland was repelled in the outskirts of Warsaw in August, 1920, Soviet Russia turned its attention to Asia where Lenin hoped to organize the nationalist unrest of the Oriental peoples for a decisive struggle against the West.[n] On February 26, 1921, he concluded a treaty of friendship with Persia which abrogated all the capitulations and concessions enjoyed previously by Russia there, wiped out Persia's debts to Russia and transferred to the Persian government the roads and railways built by Russia in northern Persia. The next month, on March 16, a similar treaty of friendship with Turkey followed. "Recognizing that national movements in the Orient are similar to and in harmony with the struggle of the Russian workers for the new social order," article 4 of the treaty stated, "the two contracting parties assert solemnly the rights of these peoples to freedom, independence, free choice of such forms of governments as they themselves desire to have." In June, 1921, Soviet Russia established the first people's republic in Mongolia and on November 5, 1921 concluded a treaty of alliance with it. By the end of 1922 the government of Moscow had re-established control over all former Russian territory in the Far East and was working for an alliance with China. Its efforts in Asia were directed against the position which the Western powers had gained in World War I and in the peace treaties following it. The same goal prompted the conclusion of the Rapallo agreement with Germany on April 16, 1922. All these steps tried to destroy the system of Versailles and the League of Nations, the very system to which Czechoslovakia, Poland and Yugoslavia owed their existence.

This "anti-imperialist" attitude was also expressed in the rewriting of the history of Russia and of the world by the Marxist school of historiography in the Soviet Union led by Mikhail Nikolaevich Pokrovsky (1868–1932). He joined the Bolshevik party as early as 1905. After 1917 he became one of the leaders and organizers of the new educational system. The *Russkaya istoriya v samom szhatom ocherke* (Brief Russian History) which he published in Moscow in 1920 and which appeared in its 10th edition in 1931, was dignified by Lenin with an enthusiastic letter of recommendation: "I like your new book immensely. . . . It should, in my opinion, be translated into the European languages. I will permit myself one slight remark. To make it a textbook (and this it must become), it must be supplemented with a chronological index." [n] The article devoted to Pokrovsky in the *Encyclopaedia of the Social Sciences*, written in 1933, stated that in his works Pokrovsky developed "an Orthodox Marxist interpretation of Russian history which serves today as the historical justification for the Soviet Union. . . . He labored successfully to stabilize Marxism-Leninism-Stalinism as the principle of scientific investigation and doctrine and to organize the class struggle on the 'scientific,' the 'general ideological' and particularly the 'historical' fronts." [n] The *Malaya Sovyetskaya Entsiklopediya*, published in Moscow in 1930, described Pokrovsky as "the most distinguished Marxist historian not only in the USSR but in the whole world," probably a true description.

Pokrovsky's interpretation of history was entirely free of any nationalist sentiment or any glorification of Russia. He rejected Tsarist policy and Tsarist heroes, regarded the Russian rulers as oppressors and their policy as repeatedly guilty of aggressive wars and imperialist exploitation. He opposed the patriotic legends of other Russian historians and writers.

At the first All-Soviet Conference of Marxist Historians he declared that the annexation of Georgia by Russia in 1801 was a crude imperialist grab which could not be defended as protection of Georgia against Turkey or Persia. Such a defense would be as bad as defending Russia's war against Turkey in 1877 as an altruistic support for Bulgaria while in reality it was dictated by the self-interest and appetite of Russian imperialism. "In the past we Russians—and I am a most pure blooded Great Russian—were the biggest robbers imaginable." He regarded Tsarist Russia as chiefly responsible for the outbreak of World War I.

All that suddenly changed in 1934. Pokrovsky's disciples who had tried to liquidate "bourgeois" historians were now as mercilessly persecuted themselves. Pokrovsky's theories were subjected to violent official attacks as anti-Marxist and unbolshevik. Pokrovsky maintained that Russian history was not distinct or different from other, especially Western, history, but that it repeated with a time-lag the general development; any peculiar traits of Russian history or structure could be explained by Russia's backwardness. In 1934 the Soviet government directed the rewriting of Russia's history and of her relationship to the outside world. The old nationalist concept of the originality and unique character of the Russian past and people was restored to full honor and the national roots and purpose of the Russian Revolution were discovered.[n] Soon this reinterpretation of history encompassed the totality of Russian and Soviet life. On November 14, 1936, the successful comic opera "Bogatyri" (The Valiant Knights) by Demyan Bedny, the most popular Bolshevik poet,[n] was suddenly withdrawn from the stage of the Moscow Kamerny Theatre where it had been presented by Alexander Yakovlevich Tairov, the founder of the theatre and one of the three most famous Russian stage directors.

In the play Bedny had made fun of the old legendary heroes and of the Christianization of Russia, an attitude which until then had been steadily propagated by the Soviet government. Now, however, Bedny was accused of having caricatured the "magnificent heroes" of the Russian folk legends, the bylini, who represented "the courage, the generosity and the ingenuity of the Russian people in their glorious struggle against the Tartar invasion." Nor could it be tolerated, the surprising new official point of view went, that the conversion of the Russians to Christianity under Vladimir the Saint (around 990) be mockingly depicted as having originated in a drinking bout.[n] A few months later on March 28, 1937, *Pravda* took Pokrovsky to task for having asserted that "the conquest of Russia by the Tartars was not the invasion, as Solovyev taught, of an agrarian country by the savages of the Steppes, but the encounter of equal civilizations, of which it would be difficult to say which of the two was superior to the other." [n] Pokrovsky's statement that the Great-Russian nationality which had founded the Moscow state originated largely in an intermingling of Slav and Finnish blood, was branded as an "anti-national heresy." At the same time the pre-revolutionary Russian historian Yevgenii Viktorovich Tarle, in 1931 attacked as "a class enemy, an imperialist and a foe of Bolshevism," was recalled from exile in Asia and became the celebrated historian of the defense of the Russian motherland by a patriotic people against the invaders of 1812 and of 1854.[n]

In a new and unprecedented way Stalin from 1936 on simultaneously appealed to the class consciousness of socialism and the traditional emotionalism of nationalism. The textbook on the history of the Soviet Union *Istoriya USSR. Kratky kurs* (A Brief Course in the History of the USSR) by Prof. A. V. Shestakov, which was chosen as the most satisfactory textbook by a special government commission on August

22, 1937, opened its introduction with the statement: "The USSR is the land of socialism. There is
only one socialist country on earth—it is our motherland." And the introduction concluded: "We love
our motherland and we must know well her wonderful history. Whoever knows history will better understand the present, will better fight the enemies of our
country, and will consolidate socialism." [n]

National holidays of the past, entirely uncon-
nected with the class struggle or with the progress of
human liberty or of social justice, were from 1937
on officially celebrated with greatest emphasis. In
September, 1937, the 125th anniversary of the battle
of Borodino, a village 70 miles southwest of Moscow, where the Russian army under Mikhail Illario-
novich Prince Golenishchev Kutuzov (1745–1813)
tried to block Napoleon's march on Moscow, was
made the occasion of great national celebration and
rejoicing.[n] In the same year the one-hundredth anniversary of the death of Pushkin, and in May, 1938,
the 750th anniversary of the famous mediaeval
Russian *Word of the Campaign of Igor* became national holidays. The *Word* (Slovo o polku Igoreve)
glorifies the expedition of Prince Igor, son of Svyato-
slav and grandson of Oleg, who lived approximately
from 1151 to 1202, against the Polovtsy in 1185.
Izvestiya characterized the *Word* as "the incarnation
of the power of the political and national consciousness of the Russian people," and *Pravda* praised it,
as the Slavophiles had done before, as proof carried
by the Russian people in defending Europe against
Asiatic hordes. "The history of their people is dear
to Soviet men, to the patriots of the socialist fatherland. With a sacred respect and with love we turn
the pages of the old legends which speak of the fear-
lessness, the courage and the glory of our ancestors." [n]

This new chant to the glory of the fatherland and
of racial ancestors replaced in the 1930's, the spirit

of the International. "His Life for the Tsar," the
famous opera by Mikhail Ivanovich Glinka (1803–
57) which had first been performed on October 9,
1836, and with which modern Russian nationalist
music had begun, was once again staged in Moscow.
The libretto by Baron George Rosen (1800–66),
praising a peasant loyally sacrificing his life for the
Tsar during the Polish invasion of Russia in the early
17th century, was retained, but the name of the
opera was changed to "Ivan Susanin" and the former
chorus

> *Glorify thyself, glorify thyself, Holy Russia!*
> *Upon the Russian throne ascends*
> *Our legitimate Russian Tsar!*
> *He comes to us in glory,*
> *Our Orthodox sovereign Tsar!*

was modernized into

> *Glorify thyself, native soil.*
> *Glorify thyself, my native land.*
> *May for ever and to eternity be strong*
> *Our beloved native land.*

Was this nationalist emphasis due only to the fear
of Hitler's plans?[n] Or did Stalin recognize how
slight, in spite of a quarter of a century of indoc-
trination and terror, the impact of socialist education and class consciousness was on the Russian people? Lenin had learned his international class
theory from Marx and Engels; was Stalin now impressed by the powerful appeal of the national past
with the help of which Hitler cemented the Germans into a unified and dedicated instrument of his
will? The Slavophiles and the early Russian nationalists had drawn their inspiration from the West,
from the German romanticists and the French tra-
ditionalists. The later Russian nationalists, the generation of Danilevsky and Katkov, were impressed
by Bismarck and pan-Germanism; the new Stalinist

nationalism with its chauvinistic fixation on Russian originality and priority and its anti-plutocratic and anti-Western appeal to the masses probably owed much to the triumph of Hitler.

Less ideological and more realistic was the change of Soviet diplomacy from the pre-1933 pattern in reply to the rise of Hitler. The famous "Popular Front" policy brought a *rapprochement* with the democracies; the Soviet Union entered the League of Nations; Maxim Maximovich Litvinov, People's Commissar of Foreign Affairs from 1930 to 1939, negotiated a treaty of friendship with the United States. At the seventeenth congress of the Communist Party of the Soviet Union, in January, 1934, Stalin declared: "Some people think that war must be prepared by the superior race, i.e., the Germanic race, against the inferior races and especially against the Slavs." Less than twenty years after the murder in Sarayevo which had unleashed what many regarded as a war between the Germanic and the Slav races, the ominous words were heard again, this time not only in Germany and from racialists but from an unexpected quarter, from the heir of the November revolution. Litvinov was more circumspect when he addressed the Czechoslovaks on January 3, 1935: "I will not speak of the ties of race and of language which exist between the most important peoples of our Union and the Czechoslovak people. The reason I will not speak of them is that, in the past, these motives have more than once been exploited for imperialist ends, and even today racial theories sometimes serve to cover barbarian ideologies and regimes. Nevertheless, these affinities do exist."

Again, as in the 1860's, Pan-Russian nationalism was to prove much stronger in Russia than Pan-Slavism. The Kremlin thought of itself, not of the Slav "brothers." The spirit of Rapallo was revived. The Soviet-German treaty of August 23, 1939, abandoned the Western Slavs to the Germans. Once more

Germans and Russians united in their rejection of the West, in their opposition to "Anglo-French imperialism," and in their disregard for the Western Slavs. Germans and Russians were now presented to the Soviet public as the two nations which had suffered most from World War I, the real victims of that war to which the Western Slavs owed their new national existence. Stalin answered the congratulatory message which Joachim Ribbentrop, German Foreign Minister, sent him on the occasion of his sixtieth birthday with unusual warmth: "The friendship of the peoples of Germany and the Soviet Union, cemented by blood, will long remain firm." Obedient to Moscow's directions, the communists in all lands tried to undermine the war effort and to slow preparations against Hitler's fascism and directed all their attacks against the democracies which resisted German aggression. Instead of fighting German fascism the French communist leader Maurice Thorez set an example; he deserted the French army and fled to Russia. The British government, fighting for the survival of the last bastion of liberty against the victorious onrush of national socialist forces, had to suspend publication of the *Daily Worker* on January 21, 1941, because it systematically published matter "calculated to cement opposition to the prosecution of the war to a successful issue."

The Communist attitude to Hitler and the democracies changed overnight with the sudden attack of Germany on the Soviet Union on June 22, 1941. The situation was entirely different from 1914. Then the Russian Empire entered the war at least partly in defense of a small Slav nation. Nevertheless in its propaganda it made officially no use of Pan-Slavism. This time, however, Stalin had done everything possible to maintain good relations with Hitler's Germany in spite of German aggression and barbarity in Bohemia, Poland and Serbia; only when he

failed in his efforts at friendship with Germany,
Stalin appealed to Pan-Slavism in a way never accepted by any previous Russian government. Thus
it came about that World War II—though again
some Slav peoples, Bulgarians, Croatians and Slovaks, fought on the German side—was the first time
that Pan-Slavism was propagated from Moscow as
an official doctrine. And again World War II ended,
at least in central-eastern Europe, in an unforeseen
way: it entirely undid the results of World War I
and the victory of the West Slavs; the Pan-Slav
dreams of the Moscow Congresses of 1867 and of
Danilevsky seemed realized in 1945, when the Eastern Slavs, the Russians, emerged as the victors over
the Germans and over the Western Slavs and Russian influence reached that very line from Stettin to
Trieste which some Russian nationalist dreamers
had fixed as the frontier in the late 1860's.

3

The Triumphs of the East-Slavs After World War II

FROM AUGUST, 1939, to June, 1941, the Soviet Union followed definitely a Russian and neither an anti-fascist nor a Pan-Slav policy. Not the slightest sympathy for the Czechs and Poles suffering under German occupation was expressed. The Russian ascendancy was enforced at home when in 1939 the Mohammedan peoples of the Soviet Union who had previously in the "progressive" internationalist phase of Leninism, replaced their Arabic alphabet by Latin had to adopt instead the Russian script. In international relations Leninist communism conducted during World War I a violent defeatist propaganda in both warring camps. In 1939, subversive communist propaganda was resumed, but only against the democratic powers. "Moreover, officially even ostentatiously, help was granted to the camp of fascism so that, from 1939 to 1941, the Soviet Union could be considered a non-belligerent partner of the Axis. From the policy of benevolent neutrality towards the Axis the Soviet Union was removed against its will. Circumstances made it an ally of the democracies. This change was performed reluctantly, only because no other choice was left." [n] The communist leadership was convinced even as late as May, 1941, that its policy of neutrality would safeguard Russia's peace.[n] It was sorely wrong, which of course did not prevent it from boasting, in January, 1945, of having always correctly foreseen the course of events and of being alone able to recognize how and whither events must develop in the future.[n] Stalin in his report to the Moscow Soviet on November 6, 1941, justifiably accused the German invaders of having "perfidiously attacked our peace-loving country." [n] Against its foresight and will, the Soviet leadership was forced to enter a war, not for social justice, for democracy or for proletarian revolution, but a "war of national liberation," "the great patriotic war," called by the same name as the one given by the Russians to the war fought by Tsarist Russia in 1812. In his report to the Moscow Soviet mentioned above, Stalin officially used words not heard since the "Great October Socialist Revolution," the twenty-fourth anniversary of which the Soviet was celebrating. Hitler, he said, was out to "exterminate the Slav peoples, the Russians, Poles, Czechs, Slovaks, Bulgarians, Ukrainians and Byelorussians." The Nazis had the audacity "to call for the annihilation of the great Russian nation, the nation of Plekhanov and Lenin, Belinsky and Chernyshevsky, Pushkin and Tolstoy, Glinka and Tschaikovsky, Gorky and Chekhov, Sechenov and Pavlov, Repin and Surikov, Suvorov and Kutuzov." The next day in his address to the Red Army Parade he called upon the Soviet soldiers to let themselves be inspired in this war by "the manly images of our great ancestors—Alexander Nevsky, Dmitri Donskoy, Kuzma Minin, Dmitri Pozharsky, Alexander Suvorov, Mikhail Kutuzov." The feudal saints of the Orthodox Church and the generals serving Tsarist reaction, all of them exclusively Russian, were proclaimed as the ancestors of the supra-national revolutionary Red Army.[n]

In the war years the Russian fatherland completely overshadowed the Soviet fatherland.[n] Traditional national values were restored without any reference either to class war or to the revolutionary struggle and without regard for the national feeling of the non-Russian Soviet nationalities. To the nationalist heroes and warriors of the past, everything was forgiven. The Russian General Prince Peter Bagration who was mortally wounded in the battle at Borodino was presented at the end of S. Golubov's novel *General Bagration* (1943) as kissing the Emperor's signature on a letter of thanks just brought to him and as dying with the words: "Soul and body alike and my blood to the last drop, I give all to my fatherland and to His Majesty's service." [n] Field Marshal Count Alexander Vasilyevich Suvarov (1729–1800) who on the Tsar's behalf, subdued with unsparing cruelty the peasant rebellion of Pugachev and the last resistance of free Poland— his sack and massacre of Ismail in Bessarabia in 1790 equalled in horror the notorious excesses of history —became the greatest hero of the communist youth; even General Alexei Brussilov who, in May, 1917, had been appointed Commander-in-Chief of the Russian army which the Bolsheviks had done everything at that time to undermine, was honored by a great war novel and by the "deep respect" which the Red Army paper, *Krasnaya zvezda*, expressed on September 3, 1943 for "the man who in the stern years of the last war upheld with dignity the honor and glory of the Russian army."

Russian nationalism did not confine itself to a defensive patriotism, the chauvinism of which might be explained by the military catastrophe facing the country. It immediately asserted itself in an aggressive way. The annexation of eastern Poland, of Bessarabia and of part of Bukovina could be "justified" by nationalism, by the desire of uniting all Ukrainians and Byelorussians under the Soviet flag (though this unification deprived the Soviet Ukrainians of that consideration which they had received from Moscow when the Soviet Ukraine was yet to attract the "brothers by race" living in Poland and Rumania). No similar justification existed for the annexation of the Baltic Republics. Naturally many Russian non-Bolshevik nationalists acclaimed this step. People who had pleaded for the independence of the Magyars or the Irish, accepted the control by Moscow of Transcaucasia, of the Baltic coast and of the Ukraine, as justified by Russian needs for security and economy. The fate of the small Baltic peoples which in their twenty years of independence had achieved relatively high standards of living but had no historical past and no friends abroad to whom to appeal, was especially cruel.ⁿ Under these circumstances it was only natural that the International was abolished as the national anthem of the Soviet Union. Its ringing call "the International unites the human race" sounded strange in an atmosphere satiated with the glory of Velikaya Rus, the great Russia as distinct from the rest of mankind. The daring challenge to the self-reliance of the masses, "Nobody will bring us liberation, neither a Tsar, nor a God, nor a hero," became unacceptable in the era of Veliky Stalin, the great Stalin, Tsar, God and hero to his people and, what no Tsar had claimed, to all of progressive mankind.

In his election speech broadcast from Moscow on February 9, 1946, Stalin praised the "Soviet multi-national state system" as having survived successfully the test of the war, because it was built on foundations promoting the feeling of friendship and fraternal collaboration between the various peoples of the USSR. But in June, 1941, the Soviet government thought itself obliged to apply against one of these peoples a "barbarous measure" which the Tsarist government had long hesitated to decide upon. These were the Russian Germans who since the later eighteenth century had been settled along the lower Volga and had developed there a prosperous community. In 1916, two years after the outbreak of World War I, the Russian government made up its mind to remove the Volga Germans temporarily for the duration of the war, but the March Revolution intervened before the plan could be carried out. After November, 1917 Lenin, grateful to German socialism, singled out these Volga Germans for especially favorable treatment. The Volga German Oblast was the first autonomous unit created by the Communist Government (in July, 1918) and was raised in 1924 to the status of an autonomous republic of the RSFSR. The city of Pokrovsk was renamed "Engels" and became the capital of the Republic; the other large town, Katherinenstadt, named after Catherine II who settled the Germans there in 1764, was rebaptized Marxstadt." In June, 1941, Stalin apparently became convinced that two decades of Soviet life and education and of his leadership which supposedly promoted the friendship and fraternal solidarity of peoples were a complete failure. While Hitler's armies were still far away in western Russia, Stalin ordered, without any proof of collective treason or any public or secret trial, the permanent eviction and dispersion of the Volga Germans. The autonomy granted with such great promises two decades before proved to be nothing but a scrap of paper. The region was cleared of all traces of German culture and ruthlessly Russified. Not even the names of Marx and Engels protected the cities from a Russian nationalist re-baptism. This policy of wholesale destruction of a cultural and political entity created by the Bolshevists themselves was not carried through on a class but purely on a racial basis.

Somewhat different was the case of four Mohammedan peoples in the Soviet Union. On December 17, 1917, a proclamation of the new Soviet government signed by Lenin and Stalin was addressed to the Moslems of Russia and the East: "The rule of the robbers and enslavers of the peoples of the earth is about to end. . . . A new world is being born, a world of workers and free men . . . Moslems of Russia, Tartars of the Volga and the Crimea, Kirgiz and Sarts of Siberia and Turkestan . . . Chechens and mountaineers of the Caucasus—all those whose mosques and chapels have been destroyed, whose beliefs and customs have been trampled under foot by the Tsars and oppressors of Russia! Henceforth your beliefs and customs, your national and cultural institutions, are free and inviolable. Build your national life freely and unhindered." In 1943 and 1944, four of the Mohammedan autonomous Soviet states, the Kalmyk ASSR, the Crimean Tartar ASSR, the Chechen-Ingush and the Karachayev autonomous regions in the northern Caucasus, were all removed from the map and from life, extinguished without leaving a trace in their ancient homes, the survivors transported to unknown regions in northern Asia, their languages eradicated, their cities and villages renamed. No memory was to remain of these historical communities. The lands were re-settled by Russians. No reasons were given for these nationalist excesses, all apparently based upon the assumption of a collective racial "guilt." As these territories were reached by the invading German armies, it can be assumed that parts of the populations collaborated with the Germans. In any case, many Soviet citizens of all nationalities went over to the German side; if Hitler had followed a less beastly policy of human extermination and degradation, the number of the elements disloyal to Stalinism would have been probably much larger and might have decided the war. Under these circumstances Stalin apparently became convinced that he could count only upon the support of the Great Russians, to whose nationalist emotions the annexations of the years 1939–41 had appealed and among

whom some began to look upon Stalin as the
leader who would fulfill both the Pan-Slav and Pan-
Asian expansion hopes of the extreme Russian
nationalists of the nineteenth century, and the utopia
of universal social justice dreamt of by some Slavophile messianists.

Stalin, conscious of the debt which he owed to
the Great Russians, acknowledged it publicly in the
toast with which he concluded the Kremlin banquet
for Red Army commanders on May 24, 1945: "I
should like to drink to the health of our Soviet people . . . and first of all to the health of the Russian
people. I drink first of all to the health of the Russian people because it is the most outstanding nation
of all the nations forming the Soviet Union. . . .
It has won in this war universal recognition as
the leading force in the Soviet Union among all the
peoples of our country . . . The confidence of the
Russian people in the Soviet government was the
decisive force which ensured the historic victory
over the enemy of mankind—fascism." The historical sorrows and triumphs of Russian imperialism
now became officially Stalin's. After he had attacked
Japan in August, 1945—breaking his pact of friendship and non-aggression of 1941 with Japan as treacherously as Hitler had broken his with Stalin—he
celebrated the quick victory in a broadcast from
Moscow on September 2, in which he said: "The
defeat of Russian troops in 1904 in the period of the
Russo-Japanese war left grave memories in the minds
of our people. It was a dark stain on our country.
Our people trusted and awaited the day when Japan
would be routed and the stain wiped out. For forty
years have we, men of the older generation, waited
for this generation, waited for this day. And now this
day has come." This astonishing declaration, which
resembled so closely Mussolini's triumph over wiping
out the stain of the battle of Adua forty years later
in the victorious war against Ethiopia, was a com-

plete reversal of the official attitude of Russian socialists in 1905, an attitude still taught in the high-school
textbooks published by the Soviet government in
1941: "Lenin and the Bolsheviks worked for the
defeat of the Tsarist government in this predatory
and shameful war (the Russian war against Japan
in 1904), because the defeat facilitated the victory
of the revolution over Tsarism. In one of his leaflets
against the war, Comrade Stalin wrote about the
necessity of defeat: 'Let us wish that this war will
become a still greater disaster for the Tsarist regime
than was the Crimean War. . . . Then serfdom was
ended. Now, as a consequence of this war, we will
bury the child of serfdom, the Tsarist regime with
its stinking secret police and gendarmes.' " [n]

Thus the Soviet Union after thirty years revived
the language and aspirations of old Russia—assumed
to have been definitely buried in the ten November
days of 1917 which shook the world—and revived
them at their most nationalist and imperialist mood,
a mood never before sanctified as official policy and
always resisted by strong liberal and humanitarian
trends of thought. But the new Stalinist nationalism
did not shed the world-wide implications and ambitions of Leninism. What emerged, was akin to the
universal Russian monarchy which Palacký had
dreaded, but with a new kind of monarch at its head,
a man of the masses, a bearer of the social gospel,
and endowed with such qualities of "genius" and
"omniscience" as no Russian ruler and no leader of
a people had ever claimed. It was only natural that
in such an atmosphere the ghost of Pan-Slavism
should rise again—not the Pan-Slavism of the West
and of 1848, but the Pan-Slavism of Moscow and
of 1867, a Pan-Slavism which preached the liberation
of the other Slavs from alien influences by the Russian people, a Pan-Slavism which was a Pan-Russism.
The chairman of the Commission on credentials of
the Council of Nationalities of the Supreme Soviet,

P. A. Sharia, according to *Izvestya*, March 15, 1946, enlarged on Stalin's statement of the Russian people as the leading force of the Soviet Union. "Every people in the Soviet Union understands perfectly well that the main decisive role in the achievement of victory over the enemy in the Great Patriotic War . . . was played by the great Russian people. For this reason the prestige of the Russian people is so immeasurably high among the other peoples; for this reason the peoples of the USSR bear toward it boundless confidence and a feeling of tremendous love and gratitude." The same love and gratitude was expected from the younger Slav brothers who had been liberated by the Russian army and its victory over the enemy.

The new Pan-Slavism, turning away from the West and looking to Moscow, was also justified by the unique position of Russian culture. Andrei Alexandrovich Zhdanov (1896–1948), in his last years probably the second most influential man in the Soviet Union, wrote in *Pravda* on September 21, 1946: "Naturally our literature which reflects a system much higher than any bourgeois democratic system, a culture many times higher than any bourgeois culture, has the right to teach others a new universal morality. Where can you find such a people or such a country as ours?" The following year, on June 27, 1947, *Pravda* wrote: "We may say with confidence that the center of artistic culture of the world has moved to Moscow. From here mankind receives the art of the most advanced thought, of great feelings, of higher morality and noteworthy artistry." This highest culture on earth had found its instrument in the Russian language. Therefore "the future belongs to the Russian language as the language of socialism," *Moskovsky Komsomolets* wrote on March 6, 1945, "the democratic peoples are learning the Russian language, the world language of internationalism." Could not the Slav peoples of the West be expected gladly to accept the Russian culture and the Russian language, akin to them by blood and tradition and at the same time the most advanced on earth?

Less than two months after the German attack on the Soviet Union a Pan-Slav committee was formed in Moscow and on August 10, 1941, it held its first meeting under the chairmanship of General Alexander Semyenovich Gundorov. Though no official Soviet leaders participated, the Russian communist intelligentsia was well represented by some of the foremost names among them, the authors Nikolai Semenovich Tikhonov, the first writer to receive the Order of the Patriotic War, First Class, Alexander Alexandrovich Fadeyev and Alexei Tolstoy, and the composer Dmitri Shostakovich. The Poles were represented by Wanda Wassiliewska, the wife of the Ukrainian playwright and communist leader Alexander Korneichuk; the Czechs by Zdeněk Nejedlý, professor of musicology at Prague University and biographer of Smetana and Masaryk, and by Jan Šverma, a communist who died in 1945 while fighting in Slovakia. In his opening words, Tolstoy "rejected the old ideology of Pan-Slavism" as reactionary and contrary to the principles of equality among the nations. "Slavs, let us unite, that each Slavonic nation may be entitled as the other nations are, to a free peaceful existence, that the culture of our nations may flourish without restraint." The main emphasis of the meeting was on the fight against the German enemy, a call upon all Slavs to establish armed forces and to sabotage the enemy's efforts.

Much more representative and more carefully prepared was the second meeting of the Slavs in Moscow on April 4 and 5, 1942. Shostakovich issued a call to arms: "I am proud to be a Russian, I boast of being a Slav. . . . May all the spiritual forces, all the intellectuals of the glorious family of the Slavonic nations fearlessly fulfill the great mission entrusted to them by history!" And Tolstoy summed up the revised Slavophile interpretation of history in an article in *Pravda*: "We must revise the whole history of the Slav peoples. . . . During one thousand years, our young blood vitalized decrepit Byzantium. Thanks to the Slavs, Byzantium preserved ancient civilization and transmitted it to feudal Europe. The Slav peoples, hard-working, lovers of liberty, peace and culture, had as their neighbors on the east, nomadic empires which always cherished the utopian design of world conquest, and in the west, mediaeval emperors whose imposing cavalcades were equally vain. These aggressions from east and west broke against the fearless resistance of the Slav world. The role of the Slav peoples in the formation of European humanism has not yet been appreciated at its true value. . . ." [n]

What no previous Slav congress had accomplished, was now realized thanks to official government support. A monthly periodical *Slaviane* (The Slavs) began to appear in Moscow in January, 1943; special committees to work among Slav youth, Slav scholars, and Slav women were formed; Slav scholarship and publications were encouraged in the Soviet Union under the leadership of Professor Nikolai Sevastyanovich Derzhavin, who published since 1898 numerous works on Slav history, especially on the Bulgarians, and was awarded the Order of Lenin in 1945; above all the Pan-Slav propaganda was carried to Britain, Canada, Latin America and the United States, appealing to the racial solidarity of citizens of Slav descent, as Hitler had done to the Germans. A congress of Slavonic nations met in London on May 25, 1944, under the chairmanship of R. W. Seton-Watson and was attended mostly by Slavs living in England in temporary exile. Of much greater importance was the American Slav congress which took place in Detroit on April 25 and 26, 1942. It made use of the wartime enthusiasm for "The Russian ally," and tried to organize the ten million Americans of Slav descent for the time being in support of the common American-Russian struggle against Hitler and permanently in support of the Soviet Union and its policy.[n]

The official recognition of the Russian Orthodox Church in September, 1943, by the Soviet government and the elevation of the Metropolitan Sergius of Moscow to the dignity of a patriarch of all Russia made them, as among the Pan-Slavs of the second half of the 19th century, an instrument of Russian imperial policy. Patriarch Alexei who succeeded Sergius in May, 1944, praised Stalin as "a wise leader, placed by the Lord over our great nation." All churches were ordered to offer prayers "for the health and well-being of the God-sent leader of the people of our Christ-loving nation." As in the 19th century, Pan-Orthodoxism was to support Pan-Slavism. Orthodox churches everywhere were to be united under Moscow's leadership. Patriarch Alexei, at whose coronation the Patriarchs of Alexandria, Antioch and Georgia participated, visited the Near East in 1945 to renew the ties which had existed in the time of Tsarist Russia. Orthodox churches in Europe and America which had split away from the Moscow patriarchate were warned to re-enter. In the same year Roman Catholics in Czechoslovakia held a conference at Velehrad in Moravia—the place where St. Cyril and St. Methodius worked in the ninth century for the Christianization of the Slavs and where the Pan-Slav enthusiasm of the 19th century had led to many demonstrations of Slav spiritual solidarity—the keynote address of which called on all Catholic theologians of Slav descent to join "the general eastward orientation of the country."

The victories of the Soviet Union in 1944 and 1945 in the Balkans, in the Danubian Basin and along the Vistula completely changed the history and political configuration in central-eastern Europe.

The Russian army entered Königsberg, the cradle of the Prussian monarchy, and Berlin, Budapest and Vienna; the Kremlin claimed the legacy of the Habsburg and the Hohenzollern. Though the Soviet Union did not enter the war for any purpose of liberation, nevertheless it demanded the gratitude of the Slavs as their "liberator." From London, King Peter of Yugoslavia declared on January 11, 1945, that "fraternal union with Russia is one of the most deeply rooted sentiments of the Slav peoples." With greater clarity the new situation was explained by a Bulgarian writer: "For one hundred and fifty years the Slav idea served the private interests of two parasitical classes, the landowners and the bourgeois, i.e., it was exploited to the harm of the Slav peoples themselves. Today for the first time in 1300 years, Slavdom lives through a propitious moment which will make its security forever possible. The German danger has disappeared. The governments which fanned hatred among the Slav peoples, have been thrown out. Now the Slavs can proceed to build up their society. What should be their program? The Slavs form a racial, linguistic and cultural group with a common character. They constitute a geo-political and economic block which can be an important factor in the preservation of European peace. The Slav nations, in order to liberate themselves from German capitalism, must build up technically perfected national economies which will secure their independence. Their inner structure must be democratic, freedom-loving and socially just. The Slav nations have to work out a political system for Pan-Slav co-operation, the principle of which ought to be full equality of small and great nations. The USSR should organize and lead this Slav society." [n] Pan-Slavism was to become the vehicle of a common civilization, the civilization of communist Russia, of the Soviet Union and of its leading people, the Great Russian people.

In 1946 the Soviet Union controlled all of Europe east of a line running from Stettin on the Baltic Sea to Trieste on the Adriatic Sea. Behind this line there were not only all the Slav peoples but as Danilevsky and other Pan-Slavs had demanded, the Magyars, the Rumanians, the Albanians. That the Greeks and Constantinople did not live up to Danilevsky's expectations, was due not only to their own will to resistance but also to the farsighted statesmanship of Winston Churchill and Ernest Bevin. Yet Königsberg had become Kaliningrad; Potsdam was under communist domination; the two western Slav nations, Poland and Czechoslovakia, emerged from the War with much diminished territory and (under communist inspiration) on a purely racial basis, having driven out the Germans and other national minorities; Moscow claimed the right— which fell in 1919 to the Western democracies and in 1939 was exercised by Hitler's Germany—of settling all territorial and other disputes in the area; and by the annexation of Carpatho-Ukraine from Czechoslovakia. Russia became the immediate neighbor of Czechoslovakia and of Hungary, commanding a strategic foothold in the Danubian plain south of the Carpathian Mountains and establishing frontiers there and along the Oder-Neisse line. This position conjured up the racial past of many centuries ago, as the fascist dictatorships had hoped to do. Of all the Slav peoples only the Poles abroad and the Polish government in London raised a passionate protest. As so often in the last two hundred years the Polish national traditions and hopes had to live on in exile. In the homelands the Slav spokesmen stressed the "democratic" and "peace-loving" character of the Slavs. This was no new melody. The romanticists among them had sung it since the time of Herder. It had been the constant chant of the Slavophiles. It was not changed substantially now by being communist-directed. But a hope was held out to all peoples that they might partake in this "democratic" and "peace-loving" community of nations if they would affirm, as the Slavs did, the undying gratitude and the indissoluble attachment to the great leader of the Slav world and of progressive mankind, Soviet Russia under Stalin.

In this atmosphere a Pan-Slav Congress met in Belgrade for five days beginning on December 8, 1946. It marked the third great Congress in the history of the Pan-Slav idea; the first in Prague represented the Western democratic trend of 1848; the second in Moscow expressed the Russian nationalism of the 1860's; the third, in the Yugoslav capital, was the triumphant affirmation of Moscow's hold over the Slav world. Of all its members, the Yugoslavs and their wartime leader, the old and trusted communist fighter and organizer, Marshal Tito, received the highest consideration, second only to that of Russia and Marshal Stalin. It was not by accident that Belgrade was chosen as the seat of the Pan-Slav Congress, the center of the new Pan-Slav movement, and after September, 1947, also the home of the newly established Cominform (Communist Information Bureau) and of its official magazine the first issue of which appeared there on November 15, 1947. The Yugoslavs were regarded as the second ranking Slav nation, a position which the Congress was to confirm. The program comprised three points: the Slav peoples in the world struggle for peace and democracy; the contribution of the Slav peoples to world culture; organizational problems of Slav co-operation. For the first time in the history of Pan-Slavism, the Congress was regarded as an official and not a private manifestation; for the first time too it was world-wide and Slav delegates from the United States, Canada, South America, Australia and New Zealand attended, *Auslandsslaven* similar to the *Auslandsdeutschen*, the men and women of German descent and loyalty, though citizens of non-German countries, of Hitler's time. Interestingly enough the Slav representatives were organized not on a basis of nationality but of states. There was a representation from the Soviet Union (including Ukrainians and Byelorussians, without, however, accounting for the many non-Slav nationalities of the Soviet Union, which now acted officially as a Slav state), Yugoslavia (comprising Serbs, Croats, Slovenians and Macedonians), Poland, Czechoslovakia (comprising Czechs and Slovaks), and Bulgaria. The official state concept replaced the formerly predominant nationality concept.

The Congress was opened by Marshal Tito who was received according to the official report, with "long-lasting ovations." "Equally enthusiastic" was the reception accorded to Marshal Fyodor Ivanovich Tolbukhin who commanded the Soviet armies which had victoriously entered Rumania, Bulgaria, Belgrade and Vienna and thus "liberated" the southern Slavs. In his opening address Marshal Tito said: "What would have happened if the glorious Red Army had not existed? What would have happened if this state of workers and peasants with Stalin, the man of genius, at its head, had not existed, which stood like a wall against fascist aggression and which with innumerable sacrifices and rivers of blood liberated also our Slav nations in other countries. For this great sacrifice which our brothers in the great Soviet Union made, we other Slavs thank them . . ." He finished his talk with a three-fold toast, to Slav solidarity (using the word which Kollár coined), to our greatest Slav brother, the Soviet Union (forgetting that the Soviet Union was not Slav but supraracial), to its leader of genius, Stalin (a climax of personal adulation unthinkable at the Moscow Congress of 1867).

Marshal Tito was followed by the two main speakers, the Yugoslav Milovan Djilas, who discussed the struggle of the Slavs for peace and democracy, and

Professor Boris D. Grekov of the Academy of Sciences of the USSR, who read a long catalogue of names as "Slav contributions to world culture." The trite verbosity and the lack of ideas in these papers distinguished the Belgrade congress from the 19th century Pan-Slav Congresses as much as did the harmonious unanimity manifested in all discussions and decisions. At the end a Pan-Slav committee was elected, in which each of the five states was represented by five members. A Yugoslav Major General Bozhidar Maslarić, became its president; a Russian, a Pole, a Czech and a Bulgarian were elected vice-presidents. Belgrade, and no longer Moscow, was designated as the seat of the Pan-Slav committee. The former Pan-Slav committee in Moscow was reorganized in March, 1947, as the Slav committee of the USSR with Gen. A. S. Gundorov as its chairman, and three vice-presidents: Alexander A. Voznesensky, Rector of the University of Leningrad, Alexander Vladimovich Palladin, President of the Ukrainian Academy of Sciences, and Yakub Kolas, a Byelorussian poet and Vice-President of the Byelorussian Academy of Sciences. The monthly *Slaviane*, which so far had appeared as the organ of the Pan-Slav Committee in Moscow, became in 1947 the organ of the Slav Committee of the USSR.

The Pan-Slav Congress in Belgrade represented the crest of the Pan-Slav tide after World War II. Its resolutions, plans and hopes came to naught as had those of all the previous Congresses. The far-reaching designs broke upon the rocks of reality. One more success could be registered by Moscow's Pan-Slavism, interestingly enough among the Czechs whose conciliatory realism and spirit of political maturity were unique among the Slavs. But Bohemia and Moravia, the Czech parts of Czechoslovakia, were the only countries in Europe where the communists achieved in free elections—held on May 26, 1946—a vote of 40.17 per cent. Wide circles expected a recession of the communist vote in the forthcoming elections of May, 1948. It might have been the fear of such a defeat which prompted the communist leadership in February, 1948, to seize the total control of the country, a coup facilitated by the fact that the government of Dr. Beneš had conceded the commanding positions of the administration to communists and had with dangerous ambiguity recognized the communists as a "democratic" party, at the same time outlawing "fascist" parties. Czechoslovakia now became an integral part of the Moscow directed Pan-Slav Empire and adjusted quickly and fully to the intellectual, moral and political model set by the Kremlin. But this success, achieved against the most Westernized Slavs,[*] was more than balanced by the event of June 28, 1948 which was a surprise and which revealed an open and widening rift between Moscow and Belgrade, between Marshal Stalin and Marshal Tito, the two most prominent leaders of the new Pan-Slavism.

The Yugoslav defection created in the Slav "family of nations" a situation similar to that which between 1830 and 1945 existed as a result of the enmity of Poles and Russians. Like Poland then, Yugoslavia now became the "Judas" and "traitor" to the Slav cause and the "tool" of "Western scheming" against the Slav world which the Russians then as now magnanimously identified with Moscow. The similarity, even to the very words used, between the diatribes by Katkov and his generation and those now used by Stalin's spokesmen was astonishing. While the Polish communists acknowledged that it was only owing to Moscow that Poland could end the "feudal" age, and that Poland's liberation from German occupation was only due to the Red Army—forgetting that it was Soviet Russia's co-operation in 1939 which facilitated Poland's subjugation by Hitler—the Serbs could point to a long tradition of peasant proprietorship and to their courageous fight, independently from Russian help, waged against Turks and Germans for independence. The communist leadership in Belgrade refused to admit that their country owed its liberation and its new order for "social justice" only, or above all, to Russia's help and guidance. They denied the thesis propagated from Moscow that the Slav peoples could not preserve their independence except under Russia's protection. They did not wish to subordinate the economic modernization of their country to the needs of "the motherland" of the Slavs and of the socialist world revolution.

Thus the new Pan-Slavism, aroused in 1941 in Moscow and apparently triumphant in 1946 in Belgrade, came to an end. Tito's defection had repercussions also in the Pan-Slav Congress in the United States; some of its most active leaders like Louis Adamic sided with the dissident communists. The growing hostility of the Kremlin to the democracies made the American people more aware of the threat to the West implied in the theory and actions emanating from Moscow, the center of the now intimately fused movements of Pan-Slavism and world communism. As a result, the American Pan-Slav Congress ceased most of its activities. The period of Pan-Slavism in its third, communist Pan-Russian form, came to its end. But even in its heyday it was unable, in spite of all totalitarian pressure and conformity, to solve the old problems of dispute among the Slav peoples, the control of Teschen as between the Czechs and Poles, the allegiance of Macedonia to Yugoslavia or Bulgaria, and the desire of the Ukrainian people for independence from the Great Russians.

The Pan-Slavism of the war years, promising the equality of all Slav peoples, was openly replaced after 1947 by a Pan-Russism which imposed Russian predominance and leadership on the Slav peoples first, but also on Magyars and Rumanians, on

Uzbeks and Caucasians. The new Soviet patriotism hardly distinguished between "Russian" and "Soviet." [n] Soviet historiography had to follow the trend; books written and praised as recently as 1941, were rejected in 1947 as not patriotic enough. As the Czechs exploited the famous forged manuscripts in the first half of the 19th century for a romantic glorification of the past—due to the immaturity of Czech scholarship at that time and quickly discarded when under Gebauer, Goll, and Masaryk Czech scholarship reached the highest Western standards in the 1880's—Russian scholarship now began to extol the Russian past beyond anything that the most extravagant cases of former Russian historiography had ever attempted. The Kievan state was no longer regarded as the first state of the eastern Slavs on Russian soil; its rise originated in a high east Slav civilization, much superior to its neighbors; the multi-national and yet centralized Russian state was dated back for many centuries, even before the 16th century, with the Great Russians, owing to their cultural superiority, the leading element.

The Great-Russian people was now generally called the great Russian people. More and more emphasis was being put on the fact that the Russians owed their whole development to their own creative originality and initiative. "Der sowjetische Reichsgedanke eines Imperiums der 'sozialistischen' Völker sättigt seine etwas dünn gewordene geistige Substanz durch eine Aufnahme des altrussischen Staatsgedankens mit all seinen expansionistischen und zentralistischen Tendenzen in seine Gesamtkonzeption. Dass das russische Volk nunmehr—anders als Lenin sich die Entwicklung dachte—zum eigentlichen Träger der weltrevolutionären Aufgaben des Marxismus geworden ist, muss den anderen Völkern der Sowjetunion auf jede Weise plausibel gemacht werden. Der 'grosse Bruder' steht vor ihnen als Führer auf dem

Wege der Fortschritts und der Freiheit. Das 'geringere Übel' der Unterjochung unter Russland ist kein Übel mehr, sondern eitel Glück and Segen." (The Soviet imperial idea of a union of socialist peoples enriches its thinned spiritual substance by incorporating the old Russian imperial idea with all its expansionist and centralizing trends. It must be made acceptable by all means to the other peoples of the Soviet Union that the Russian people—differently from Lenin's idea—has now become the true bearer of the world revolutionary tasks of Marxism. The great brother is now the leader on the road to progress and liberty. What had been formerly the lesser evil of the subjection to Russia, has now become no evil at all but sheer good fortune and bliss.)[n]

Professor Militsa Vasilyevna Nechkina, one of the well known younger historians of Russia, author of many works on the Decembrists and editor of Volume II, covering the 19th century, of the official textbook *Istoriya USSR*, wrote in the official organ of the Soviet historians, *Voprosy istorii*, in 1951, that the conquest of colonial peoples by Tsarist Russia had been not only "the lesser evil" compared with the conquest of Britain or Turkey to which they might have otherwise succumbed—the official Soviet theory since 1934—but a positive good. The Ukrainians, Georgians, Armenians or Uzbeks were actively helped in their economic progress by their inclusion in the Russian Empire. Tsarism oppressed all the peoples, above all the Russian people, "the older brother of all the peoples of the Soviet land." The struggle against the common enemy, Tsarism, a struggle led by the Russian people, became the foundation of a fraternity of all the peoples devoted to the common construction of a new socialist society. The education of the non-Russian peoples by the Russians created the condition for their liberation and progress. To elucidate these more profound

aspects of the annexation of the non-Russian peoples
by the empire, was one of the great tasks for Soviet
historiography."

In 1931 Sergei A. Piontkovsky, *Burzhuasnaya istoricheskaya nauka v Rossii* (Bourgeois Historical Science in Russia), p. 92, violently attacked the well
known book by Matvyei Kuzmich Lyubavsky (1860–
1936), *Obrazovanie osnovskoi gossudarstvennoi ter-
ritorii velikorusskoi narodnosti* (The Development
of the State Territory of the Great Russian Nationality, Leningrad: Academy of the Sciences of the
USSR, 1929) because it stressed "chauvinistically"
the Great-Russian element in the history of the Russian state. The book was characterized by the disciple
of Pokrovsky as the "political program of the NEP
bourgeoisie." A few years later Pokrovsky and Piontkovsky were regarded as un-Marxist and un-scientific,
and present-day Russian historiography goes infinitely
further than Lyubavsky and his generation in glorifying the Russian national element. *Voprosy istorii* in
1950 praised the thesis of Lt. Col. L. G. Beskrovny,
Professor of the history of warfare at the Military
Frunze Academy, "Stroitelstvo russkoi armii v XVIII
veke" (The Building of the Russian Army in the
18th Century). In it the author rejected the "cosmopolitan" views of "bourgeois historians," according
to which Peter I built the Russian army after German models. On the contrary, Russia produced in
the 18th century the best arms in Europe and made
many inventions in the field of artillery; the Russian
army was then trained according to its own national
system, which was the most progressive in Europe;
the leading officers were Russians and not foreigners,
Napoleon learned much from the tactics and the
strategy of Suvorov."

The same issue of *Voprosy istorii* bestowed similar
praise on a symposium on the "Progressive Influence
of the great Russian Nation on the Development
of the Yakut Nation." "The Yakuts, as a result of

their inclusion into the centralized Russian state, entered the most advanced culture of the period and accelerated thereby the process of their social-economic and cultural development. The concrete elucidation of this question has at present, besides its purely scientific interest, great political significance. The study of the process of the historical development of the nationalities in the light of their historical interaction appears as one of the important moments in the education of the workers of our country in Soviet patriotism." [n] It is hardly astonishing that in an official programmatic article about the tasks of historical science, I. Kon wrote in the June issue of V*oprosy istorii* in 1951: "Marxist historical scholarship must wage an incessant war against the falsification of history by the bourgeoisie. This war which places the Soviet historians on the firing line is being conducted (and must be conducted) in all fields of historical science. . . . Soviet historical science develops under the constant and close leadership of the Soviet state, the Bolshevik party and Stalin himself. . . . All Soviet scholarship works under the guidance of Lenin and Stalin for the welfare of our nation." [n]

The historians onto the firing line, was not a new slogan. It fully corresponded to Lenin's attitude. The difference was in what they were firing at. The *Bolshaya Sovyetskaya Entsiklopediya*, the great depository of communist scholarship, devoted to Pan-Slavism a short article, less than a column, in 1939. There it quoted Marx and Engels as pointing out that "the immediate goal of Pan-Slavism appears to be the creation of a Slav empire from the Erzgebirge and the Carpathian Mountains to the Black, Aegean and Adriatic Seas under Russia's rule." The article stressed the reactionary and expansionist character of Pan-Slavism; Marx and Engels were reported to have looked with horror on its results which would make all Slavs share "the terrible fate of the Polish nation." [n] For once Marx and the Communist Encyclopaedia seemed right in their characterization of Pan-Slavism as Russian imperialism which would subject the other Slavs as the Poles had been subjected during Marx's lifetime.

As in the worst period of Tsarist nationalism, the right of national originality was claimed for, and reserved to, the Russians alone; the other Slav nations, Poles and Ukrainians, had to adapt themselves to Russian nationalism. In the case of the Poles this was clearly expressed at the seventh congress of Polish historians which met in Breslau from the 19th to the 22nd of September, 1948. "It is interesting to note that, while the campaign for the cultural and national distinctness (of Russia) was being trumpeted, at least one significant exception was made. The seventh congress of Polish historians . . . was criticized principally for writing history from a nationalist point of view and for contrasting Russian and Polish culture rather than drawing comparisons between their fundamental similarity." [n] Even the Poles who after 1945 propagated the new Pan-Slavism came in for sharp criticism. Henryk Batowski, editor of the Pan-Slav magazine *Życie Słowiańskie* (which began publication in January, 1946) and author of *Historia Wspołpracy Słowiańskiej* (History of Slav Cooperation), was branded a bourgeois nationalist because he over-emphasized Poland's role in the Slav world and glorified past instances of Slav co-operation at the expense of the present. [n]

Had Stalin forgotten the warning which he voiced in his "Report on National Factors" before the 12th Congress of the Russian Communist Party on April 23, 1923? He then regarded Great-Russian chauvinism, "a force that is gaining in strength," as a factor impeding the amalgamation of the Soviet peoples, undermining the confidence of the "formerly oppressed peoples" in the Russian proletariat. "This is our most dangerous enemy, which we must over-

come; for once we overcome it, we shall have overcome nine-tenths of the nationalism which has
survived and which is developing in certain republics." [n] In the discussion at the Congress Bukharin
went even further: "In the capacity of a former great
power nation we must counter nationalist ambitions
and place ourselves in a position of inequality, in
the sense of making still greater concessions to national tendencies. By such a policy alone . . .
whereby we artificially place ourselves in an inferior
position as compared with others, only at such a
price can we purchase the real confidence of the
formerly oppressed nations." Stalin opposed this
point of view: "We must not overshoot the mark in
politics, just as we must not undershoot it." Thirty-
seven years later, it seems that Stalin has more and
more undershot the mark. In spite of all totalitarian
control and of the ever-growing purges of "local nationalists," Great Russian chauvinism has apparently
aroused and strengthened the opposition of the Slav
and non-Slav peoples subject to Moscow. [n]

Soviet patriotism, the official term most frequently
used, was more and more tinged with Slavophile
Russianism. *Izvestiya* on August 13, 1947, published
a lecture by C. Kovalev on the Soviet people's national pride, delivered in the Moscow All-Union Society for the Dissemination of Political and Scientific
Knowledge. "In the process of socialist construction
in our country, the Soviet people have worked out
their own world outlook, peculiar to themselves
alone. One of its most important characteristics is
Soviet patriotism, a feeling of the most profound
love for and devotion to the Socialist Motherland.
A most important peculiarity of Soviet patriotism
is the profound understanding of the superiority of
the Soviet system over the bourgeois and all other
class systems. . . . It is precisely this peculiarity
which above all characterizes Soviet patriotism as patriotism of the highest kind . . ." Like the Slavo-

philes, he attacked Peter I for his Western reforms and the 19th century Westernizers for their "worship of the West." "Great are the services of our people to history. Our people have repeatedly saved Europe from destruction by barbarians. . . . The great Russian people, as well as the other peoples of Russia, was also in the past not dependent on other peoples in the struggle for progress, for the development of science, literature and art." Kovalev, the official report went on, "dwelled in detail on Russia's priceless contributions to world civilization in all spheres of culture." [n]

Pravda of the same day said editorially: "For centuries Russian intellectuals fell over themselves in servility and obsequiousness before everything foreign. For centuries their consciousness was poisoned with absurd prejudices which attributed leadership in science, technology and culture to the West . . . This most harmful survival from the past can still be found among a certain section of our intellectuals. Bolshevik propaganda must utterly destroy this survival. Our intellectuals must be daily educated and strengthened in their feeling of Soviet national pride." In spite of all these educational efforts, some Soviet intellectuals continued to succumb to the sin of "cosmopolitanism." L. Knipper wrote a long article "Protiv kosmopolitizma, za russky natsionalny stil" (Against Cosmopolitanism, for a National Russian Style) in *Sovyetskaya Muzyka* (Soviet Music, Moscow, 1951, no. 2), in which he asked: "Can it be that Russian music is no longer Russian music because it became Soviet music? The Russian nation which has changed in some respect in the last thirty-three years, has in no way ceased being Russian by becoming Soviet. . . . For there can be no art which is not rooted nationally. . . . We own the treasure of the truly popular art of our great Russian classics. Only by going back to these glorious traditions, can we find new ways for the development of the Russian song of the Soviet era. . . . In the brotherly family of the Soviet republics, the Russian culture is the first among equals. The national cultures not only of the Soviet republics but also of the people's democracies, orient themselves after the Russian culture and grow to strength through it." [n]

The famous directives of Stalin on the question of language in 1950 had one purpose, to make clear that the "international" language of socialism would be Russian. David Zazlavsky wrote in an article, "The Great Language of our Epoch," in the *Literaturnaya Gazeta* of January 1, 1950: "The Russian language is the first world language of international significance, which rejects sharply the destruction of the national character by cosmopolitanism. . . . Nobody can regard himself as educated in the full and true sense of the word, if he does not understand Russian and cannot read the creations of the Russian mind in the original language." The Russian nationalism of 19th century Pan-Slavs never voiced such uncompromising claims on behalf of the great Russian nation and of Moscow, the Third Rome.

In the 19th century even the Slavs who were most friendly to Russia never went so far as to back Russia's claims to leadership. At the Pan-Slav Congress in Moscow in 1867 much milder pretensions aroused strong opposition on the part of the Czech spokesmen. Now, however, the Prague communist organ *Rudé Právo* reported on March 4, 1952, a long speech by the Minister of Information Václav Kopecký delivered before a conference of teachers, in which he said: "It is known to us that one of the main weapons in America's ideological war is cosmopolitanism, which destroys the ties to one's native land and people . . . The case of the miserable traitors Slánský . . . has shown how the malicious agents of Western imperialism tried to use cosmopolitanism in its Trotzkyite-Zionist form. Therefore we must resolutely destroy cosmopolitanism, this

ideological monster which is today put to the service
of American war barbarism. We know too that the
Western imperialist enemies in their preparations
for a criminal war, besides cosmopolitanism use another ideological weapon, nationalism . . . The
Judas-treason of the Tito clique in Yugoslavia . . .
and the case of Clementis . . . prove that American
imperialism . . . tries in this way to loosen the
close ties of the people's democracies with the Soviet
Union. . . . Today the question of a just and an
unjust war and the question of patriotism is before
all the workers of the world, and this in the sense,
that every action against the Soviet Union is unjust,
but that every action of the Soviet Union is sanctified with the seal of supreme justice, because its
goal is the welfare of the workers, of the whole
working population of the world, the welfare of all
peoples and of all mankind. . . ." [n]

After 1950 communist dialectics had to solve the
difficulty of harmonizing Russia's nationalist uniqueness and the glorification of Russia's past with the
condemnation of the slightest emphasis on the national originality of other peoples. This may explain
the violence of vituperation, unusual even for communist language, used against violators of the new
line, which added to the uncertainties of Soviet
policy. The Western Slavs faced the possibility of a
new German-Russian *rapprochement* sacrificing
them to Moscow's interests, a possibility fore-
shadowed in Stalin's wire of October 13, 1949, to
Wilhelm Pieck and Otto Grotewohl on the occasion
of the establishment of the German Democratic
Republic: "The experience of the last war has shown
that the German and the Russian peoples have borne
the greatest sacrifices in that war and that these two
nations dispose of the far greatest potential forces in
Europe for the accomplishment of great actions of
world significance."

In their reply the two German communist leaders acknowledged, on behalf of the German people, its historical guilt which it assumed by attacking the Soviet Union. Thus a positive and a negative community of fate was again established between the two peoples: they had been in 1945, as in 1918, the two chief victims of the World War, and Germany had become guilty not by her march into Prague nor her dismemberment and subjection of Poland (helped by the Soviet Union) but only by her aggression of June 22, 1941. The little Slav brothers were bound to realize their dependence on the self-centered policy of the older brother, with whom Yugoslavia had broken because it felt itself treated as a colony and its communist party used as an instrument for the country's exploitation in the economic, military and political interests of Moscow. By 1950 Pan-Slavism was hardly mentioned any more in the Soviet orbit. Moscow's policy toward Poland and Czechoslovakia differed as little from that toward Hungary or Rumania as its attitude toward the Ukraine differed from that toward its Mohammedan subject nationalities.

In June, 1951, a "decade" of Ukrainian art was celebrated in Moscow, fifteen years after the 1936 "decade," which closed the terrible persecution of the Ukrainian peasantry and intelligentsia, begun in 1929. The new "decade," which culminated in a glorification of Stalin, of Soviet patriotism, and of the Pereyaslav Council of 1654 which decided on the union of the Ukraine with Moscow, coincided with a new attack on the Ukrainian writers and the Ukrainian Communist Party for "nationalist deviation." Volodimir Sosyura, one of the most respected older working class poets of the Ukraine, had written in 1944 a poem, "Love the Ukraine," sentimental and patriotic as thousands of Russian poems were at that time:

. . . *The Ukraine lives for us in the songs which we*
  sing,
In the stars and in the willow trees along the rivers,
And in the beat of our heart.
How can one love other peoples,
If one does not love her, our Ukraine.
We are nothing without her, like dust of the fields
  or smoke,
Eternally driven away by the winds.

For seven years the poem was many times reprinted in the Ukraine, widely praised, and even
twice translated into Russian. Only in July, 1951,
however, *Pravda* discovered the "nationalist deviation" in the poem and bitterly attacked the author
and also Alexander Prokofiev whose translation appeared in May, 1951, in the Leningrad literary magazine *Zvezda.* The poem was criticized for neglecting
to praise the socialist transformation of the Ukraine
under the leadership of Stalin. "It is the duty of
Soviet writers," *Pravda* wrote, "to fight implacably
against all forms of nationalism . . . and to sing in
their works the heroic deeds of our great fatherland,
which builds communism." *Pravda* did not say how
to reconcile the implacable fight against all forms
of nationalism with the glorification of the great
and unique Russian people and its past.

Its article opened a whole series of attacks on
"Ukrainian nationalism." [n] Even Alexander Korneichuk and Wanda Wassilievska were accused of
having not sufficiently stressed the pre-Russian
character of the Ukrainian liberation struggle against
Poland under Hetman Bohdan Khmelnitski in the
libretto to an opera of that name composed by
Konstantin Dankevych. Immediately a meeting of
the central Ukrainian Union of Soviet writers in
Kiev was called in which the great importance of
the *Pravda* article for the development of Ukrainian
literature was recognized and all those present in-

dulged in a "profound analysis" of their "mistakes."
A Ukrainian literary critic Leonid Novichenko
summed up the accusations against Sosyura for not
having "freed himself from the influence of hostile
bourgeois nationalistic ideology, which also finds a
more complete reflection in the corrupt poem 'Love
the Ukraine' . . . He represents the Ukraine as
standing alone . . . without connection with the
Great Russian people and the other peoples of the
Soviet Union. . . . He refuses to see that in the
battle to free the Ukraine the sons of all the peoples
of the Soviet Union, and in the first instance the
sons of Great Russia, took part; about them he
crudely and insultingly keeps quiet. . . . While
praising a certain exclusiveness of the Ukrainian
language, he considered it possible not even to mention the Russian language, which is to every
Ukrainian as much a native language as is Ukrainian
itself." [n]

This last sentence is revealing for the new trend.
When Professor Alexander Vladimirovich Palladin,
President of the Ukrainian Academy of Sciences and
Ukrainian representative in the Soviet Pan-Slav Committee, returned from the International Congress of
Physiology in England in 1947—one of the many international scholarly congresses which the aged
scholar had attended—he reported in the *Literaturnaya Gazeta* how he had there scored a nationalist triumph. Though he knew French and English perfectly well, he refused to use either of these official
languages. "We firmly rejected all these arguments,
and said we could not accept such a humiliating
treatment of Soviet science and of the Russian
language. This we said, was the language of a great
victorious nation, and of the nation which had
created the greatest and most advanced form of
state in the world, and this language must receive
its legitimate place in the work of the congress. We
scored our point. We read our papers in our lan-

guage." What strikes one in this statement is not only the spirit of nationalist pride and intransigence shown at an international scientific gathering ("This episode showed," Professor Palladin continued, "how important it is never for a moment to yield on points affecting our national honor and dignity, nor must we ever tolerate any kind of toadying to the West") —but the fact that the president of the Ukrainian Academy of Sciences, an avowed nationalist, is not a Ukrainian nationalist, but a Russian nationalist, who regards Russian as "our" language and reads his paper, in defiance of the rules of international courtesy, in Russian not in Ukrainian.[n]

A similar revaluation of their history and culture was imposed by Moscow on the non-Slav Soviet peoples. Until recently Shamil, the famous fighter for the independence of the North Caucasus (1834 to 1859) and Kenesary Kasymov who led the Kazakh revolt against Russian conquest (1837 to 1846) were recognized as heroes of liberty. Soviet Russian historians agreed with the new Kazakh and Daghestani communist intelligentsia in praising the "anti-colonial" and "progressive" character of these wars for independence. But in 1950 it was found out that these national heroes were no liberators; "objectively, Russia fills the role of liberator of the Caucasian peoples from the cruel and arbitrary oppression of the Iranian and Turkish bandits." It was only natural that the new Soviet scholarship suddenly discovered that "the longing of progressive people in the Causasus for union with Russia had reflected the feelings of the broad masses," and that "Shamil was forced to overcome the stubborn resistance of the people, which expressed its sympathy for Russia, the savior of Daghestan from the eastern brutes." [n] No lesser body than the "presidium" of the Academy of Sciences of the USSR adopted in November, 1950, a resolution blaming leading Russian historians, among them the academy member, Anna

Mikhailovna Pankratova, for having idealized and misrepresented the "war of liberation" of the Caucasian mountaineers under Shamil's leadership." Therein was seen a remnant of the "un-Marxist" school of Pokrovsky who had not understood the importance of the Black Sea and the Caucasus for the security of (Tsarist) Russia. These independence movements of the Mohammedan people against Russian control were not progressive for they allegedly played into the hands of pan-Turanism and of British imperialism, the dark foes of mankind.

The new communist intelligentsia among the non-Russians had been encouraged, at the beginning of the Soviet domination, to explore the past and especially the folk songs and epic poems of their people. The various state publishing houses and academies of sciences of the national republics had published, and glorified, such epic poems and heroic songs as *Altamysh* (Uzbek), *Dede-Korkut* (Azerbaijan), *Korkut-Ata* (Turkmenistan) and *Gesser Khan* (Buryat-Mongol). But while the Russians were exhorted after 1934 to take pride in the unique beauty of the "Song of the Expedition of Igor" and of the byliny (oral popular poetry celebrating the exploits of the pre-Tartar Russian princes), the epic poems of the other peoples were unmasked after 1949 as reactionary. In his Russian translation of the *Altamysh*, M. Sheikhsade had characterized it as the revelation of "the best traits of character of the working population in the past, of its unceasing longing for social justice, for happiness and for the good, a symbol of all the heroic and noble aspirations which lived among the working masses of Uzbekistan." Now it was condemned as was the similar *Gesser Khan* epos." "The epos cultivates a hostile attitude towards the Russian people. The Buryat-Mongol people, which owes its freedom and happiness to the great Russian people, cannot tolerate that its sentiments for the fraternal Russian people be hurt. . . . Only under the protection of the Soviet power . . . could the culture of the Buryat-Mongol people . . . flower as never before. It forms an indissoluble part of the united harmonious Soviet family of peoples and progresses towards communism thanks to the support of the great Russian people under the leadership of the party of Lenin and Stalin."

Historians of these Mohammedan peoples who pointed to the influence of Arab, Iranian and Turkish civilizations, were accused of being "cosmopolitans." According to the new theory, the Uzbeks and Kazakhs, the Tadjiks and Turkmens, developed independently until the 19th century when they came under the benevolent influence, not of the Russian Tsars it is true, but under that of the Russian people and the Russian culture. Kazakh communist historians who had regarded the struggle of their people for independence from Russia as a school for the political education of the masses, were censored because "they failed to recognize the deep progressive significance of the Union of Kazakhstan with Russia. . . . The Kazakh working class had the greatest interest in this union. The activities of the Kassymovs (leaders of the independence movement) who wished to hinder the union, were in sharp opposition to the desires of the progressive part of Kazakh society." [n]

4

Conclusion

IN ONE HUNDRED and fifty years Pan-Slavism has travelled a long and tortured road from Herder to Stalin. In 1800 the Slav world, apart from the Great Russians, offered the spectacle of subjection and multiple division. In 1950 the Slav world, except for the Yugoslavs, was united under the control of the Great Russian people. In 1800 their literatures and cultural activities were undeveloped, except for the Poles. In 1900, these gifted peoples had contributed to Europe great cultural achievements, among which the Russian novel and Russian poetry ranked first. By 1950 their cultural life suffered from confinement in a common strait jacket of narrow conformity. In 1826 the word Pan-Slavism was first used. Like similar words—nationalism, socialism, etc.—it owed its origin and its spread to the early 19th century. So far, at least, the Pan-Slav program of a union of all Slavs into a powerful whole, shaping the political and cultural destinies of mankind, has never come near realization except in the brief period from 1945 to 1948 when for the first time in history it became part of the official ideology of a powerful government. Otherwise, the Pan-Slav aspirations foundered on the rock of the national diversities of the various Slav peoples, of their different traditions and interests. The ill-defined movement aroused hopes in some, fears in others; it rarely was an effective force, politically, economically or culturally.

The future of Pan-Slavism is uncertain. In 1930 it seemed a dead issue. World War II brought an unexpected revival in an unprecedented breadth and intensity. There was some hope of a Pan-Slavism based upon the equality and the free development of the various Slav peoples: Dr. Beneš and Jan Masaryk apparently believed in its possibility. In fact the Czech democrats were the only sincere Pan-Slavs at that time. They identified the Pan-Slavism of World War II which had emanated from Moscow with the neo-Slavism of the last decade before World War I. Thus Hubert Ripka, a follower of Dr. Beneš, declared on November 7, 1947, that Soviet Russia would respect "the independent Slav nations administering their own affairs in their own way, according to their own law and their own national tradition." Beneš, himself, was convinced that "the new Slavism" was an expression of Slav solidarity and equality and would be the leading tenet in Soviet post-war policy. The Russophile Czech democrats misread Soviet intentions completely. They paid for it with their downfall, death, and exile."

What emerged in reality immediately after World War II was a Pan-Russism of the kind preached by the extreme Pan-Slavs of the 19th century but never adopted by the Russian government and always combatted by liberal and humanitarian trends among the Russians themselves and by the nationalism of Ukrainians and Poles, Czechs and Serbs. Now, however, a new dimension has been added to the exclusive and all-inclusive state-religion of the Soviet Union. Before World War II, Soviet citizens had to worship the party of Lenin and Stalin and the great Stalin himself. After the war, a compulsory obsequious deference to the "great" Russian people has been imposed on all its "younger brothers," a category in which all non-Slavs had to enter. In that respect the Pan-Slav frame was broadened and racial equality throughout the Soviet empire maintained. All its peoples, whether white or colored, Slav or Turk, Christian or Mohammedan, have equally and continually to pay their deep respects to the Russian people and even to the Russian past.

Yet there are signs—in Titoism, in the ever-repeated official accusations by Moscow against Polish and Ukrainian, Uzbek and Caucasian writers and historians—that the non-Russian peoples, Slavs as well as non-Slavs, do not sufficiently appreciate being constantly reminded of the deep gratitude which they owe to the "Great Russian people," of the immutable dependence upon the leadership of the Russian people. It is not impossible that this enforced conformity and loyalty may prove a weakening factor in the vast Moscow Empire and may help to restore there one day the principles of liberty, equality and diversity, on which the Pan-Slav movement insisted in 1848. This day is still very far away, yet the policy of de-Stalinization followed by Nikita Khrushchev led to a lessening of the emphasis on the leading role of the Great Russian people among the Slav and non-Slav peoples within the Soviet orbit. The October revolutions in Poland and Hungary in 1956; the truce established between Moscow and Belgrade on the initiative of Khrushchev; and finally the strength of the Communist regime in Peking did not result in a growth of liberty, which cannot take place in an authoritarian and dogmatic regime, but they helped to produce a mild degree of diversity in the Communist and in the Slav world, a diversity which would have been unacceptable to Stalin at the end of World War II when the Communist movement presented a strictly monolithic framework into which all Slav elements, even those living abroad, were to be absorbed.

THE SLAVS 1960

Nationality	Estimated Number	Religion	Citizenship
	EASTERN SLAVS		
Great Russians	95,000,000	Greek Orthodox	USSR
Ukrainians	36,000,000	Greek Orthodox and Greek Catholic	USSR
Byelorussians	8,000,000	Greek Orthodox	USSR
	WESTERN SLAVS		
Poles	24,000,000	Roman Catholic	Poland
Czechs	8,000,000	Roman Catholic	Czechoslovakia
Slovaks	3,000,000	Roman Catholic	Czechoslovakia
Lusatians		Protestant and	Eastern
(Sorbs or Wends)	100,000	Catholic	Germany
	SOUTHERN SLAVS		
Serbs	7,500,000	Greek Orthodox	Yugoslavia
Croats	4,500,000	Roman Catholic	Yugoslavia
Slovenes	1,400,000	Roman Catholic	Yugoslavia
Macedonians	1,000,000	Greek Orthodox	Yugoslavia
Bulgarians	6,500,000	Greek Orthodox	Bulgaria

Thus the total number of Slavs can be estimated in 1960 at 195,-000,000. Of them the Great Russians represent about half of the total. At the beginning of 1948 all these Slavs lived under Communist regimes directed from Moscow. Since then the four Slav nationalities of Yugoslavia, though continuing to live under a communist regime, have emancipated themselves from Moscow's control.

Notes

Bibliography

NOTES TO INTRODUCTION

Page ix, line 9
See Hans Kohn, "Arndt and the character of German
Nationalism," *American Historical Review* LIV (July,
1949), 787–803; "The Paradox of Fichte's Nationalism," *Journal of the History of Ideas* X (June, 1949),
319–343; "Romanticism and the Rise of German Nationalism," *The Review of Politics* XII (Oct., 1950),
443–472. Arndt's song "Was ist des Deutschen Vaterland? So nenne mir das grosse Land! So weit die
deutsche Zunge klingt . . ." was as popular as Theodor
Körner's "Uns knüpft der Sprache heilig Band . . . "

p. x, l. 18
See Hans Kohn, *The Idea of Nationalism* (New
York: Macmillan, 1944) 427–441; Konrad Bittner,
"J. G. Herder's Ideen zur Philosophie der Geschichte
der Menschheit und ihre Auswirkungen bei den slav-
ischen Hauptstämmen," *Germano-slavica* II (Brünn:
R. Rohrer, 1932–33), 453 ff. On the influence of the
University of Jena on the Slavs see Othmar Feyl:
*Beiträge zur Geschichte der slavischen Verbindungen
. . . der Universität Jena* (Jena: Gustav Fischer, 1960).

p. xii, l. 1
See Alfred Fischel, *Der Panslawismus bis zum Weltkrieg* (Stuttgart: Cotta, 1919) 29–39; Anatole Mazour,
An Outline of Modern Russian Historiography (Berkeley: Univ. of California Press, 1939) 5–11.

p. xiii, l. 9
See J. G. Fr. Cannabich, *Lehrbuch der Geographie
nach den neusten Friedensbestimmungen*, 12th ed.
(Illmenau: B. F. Voigt, 1829) 624.

p. xiii, l. 24
See *The Idea of Nationalism*, pp. 546 ff. In addition
to the bibliography given there p. 720, *n.* 153, see Mich-

ael B. Petrovich, "Juraj Križanić, a Precursor of Panslavism," *The American Slavic and East European Review* VI, 18/19 (1947), 75–92; V. Vondrak, *Slovenská myšlenka u Križaniće a jeho soud o Slovanech vůbec* (The Slav Idea of K. and his Judgment on the Slavs in general. Inauguration Address, Masaryk University, Brno, 1921); H. I. A. Van Son, *Autour de Krizanic. Etude historique et linguistique* (Paris: Medicis, 1934); Louis Léger, "Un précurseur du panslavisme au XVII siècle" in his *Nouvelles Etudes Slaves* (Paris: E. Leroux, 1880) 1–47; Oscar Halecki, "The Renaissance Origin of Panslavism, *The Polish Review* (New York) vol. III, nos. 1–2.

p. xiv, l. 18
"Un système fédératif des nations Slaves est le grand et unique but auquel elle doit nécessairement tendre." He proposed to name Alexander I "Protecteur des Slavs et d'Orient." Theodor Schiemann, *Geschichte Russlands unter Kaiser Nikolaus I* (Berlin: G. Reimer, 1904) I, 266, *n.* 1; *Mémoires* du Prince Adam Czartoryski et correspondance avec l'Empereur Alexandre I (Paris: Plon, 1887) II, p. 65.

p. xiv, l. 37
On this Obshchestvo Soyedinennikh Slavyan see V. J. Semevskij, *Politicheskiya i obshchestvenniya idei dekabristov* (The Political and Social Ideas of the Decembrists; St. Petersburg: Tip. Pervoi Trudovoi Arteli; 1911) p. 522; P. Gronskij "L'idée fédérative chez les Décabristes," *Le Monde Slave*, N. S., III, 6 (June, 1926) 368–82. M. V. Nechkina, *Obshchestvo soedinennikh Slavyan* (Moscow: Goss. Izdat, 1927).

p. xv, l. 36
Jan Herkel published in Buda in 1826 *Elementa universalis linguae Slavicae e vivis dialectis eruta et suis logicae principiis suffulta.* There he proposed a common Slav literary language which would make possible a "unio in literatura inter omnes Slaves sive verus panslavismus."

NOTES TO PART ONE

Page 5, line 22
The Catholic Slovaks used the Western Slovak dialect as a literary language. This movement was started by the Catholic priest Anton Bernolák (1762–1813) who published in Pressburg in 1787 *Dissertatio philogico-critica de litteris Slavorum cum adnexa lingue Slavonicae per regnum Hungariae usitatae compendiosa simul et facilis orthographia.* He founded in Trnava a Slovak Learned Society (Učené Slowenské Towarišstwo). His most gifted disciple was the priest and poet Jan Hollý (1785–1849). He wrote in 1826 an ode to Bernolák and celebrated in three poems Slovakia's greatness of one thousand years ago, "Swatopluk" (1833), "Cirillo-Metodiada" (1836), and "Sláwon" (1839). He collaborated in the four issues of the literary almanac "Zora" (Dawn) which the Catholic Slovaks published in Pest 1935–40 and in which also Kollár wrote.

Slovak Protestant cultural life centered in Pressburg where Palkovič published since 1812 a weekly paper *Cisařské Královské Národni Noviny* (Imperial Royal National Newspaper), replaced later by *Tatranka*, and in *Banská Bystrica*. There Karel Kuzmány published the periodical *Hronka* (1836–38 where Kollá's "Wechselseitigkeit" was first published.

p. 5, l. 34
Paměti (Recollections) in Kollár: *Sebrané Spisi* (Collected Writings, Prague: (1863), IV, p. 203.

p. 6, l. 23
See *The Idea of Nationalism*, p. 557 f. To the celebration of the hundredth anniversary of Dobrowsky's death, the first congress of Slav philologists was called in Prague and the Slav Seminar of the Charles University in Prague published a symposium on Dobrowsky's

influence on Slav languages and literature, *Josef Dobrovský* (1753–1829), ed. by Jiří Horák, Matyáš Murko,
and Miloš Weingart (Prague, 1929). Jaroslav Ludvík-
ovský, *Dobrovského klasická humanita* (Dobrowsky's
Classical Humanism), Publications of the Philosophical
Faculty of the Komensky University in Bratislava, XII
(Bratislava, 1933), points out that the classical humanism and Ciceronian liberalism of Dobrowsky lived on
in the Czech national movement though the romantic-
Herderian current proved stronger. The author believes
that in the romantically influenced work of Palacký
and Masaryk, Dobrowsky's Greco-Latin ideal of inner
liberty and faith in the spirit and in the European
culture survives. "Faced by Leninism, Hitlerism and
the plebeian mass movements, the more verbal differences [between Dobrowsky's classicism and the romantic
humanitarianism] recede and only the voice of Europe
is heard which calls to the defence of classical as well
as of Christian humanity. There is hardly another figure
of our past which obliges us more to participate in this
struggle than Josef Dobrowsky, whose enlightened humanism has so much contributed to the indissoluble
union of Czech national thought with the European
classical tradition" (p. 146).

p. 9, l. 4
   The first edition, published in Budapest in 1824 in
the Royal University Press, consisted of 151 sonnets,
divided into three parts, named after the three main
Slav rivers in Central Europe, the Saale, the Elbe, and
the Danube. The second much enlarged edition consisted of 615 sonnets, and had two parts added, one
called Lethe which represented a Slav heaven where the
good Slavs and their friends were placed, and the other
called Acheron, the Slav hell, where Slav traitors and
enemies were condemned to horrible suffering. A great
number of explanatory notes enlarged the volume.
Further editions with additions appeared in 1845 and
1852. The best modern edition is by Jan Jakubec
(Prague: J. Otto, 1903). See on Kollár, Roderick A.
Ginsburg, *Jan Kollar, a Poet of Pan-Slavism* (Chicago:
Czech Literary Press, 1942); Louis Leger, "Jean Kollár

et la poésie Pan-slaviste au XIXe siècle" in his *Russes
et Slaves. Études politiques et littéraires* I (Paris:
Hachette, 1890), pp. 277–346; Albert Pražák, "The
Slovak Sources of Kollár's Pan-Slavism," *The Slavonic
Review,* VI, 18 (March, 1928), 579–92; M. Murko,
"Hundert Jahre der 'Slavischen Wechselseitigkeit' J.
Kollár's," *Slavische Rundschau* IX, 1 (Prague, 1937),
pp. 13–23; *Jan Kollár 1793–1852,* Sborník statí o
životě, působení a literární činnosti pěvce Slávy Dcery
na oslavu jeho stoletých narozenin (A collection of
articles on the life, the influence and the literary activity
of the author of "The Daughter of Slava" on the occa-
sion of the centenary of his birth), ed. by František
Pastrnak (Czech Academic Society in Vienna and the
Slovak Academic Society Tatran in Vienna, 1893);
Miloš Weingart, "Le Passé et le présent de la solidarité
Slave," *Le Monde Slave,* N. S., III, 2 (Feb., 1926),
187–210.

p. 11, l. 9

From Prague on Feb. 21, 1836, Šafařík wrote to his
Russian friend M. P. Pogodin who had invited him to
Moscow to occupy there the chair of Slav studies: *"Ich
bin in einem Alter und im Erlernen der Sprachen so
schwerfällig, dass ich nicht hoffen kann, in Russland
als Lehrer und Schriftsteller in russicher Sprache je
auftreten zu können, und als ein Fremder, Deutscher,
mag und will ich dort nie, nie auftreten. Endlich, was
das Wichtigste ist, ich bin an Prag, Böhmen und den
österreichischen Kaiserstaat durch so viele Bandes des
Dankes und der Liebe gebunden, dass ich dieselben
freiwillig und so lange ich hier meinen Landsleuten
nützen kann, nie verlassen werde."* (I am too old and
have too little ability to learn foreign languages easily,
that I cannot hope to teach and write ever in Russia in
Russian. And I do not wish ever to appear there as a
foreigner or German. Finally, what is most important,
I am bound to Prague, Bohemia, and the Austrian
monarchy by so many ties of gratitude and love that I
shall never leave them voluntarily and as long as I can
be of any use here to my fellow citizens.) "Pis'ma k
M. P. Pogodin iz slavyanskikh zemel' 1835–61" (Letters

to M. P. Pogodin from the Slav countries), part II, Letters by Šafařík, ed. by Nil Popov. *Chteniya* (Papers read in the Imperial Society for the History and Antiquities of Russia at the Moscow University), 1879, Oct.-Dec., no. 4, p. 152.

Some of the other Pan-Slavs of the same generation did not show the political restraint of the leading figures, f.i. Václav Hanka (1791–1861), who "found" in 1817 the famous Königinhofer manuscript and also forged the other manuscript "Libuša's Judgment" found in 1818. These two manuscripts played a great role in arousing Czech national pride. They were, against much nationalist resistance, definitely proven in the 1880's to be forgeries by three great Czech scholars, the philologist Jan Gebauer, the historian Jaroslav Goll, and T. G. Masaryk. Ernest Denis in his excellent *La Bohême dépuis la Montagne-Blanche*, 2 vols., (Paris: 1902–3) makes a comment that can be applied generally in the age of nationalism: "Generally it is infinitely better to have no history than to keep up in the people the inclination to falsehood. It is a wrong piety to wish to cover up the errors of our forefathers; the only means of honoring the memory of our fathers consists of abandoning their mistakes." Quoted from the authorized and much enlarged Czech translation by Jindřich Vančura, 4th ed. (Prague: Šolc & Šimáček; 1931), part II, book 1, p. 114.

p. 11, l. 16
The book was first published in Czech in 1836 in a Slovak periodical *Hronka, Podtatranská zabavinice*, part I, no. 2, pp. 39–53, but the German edition is much expanded (132 pp.) and was written as an original. The first edition (Pest; 1837) was followed by a second revised edition in Leipzig, 1844. Šafařík wrote to M. P. Pogodin on June 18, 1837, pleading for an immediate translation of Kollár's new book: "Sorgen Sie doch dafür, dass es (das Werklein) unverzüglich ins Russische übersetzt und gedruckt wird. Da die Pièce deutsch und sehr klein ist, so wird die Sache, hoffe ich, gar keine Schwierigkeiten haben." (Please see to it that the little book is immediately translated into Russian and

printed. As it is written in German and is very short,
the matter, I hope, will present no difficulty). *Chteniya,
loc. cit.*, p. 202.

p. 14, l. 6
Ernest Denis, *loc. cit.*, p. 130.

p. 14, l. 27
In Taras Shevchenko: *The Poet of Ukraine.* Selected
Poems, tr. by Clarence A. Manning (Jersey City:
Ukrainian National Association; 1945), p. 146 f. Dr.
Manning sees in this dedication with its mention of a
free sea in which all the Slavic rivers will gather, a
direct answer by the Ukrainian poet to Pushkin's poem
demanding that all the Slav rivers flow into the Russian
sea.

p. 15, l. 12
See H. Tourtzer, *Louis Štúr et l'idée de l'indé-
pendance Slovaque,* 1815–1856 (Thèse, Paris 1913;
Cahors & Alençon: A. Coeurant, 1913). Josef Miloslav
Hurban, *Ludovit Štúr,* 3 vols. (Turčianský Sv. Martin,
1928–1942). On Slovakia see *Slovenská vlastiveda,* 5
vols., ed. by the Slovak Academy of Sciences and Art
(Bratislava 1943–48), especially vol. IV by Frant. Bokes
on History and vol. V, 1 by Andrej Mraz on the History of Literature; Ernest Denis, *Les Slovaques* (Paris:
Delgrave, 1917); J. Hanák, "Slovaks and Czechs in the
early 19th century" *The Slavonic Review* X, 30 (April,
1932), 588–601.

p. 16 l. 5
        The popular song began:
        Nitra milá, Nitra, ty vysoká Nitra!
        Kde že sú tie časy, v ktorých si ty kvitla? . . .

Štúr himself wrote poems glorifying Nitra: see Josef
Ambruš, "Poezia L'udovíta Štúra," *Sbornik Matice
Slowenskej,* XV (1937), p. 420.

p. 16, l. 33
Besides his *Nárečja slovensko alebo potreba písanja
v tomto nárečí* (Pressburg: K. F. Wigand, 1846) which

is mentioned in the text, Štúr published in the same year a grammar of the Slovak language. His newspaper had an important literary supplement "Orol Tatranski" (The Eagle from the Tatra). Hurban published an almanac *Nitra* in the new language and later edited the first scholarly review in Slovak, *Slovenskje pohlady no vedi, umenja a literatúru* (Slovak Views on Science, Art and Literature). The Czech writers and scholars, among them also Kollár, Šafařík, Palkovič, published in 1846 a strongly worded "Voices about the Need of the Unity of a Literary Language for the Bohemians, the Moravians and the Šlovaks." Štúr answered it in *Orol Tatranski*, vol. II (1846), pp. 274–76, 282–84. Kollár published in the *Narodní Noviny* on May 2, 1848 an article "Slavočech," in which he pointed out that the Bohemians (Czechs) were the trunk, the Moravians, the Silesians, the Lusatian Wends and the Slovaks were the boughs of the tree of Slav solidarity. They should be Moravians, Silesians, Wends and Slovaks at home but as a nation they must all be one: Slavoczechs.

p. 18, l. 28

The translation by Vladimir Ivanovich Lamansky (1833–1914) was published in the *Chteniya, op. cit.,* 1867, Jan-March, vol. I, pp. VI-191, under the title "Slavyanstvo i mir budushchavo. Poslanie slavyanam s beregov Dunaya" (Slavdom and the World of the Future. A Message to the Slavs from the Shores of the Danube). The German original appeared as *Das Slawenthum und die Welt der Zukunft,* ed. by Josef Jirásek (Bratislava, 1931). See also Michael B. Petrovich, "Ludovit Štúr and Russian Panslavism," *Journal of Central European Affairs,* XII (1952), 1, 1–19.

p. 20, l. 2

At the beginning of the nineteenth century it was generally believed that the Slavs formed one nation with one language. Thus Cannabich *op. cit.* (Intr., note 4), maintained that Russia's "Hauptsprachen sind die Slavische Sprache (vorzüglich die Hauptdialekte derselben,

die Russische und Polnische Sprache), die Finnische,
Tartarische . . . " (p. 625), or in speaking of Austria,
"Ausserdem werden in dieser Monarchie folgende
Sprachen geredet: die Slavische in fünf verschiedenen
Dialekten, dem Windischen, Böhmischen, Polnischen,
Russischen und Serbischen (letzterer in Slavonien,
Kroatien etc.), die Ungarische, die Wallachische (ein
Gemisch von Römischem und Dacischem Dialekte)
und die Italienische." (p. 235). But by 1850 it had
been generally accepted that the Slav languages were
independent languages like the Romance languages and
that the Slavs were divided into a number of different
nations.

p. 20, l. 23

Palacký began to write his History in German, but
from March, 1848 on (a significant date) it appeared in
Czech and the title was changed from "History of
Bohemia" to "History of the Czech Nation" (*Dějiny
národa Českého*). Both editions comprised five volumes; the last volume of the Czech edition appeared
in 1876, shortly before the author's death. T. G.
Masaryk wrote in *The Making of a State* (New York:
Frederick A. Stokes, 1927): "My guide and master
was Palacký, the father of the fatherland, who gave us
the philosophical history of our nation, understood its
place in the world and defined our national objective."
(p. 472). On Palacký see the article by Josef Pekář in
Ottův Slovník Naučný, reprinted in *Světová knihovna*,
nos. 1025–6; T. G. Masaryk, *Palackého idea národa
českého* (Prague: Čin, 1926)—this pamphlet "Palacký's
Idea of the Czech Nation" appeared first in 1898—;
Josef Fischer, *Myšlenka a dílo Františka Palackého* (The
Thought and Work of F. Palacký), 2 vols. (Prague:
Čin, 1926–27).

p. 22, l. 24

T. G. Masaryk wrote "the conviction that the Czech
people cannot become politically independent is one of
the fundamental political conceptions of Palacký."
("Palacký's Idea of the Czech Nation," *loc. cit.*, p. 42 f).
Palacký knew well that the Czechs did not lose their

national existence by the union with Austria in 1526. On the contrary, this union put an end to the possible conflicts of the different neighboring peoples. But even the Battle of the White Mountain in 1620 cannot be regarded as a defeat and extinction of Czech nationalism. In that battle the Catholic Habsburgs defeated a Protestant Bohemian king who was a German. It is an open question whether the Czechs, if they had remained Protestants, would not have come very strongly under German influence and would not have been incorporated into German life, whereas in the Habsburg state they escaped the fate of Germanization more easily.

p. 23, l. 10

See *Politické výroky a zásady Františka Ladislava Riegra*, ed. by Jan. J. Langer (Prague, 1913), p. 16. (Political Declarations and Principles of F. L. Rieger).

p. 25, l. 39

Already in Moscow Havlíček wrote a poem on December 23, 1843 against Kollár's Pan-Slavism ("Tyš bratr náš" in *Basnické spisy Karla Havlíčka*, ("The Poetical Works of K. H."), ed. by Ladislav Quis, Prague, 1897, p. 10). See on Havlíček T. G. Masaryk, *Karel Havlíček*, 3rd ed. (Prague: Jan Laichter, 1920), a detailed study regarding H. as a forerunner of Masaryk's "realistic" policy. Among the famous satirical poems by H. is *Křest sv. Vladimira* (The baptism of St. Vladimir), a sharp attack on the Russian Church, on Russian autocracy and on Cesaropapism. He began to write it while he was in Russia and completed it during his last years.

See also Jiří Polivka, "Havlíček a Rusko" (H. and Russia), *T. G. Masarykovi k 60. narozeninám* (T. G. M. to his 60th Birthday), ed. by E. Beneš, F. Drtina et alii, 2nd ed. (Prague: Čin, 1930), pp. 218–226. Havlíček wrote in 1848: "Especially Russian literature remains to us mostly inaccessible and as far as is known, only one Russian periodical arrives regularly in Bohemia, and this is one which has no great importance among the Russians themselves." This periodical was Pogodin's Pan-Slav *Moskvityanin*.

p. 26, l. 16

While an editor of the official newspaper before March, 1848, Havlíček often referred to the Irish national movement, especially to Daniel O'Connell's agitation for the repeal or annulment of the Articles of Union (1800) between Great Britain and Ireland. The word "repeal" became under his influence a widely accepted slogan among the Czechs of that time. Ironically enough, this veiled repeal agitation was used after 1918 by the Slovaks against the Czechs.

In his religious program, Havlíček demanded the "nationalization" of the Church, the use of Czech instead of Latin in its services, and the end of the celibacy for the priests. His *Národní Noviny* was stopped by the government on January 18, 1850. Havlíček founded a new paper *Slovan* in Kutná Hora which appeared twice a week but ceased on September 14, 1851. At the end of the same year he was arrested and exiled to Brixen in Tyrol. "Brixen was not a concentration camp like those in the dictatorships in which today political adversaries are thrown. It was neither Oranienburg nor Bereza Kartuska nor the shore of the White Sea. The political prisoner lived there in a house where he rented an apartment. He received several hundred florins yearly and had the opportunity to circulate freely in the near environment. From the point of view of today's fate of political prisoners the government of Bach (the Austrian absolutist and reactionary government of Alexander Freiherr von Bach, 1851–1859) was a very enlightened and civilized government." Václav Cháb, *Karel Havlíček Borovský* (Prague: Volná Myšlenka, 1936), p. 79. In his exile Havlíček returned to literature and the period was on the whole fertile for his productivity. In April, 1855, he was allowed to return to Bohemia where meanwhile his wife had died of tuberculosis, an illness to which he himself succumbed in July, 1856, the same illness which ended another brilliant career, that of Belinsky.

p. 26, l. 23

Modern Czech historiography has upheld the Western orientation and the sober sense of responsibility of Palacký and Havlíček. The founder of the school of modern Czech historiography Jaroslav Goll (1846–1929) maintained that the Czechs, except for the very early period when they underwent Byzantine influences, were since the Gothic period historically and culturally connected only with the West. His leading disciple Josef Pekář (1870–1927) declared in his address as rector of the Charles University in 1931 that "the whole Czech history is in its essence a product of Western European influences and interrelations." ("Zur Periodisierung der tschechoslovakischen Geschichte," *Prager Rundschau*, I, 6 (1931), 481–495). After 1918 Pekář had the courage to protest against the agrarian reform which the Czechoslovak Republic carried through primarily as an expropriation of German landowners to the profit of Czech peasants. "Ich bin ein gläubiger und wahrhaftiger Nationalist, aber ich gehöre gleichzeitig zu jenen, die überzeugt sind, dass Gewalt und Unrecht die ungeeignetsten Waffen im nationalen Ringen sind, namentlich heute, nach dem grossen Kriege, in dem wir die Selbständigkeit unter einer Losung erlangt haben, in der sich unser altes nationales Programm Palackys und Riegers mit dem Befreiungsprogramm der grossen westlichen Demokratien in Übereinstimmung befunden hat." (I am a faithful and true nationalist but I belong at the same time to those who are convinced that force and injustice are most inept weapons in the national struggle, especially today, after the great war, in which we have achieved independence in a way in which our old national program of Palacký and Rieger was in agreement with the liberation program of the great Western Democracies). See the necrologue by Kamil Krofta in *Prager Rundschau*, VII, 2 (1937), 81–102. See also S. Harrison Thomson, "T. G. Masaryk and Czech Historiography," *Journal of Central European Affairs*, X, 1 (April, 1950), 37–52.

p. 28, l. 11

See Robert F. Arnold, *Geschichte der deutschen Polenliteratur von den Anfängen bis* 1800 (Halle: Max Niemeyer, 1900). On the Polish nationalism of that period in general see *The Idea of Nationalism*, pp. 518–526; W. Feldman, *Geschichte der Politischen Ideen in Polen seit dessen Teilungen* 1795–1914 (Munich: R. Oldenbourg, 1917); Wacław Lednicki, "Poland and the Slavophile Idea," *The Slavonic Review*, VII (1928–29), 128 ff; Zofja Klarnerowna, *Słowianofilstwo w literaturze polskiej lat 1800 do 1848* (Warsaw: Studja z zakresu historji literatury polskiej, IV, 1926), Marcel Handelsman, "La politique slave de la Pologne aux XVIIIe et XIXe siècles," *Le Monde Slave XIII* (Dec. 1936), pp. 426–455; Julian Krzyzanowski, *Polish Romantic Literature* (London: Allen & Unwin, 1930). An excellent selection of important Polish writers is *Wiek XIX. Sto lat myśli polskiej* (The 19th Century, One Hundred Years of Polish Thought) 8 vols. (Warsaw: Gebethner & Wolff, 1906–1913).

p. 29, l. 19

Victor Hugo, *Actes et Paroles. Avant l'exile 1841–1851* (Paris: Michel Lévy Frères, 1875), p. 68 f.

p. 29, l. 28

See Hannah Alice Straus, *The Attitude of the Congress of Vienna toward Nationalism in Germany, Italy and Poland* (New York: Columbia University Press, 1949).

p. 29, l. 36

Samuel Gottlieb Linde (1771–1847) who had studied philology in Leipzig and was later lecturer in Polish there, came in 1803 to Warsaw as director of the Lyceum. There he wrote his famous Dictionary of the Polish Language (*Słownik języka polskiego*, 6 vols., 1807–14). This dictionary laid the foundation for Slavic lexiography and included the vocabulary of all Slav languages. He wrote also a "Historical Survey of the Literature of the Slav Peoples", 1825. Early scholarly interest in the Slavs was evinced by Adam Czarnocki who in

his O Słowiańszczyznie przed chrześcijaństwem (About
the Pre-Christian Slavs, 1818) glorified the Slav people
of the early past. Wenceslas A. Maciejowski (1793–
1883) developed in his Historja prawodawstw słowiań-
skich (History of Slav Law, 4 vols. 1832–35) and other
works the thesis of the superiority of Slavs over the
West.

p. 31, l. 5
    See W. M. Kozlowski, "Der Tschechische Humani-
tismus und der Polnische Messianismus", *Festschrift
Th. G. Masaryk zum 80. Geburtstage* (Bonn: Friedrich
Cohen, 1930), II, 49–104; Nikolai O. Lossky, *Three
Chapters from the History of Polish Messianism* (International Philosophical Library, 11, 9, Prague 1936)
and *Three Polish Messianists* (International Philosophical Library, III, 11, Prague 1937). A late representative
of this Polish-centered Slavism was Wincenty Lutosław-
ski. In his *The Polish Nation* (A lecture delivered at
the Lowell Institute in Boston on October 21, 1907.
Paris: Boyveau & Chevillet, 1917) he wrote: "The
Poles as Aryans have this in common with the other
Western Aryans, that they are in many respects the heirs
of Rome. . . . Therefore, if you wish to understand a
Pole, be careful to distinguish him from Orientals like
the Jews and Russians or Muscovites, and regard him as
one of that great Western family which gave to mankind the Greeks, the Romans, and the English. . . .
Among the Slavs the Poles occupy the central position.
Poland was probably the original home of the Slavs and
there is no evidence whatever that the Poles came from
elsewhere. While the eastern and western and southern
Slavs have been conquered by other nations and long
ago lost their independence, the Poles alone formed an
independent state for a thousand years, and have had an
opportunity for carrying out Slavic ideals of political
organization, based on brotherhood and freedom. Those
who believe that the day of Slavic influence in the world
will come, after the other branches of the Aryan race
have contributed their share to the life of mankind, must
look towards the Poles as the purest Slavs and not expect from the Russians who are not Slavs or Aryans, the

fulfilment of the Slavic mission." (p. 45–48). He believed that the Great Russians were Turanians among whom the Moscow princes introduced the Slav language. Thus they became "Russian in language while remaining thoroughly Turanian in feeling and tradition."

p. 31, l. 9
On this glorification of the people in the nationalist movements in the 1830's and 1840's see Hans Kohn, *Prophets and Peoples* (New York: Macmillan, 1946), especially the chapters on Michelet and Mazzini. Mickiewicz declared in his lecture of January 9, 1844: "It is possible to be dressed in rags like a Slav peasant or in the overalls of the French workman, and not to belong to the people. It is possible to shine in the splendor of gold and to be of the people. The people, that is the man who suffers, the man who longs for the higher life, the man who possesses liberty of mind. . . . For that reason the people sees the truth so quickly and so infallibly in the decisive moments. . . . A man whose heart beats not faster when he hears the words of Gracchus or St. Paul, such a man is not of the people." The people is a mystical entity destined to realize the most sublime hopes and the most nationalist imaginations of the great poets and agitators of the nationalism of the period.

p. 32, l. 14
Marcel Handelsman, "La Politique slave de la Pologne aux XVIIIe et XIXe siècles," *Le Monde Slave* XIII (Dec. 1936) 426–455, p. 440.

p. 33, l. 20
Hoene fought as a boy in the Polish army with Kościuszko and was taken prisoner with him in 1794. Later he tried to join the Polish legions in France. He dedicated his first writings to General Henryk Dąbrowski, the commander of the Polish legion who advised him to devote his talents to a work "about the necessity of the re-establishment of Poland for Europe's happiness." He developed his system in 1818 in an essay

dedicated to Alexander I. There he called his system
"Sehelianism," a name which he derived from the
Hebrew word "sekhel," "reason." The word "messianism" was first used in his *Prodrome du messianisme.
Révélation des destinées de l'humanité* (Paris 1831. A
German translation *Prodrom des Messianismus oder
die absolute Philosophie* appeared in Oldenburg: Gerhard Stalling, 1930). One of his last writings, "Document Historique secret sur la révélation des destinées
providentielles des nations Slaves," he dedicated to Emperor Nicolai I. See F. Warrain, *L'Armature métaphysi-
que, établie d'après la Loi de Création de Hoene-Wron-
ski* (Paris: Alcan, 1926); Józef Ujejski, *Dzieje polskiego
mesjanizmu do powstania listopadowego włącznie* (History of Polish Messianism up to the November Uprising.
Lwów: Zakład narodowy imienia Ossolińskich, 1931).

p. 34, l. 23
His main work was called *Ojcze-Nasz* (Paris: Maulde
& Renou, 1848), because the Lord's Prayer in its seven
petitions contains the foundations of the Kingdom
which will come not in heaven but here on earth. There
is a French translation by the author's son and M. V.
Gasztowtt, *Notre Père*, 3 vols. (Paris: Société Française
d'imprimerie et de librairie, 1906, 1927, 1928). The
passage on the Slavs is vol. I, pt. 3, chs. X–XI, pp. 261–
294. See the valuable book by Walter Kühne, *Graf August Cieszkowski, ein Schüler Hegels und des deutschen
Geistes* (Berliner Universität, Slavisches Institut. Veröffentlichungen XX, Leipzig: Harrassowitz, 1938). The
book contains an important correspondence between C.
and Michelet covering the years 1836–1873.

p. 35, l. 38
Trentowski published in 1842 *Chowanna czyli system
pedagogiki narodowej* (Chowanna or the System of National Education) where he proposed a new system of
education for the Poles to transform the national psychology to a voluntaristic bent. Man's value consists not
in what he thinks or feels but in what he does. Another
Polish philosopher who fused a philosophy of activism

based upon intuition with nationalism, democracy and social messianism was Karol Libelt (1807–1875).

p. 37, l. 23

Of practical statesmen and leading politicians Poland had only two in the years between 1830 and 1865. Neither of them had any large popular support. The old Prince Adam Czartoryski became after 1831 in exile in Paris the leader of the conservative aristocratic movement for the restoration of Poland, violently opposed to Russia. Nothing remained of his former friendship of his youth for Alexander I. With the help of Władysław Zamoyski (1803–1868), Czartoryski tried to win over the Balkan Slavs to a Pan-Slavism directed against Russia. His numerous agents were active, especially in the years preceding the Crimean War. Czartoryski wrote on Feb. 15, 1844, to Lord Dudley (1803–1854), a member of the British Parliament for many years and well known as a devoted friend of Polish independence: "The cause of Poland should no longer be separated from that of several other Slav peoples, where it has been received with interest and where it has produced an anti-Russian reaction. It is extremely fortunate for the liberty of Europe that the so remarkable and very serious movement which agitates all the Slav countries, has been liberated through our efforts more and more from Russian influence. . . . I wished that . . . the services rendered to mankind by Poland be appreciated, not only as a chain tied to the feet of Russia and which does not allow it to advance, but also as a zealous agent which has shown to all the Slav peoples Russia as it really is and has broken the spell which Russia exercises on the Slavs." Quoted by J. A. Teslar in *The Slavonic and East European Review* XXIX, 72 (Dec. 1950) p. 164. See also M. Kukiel, *Czartoryski and European Unity 1770–1861* (Princeton Univ. Press, 1955).

On the other hand, Alexander Ignacy Marquis Wielopolski (1803–1877), a legitimist like Czartoryski, turned violently against Austria and Germanism in his famous "Lettre d'un gentilhomme polonais sur les massacres de Galicie addressée au prince Metternich," Paris, 1846.

He regarded Poland as too weak for political independence. The Poles should turn to Russia where they could help to bring about the necessary changes and thereby strengthen the common Slavdom of the two peoples. "Each of these nationalities could perhaps become better and richer than they are now when they procede separately. The Russian state would through us gain an influence on all the lands inhabited by our brothers and thereby also on other Slav peoples in the south and west. The Polish nobility will without doubt prefer to march with the Russians at the head of the young strong Slav civilization which possesses the future instead of dragging along, being pushed around, offended, despised and hated, at the tail of your decaying, noisy and conceited civilization." See Henryk Lisicki, *Le Marquis Wielopolski, sa vie et son temps* (Vienna: Faesy & Frick, 1880) 2 vols.; A. M. Skalkowski, *Aleksander Wielopolski w świetle archiwów rodzinnych* (Poznań: Poznańskie towarzystwo przyjaciół nauk, 1947) 3 vols.

p. 38, l. 17
See M. Handelsman, *Les idées françaises et la mentalité politique en Pologne au XIXe siècle* (Paris: Alcan, 1927).

p. 39, l. 1
On the importance of this address "O narodowości Polaków" see Bronislas Chlebowski, *La littérature polonaise au XIXe siècle*, ed. by Manfred Kridl (Paris: H. Champion, 1933. Bibliothèque polonaise de l'institut d'études slaves, III), p. 72 f. Brodziński collected and translated Czech, Slovak, Serb and Ukrainian folksongs. In his introduction he proclaimed his conviction that "the folksongs of the Slavs as well as their habits and customs, can lead faster and with greater certainty to poetry than the German folksongs. Today only the Slavs recall by their customs, their taste and their national songs, ancient Greece."

At the same time in Bohemia František Ladislav Čelakovský (1799–1852) under the influence of Kollár collected Slav folksongs. In 1829, when the Russians advancing against the Turks crossed the Danube, he published his collection of Russian songs *Ohlas písní ruských*. His "Slav Folksongs" (*Slovanské národní písně*) appeared in three volumes, 1822, 1825 and 1827. In his last year he published *Mudrosloví národu slovanského v příslovích* (The Wisdom of the Slav Nation in Proverbs). There he still spoke of one Slav nation.

p. 41, l. 4

Certain passages in Mickiewicz sound familiar today, as when he writes that the gendarme "usually arrives at night and carries off the suspected person never informing him of his destination. The kibitka (wooden carriage without springs) is provided with a bell. A person who has never lived in Lithuania can scarcely imagine the terror that prevails in every house at the door of which the sound of the post bell is heard." And again: "The common folk of Russia are fully convinced that the Tsar is quite equal to carrying off any other monarch in a police kibitka." A Russian dignitary whom Mickiewicz hated, was reported to have said: "There will never be peace until we so organize Europe that one of our Feldjägers can execute identical orders in Wilna, Paris, and Istambul with equal ease."

p. 42, l. 3

George Rapall Noyes in the introduction to his edition in English of *Poems by Adam Mickiewicz* (New York: Polish Institute for Arts and Sciences, 1944), pp. 30, 14 f. Prof. Manfred Kridl writes on that subject: "In the moral sphere, in the field of certain established feelings and attitudes, the spirit of Mickiewicz continues to rule over us. The same holds true for our relationship to Russia and the Russians, which was largely determined by part III of *Forefathers' Eve*. And this is also true of Polish patriotism which to strangers may appear too 'romantic,' too idealistic or fantastic. We were taught this patriotism above all by the works of Mickiewicz."

English readers are fortunate to have the translation of Mickiewicz, including part III of *Forefathers' Eve*, in the above mentioned edition by the late Prof. Noyes. He also published in Everyman's Library a translation of *Pan Tadeusz*. See also the newer translations of

Selected Poems, ed. by Clark Mills, intro. by Jan Le-
chon (New York: Noonday Press, 1955) and of *The
Great Improvisation* from Part III of Forefathers by
Louis Vàrise (New York: Voyages, 1956); Manfred
Kridl, ed., *Adam Mickiewicz, Poet of Poland* (New
York: Columbia University Press, 1951); Arthur P.
Coleman and Marion M. Coleman, *Mickiewiczana,
Articles, Translations, Bibliographies* (New York: Klub
Polski, 1946); Jósef Kallenbach, *Adam Mickiewicz,* 3rd
ed., 2 vols. (Lwów: Ossoliński Institute, 1923); *Adam
Mickiewicz: In Commemoration of the Centenary of his
Death* (Paris: UNESCO, 1955); Abraham G. Duker,
Mickiewicz's Jewish Mystique (Hague: Mouton & Co.,
1956); Edouard Krakowski, *Adam Mickiewicz, phil-
osophe mystique. Les sociétés secrètes et le messianisme
européen après la révolution de 1830. 2nd ed. (Paris:
Mercure de France, 1935); Gleb Struve, "Mickiewicz in
Russia," *The Slavonic and East European Review,*
XXVI, 66 (1947), pp. 126 ff.; Waclaw Lednicki,
"Mickiewicz at the Collège de France," *The Slavonic
Yearbook* (The Slavonic and East European Review,
XX, 1941), 149–172; Mieczysław Jastruń, *Adam Mickiewicz* (Warsaw: Państwowy Instytut Wydawniczy,
1949). There are two anthologies which make the Polish
literature of the period accessible, *A Polish Anthology*
(Polish text selected by T. M. Filip and English transla-
tion by M. A. Michael), (London: Duckworth, 1944);
Le Chant de la Pologne (Fribourg: Fragnière Frères,
1940).

p. 44, l. 15
  Quoted by John N. Washburn in M. Kridl (editor),
Adam Mickiewicz, loc. cit., p. 147 f. Mickiewicz' lectures
were published as *Les Slaves,* Histoire et littérature des
nations polonaise, bohême, serbe, et russe, cours professé
au Collège de France, 1840–42, 3 vols., (Paris: Librairie
du Luxembourg, 1866); *L'Eglise officielle et le Messianisme,* 2 vols. (Paris: Au Comtoir des Imprimeurs
Reunis, 1845); *Vorlesungen über Slavische Literatur
und Zustände,* 4 vols. (Leipzig: Brockhaus & Avenarius,
1843–45).

p. 45, l. 39
Quoted by Karel Krejčí in M. Kridl, *op. cit.*, p. 191.

p. 46, l. 4
See Krasiński's letter to Countess Delfina Potocka of
March 20, 1848, *Listy do Delfiny Potockiej*, ed. by A.
Żółtowski (Poznań, 1938), III, 659–661.

p. 47, l. 11
The Writings of Margaret Fuller, ed. by Mason
Wade (New York: Viking, 1941), p. 463 f.

p. 48, l. 9
See Hans Kohn, *Prophets and Peoples*, *op. cit.*, p.
188.

p. 48, l. 36
See the article on messianism in *The Encyclopaedia
of the Social Sciences*. On the identification of the Puritans with Israel see *The Idea of Nationalism*, 166–178,
269–271, 278–79.

p. 49, l. 23
Mickiewicz, *Les Slaves*, *op. cit.*, III, 365.

p. 50, l. 14
Mickiewicz, Cours professé au Collège de France,
1842–1844, *L'Église officielle et le messianisme*, Philosophie et Religion; L'Eglise et le Messie, Religion et Politique (Paris: Musée Adam Mickiewicz, 1914), pp. 5, 11,
284. This book which under the influence of Towiański
came to be regarded as containing much which was unacceptable to the Church was put on the Index by a
decree of April 15, 1848. Mickiewicz regarded Napoleon
as the Man who had most completely in his person
realized the past era and had surpassed it by his genius.
"Of all men of the past epoch, Napoleon was the most
miraculous. The peoples felt instinctively that this man
accomplished within himself a work unknown to the
priest and to the pope, that he was more advanced in
the knowledge of the secrets of heaven than the official
Church, and that he therefore could help the peoples to

approach . . . the kingdom of the Gospels, Heaven.
They understood that the work he did was a continuation of the work of Jesus Christ." *ibid.* 317, 357.

p. 50, l. 20
  Les Slaves, op. cit., III, 335–340, 356–368.

p. 53, l. 23
  In his beautiful and violent poem "Agamemnon's
Tomb" Słowacki expressed all his despair in comparing
the Poles with the Spartans. "The legion of the Spartan
dead might well drive me from the tombs of Thermo-
phylae, for I am from a sad land of Helots, from a land
where despair builds no memorials to fame, from a land
where, on the morrows of misfortune, there always remains a melancholy half—of knights—alive. . . . At
Thermopylae, what account would I give, if men were
to be standing on the graves, who showing me their
bloody breasts should bluntly ask: You were many?
. . . If they asked me that, what should I say?"

p. 54, l. 21
  See Wacław Lednicki, *Jules Slowacki* (Brussels: Editions de la Revue de l'Université de Bruxelles, 1927);
Francis J. Whitfield, "The Author of Anhelli", *The
American Slavic and East-European Review,* VIII (Dec.,
1949), 317–327; Albert M. Wagner, "Undivine Comedy: Zygmunt Krasinski and German Expressionism",
The American Slavic and East European Review, VI
(1947), 95–109. Many of that period rejected Pan-
Slavism and Polish messianism. The *Demokrat Polski*
wrote on January 13, 1849; "Pan-Slavism means a return to the times of barbarism, when humanity was
divided into races, and when not thinking but blood
was the only link between people." Quoted by Henryk
Batowski, *The Slavonic and East European Review,*
XXVII, 69, (May, 1949), p. 413. And in the camp of
the rightists in 1842 Karol Sienkiewicz wrote in the introduction to his historical studies about the Slavs:
"There are Slav languages, literatures, and there are also
several Slav fatherlands. But because these fatherlands
have not known each other for centuries or because

hatred, oppression and difference of languages exist
among them, . . . there is today neither a Slav language, nor a Slav literature, nor a Slav fatherland. . . .
To put the Polish idea under the protection of a Slav
idea which in reality does not exist, . . . would lead
Poland astray." Quoted in W. Feldman, *op. cit.*, p.
144 f.

p. 59, l. 5

See *The Idea of Nationalism*, pp. 543–551; Ferdo
Šišić, *Jugoslovenska Misao*, A History of the Idea of the
Unification and Liberation of the Yugoslav Peoples from
1790 to 1918 (Belgrad: Balkanski Institut, 1937); Josip
Horvat, *Politička povijest hrvatske* (Political History of
Croatia), (Zagreb: Binoza-Svjetski Pisci, 1936); Tomi-
slav Kokorić, *Narodno jedinstvo Srba, Hrvata, Slovenaca
i Bulgara* (The National Unity of Serbia, Croatia, Slove-
nia and Bulgaria, considered from a Historical Point of
View) (Prague: Ed. Grégr & Son, 1937); Aurelio F.
Palmieri, "Growth of Croatian Nationalism," *The
Catholic World*, no. 109 (New York, 1919), pp. 344–
359; Hermann Wendel, *Der Kampf der Südslawen um
Freiheit und Einheit* (Frankfurt a.M.: Societäts-Drucke-
rei, 1925); Émile Haumant, *La Formation de la Yougo-
slavie* (Paris: Bossard, 1930); Dinko Tomasic, *Personality and Culture in Eastern European Politics* (New
York: George W. Stewart, 1948); Gellia Cassi, "Les
populations Juliennes-Illyriennes pendant la domination
Napoléonienne, 1806–1814," *Revue des études napo-
léoniennes*, Oct.-Dec., 1930, pp. 193–212, 257–275,
335–369.

p. 61, l. 10

The best brief discussion of the complex language
question among the southern Slavs is by George R.
Noyes in Robert J. Kerner (ed.). *Yugoslavia* (Berkeley:
University of California Press, 1949), pp. 279–317. See
also Boris Unbegaun, *Les Débuts de la langue littéraire
chez les Serbes* (Paris: Institut d'Études Slaves, 1935)
and V. Čorović, "Vuk Karadžić," *Slavonic and East
European Review*, XVI, 48 (April, 1938).

p. 62, l. 13

Professor **Philip** E. Mosely published in *American Historical Review*, XL (1935), 704–716, a Pan-Slav memorandum written by Gaj on November 1, 1838. There he wrote: "Das politisch nationale Interesse aller slavischen Völker kann und muss mit jenem Russlands nur ein und dasselbe sein, jedes andere mit diesem Interesse unvereinbare Streben ist antislavisch, ist ein Verrat an der eigenen Nation, ist ein moralischer Selbstmord, ist daher ein Verbrechen, das früher oder später in fremden Fesseln gebüsst werden muss. . . . Wenn wir dem feindseligen Prinzip Europas, welches schon in den ältesten Zeiten die grössten slavischen Reiche zertrümmerte, und in unserer Zeit, durch Russlands Grösse neuerderdings geweckt, mehr als je, selbst in den entferntesten Himmelsstrichen, gegen alles, was slavisch ist, zerstörend intrigiert, kraftvoll widerstehen und eine unserer Nation würdige Stellung behaupten wollen, so müssen unsere Stämme mit Aufopferung aller Separat-Interessen und mit Unterdrückung aller Parteiungen zu der bereits festbegründeten Zentral-Macht streben und sich mit einer dem slavischen Gemüt allein ensprechenden kindlichen Hingebung um Einen Vater, der allein sie zu beglücken vermag, Hand in Hand gruppieren. Wer diese grossartige Zentralisierung des gesamten Slaventums um Einen Herrscher für eine unpraktikable Idee hält, kennt nicht die Ursachen der Melancholie, die sich im Leben und Liede aller Stämme kundgibt, welche so vielmal an der Ausführung derselben, zu der sie vermöge ihrer patrioarchalischen Gemütsart von Natur aus bestimmt sind, teils gewaltsam, teils durch Einimpfung fremdartiger Grundsätze, gehindert wurden; der kennt nicht das de facto in den rein illyrisch-slavischen Provinzen bestehende echt nationale Familienleben im Grossen, wo um seine Gospodare oft mehr als 160 Familienmitglieder in Eintracht und kindlichem Gehorsam versammelt leben,—was dem heutigen Westeuropa fremd ist."

p. 62, l. 36

See letter from Rev. Malcolm MacColl to Gladstone written September 25, 1876, from Diacovar in *The*

Slavonic and Eastern European Review, XIV, 2 (April, 1936), p. 689. "What he (Strossmayer) himself would prefer is that Bosnia should be given to Serbia and Herzegovina to Montenegro. He has the highest possible opinion of the Serbians. He says . . . that they are about the most tolerant people in the world and are possessed of great political and administrative capacity." This opinion would hardly have been shared by the Croats half a century later in independent Yugoslavia. In a letter by the Bishop of August 5, 1886, to a Russian correspondent he wrote: "Nos slavi nec culpa, nec merito nostro ad utramque ecclesiasm spectamus; quod equidem multi ad defectum nostrum referant, mihi autem hocce ad commodum et utilitatem nostram spectare videtur, quia sic nobis bini orbes binique altioris culturae fontes patent. Omnem tamen in casum ego hocce ad providentiam divinam refero, quae vult ut gravissimum illud damnum, quod christianae fidei et ecclesiae Graecorum et Latinorum culpa infulit, Slavorum pietate, virtute, religiositate et initiatione reparetur. In hocce divino opere, fateor, prima pars praecipuumque munus et veri nominis initiatio ad Slavos Russos pertinet. Slavi hocce deficiente saeculo 19. et vicesimo etc. evidenter primas partes ac praecipuas in Europa aeque ac in Asia tenebunt. Haec hora evidenter eorum est, quam Pater aeternus in sua tenet potestate, nec quisquam eidem efficaciter obesse potest. . . . Vult evidenter Deus, ut Slavi et ecclesia Orientis, in fraterno utique cum ecclesia Occidentis foedere, sint Europae salus et secunda quodammodo post naufragium tabula; ut Asiae et feris ejusdem gentibus sint regeneratio, divinioris item vitae et salutis per christianam religionem fons. Quoad Europam, ea evidenter senescit et veluti decrepita est." Quoted in D. Stremooukhoff, *Vladimir Soloview et son Oeuvre Messianique* (Publications of the Faculty of Letters of the University of Strasbourg, 69, Paris: Les Belles Lettres, 1935), p. 317.

p. 63, l. 26

See Dragotin Loncar, *The Slovenes: a Social History*, tr., by A. J. Klancar (Cleveland: American Yugoslav Printing Co., 1939).

p. 64, l. 36

It was in Novi Sad that the *Serbski Letopisi* were founded which appeared regularly as a quarterly from 1826 to 1848, then later irregularly. There too, for their distribution, the *Matica Srpska* was founded in 1826 to publish books, both scholarly and popular. This *Matica (Queen Bee)* was later imitated in other Slav lands. After 1848 Svetozar Miletić (1826–1901) became the militant leader of the Vojvodina Serbs with his newspaper *Zastaba* (The Standard). He was supported by the youth movement of the Omladina which was founded in 1866 and was active for a few years.

p. 65, l. 7

See Emile Haumant, *op. cit.*, pp. 278, 293, 341 f.

p. 68, l. 10

On the Bulgars see James F. Clarke, "Serbia and the Bulgarian Revival, 1762–1872," *The American Slavic and East European Review*, IV (Dec., 1945), pp. 145–162; Cyril E. Black, *Establishment of Constitutional Government in Bulgaria* (Princeton: University Press, 1943); George Hateau, *Panorama de la littérature bulgare contemporaine* (Paris: Sagittaire, 1937); M. Arnaudov, *Aprilov. Zivot, dejnost', sŭvremennici* (Aprilov. Life, Activity, Contemporaries. Sofia: Ministry of National Education, 1935). Paisii (see *The Idea of Nationalism* p. 543 f.) was rediscovered only in 1871, until then Venelin could be regarded as the pioneer. From 1806 to 1834 an average of less than one book annually was published in Bulgarian: the highest number in any year was three; in 1834 fifteen books were published, mostly textbooks.

p. 71, l. 17

Michael Hrushevsky, *A History of Ukraine*, ed. by O. J. Frederiksen (New Haven: Yale University Press, 1941); Clarence A. Manning, *Ukrainian Literature* (Jersey City: Ukrainian National Association, 1944); Taras Shevchenko, *Selected Poems*, tr. by Clarence A. Manning (Jersey City: Ukrainian National Association, 1945); Elie Borschak, "Le mouvement national ukrainien au XIXe siècle," *Le Monde Slave*, Oct., Nov. and Dec., 1930.

p. 72, l. 6

Zdeněk Tobolka, *Slovanský sjezd v Praze roku 1848* (The Slav Congress in Prague in 1848, Prague: F. Šimáček, 1901); Josef Vaclav Frič, *Paměti I: Do třiceti let* (Memoirs I: To my Thirtieth Year) 4 vols. (Prague: B. Grund, 1886–87); František Roubík, *Český rok 1848* (The Czech Year 1848; Prague: L. Kuncíř, 1931); V. Čejchan and others, *Slovanský sjezd v Praze* (The Slav Congress in Prague: Prague 1848); Alexandre Thomas, "La Praguerie de 1848," *Revue des Deux Mondes*, Sept. 1, 1848; Hippolyte Desprez, "La Russie et le Slavisme, "*Revue des Deux Mondes*, May 1850, pp. 526–542.

p. 73, l. 28

See Palacký, *Radhost*, Collected Shorter Essays on Czech Language and Literature, Esthetics, History and Politics, 3 vols. (Prague: B. Tempský, 1873), vol. III, p. 9. In this revolutionary spring everything seemed possible. Šafařík wrote to Pogodin on April 1, 1848: "Es hängt, so scheint es, alles an einem dünnen Faden, ein kleiner Anstoss—und das Jüngste Gericht bricht an." *Chteniya, op. cit.*, 1879, p. 361.

p. 74, l. 7

See *The Idea of Nationalism*, p. 527. The ideal of a supranational state as against the nation-state of the 19th century was emphasized by Lord Acton, "Nationality" (1862) in his *The History of Freedom and Other Essays* (London: Macmillan, 1907), pp. 270–300. On similar ideas expressed at the same time by the French philosopher Charles Renouvier, see Hans Kohn, *Prophets and Peoples* (New York: Macmillan, 1946), p. 167.

p. 75, l. 16

See Max Lehmann, *Bismarck, eine Charakteristik* (Berlin: Oswald Arnold, 1948) and Hans Kohn, "Re-Thinking Recent German History," *Review of Politics*,

July, 1952. Hans von Perthaler (1816–1862), an Austrian, wrote in his "Das Erkaisertum in Kleindeutschland": "Die äussere Linie der deutschen Politik darf sich nicht auf den ethnographischen Begriff von Deutschen beschränken, sondern sie muss sich ausdehnen bis zu dem Punkt, wo sie hart an Frankreich und hart an Russland grenzt . . . Die zwischen dieser Linie liegenden Völker können ein eigentümliches nationales Leben nur unter dem Einfluss des deutschen Volkes führen.—Es darf in Mitteleuropa nur eine Politik geben: weil das deutsche Volk das einzige mächtige Volk in Mitteleuropa ist, muss diese Politik eine deutsche sein." Joseph Redlich, *Das Oesterreichische Staats- und Reichsproblem*, 2 vols. (Leipzig, 1920–26), vol. I, part II, p. 30.

p. 75, l. 19
The invitation to Palacký was sent by the Fünfziger Ausschuss of the German Vorparlament on April 6. His reply was dated April 11 and was addressed to Alexander von Soiren, the chairman of the Ausschuss. It is reprinted in *Radhost, op. cit.*, III, pp. 10–17. There also appears his opening speech of June 2, pp. 31–33, and the manifesto to the nations of Europe, pp. 34–37.

p. 88, l. 24
See Johannes Urzidil, "Das tschechisch-deutsche Problem einst und jetzt," *Preussische Jahrbücher*, vol. 200, no. 1 (April 1925), pp. 1–12. The anonymous article appeared in the second volume of *Revue österreichische Zustände*, published by Phil. Reclam in Leipzig. The author pleaded also for the Poles, and in a strange foresight he predicted that Poland would be politically revived only as a result of a conflagration starting among the southern Slavs. "The Polish nobility," he warned, "must understand that in our age the single class can do nothing but the people as a whole (die Gesamtmasse) can do everything. The Messiahs of the new times will not be born in a royal house but as in ancient times in a manger; the people is the only true sovereign."

p. 89, l. 13
  See R. R. John Rath, *The Viennese Revolution of 1848* (Austin: University of Texas Press, 1957, p. 262 f.

p. 89, l. 27
  See Robert A. Kann, *The Multinational Empire. Nationalism and National Reform in the Habsburg Monarchy 1848–1918* (New York: Columbia University Press, 1950), vol. II, pp. 42–47. See also Prof. Kann's brilliant analysis of the consequences of the misreading of historical forces by Marx and Engels by the Austrian and German Social Democracy, *ibid.*, p. 49 f.

p. 90, l. 29
  Ludwig Feuerbach, "Fragmente zur Charakteristik meines philosophischen Curriculum vitae," 1835: Voraussetzungen über die Geschichte der neueren Philosophie, *Sämtliche Werke*, 10 vols., Leipzig, 1846, vol. II, p. 400 f. See there also, p. 409; "Die Gegenwart erkennst du nicht aus der Geschichte; denn die Geschichte zeigt dir nur die Ähnlichkeit einer Erscheinung mit einer bereits dagewesenen, aber nicht ihren Unterschied, ihre Individualität, ihre Originalität; die Gegenwart kann nur unmittelbar durch sich selbst erfasst werden. Und du verstehst sie nur, wenn du selbst nicht bereits zur Vergangenheit, sondern zur Gegenwart, nicht zu den Toten, sondern zu den Lebendigen gehörst."

p. 91, l. 15
  Josef Pfitzner, *Bakunin Studien* (Prague: Verlag der Deutsche Gesellschaft der Wissenschaften und Künste für die Tschechoslovakische Republik, 1932) pp. 94–105; Michael Bakunin, *Zwei Schriften aus den 40er Jahren des XIX. Jahrhunderts* (Prague: Internationale Bibliothek für Philosophie, II, no. 11–12, 1936); Joseph Billig, *Der Zusammenbruch des deutschen Idealismus bei den russischen Romantikern: Bjelinski und Bakunin* (Berlin: C. Heyman, 1930).

p. 91, l. 31

17e anniversaire de la révolution polonaise. Discours prononcé à la réunion tenue à Paris pour célebrer cet anniversaire le 29 Nov. 1847 par M. Bakounine, réfugié russe (Paris: au bureau des affaires polonaises, 1847). See also Benoit-P. Hepner, *Bakounine et le panslavisme révolutionnaire* (Paris: Marcel Rivière, 1950). The best edition of Bakunin's works is *Sobranie sochinenii i pisem 1826–1876*, ed. by Ju. M. Steklov, 4 vols. (Moscow: Publishing House of the All-Union Association of Political Prisoners and Deportees, 1934–35). Vol. III contains the writings from 1840–49; vol. IV the writings of 1849–61, the period of his imprisonment and exile. The famous *Confession* of Bakunin was found in the secret archives of the Chief of the Third Division of the Chancellery of the former Tsar and published in Russian by V. Tolonski. It was translated into German, *Michael Bakunin Beichte aus der Peter-Pauls Festung an Zar Nikolaus* I by Kurt Kersten (Berlin: Deutsche Verlagsgesellschaft für Politik und Geschichte, 1927), and into French by Paulette Brupbacher with introd. by Fritz Brupbacher and notes by Max Nettlau (Paris: Rieder, 1932); his *Social-politischer Briefwechsel mit Alexander Iw. Herzen und Ogarjow*, ed. by Michail Dragomanov, was translated into German by B. Minzes (Stuttgart: Cotta, 1895). There are reprinted, in addition to Bakunin's address on the anniversary of the Polish Revolution and his "Aufruf an die Slaven von einem russischen Patrioten," also his "Statuten der neuen slavischen Politik" from Jordan, *Slavische Jahrbücher*, 1848, and in an abbreviated form his "Russkim, polskim i vsem slavyanskim druzyam" ("To the Russian, Polish and all Slavic Friends"), published first on Feb. 15, 1862, in Herzen's *The Bell*. Also reprinted in German translation are Bakunin's speeches at the congresses of the League for Peace and Freedom, in Geneva in 1867 and in Berne in 1868. The latter speech was also published in the French original in Bakunin, *Die Bekämpfung des Zarismus*, Rede gehalten auf dem Kongres der Friedens- und Freiheits-Liga in Bern 1868, ed. by Ernst Drahn (Berlin: R. L. Prager, 1925).

p. 92, l. 15
On Bakunin in 1848 see Václav Čejchan, *Bakunin v Čechách* (Prague, 1928) and his "Revoluční slovanství M. A. Bakunina," *Slovanský přehled*, XXXII (1942), no. 5–6, pp. 266–284. In that period Bakunin stressed the Germans as the "natural" enemies of the Slavs and even spoke of Slav racial hatred of the Germans. He went so far—perhaps from his Russian point of view—as to regard the English as instinctively hostile to the Slavs and as imbued with the feeling of superior civilization. The French are neither hostile nor friendly to the Slavs, they think only of themselves. That was the content of Bakunin's last appeal to the Czechs in May, 1862, to abandon the Austro-Slavism of Palacký and Rieger. "The only ideal which can move the Slavs is the renovation of the ancient Slav freedom in the framework of the great Slav world. . . . That we may achieve a final victory over our enemy of the ages (the Germans), the whole Slav world must unite and rise."

p. 97, l. 11
The pamphlet was originally written for Herzen's periodical *The Bell* and was published by Trübner & Co., London, 1862. On the sincerity of Bakunin's Confession see the good arguments in E. H. Carr, *Michael Bakunin* (London: Macmillan, 1937), p. 213.

p. 98, l. 9
It is interesting to note how far Bakunin in the Appeal of 1870—the year of Lenin's birth—anticipated Lenin: "Dans mon appel aux jeunes frères russes je disais que le Stenka Razine qui si mettra à la tête des masses populaires pendant la destruction si visiblement prochaine de l'empire russe, ne sera plus le heros individuel, mais un Stenka Razine collectif. Tout homme qui n'est pas un sot, comprendra facilement que je parlais d'une organisation secrète existant et agissant déjà en ce moment, forte par sa discipline, par le dévouement et l'abnégation passionnée de ses membres, et par l'obéssance passive à toutes les dispositions d'une Comité unique que connaît tout et n'est connu de

personne . . . Comme les Jésuites, non dans le but de l'asservissement, mais dans celui de l'emancipation populaire, chacun d'eux a renoncé même à sa propre volonté. Dans le Comité . . . ce n'est pas l'individu qui pense, veut et agit, mais la collectivité . . . Un membre sérieux comprendra qu'ene telle discipline . . . seule est capable . . . de créer une force révolutionnaire collective qui, s'appuyant sur la puissance élementaire du peuple, sera en état de vaincre la force formidable de l'organization de l'état. . . . Ainsi le programme est prêt, il est invariable. Celui qui est pour ce programme viendra avec nous. Celui qui est contre nous est l'ami des adversaires du peuple, . . . le bourreau du Tsar, notre ennemi . . . Celui qui n'est pas pour nous est contre nous. Choisissez." Bakunin's *Social-politischer Briefwechsel mit Herzen, op. cit.,* pp. 364–369.

p. 98, l. 26

Later Bakunin lost his Pan-Slav ardor, largely under the influence of the Polish Revolution of 1863 and of the Russian and Polish chauvinism shown during that revolution. The Slav section in Zürich of the International Association of Workers accepted in 1872 a program proposed by Bakunin in which it was said that it will fight with equal energy all the tendencies and manifestations of Pan-Slavism and of Pan-Germanism. "We wish to abolish all states. Especially for the Slavs, this is a question of life and death and at the same time the only way of conciliation with the peoples of different race, the Turks, the Magyars or Germans." No longer were the Slavs to form a world of their own with a mission of its own. The task now was to make Slav peoples enter the common family of nations. In his last years Bakunin put his faith more and more in the Latin peoples. His faith in the Slavs had vanished. To the Germans he always remained indifferent or skeptical. In the first of the four speeches which Bakunin delivered at the Berne Congress of the League for Peace and Freedom in 1868 he said: "I hate communism because it is a negation of liberty and because humanity is unthinkable to me without liberty. I am not a communist because communism concentrates and swallows up in itself for the benefit of the state all the forces of society, because it inevitably leads to the concentration of property in the hands of the state whereas I want the abolition of the state, the final eradication of the principle of authority and patronage proper to the state which under pretext of making men more moral and civilized, has so far only enslaved, persecuted, exploited and corrupted them. I want to see society a collective or social property organized from below upwards, by way of free association, not from above downwards, by means of any kind of authority whatever." The fourth of his speeches attacked Russian Pan-Slav imperialism.

p. 98, l. 33
Josef Macûrek, "The Achievements of the Slavonic Congress," *The Slavonic and East European Review,* XXVI, no. 67 (April, 1948), pp. 329–340.

p. 99, l. 25
G. W. F. Hegel, *The Philosophy of History,* tr. by J. Sibree, rev. ed. (New York: Wiley Books, 1944), p. 350.

p. 100, l. 14
Franz Mehring, *Aus dem literarischen Nachlass von Karl Marx, Friedrich Engels und Ferdinand Lassalle,* 4 vol. (Stuttgart: J. H. W. Dietz Nachf., 1902), III, pp. 231, 245, 269, also pp. 134–182; Solomon F. Bloom, *The World of Nations* (New York: Columbia University Press, 1941); H. Malcolm Macdonald, "Karl Marx, Friedrich Engels, and the South Slavic Problem in 1848–9," *University of Toronto Quarterly,* VIII, no. 4 (July, 1939), pp. 452–460; "Karl Marx und Friedrich Engels über die Polenfrage," ed. by N. Rjasanoff, *Archiv für die Geschichte des Sozialismus und der Arbeiterbewegung,* vol. VI., (1915–16), pp. 175–221. Marx despised not only the Austro-Slavs, he heaped even greater contempt upon the Russian Empire, on the pre-Petrinian of Moscow as well as the Petrinian of St. Petersburg. In the pamphlet *Secret Diplomatic History of the 18th Century,* (London: Swan Sonnenschein,

1889), in which his daughter republished the articles Marx contributed to Urquhart's *Free Press* from August 16, 1856, to April 5, 1857, he wrote that Moscow-Russia was born in "the bloody mire of Mongolian slavery, not the rude glory of the Norman epoch," probably equating Norman with Germanic influences. In the pamphlet there is no mention of economic reasons for the "Drang zum Meere," the push for sea ports of the land-locked Moscow Empire. Peter created the new Russian Empire according to Marx in order that "the traditional limits of the Muscovite policy could be superseded and merged into that bold synthesis which, blending the encroaching method of the Mongol slave with the world-conquering tendencies of the Mongol master, forms the life-spring of modern Russian diplomacy."

p. 101, l. 37

Even in his last years Palacký, in spite of all his disappointments in Austrian policy and the justified fears aroused in him by the events of 1866 and 1867, the rise of a great German military power and the dominant place conceded to the Magyars in the Austro-Hungarian Ausgleich, reiterated his loyalty to a federal Austria. In his "Political Testament," which he published as a "Postscript in Place of a Preface" to the collection of his essays *Radhost*, he rejected the demand raised by some Russians that the other Slavs should accept the Russian language or at least the Russian alphabet, and insisted on a separate nationality for the Czechs and the southern Slavs. "Whoever reflects on the conditions under which it (the Russian universal monarchy) could be established, will not be astonished, and even less bear me a grudge, because I looked at it (in 1848), and would look at it also today, as an unspeakable evil. . . . Because all nations would resist it with their last cent and their last drop of blood, it would mean nothing less than the violent overthrow, the total subjugation and enslavement of all educated Europe, the suppression and suffocation of all free and noble thoughts and aspirations in the human race." This feeling was on the whole shared by Dr. František Ladislav Rieger (1818–1903) who married in 1853

Palacký's daughter Maria and was chairman of the
Czech Club in the Austrian Reichsrat from 1879 to
1891. In his "Political Testament" in 1872 Palacký
also bitterly attacked the uprising of Whitsun-Day
1848 which he regarded as a catastrophe for the Czech
nation. He referred again to his repeated requests in
May, 1848, "that we do not abandon our moral position
and refrain from all appeal to violence." *Politisches
Vermächtnis* (Prague, 1872), p. 9.

p. 103, l. 17

On Napoleon's interest in Constantinople see Vernon
J. Puryear, *Napoleon and the Dardanelles* (Berkeley:
University of California Press, 1951); on the year
1848 in Russia see Isaiah Berlin, "Russia and 1848,"
The Slavonic and East European Review, XXVI, no. 67
(April, 1948), pp. 341–360.—On Urquart and English
public opinion between 1829 and 1841 see John Howes
Gleason, *The Genesis of Russophobia in Great Britain*
(Cambridge: Harvard University Press, 1951). Most
outspoken, however, were not the friends of Turkey
like Urquhart but the friends of Poland. Thomas Att-
wood, M. P., wrote to Lord Dudley Coutts Stuart
(1803–1854), a stout friend of Polish independence, on
November 4, 1838: "(I) shall never be satisfied until
I see the honour of England vindicated and her interest
seconded by the full and entire restoration of Polish
independence. This great object might have been secured
without war, but now the opportunity is lost. *War we
must have for Poland today and for England tomorrow.*
There is no longer a middle course. We must humble
Russia in the dust; or we must be driven step by step
from every position of honour and security, until at last
we shall ourselves be crushed into earth. And even then,
I doubt not that we shall find men in England bad
enough to propose to buy off the Russians as our forefathers did the Danes and Saxons." *The Slavonic and
East European Review*, XXIX, no. 72 (Dec., 1950),
p. 173.

p. 104, l. 5

The Works of Oliver Goldsmith, ed. by Peter Cun-

ningham, 4 vols. (London: John Murray, 1854), vol.
II, p. 378.

p. 104, l. 9

The Testament of Peter the Great was written in
1797 by the Polish General Michael Sokolnicki who
submitted in 1797 to the French government a memorandum on Russia's plan to conquer all of Europe in
which he incorporated what he maintained he had
learned from secret Russian documents captured in
Warsaw in April, 1794. It was first published in a
serious and detailed work, *Des Progrès de la Puissance
Russe depuis son origine jusqu'au commencement du
XIXe siècle* (Paris, 1812). See Alexander Petrunkevich,
"Zaveshchanie Petra Velikogo (The Testament of Peter
the Great)," *Novy Zhurnal*, XXIII (New York, 1950),
pp. 215–237. The Testament was first proved a forgery
by Harry Bresslau in the *Historische Zeitschrift*, 1879.

p. 104, l. 28
The Graphic, March 21, 1914.

p. 105, l. 17
Obras de Donoso Cortés, ed. by Orti y Lara, 4 vols.
(Madrid, 1903–04), vol. II, p. 170 f. His judgments
about Germany are not without interest. He wrote to
his friend Count Athanasius Raczynski (1788–1874)
who was Prussian minister in Madrid: "I like neither
Prussia nor its policy, nor its aggrandisement, not even
its existence. I see in Prussia a power which dedicated
itself from the first days of its existence to the devil,
and if I consider the peculiar and enigmatic development of this state, then I become convinced that it
will remain thus also in the future." (Letter of May 24,
1852) "The moral anarchy, the anarchy of ideas will
grow and develop in Germany to the day of its victory."
(Letter of March 1, 1849) "The revolution will be
victorious everywhere, but in Germany it will be more
comprehensive and more profound than anywhere else."
(Letter of Oct. 25, 1849) Cortés was Spanish minister
in Prussia in 1849. See Adhémar d'Antiocse, *Deux*

Diplomates. Le Comte Raczynski et Donoso Cortés
(Paris, 1880), pp. 306, 67, 118.

p. 105 l. 39
Joseph de Maistre, *Quatre chapitres inédits sur la
Russie*, ed. by Rodolphe de Maistre (Paris: A Vaton,
1859), p. 19. See also Peter Struve, "Russia," *The
Slavonic Review*, I (1922–23), no. 1, pp. 24–40.

p. 106, l. 29
Friedrich Bodenstedt, *Russische Fragmente. Beiträge
zur Kenntnis des Staats- und Volkslebens in seiner his-
torischen Entwicklung*, 2 vols. (Leipzig: F. A. Brockhaus, 1862), vol. I, p. 8 f. Bodenstedt was convinced
of the superiority of Russian diplomacy and wished to
divert Russian interests to Asia to protect Germany.

p. 109, l. 15
The articles by Marx were reprinted as *The Eastern
Question*, ed. by Eleanor Marx Aveling and Edward
Aveling (London: Swan Sonneschein & Co., 1897).
In his article printed on April 12, 1853, Marx opposed
Western liberty, as inaugurated by the Revolution of
1789, "the explosive force of democratic ideas and
man's native thirst for freedom," to Russian absolutism.
". . . let Russia get possession of Turkey, and her
strength is increased nearly half, and she becomes
superior to all the rest of Europe put together. Such
an event would be an unspeakable calamity to the
revolutionary cause. The maintenance of Turkish independence, or, in case of a possible dissolution of the
Ottoman Empire, the arrest of the Russian scheme
of annexation, is a matter of the highest moment. In
this instance the interests of the revolutionary Democracy and of England go hand in hand. Neither can
permit the Czar to make Constantinople one of his
capitals, and we shall find that when driven to the wall,
the one will resist him as determinedly as the other."
Engels wrote in the *Neue Oderzeitung* on April 21,
1855: "Der Panslawismus hat sich jetzt umgewandelt
aus einem Glaubensbekenntnis in ein politisches Programm mit 800,000 Bajonetten zu seiner Verfügung.
Er lässt Europa nur eine Alternative: Unterjochung

durch die Slawen oder Zerstörung für immer des Zentrums ihrer Offensivkraft: Russlands." (Pan-Slavism has now transformed itself from a creed into a political program with 800,000 bayonets at its disposal. It leaves to Europe only one alternative: subjection by the Slavs or destruction forever of the center of their offensive power: Russia.) Engels attacked Russian foreign policy and diplomacy in 1890 in a letter published in Russian in the organ of the Russian Marxists. Recently this point of view of Engels was rejected by F. I. Kozhevnikov in *Sovyetskoye gosudarstvo i pravo*, December 12, 1950. According to the present doctrine, Russian Tsarist expansion was a progressive movement and beneficial for the peoples annexed to Tsarist Russia.

p. 111, l. 14

On Michelet (1798–1874) see Hans Kohn, *Prophets and Peoples* (New York: Macmillan, 1946), pp. 43–76. The quotations are from his *Légendes démocratiques du Nord. La Sorcière* (Oeuvres complètes, édition définitive, Paris: E. Flammarion, n. d.) pp. 11, 43–46, 102, 105, 110, 162, 180, 226.

p. 112, l. 16

J. Michelet, *Légendes démocratiques du Nord. La France devant l'Europe* (Paris: Calman Lévy, 1899), pp. 384, 480. In 1871 the liberal Italian nationalist Giuseppe Mazzini demanded a similar union of Europe and especially of the Western Slavs—with Italian help and guidance—against Russia. See *Prophets and Peoples*, pp. 94 and 188: Pan-Slavism under Russian leadership would result in a "gigantic attempt to make Europe Cossack; a long and fierce battle waged by despotism against all the liberties we have already won; a new era of militarism; . . . the creation of a hostile Pan-Slav unity, governed by one despotic will, instead of a barrier erected against tyranny by the organization of free men from the Baltic to the Adriatic." Thus in the very same year (1871) the two men expressed the same fears and hopes as regards Russia. Similarly Erard de Choiseul-Gouffier warned in his *La Russie et le Panslavisme*

(Nancy: Sordoillet et fils, 1870) after the French defeat
against Russian-Prussian domination of Europe.

p. 112, l. 18
   Michelet himself protested in *La Pologne Martyre*
(Paris: Dentu, 1863) against the subordination of Poles,
Czechs and other Slavs to "la tribu finno-tatare, le
Kremlin byzantino-mongol."

p. 112, l. 20
   The book was published in Paris: Friedrich Klinck-
sieck, 1864.

p. 113, l. 11
   The book was published in Paris: Furne, Jouvet &
Cie., 1866. See there p. 316 ff. The opinion that Russia's future was more "Turanian" than "European" was
shared by some Russians like the admirer by Byzantium and of the Turanian Turks, Konstantin Nikolaevich Leontev (1831–1891), and, after World War I,
the Eurasian movement started in 1920 by Prince N. S.
Trubetskoy. The Eurasians regarded Muscovy as a
successor of the great Tartar empire and stressed the
close relationship throughout history of the Russian
Slav settlers of the forest and the Turanian nomads of
the steppe.

p. 113, l. 17
   Cyprien Robert, *Le Monde Slave, son passé, son état
présent et son avenir,* 2 vols. (Paris: Passard, 1852).
The German Orientalist Jakob Philipp Fallmerayer
(1790–1861), one of the most liberal members of the
Frankfurt Assembly of 1848, wrote in 1830 in his
Geschichte der Halbinsel Morea im Mittelalter, vol. I,
p. V, Untergang der peloponnesischen Hellenen und
Wiederbevölkerung des leeren Bodens durch slavische
Volksstämme (Stuttgart: Cotta, 1830), that he saw
the domination of the globe being transferred from the
Germanic and Latin peoples to the Slavs.

p. 113, l. 23
   Krasiński, *Panslavism and Germanism* (London:

T. C. Newby, 1848). The book appeared in a German translation by Wilhelm Adolf Lindau (Dresden: Arnoldische Buchhandlung, 1849). A different stress was put on Pan-Slavism by an anonymous Polish author in his *Panslavismus im Gegensatz zum Allslaventhum und die politische Bedeutung der polnischen Bevölkerung ausserhalb der russischen Zwingherrschaft* (Strasburg i. Pr.: C. A. Köhler, 1870). He regarded Pan-Slavism as a despotic and centralizing movement promoted by the Russians, and Allslaventum as a liberal and federal movement which could be based on the Western Slavs. The Germans make a serious mistake by oppressing the Western Slavs and driving them thus into Russia's arms. The Germans based their relationship with the Slavs on conquest, but this is an insecure foundation: "Was mit dem Schwerte genommen wurde, kann mit dem Schwerte wieder genommen werden. Furchtbar waltet und richtet hier die Geschichte." The anonymous Polish author ended his pamphlet with a plea for the cooperation of the Germans and the Western Slavs on the basis of equality, enlightenment and liberty, without regard for race or nationality. A similar plea was voiced in the same year (1870) by Richard Böckh (1824–1907), a Prussian statistician, who protested in his *Die Ausbreitung der deutschen Nation* against the suppression of the national tongues and civilizations by the conquerors, pointed to Switzerland as a model for the cohabitation of several nationalities in harmony and liberty, and saw in the oppression of national minorities a threat to peace.

p. 114, l. 15
Krasiński, *Is the Power of Russia to be Reduced or Increased by the Present War? The Polish Question and Pan-Slavism* (London: Chapman & Hall, 1855), p. 218. Another Polish count who lived in America, Adam Gurowski, at that time described Russia to the Western world: "This mighty colossus, overtopping Europe and Asia, is for many but a dark cavern filled with demoniac forces, which, let loose, are to extinguish light, engulf civilization, and stop the onward progress of the European world, spreading over it all the plagues

and curses of darkness." *Russia As It Is* (New York: Appleton, 1854) p. III. Count Gurowski himself was an ardent Russophile, but his words aptly characterize the widespread opinion of Russia then held in Europe and America.

p. 114, l. 18

This Polish attitude is old. King Sigismund-August of Poland wrote to Queen Elizabeth of England on July 13, 1567, that he could not allow British trade with Russia through Danzig, for "the more the Moscovite power will grow, the more dangerous will it become not only to us but to the whole of Christianity. . . . One supplies them with munitions of war, with arms the use of which they did not know, and what appears most dangerous to us, one procures to them adroit engineers. . . . These engineers would easily construct even in this barbarous country all the machines needed for war and so far unknown to that people. One must therefore apprehend lest these works are not carried out for the ruin of the Christian states before one expects it." Comte Renaud Przezdziecki, *Diplomatie et protocole à la Cour de Pologne* (Paris: Les Belles Lettres, 1937), vol. II, p. 361.

p. 114, l. 29

Pierre Joseph Proudhon (1809–1865) had in 1848 taken sides with the Poles. In *Le Peuple*, no. 4, Nov. 5, 1848, he wrote: "The struggle between the German democracy and the Moscovite Pan-Slavism is, above all, the struggle of progressive civilization against reactionary barbarism." But in his great book *La Guerre et la Paix*, 3rd ed. (Paris: E. Dantu, 1861), vol. II, p. 412, he compared the resurrection of Poland to the resurrection of the Saxony of Widukind or the kingdom of the Visigoths. Generally in the section which he calls "La Démocratie et la guerre" (pp. 402–415) Proudhon opposes the bellicosity of the democrats of his time, especially exercised in favor of the principle of nationalism and of national self-determination, which he regards as hostile to economic progress and to individual and federal liberty. "Les nationalités doivent aller s'effaçant de plus en plus par la constitution économique, la décentralisation des États, le croisement des races et la perméabilité des continents." Proudhon was attacked on behalf of the Polish emigration by Élias Regnault (1801–1868), *L'Odysée Polonaise precédée d'une lettre à M. Proudhon* (Paris: Dantu & Franck, 1862).

p. 115, l. 3
The book of 437 pages appeared in London in October, 1854, without mentioning a publisher or printer. It is well printed with few printing errors though the author could not revise the proofs.

p. 115, l. 23
Ibid., p. 21. Coeurderoy welcomes the Russians as the redeemers on behalf of his "Dieu des criminels, des opprimés, des révoltés, des pauvres, de tous ceux qu'on torture."

p. 116, l. 15
Ibid., pp. 60–66. Coeurderoy in his disillusionment in the crisis of 1848 anticipates the young Rimbaud writing in the crisis of 1870 and the old Sorel writing in the crisis of World War I and praising Lenin. In comparing the Latins with female races and the Slavs with male races, Coeurderoy forgets the Germans who a few decades later regarded themselves as *the* male race.

p. 116, l. 26
ibid., pp. 189–195.

p. 117, l. 8
ibid., p. 351.

p. 117, l. 35
ibid., pp. 400–405.

p. 118, l. 24
In these concluding words Coeurderoy recalls the later Nietzsche, a prophet and a law-giver. Both despaired of the pettiness of historical civilization and appealed to nature against history, to the natural man

before the rise of Greek society and Christian ethics against the fatigued and nihilistic civilized man. Coeurderoy thought that he recognized this natural man in the Russian; Nietsche was free of all nationalist or racial illusions.

p. 119, l. 24

Custine, *La Russie en 1839*, 4 vols. (Paris: Amyot, 1843), vol. III, pp. 386, 404.

p. 120, l. 12

The *Lettres sur la Russie* (*La Russie en 1839*) were widely read throughout Europe and the United States in the 1840's. They abound in pithy remarks. "Le gouvernement russe c'est la discipline du camp substituée à l'ordre de la cité, c'est l'état de siège devenu l'état normal de la sociéte." (vol. I, p. 278) Or "l'autocratie russe qui n'est qu'une démocratie idolâtré." "Sous le despotisme russe, c'est le gouvernement qui est révolutionnaire, parceque la révolution veut dire régime arbitraire et pouvoir absolu." A decade later another Frenchman, Emile Montégut, made similar observations speaking about Russia: "L'égalité par la force, sinon autrement; la fraternité par le knout, sinon autrement" (*Revue des Deux Mondes*, July, 1854); "Un islamisme matérialiste, volià la forme nouvelle qui revêt la démocratie" (*Libres opinions morales et historiques*, Paris, 1888, p. 374). A shortened edition of Custine's book was published in Paris: La Nouvelle France, 1946; an English translation by Phyllis Penn Kohler, *Journey for our Time* (New York: Pellegrini & Cudahy, 1951). See also Bruce Hopper, "Custine and Russia—a Century after," *The American Historical Review*, LVII (January, 1952), pp. 384–392.

p. 120, l. 20

Herzen, *Polnoe sobranie sochinenii i pisem*, ed. by M. K. Lemke, 21 vols. (Petrograd, 1919–23), vol. III, p. 140.

p. 121, l. 12

Herzen, Lettre à Charles Lytton, *La Russie et le*

vieux monde (Jersey: Imprimerie Universelle, 1854), p. 18. See also, Oskar J. Hammen, "Free Europe versus Russia, 1830–1854," *The American Slavic and East European Review*, vol. XI (Feb. 1952), pp. 27–41.

NOTES TO PART TWO

Page 125, line 17

See Ernst Benz, *Die abendländische Sendung der östlich-orthodoxen Kirche*. Die russische Kirche und das abendländische Christentum im Zeitalter der Heiligen Allianz (Mainz: Akademie der Wissenschaften, 1951).

p. 126, l. 13

See Constantin de Grunwald, *Trois Siècles de Diplomatie Russe* (Paris: Calmann-Lévy, 1954), pp. 181–191. He wrote on October 20, 1838, to Carlo Andrea Count Pozzo di Borgo, a Corsican who entered the Russian diplomatic service in 1804 and was then Russian ambassador in London: "La pensée de porter atteinte à la sureté et au repos des possessions de la Grande-Bretagne aux Indes ne s'est jamais presentée à notre esprit," and he continued that it must be the concern of both powers to respect the independence of the buffer states between the two empires. In his official report for 1840, he wrote: "As we do not wish to rival the British maritime influence nor make the Mediterranean a Russian lake nor destroy the Ottoman Empire nor overthrow the British power in India, we cannot see where there could be the scene of a serious conflict between the two countries: there never existed between them anything but simple prejudices."

p. 126, l. 15

In September, 1848, Nesselrode wrote: "Si jamais l'amour des peuples devait entrer dans les calculs de la haute politique, il y aurait de quoi bouleverser l'Europe entière de fond en comble."

p. 128, l. 8

From the beginning, Russian opposition to the transfer of the capital to St. Petersburg was strong. See f.i.

J. G. Vockerodt's memorandum "Russia under Peter
the Great" which he wrote in 1737 as secretary of the
Prussian legation in St. Petersburg, in Ernst Adolf
Herrmann, *Zeitgenössische Berichte zur Geschichte
Russlands* (Leipzig, 1872), pp. 94–101. Vockerodt who
knew Russia and Russian well, defended the people
against the then widespread judgment, shared by Peter
I, that they were primitive and bestial ('wild und
viehisch"). He wrote: "Man brauche nur einen gemei-
nen russischen Bürger oder Bauer vorzunehmen, um
nachzuforschen, wie weit sich deren Verstand und
Gemütskräfte erstrecken, und man werde, finden, dass
der Russe im allgemeinen in allen Dingen, worin er
nicht durch das Vorurteil seines Vaterlandes oder seiner
Religion gefesselt ist, einen recht gesunden natürlichen
Verstand und ein reines Urteil besitze, dass er daneben
eine ungemeine Fähigkeit habe, etwas zu begreifen, eine
grosse Fertigkeit zu seinem Zweck diensame Mittel
anzuwenden und dass die meisten unter ihnen ihre auf
das tägliche Leben bezügliche Angelegenheiten sehr
wohl auszurichten wüssten, und zwar alles dies in einem
viel eminenteren Grade, als man dergleichen an gemei-
nen Leuten in Deutschland oder anderwärts zu finden
gewohnt sei." (One has only to observe a common
Russian townsman or peasant to find out how great his
intellectual and mental capacities are, and one will find
that the Russian in general in everything where he is
not limited by patriotic or religious prejudices, shows
good common sense and intelligent judgment, that in
addition he has an unusual ability of comprehension,
a great gift to use means helpful to his purpose, and
that most among them know well how to arrange their
daily affairs, all this to a much greater degree than is
being found among the common people in Germany or
elsewhere.)

p. 129, l. 4

Nikolai Mikhailovich Karamzin (1766–1826) started
as an 18th century admirer of Europe. From his journey
there (May, 1789, to Sept., 1790) he brought home
his famous "Pisma russkogo puteshestvennika" (Letters
of a Russian Traveller), 210 Letters published between
1791 and 1801. In letter CXXXVI he wrote: "We had

our Charlemagne: Vladimir; our Louis XI: Tsar Ivan; our Cromwell: Godunov; and in addition a ruler the like of which nowhere existed: Peter the Great. Their reigns form the most important epochs in our history, and even in the history of mankind." In 1802 he began to write his "History of the Russian State", the publication of which started in 1816 (*Istoria gosudarstva rossijskogo*, ed. by P. N. Polevoj, 12 vols., St. Petersburg: Evgokemov, 1892); the last (12th) volume appeared posthumously in 1827. The work was quickly translated into foreign languages. Important is also his "Memorandum on the Old and the New Russia in her Political and Civic Relationships" (Zapiska o drevnej i novoj Rossii v ego politicheskom i grazhdanskom otnosheniyakh) which he presented to the Emperor in 1811 and which was published in 1870. Karamzin was not uncritical of the reactionary trends of the later part of Alexander's reign. See Mikhail Pogodin, *N. M. Karamzin, po ego sochineniyam, pismam i otzyvam sovremennikov* (N. M. K. in his Works, Letters and Contemporary Utterances. Materials for a biography), 2 vols. (Moscow: Mamantov, 1866), vol. II, p. 450 f. In his Memorandum he wrote: "Our grandfathers . . . persevered in the thought that the Orthodox Russian is the most perfect citizen on earth and that Holy Russia was the first state. One may call that an aberration, but how did it favor the love of the fatherland and its moral forces!" And: "To try to change ancient states is dangerous; Russia has existed for about one thousand years and not in the form of a wild horde but in the form of a great empire. And one always tells us of new institutions as if we had emerged recently from the dark forests of America." See also Rudolf Bächtold, *Karamzins Weg zur Geschichte,* Basler Beiträge zur Geschichtswissenschaft, 23 (Basle: Helbing & Lichtenhahn, 1946).

p. 129, l. 28

The poem "Klevetnikam Rossii" (To the Slanderers of Russia) was written August 2, 1831, Pushkin, *Sobranie sochinenii* (Berlin: Ladyzhnikov, 1921), vol. II, p. 43. Pushkin admired Karamzin's History. As Belinsky wrote: "Pushkin had penetrated so deeply into the

spirit of this History that he had become its protector
and champion; he justified it not only as history but
even as a political Koran which does not only fit our
time in the best way but should remain for ever."

p. 130, l. 33

In A. S. Pushkin, *The Poems, Plays and Prose* (New
York: Random House, 1936), p. 51. See on Pushkin,
Centennial Essays for Pushkin, ed. by Samuel H. Cross
and Ernest J. Simmons (Cambridge: Harvard University Press, 1937); *Pushkin: Man and Artist* (New York:
Paisley Press, 1937); Ernest J. Simmons, *Pushkin* (Cambridge: Harvard University Press, 1937); Wacław Lednicki, *Poushkine et la Pologne* (Paris: E. Leroux, 1928).
Herzen said of Pushkin: "He had an instinctive faith
in the future of Russia; the shouts of triumph and
victory which struck him while still a child, in 1813 and
1814, reverberated in his soul; for some time he was
even carried away by a St. Petersburg patriotism which
boasts of the number of bayonets and leans upon
canons. It is painful to say, but Pushkin had an exclusive
patriotism; great poets were courtiers like Goethe or
Racine, but Pushkin was neither a courtier nor a member of the government; the brutal force of the state
pleased him out of patriotic instinct so that he shared
the barbaric wish to answer reasoning by bullets. Russia
is partly enslaved because it finds poetry in material
force and glory in frightening peoples." *Du développement des idées révolutionnaires en Russie* (Paris: A.
Franck, 1851), p. 79 f.

p. 131, l. 6

One of the Decembrists, Matvyej Ivanovich Mura-
vyev-Apostol wrote in 1870: "We were the children of
1812. Our heart urged us to sacrifice everything, even
life, for the love of the fatherland. There was no
egoism in our feelings. I call God as my witness for it."
Nikolai K. Schilder, *Imperator Nikolai Pervy, ego zhizn
i tsarstvovanye* (Emperor Nikolai I, his Life and Rule,
St. Petersburg: A. S. Suvorin, 1903), 2 vols., vol. I, p.
436. The prominent Decembrist leader, Pavel Ivanovich
Pestel in 1817 left the Free Mason Lodge Les Amis

Réunis and entered that of The Three Virtues because in the latter one spoke Russian while in the former French. V. J. Semevskij, *op. cit.* (note 7 to Intro.), p. 288. Regarding the political idea of the Decembrists see also G. V. Vernadsky, *Gosudarstvennaya ustavnaya gramota rossijskoi imperii 1820 goda* (Prague, 1925).

p. 131, l. 12

On the attitude of Russian society to the Decembrists see Wacław Lednicki, "Pushkin, Tyutchev, Mickiewicz," *The Slavonic and East European Review,* XXIX, 73 (June, 1951), pp. 375–401. Tyutchev's poem "To the Decembrists" was probably written in 1827. Tyutchev in all his burning Pan-Slavism took a nobler stand towards the defeated Poles in 1831 than Pushkin did. He compared in a poem the mortal blow which the Russians dealt to Warsaw, "purchasing at this sanguine price peace and unity for Russia," to Agamemnon's immolation of his own daughter.

> Pierced by a brother's shot,
> Which carried out fate's decree,
> You fell, oh eagle of our own tribe,
> Into the purifying fire.
> Believe the word of the Russian nation—
> We shall gather your sacred ashes
> And from them, like a phoenix,
> Our common freedom will be born.

p. 131, l. 37

An early Westernizer was Prince Peter Borisovich Kozlovsky (1783–1840). See about him Gleb Struve, *Russky evropeyets. Materiali dlya biografii i kharakteristiki kn. P. B. Kozlovskogo* (A Russian Westernizer. Material for the Biography and Characterization of Prince P. B. K. San Francisco: Delo, 1950). He was probably the Prince K. travelling with Custine in 1839 from Travenmünde to Kronstadt. He and other Russian Westernizers of that period like Prince Peter Andreevich Vyazemsky (1792–1878) and Alexander Ivanovich Turgenev (1785–1846) did not share Pushkin's joy over the suppression of Poland. On the other hand, Prince

Elim Mestscherski (1808–1844), a Russian diplomat and writer of excellent education who held diplomatic posts in Dresden, Turkey and France, was an early Slavophile, enthusiastic about the mission of Holy Russia. See his poetry *Les Boréales* (Paris: Belizard, Dufour & Cie., 1839), pp. 23 f., 27, 35, and André Mazon, "Knyaz Elim", *Literaturnoye nasledstvo*, vol. 31–32 (Moscow, 1937), pp. 373–490.

p. 133, l. 11

See Hans Kohn, "Romanticism and the Rise of German Nationalism," *The Review of Politics*, XII (1950), pp. 443–472, and "The Paradox of Fichte's Nationalism," *Journal of the History of Ideas*, X (1949), pp. 319–343. The affinity of German romanticism and Russian nationalism in a common anti-Western front was emphasized by many Germans. The theologian Bruno Bauer (1809–1882) came out in his *Russland und das Germanentum* (Charlottenburg: Egbert Bauer, 1853) for a Russian-German alliance to overwhelm decadent Europe and to establish world domination. In his *Die Russische Kirche* (Charlottenburg: Egbert Bauer, 1854), p. 4, he wrote: "Dieses Volk mit dem Antlitz des Menschen und mit dem Leibe des Löwen ist die Sphinx, die vor dem jetzigen Europa steht und ihm die Aufgabe gestellt hat, das Rätsel der Zukunft zu deuten. Die Augen des Ungetüms sind unverwandt und lauernd auf Europa gerichtet, seine Löwentatze ist erhoben und zum Schlage bereit; Europa beantworte die Frage und es ist gerettet;—es höre auf, an der Frage zu arbeiten, es lasse die Antwort auf sich beruhen oder gebe sie dem Zufall anheim und es wird die Beute der Sphinx, die es mit eiserner Gewalt niederhalten wird." (This people with the face of man and the body of a lion is the sphinx standing before Europe and asking it to solve the riddle of the future. The monster looks unflinchingly and impatiently upon Europe with its raised claw ready to strike; let Europe answer the question and she will be saved;—let her cease to work on the riddle or to abandon the answer to chance, and she will become the prey of the sphinx which will keep

her down with iron strength.) After 1866 Bauer abandoned these ideas. Thomas Mann who shares in many
ways was the anti-Western attitude of German romanticism wrote in 1917: "Are the Russian and German
attitudes toward Europe, the West, civilization, politics
and democracy, not closely akin? Haven't we Germans
also our Slavophiles and Westernizers? . . . If spiritual
affinity can form the foundation and justification of
political alliances, then Russia and Germany belong
together: their agreement now, their union for the
future, has been since the beginning of this war (the
war of 1914) the desire and dream of my heart. It is
more than a desirability: it is a political and spiritual
necessity should the Anglo-American alliance endure."
Betrachtungen eines Unpolitischen (Berlin: Fischer,
1920), pp. 444 ff. Mann's very characteristic point of
view can be best supplemented from the Russian point
of view by Dostoevsky's remarks in his *Dnevnik pisatela*
for May–June, 1877, in which he regarded Germany
as implacably opposed to the Western and Roman
traditions as Russia was. But Germany was, according
to the Russian writer, only a negative force, an eternal
protest against Rome and against universalism and rationalism, which could oppose and crush the West but
not save it by speaking the new word. That was Russia's
mission.

p. 134, l. 9

The best criticism of Russia from the Western point
of view was written by Masaryk, who believed that
Russian thought could become negative, but not critical.
Even the Russian rationalists thought as mythically as
the theologians, neither of them had any use for Kant.
They only changed the object of their faith when they
no longer adhered to Orthodoxy but they preserved its
intellectual and spiritual trend. The revolutionaries remained occultists in their secret organizations. "The
Russians forget very easily that their aim is not the
revolution but democracy; the Russian revolutionism
falls much too easily into anarchism and nihilism." "In
everything we see the lack of criticism, of the cautious
gradation." "I confess that I have not only learned by

studying Russia and its literature to estimate better the philosophy of Feuerbach and Hegel: Russian philosophy and literature has made me comprehend the world historical importance of Hume and Kant." T. G. Masaryk, *Russland und Europa. Studien über die geistigen Strömungen in Russland*, 2 vols. (Jena: Diederichs, 1913), vol. II, pp. 429, 430, 433, 492, 497, 511. Ivan Kireyevsky wrote to Alexandre Ivanovich Koshelev (1812–1883) on Oct. 1, 1828, that the readers of Kant in Russia were in a relation of 5 to 5,000 to the readers of Schelling. "Kant is not a poet," he added as an explanation.

p. 134, l. 23

The liberal historians of Russia criticized the romantic Slavophilism. Thus Alexander Nikolaevich Pypin (1833–1904) wrote about Karamzin's glorification of old Russia in his "Memorandum" (see above, note 5): Commenting upon Karamzin's words: "The political system of the Muscovite rulers was worthy of admiration for its wisdom" Pypin added: "though all travellers wondered at the Asiatic despotism of the authorities and the slavery, primitivity and ignorance of the people, and though Karamzin himself notes that life and property depended on the arbitrary will of the Tsar." In another passage Karamzin maintained that the people, liberated from the threats of civil war and from the foreign yoke by the new despotism, was satisfied and did not demand any rights. Pypin commented: "though it run away in great number among the Kozaks and pillaged Russia." Pypin, *Die geistige Bewegung in Russland in der ersten Hälfte des 19. Jahrhunderts* vol. I, tr. from the 2nd Russian ed. by Boris Minzes (Berlin: S. Cronbach, 1894), p. 310. In his memorandum Karamzin accused the Russians of having become cosmopolitans and of regarding the Europeans as their brothers. "Formerly we called all other Europeans infidels, now we call them brothers; I ask for whom it would be easier to subjugate Russia, for the infidels or for the brothers?" Pypin pointed out that (in 1811) there were hardly any "cosmopolitans" among the Russians. The overwhelming majority of the people and of the Russian society had remained entirely faithful to the ideas of old Russia. "In the following year (1812) Karamzin was to receive the proof for it: the people regarded Napoleon as the anti-Christ, his army as non-Christian and hardly human; one could not desire more." *Ibid.*, p. 318. See also Leonid Strakhovsky, *L'empereur Nicolas Ier et l'esprit national russe* (Louvain: Librairie Universitaire, 1928).

p. 135, l. 5

In Western languages there are two excellent studies of these important periods in Russian intellectual history, for the 1820's which end in 1835, Alexandre Koyré, *La Philosophie et le problème national en Russie au début du XIXe siècle* (Bibliothèque de l'Institut Français de Léningrad X, Paris: H. Champion, 1929), and for the 1840's which lasted from 1835 to 1848, Dmitrij Tschizewskij, *Hegel in Russland* (Veröffentlichungen der slavistischen Arbeitsgemeinschaft an der deutschen Univerität Prag IX, Reichenberg: Gebrüder Stiepel, 1934). See also Wsewoled Setschkareff, *Schellings Einfluss in der russischen Literatur der 20er und 30er Jahre des 19. Jahrhunderts* (Leipzig: Harrassowitz, 1939). 1835 was also a momentous year in the history of Slav scholarship in Russia. The first chairs in Slavonic languages and literatures were established at the Universities of Moscow, Petersburg, Kharkov and Kazan and young scholars were sent to the various Slav capitals to study there.

p. 135, l. 9

Nikolai Vladimirovich Stankevich (1813–1840) the center of the "Hegelian" circle, who died of tuberculosis and left no written work, was according to all the testimonies a most fascinating youth of luminous intelligence and saintly spirit. Belinsky, Konstantin Aksakov, Turgenev, people most different in their attitudes and characters, testified to the uniqueness of his personality. Whoever met him was morally and spiritually uplifted. Turgenev portrayed Stankevich in Pokorsky in his novel "Rudin" though he himself regarded it only as a pale reflection of the radiant reality. "They were great times then, and I don't like to think that they went for nothing! Nor did they, not even for those who afterwards were vulgarized by life. . . . How often have I happened to meet men who were my former comrades! You would think the man had become quite an animal, but you had only to mention the name of Pokorsky in his presence and all the last remnants of nobility within him began to stir, as though in a dark and dirty room you had unstoppered a forgotten phial of perfume." (*The Borzoi Turgenev*, New York: Knopf, 1950, p. 616). See on the intellectual life of the period also The Memoirs of Alexander Herzen, *My Past and Thoughts*, chs. 25 and 30, English tr. by Constance Garnett, 6 vols. (London: Chatto & Windus, 1924), vol. 2, pp. 104–150, 254–303. "The philosophy of Hegel is the algebra of revolution, it emancipates a man in an extraordinary way and leaves not a stone standing of the Christian world, of the world of outlived tradition." (*ibid.*, p. 121). On Hegel in Russia see also Boris Jakowenko, *Zwei Beiträge zur Geschichte des Hegelianismus in Russland* (Prague: International Philosophical Library I, 5–7, 1935) and *Geschichte des Hegelianismus in Russland* vol. I (Prague: Der russiche Gedanke, VI, 1938).

p. 136, l. 12
See Hans Kohn, "Father Jahn's Nationalism," *The Review of Politics*, XI (1949), pp. 419–432. Jahn in his *Deutsches Volkstum* (1810) stressed characteristically not the state of the government but "Volk, Deutschheit und Vaterland," while Count Uvarov placed religion and state first. Jahn was a Jacobin nationalist, Uvarov a conservative statesman; the Slavophiles proud of a mighty and powerful state and deeply devoted to religion, held a position between Jahn and Uvarov.

p. 136, l. 17
See the story of Uvarov's educational policy in Nikolai Platonovich Barsukov, *Zhizn i trudy M. P. Pogodina* (Life and Works of M. P. P.), 22 vols. (St. Petersburg: M. M. Stasyulevich, 1888–1910), vol. IV, pp. 82–85. Barsukov's immense work gives much more than the biography and works and letters of Pogodin, it is an

important contribution to the history of the Slavophile
movement in which Pogodin played a great role. Uva-
rov's conservative policy was supported by the then only
Russian daily, the *Severnaya Pchela* (The Northern
Bee), founded in St. Petersburg in 1825 by Faddej
Benediktinovich Bulgarin (1789–1859) and Nikolai
Ivanovich Gretsch, the editor of *Syn Otechestva* (The
Son of the Fatherland), founded in 1812. This official
policy was naturally in favor of the Russian monarchs
who had saved Russia from the Tartar yoke and had
later sought a certain rapproachment with Europe.
There were Russians to whom such a policy was much
too liberal. Mikhail Leontevich Magnitski (1778–1855)
in a series of articles "Sudby Rossii" (Russia's Destiny)
which he published in 1832–33 in *Raduga* (The Rain-
bow), called the Tartar rule "perhaps the greatest blessing in Russian history," because it had preserved the
Russian faith and saved it from Western Europe.

p. 138, l. 20
On Chaadayev see the excellent book by Charles
Quénet, *Tchaadaev et les lettres philosophiques* (Bib-
liothèque de l'Institut Français de Leningrad, XII,
Paris: H. Champion, 1931); Martin Winkler, *Peter
Jakovlevič Čaadaev. Ein Beitrag zur Russischen Geis-
tesgeschichte des 19. Jahrhunderts* (Berlin: Ost-Europa
Verlag, 1927); Alexander von Schelting, *Russland und
Europa im Russischen Geschichtsdenken* (Bern: A.
Francke, 1948); Anatole G. Mazour, "Petr Jakovlevič
Čaadaev," *Le Monde Slave*, Nov., 1937.

p. 138, l. 26
Herzen wrote movingly on the impression which
Chaadayev made, both in *My Past and Thoughts*, ch.
30, and in *Du développements des idées révolutionnaires en Russie, op. cit.*, p. 109 f: "The publication of
this letter was one of the greatest events. It was a challenge, a sign of awakening; it broke the ice after the
14th December . . . The author takes Russia to account for all the sufferings which it causes to a man
who dares to be more than a brute. . . . The author
has been accused of being hard, and that is perhaps his
greatest merit. We should not despair; we forget too

quickly our position, we are too accustomed to amuse ourselves between the walls of a prison."

p. 139, l. 6
The highly interesting story is told from the original documents in Mikhail Lemke, *Nikolaiyevskie zhandarmy i literatura* 1826–1855 (Nikolai's Police and Literature 1826–1855, Moscow: Bunin, 1908) pp. 592 ff.

p. 140, l. 38
Barsukov, *op. cit.*, vol. II, p. 189. See also Karl Stählin, "Die Entstehung des Panslavismus," *Germanoslavica*, IV (Brünn: Rohrer, 1936), pp. 1–25, 237–262.

p. 142, l. 29
Tolk: insight, understanding, good sense, fairness; *udal:* boldness, daring, inclination to take a risk.

p. 144, l. 20
A rather overdone interpretation of the treaty of Unkair Skelessi of July 5, 1833.

p. 146, l. 27
Barsukov, *op. cit.*, vol. V, pp. 165–175. Turgenev as a Westerner was hated by the Slavophiles and Pan-Slavs, especially by Dostoevsky. In the novel "Smoke" Potugin says: "Yes, I am a Westerner, I am devoted to Europe. I mean, to put it more exactly, I am devoted to its cultural standards, to those same cultural standards at which our people poke such delightful fun these days —its civilization—yes, yes, that word is still better. And I love it with all my heart, and I believe in it . . . That word . . . is both comprehensible and clean, and sacred; but all the rest, the nationality (narodnost) and the glory, stinks of blood. . . ." In another passage Potugin poked fun at the superiority complex which depreciates other nations and admires some home-grown genius whose works are only an imitation. Some "have even discovered a Russian science: why, twice two are four in Russia too and for some reason it is more clever there." To the young man returning to Russia, Potugin gave the advice: "Every time you have to turn to a

task, ask yourself: are you serving civilization—in the exact and strict meaning of the word—are you carrying through one of its ideas, has your labor that educative, European character which alone is beneficial and fruitful in our day, in our country?" (*The Borzoi Turgenev, op. cit.*, pp. 29, 77–81, 151). In his letters to Herzen, Turgenev several times attacked the Slavophile attitude. Thus in his letter of November 8, 1862: "With an extraordinary understanding you are making the diagnosis of the contemporary world, but why is it valid only for its Western half— and not in general for all bipeds? You are like a physician who after having discovered all the symptoms of a chronic disease suddenly declares that its origin lies in the fact that the patient is a Frenchman. You who are an enemy of all mysticism and absolutism are kneeling mystically before the Russian sheepskin, and you recognize in it the great blessing, the novelty and originality of the future forms of society— in one word, the absolute—that absolute of which you make so much fun in philosophy. All your idols lie in ruins, but how can man live without such an idol—and thus let us build an altar to the sheepskin, this unknown God; fortunately one does not know anything about him—and thus one can again pray, believe and hope." In another letter of December 12, 1867, he rejected the opinion that Europe was old or Russia young, and two weeks later on December 25, he criticized the Slavophile glorification of the village community, the *mir*, and of the traditional Russian industrial cooperative, the *artel*. "May God forbid that the principles of unhuman exploitation on which our *artel* are based should ever be widely accepted in our country." *Konstantin Kawelins und Iwan Turgenjews Socialpolitischer Briefwechsel mit Alexander Iw. Herzen*, ed. by Michail Dragomanow, tr. by B. Minzes (Stuttgart: Cotta, 1894), pp. 135 f., 152 f.

p. 147, l. 24

Schelling is reported to have told Peter Kireyevsky in 1829: "Russia has a great mission and never has she shown her power as completely as now. Now for the first time all Europe, or at least right-thinking Europe, looks upon her with sympathy and wishes her success;

one regrets only that her vindications in the present
situation are perhaps too moderate." "Peter Vasilyevich
Kireyevsky. Ego pisma," *Russky Arkhiv*, 1905, vol. II.
pp. 113–173 (p. 125). See also Alexander Koyré, "La
jeunesse d'Ivan Kireevski," *Le Monde Slave*, 1922, pp.
213–237; F. Stepun, "Die Deutsche Romantik und die
Geschichtsphilosophie der Slavophilen," *Logos*, 1927,
pp. 46–47; T. G. Masaryk, *Slavjanofilstvo I. V. Kiřějev-
ského* (Prague: L. Masaryk, 1889).

p. 147, l. 36
I. V. Kireyevsky, *Polnoe sobranie sochinenii*, 2 vols
(Moscow: J. P. Bakhmetev, 1861), vol. I. pp. 72 ff. A
handy collection of early Slavophile texts is in Nikola
Leontevich Brodsky, *Rannye Slavyanofily: A. S. Khomya
kov, I. V. Kireyevsky, K. S. i I. S. Aksakov* (Moscow
Istor.—lit. biblioteka no. V, 1910). There pp. 69–79
is also K. S. Aksakov's memorandum to Alexander II
(1855) on Russia's internal situation.

p. 149, l. 12
Nadezhdin wrote: "We are children, and childhood
compromises our happiness. Our history has until now
been a great poem with only one hero, one acting char
acter. . . . Remember with religious humility and
noble pride that your existence is concentrated in you
holy master. Without him you are only a line of zeros—
with that monarchical one these zeros make a billion."
Quoted in Wacław Lednicki, "Panslavism" in *Euro
pean Ideologies*, ed. by Felix Gross (New York: Phil
osophical Library, 1948), p. 821. The Slavophile belie
in the unique and exceptional character of a Russian o
rather Slav patriarchal society was stimulated by the
German economist and agrarian expert, August Freiher
von Haxthausen (1792–1866), who travelled through
out Russia on the invitation of the Tsar in 1843–44. In
his *Studien über die innern Zustände, das Volksleben
und insbesondere die ländlichen Einrichtungen Russ
lands*, 3 vols. (Hanover: Hahn'sche Hofbuchhandlung
1847–52), he came to the conclusion that while the
other European states were of feudal origin, Russia wa

a patriarchal state. "Während die übrigen Staaten Europas in ihrem Ursprunge und ihrer Fortbildung als Feudalstaaten zu bezeichnen sind, muss man Russland einen Patriarchalstaat nennen. Dieser einfache Satz schliesst unermessliche Consequenzen in sich und erklärt im Wesentlichen fast den ganzen staatlichen und socialen Zustand Russlands. Die russische Familie ist der Mikrokosmus des russischen Volksstaats. In der russischen Familie herrscht vollkommene Gleichheit der Rechte; so lange sie aber ungeteilt zusammen sitzt, hat sie ein Haupt im Vater, . . . dem allein die unbeschränkte Disposition über alles Vermögen zusteht. . . . Russland gehört nach der traditionellen Volksüberzeugung dem in Gemeinden abgeteilten russischen Volke, als einer einzigen Familie unter ihrem Haupte, ihrem Vater, dem Czar, an, dem daher auch allein die Disposition über Alles zusteht und unbedingt gehorcht wird. Eine Einschränkung des Czars ist dem russischen Volke völlig undenkbar." (The Russian family is the microcosmos of the Russian people's state. In the Russian family there is complete *equality of rights*; as long as it lives together, it has its head in the father who *alone* disposes of all its possessions without limitation. . . . According to the traditional conviction of the people Russia belongs to the Russian people organized in communes as a single family under its head, its father, the *Tsar* who therefore *alone* can dispose of everything and who is being obeyed unconditionally. A limitation of the power of the Tsar is entirely unthinkable to the Russian people. Vol. I, p. XI). Haxthausen suggested to the Russian government to pay greater attention to the *artel* ("eine Art von nationalen Associations-Fabriken") which he regarded as the realization of Saint-Simon's theories for the reform of social conditions in Europe. He was convinced that Russia would have a great future, proposed its indivisibility within the frontiers of 1840, warned, however, against further expansion. Of Moscow he wrote: "Moscow has an importance for the Russian people as no city for any other people has. It is the center of all popular (volkstümlich) and religious sentiments of the Russians." vol. I, p. 45

p. 149, l. 18

The religious theories of Khomyakov were published also in French, A. S. Khomiakoff, *L'Eglise Latine et le Protestantisme au point de vue de l'église d'Orient*. Recueil d'articles sur des questions réligieuses, écrites à différentes époques et à diverses occasions (Lausanne: B. Benda, 1872). See about him A. Gratieux, *A. S. Khomiakov et le mouvement Slavophile*, 2 vols. (Paris: éds. du Cerf, 1939); G. Samarine, *Préface aux Oeuvres Théologiques de A. S. Khomiakov*, tr. and ed. by A. Gratieux (Paris: éds. du Cerf, 1939); W. J. Birkbeck, *Russia and the English Church during the Last Fifty Years*, vol. I (London: Rivington, Percival & Co., 1895); Nikolai Alexandrovich Berdyaev, *Aleksei Stepanovich Khomyakov* (Moscow: A. I. Mamantov, 1912). Another Slavophile, Konstantin Dmitrievich Kavelin (1818–1885), a well known constitutional jurist who was a champion of the emancipation of the peasants with full land allotment and of local self-government, wrote at the end of 1858 in Herzen's *Kolokol*, no. 31: "I turn to you, young men, who are now in the schools and universities. You will have to do a lofty and unprecedented work. You will be called to save the world and to realize the true Kingdom of Christ. Start by not believing in the social sciences, especially those relating to political economy and to the natural rights of men however they may seem satisfactory to you. Learn them thoroughly in order to become convinced that they disregarded the heart; learn them in order to curse them learn them in order to overthrow them and to build a new edifice. Do not forget that the Kingdom of Christ has not yet existed on earth, that so far only the form but not the true essence existed. All societies laugh at Christ's truth, everywhere the heart feels oppressed. Only on peasant soil—only in the Russian peasant community, only in the Russian village, the heart recovers and one breathes more freely. Die if it should be necessary, die like martyrs, die for the fundamental truth as the first Christians died for the form, die for the maintenance of the equal rights of every peasant in the soil —die for the principle of the *mir*." That was written by a high official of the Ministry of Justice, author of many scholarly books, who held the chair of constitutional law in Moscow and later at St. Petersburg University. In a letter to Herzen of May 22, 1862, he wrote: "Only the common folk is good which does its work without regard for our talk. But the folk is for the Tsar. It feels instinctively that it could lose in case of a constitution or a revolution, and could win nothing." Kavelin rejected a constitution after the French model. On June 11, 1862, he wrote from Paris to Herzen: "All the horrors (in Russia) under Nikolai (I) are nothing in comparison with the systematic enslavement and demoralization of the French people." He rejected a constitution which would not assure social justice and equality; that a constitution which would safeguard personal rights and civic freedoms would be of some value, he never considered.

p. 150, l. 13

The political articles of Tyutchev in French are printed in his *Sochineniya,* 2nd ed. (St. Petersburg: A. S. Suvorin, 1900). See Ivan S. Aksakov (who married in 1865 Tyutchev's daughter Anna), *Biographia Fedora Ivanovicha Tyutcheva* (Moscow: M. G. Bolchanimov, 1880); D. Stremooukhoff, *La Poesie et l'Idéologie de Tiouttchev* (Paris: Les Belles Lettres, 1937); K. Pigarev, "F. I. Tyutchev i problemy vneshnej politiki tsarskoi Rossii," (F.I.T. and the Problems of the Foreign Policy of Tsarist Russia) *Literaturnoye Nasledstvo,* nos. 19–21 (Moscow, 1935); George Florovsky, "Historical Premonitions of Tyutchev," *The Slavonic Review,* vol. III, pp. 337 ff.; K. Pigarev, "F. I. Tyutchev o frantsuzskikh politicheskikh sobytiyakh 1870–1873," (F.I.T. on the French political Events 1870–1873), *Literaturnoye Nasledstvo,* vol. 31–32 (Moscow, 1937), pp. 753–776.

p. 151, l. 33

Aksakov, *Biografia, op. cit.,* p. 226 f. While serving in the Russian legation at Munich, Tyutchev met the Bavarian orientalist Fallmerayer. In reviewing Custine's book on Russia in the *Augsburger Allgemeine Zeitung* in January, 1844, while generally agreeing with Custine's

picture of the backwardness of Russia, Fallmerayer
warned against underestimating the strength which the
Russians drew from the Orthodox Church and their
nationalism. He recognized that Russia feared Western armies less than Western doctrines. (F. himself was
a strong liberal who later belonged to the left wing of
the Frankfurt Assembly). *Gesammelte Werke,* 3 vols.
(Leipzig, 1861), vol. III, pp. 23 ff. In June, 1844,
Tyutchev published in the same *Augsburger Allgemeine
Zeitung* a reply to Custine's book in the form of a
Letter to Dr. Gustav Kolb who edited the paper from
1837 to 1863. In it he not only, understandably,
rejected Custine's criticism, he tried also to convince the
Germans that their peace and happiness was best secured
by Russia's protection. Custine on the other hand,
(vol. III, pp. 320 ff) had come to the conclusion that
an intimate alliance between France and Russia in
which he had believed was impossible (". . . depuis
que j'ai vu de près la nation russe et que j'ai reconnu
le véritable esprit de son gouvernement, j'ai senti qu'elle
est isolée du reste du monde civilisé par un puissant
intérêt politique, appuyé sur le fanatisme religieux");
instead he proposed an alliance between the French and
the Germans.

p. 156, l. 8
The *Revue des Deux Mondes* prefaced Tyutchev's
article in its issue of January 1, 1850, p. 118, with the
following editorial comment: "Charlemagne is no longer
in Paris or in Aix-la-Chapelle, he is in Moscow or in
St. Petersburg. And one must above all keep in mind
the fact that the new Charlemagne coming to Rome
clearly pretends to bring, as the former did, a great material power, but that he has no intention of coming there
to receive a spiritual and moral consecration for his
power. Far from it; it is he who, as it were, comes to
consecrate the Papacy."

p. 157, l. 8
"The adherents of (Italian) national independence
hoped that by secularizing the Papacy completely for
the benefit of their cause, (Pius IX) who above all is a

priest would agree to become the standard bearer (gon-
falonier) of Italian liberty. . . . The naively ambitious
doctrines (of the neo-Guelphs) wished to make us believe that contemporary Italy would recuperate under
the auspices of the Roman Pontificate the universal
primacy and seize again, for the third time, the scepter
of the world. At the very moment when the Papal establishment was shaken to its very foundations, they proposed seriously to the Pope to outdo the mediaeval
world and offered him something like a Christian cali-
phate—under the condition, of course, that this new
theocracy would be exercized above all in the interest
of Italian nationality." *Sochineniya, op. cit.*, p. 594.

p. 157, l. 14
On the Third Rome of Vincenzo Gioberti and Giuseppe Mazzini see Hans Kohn, *Prophets and Peoples,
op. cit.*, ch. 3.

p. 157, l. 18
He saw the reason for French inability and governmental instability in the fact that France was a deeply
divided nation. "It is a case of a permanent, fundamental and forever insoluble antagonism which for the
last sixty years has formed, as it were, the core of
French national consciousness. It is the soul of France
which is divided."

p. 158, l. 32
"Pisma F. I. Tyutcheva k P. Ia. Chaadayevu," *Russky
Arkhiv*, 1900, III, p. 415.

p. 159, l. 12
Letter of June 23, 1845, letter no. 6 of the 21 letters
by Khomyakov to Samarin in Khomyakov, *Polnoe sobranie sochinenii*, 8 vols., (Moscow: Kishnerev, 1900–
1904), vol. VIII, p. 247.

p. 160, l. 18
Literaturnoye Nasledstvo, vol. 19–21, *op. cit.*, p.
205 f.

p. 162, l. 2

The revolutionary nature of Slavophilism was pointed out by Prince Ivan Sergeyevich Gagarin (1814–1882), a cousin of Samarin, who in 1842 joined the Catholic Church and a short time later the Jesuit order. In his pamphlet *La Russie sera-t-elle catholique?* (Paris, 1856), p. 74, he characterized the Slavophiles as "un circle où s'elaborait la formule russe nationale de l'idée révolutionnaire," because of their identification of national passions, political interests and religion. "In their domestic policy they wished to establish the most complete religious, political and national uniformity. . . . In their foreign policy, they wished to fuse all Orthodox Christians of whatever nationality, and all Slavs of whatever religion, in a great political unity, in a great Slav and Orthodox empire. . . . These strange Christians are above all preoccupied with the hegemony which their Church could exercise in the world." Gagarin accused the Slavophiles of having "turned away the principle of nationality from its natural path to serve as an instrument of the Revolution," and regarded their slogans as "the Eastern form of the revolutionary idea of the 19th century. If you compare the Old Moscovite party (the Slavophiles) with Young Italy, you will be astonished by the similarity . . . I doubt that the revolutionaries of the Occident . . . had ever proposed anything better combined to act upon the masses than Panslavism." Khomyakov discussed Gagarin in *L'Église Latine, op. cit.*, pp. 219 ff.

p. 162, l. 10

The nationalist atmosphere in which the young generation grew up is well described by Nikolai Nikolaevich Strakhov (1828–1896), Dostoevsky's close friend and collaborator: "A boundless patriotism—that was the emotional atmosphere in which I grew up and was educated in the provinces. Russia appeared to me as a country of immense strength, covered with incomparable glory, the first country of the world, so that I literally thanked God for having been born a Russian. For a long time I could not conceive that there could be men who felt and thought differently in that respect. . . .

When I finally became convinced that Europe despises us, that it regards us as semi-barbarians, and that it is for us not only difficult but impossible to convert the European peoples to a different opinion, the discovery was for me unbelievably painful, and I still feel this pain. But I never thought, even for a moment, of abandoning my patriotism or of preferring the spirit of any other land to that of my land. Though I often believed that Russia, as the poet Tyutchev says, 'cannot be understood by reason' and that one must 'believe' in Russia, I began more and more to understand why 'the haughty glance of other peoples will not recognize nor understand what glows within Russia's humble nakedness and shines forth full of secrecy'." Quoted in F. M. Dostojewsky, *Literarische Schriften* (Munich: Piper, 1920), p. 65 f. Strakhov collaborated in the nationalist periodical *Vremya* which Dostoevsky started in 1861. It was suppressed by the authorities in 1863 as the result of an article by Strakhov, "A Fateful Question," in which he pointed out that the Polish problem was a Russian problem which could be solved only by developing Russian national life so as to be able to justify it before Polish culture. Even in such an innocuous article, the Russian government saw "liberalism."

p. 162, l. 28

Alexander Ivanovich Koshelev, *Zapiski* (Diary) (Berlin: B. Behr, 1884), p. 67. See also Nil Petrov Kolyupanov (1827–1894) *Biografiya Alexandra Ivanovicha Kosheleva*, 2 vols., (Moscow: I. N. Kushnever, 1889–92) which like Barsukov's gigantic biography of Pogodin is a storehouse of information on Russian Pan-Slavism.

p. 162, l. 29

After the suppression of Pogodin's *Moskvityanin*, the Slavophiles published from 1856 to 1860 *Russkaya Beseda* (Russian Conversation), which was edited by Koshelev and Ivan Aksakov and in which Ivan Dmitrievich Beliayev (1810–1873), professor of the history of Russian law at Moscow University, and Prince Vladmir Alexandrovich Cherkassky (1824–1878) collaborated. It found little support. A weekly *Molva* (Rumor

or Report) was started by Konstantin Aksakov in April
1857 and was suppressed by the government in December of that year. The next year Ivan Aksakov founded
Parus (The Sail) which was suppressed after only two
issues. A longer life had his *Den* (The Day) which
appeared from 1861 to 1866.

p. 164, l. 34
   Koshelev, *Zapiski, op. cit.*, pp. 82–84.

p. 165, l. 32
   Alexander Ivanovich Herzen (1812–1870), *Palnoe
Sobranie sochinenii i pisem*, ed. by M. K. Lemke, 21
vols. (Petrograd and Moscow, 1919–23), vol. 8, pp.
67 ff.

p. 166, l. 20
   Ibid, vol. 8, p. 188.

p. 166, l. 38
   Herzen reprinted Chaadayev's "Letter" from the
Teleskop in vol. VI, (1861) of the yearbook *Polyarnaya
zvezda* (Polar Star), which he began to publish in London in 1855 and which he named after the literary almanac edited by Kondratij Federovich Ryleyev (1795–
1826), the leading poet among the Decembrists and
one of the five executed.

p. 168, l. 9
   Herzen, *Du développement des idées révolutionnaires
en Russie, op. cit.*, pp. 134–143. Herzen explained the
popularity of Fourier's system among the Russian youth
by its demand for immediate realization, its industrial
discipline and its regimentation of workers which recalled the Russia system of military settlements. "One
has remarked that an opposition which leads a frontal
attack upon a government has always something of its
character in an inverted sense. I believe that there is
some justification for the fear which the Russian government begins to feel of communism: communism is
the Russian autocracy turned upside down." *Ibid.*, p.
157.

p. 168, l. 17

Herzen, ed. Lemke, *op. cit.*, vol. V, pp. 388, 478. *Vom andern Ufer* appeared in Hamburg: Hoffman & Campe, 1849.

p. 169, l. 28

In 1862 an illegal paper in Russia, "Young Russia," asked the youth of Russia to prepare itself for the imminent "bloody and pitiless revolution," during which the imperial family and the "imperial party" including the "pseudo-liberal land-owning constitutionalists" would be liquidated. The revolutionary party, in case of victory, was to preserve the Tsarist centralized system, "to introduce with its help new foundations for the economic and social life in the shortest time possible. It must assume dictatorial powers and must not allow itself to be stopped by anything. The elections for the National Assembly must be held under the influence of the government which will take good care that adherents of the existing order (should they survive) would not be elected." Herzen answered in two articles of the *Kolokol*, "The young and the old Russia" in No. 139 of July 1, 1862, and "Journalists and Terrorists" in No. 141 of August 15. In the first article he wrote: "We must make use of the knowledge and experience of Western Europe for our cause. But we need as little its revolutionary declamations as the French needed the Roman Spartan rhetorics with which they spoke at the end of the last century." And in the other article: "Perhaps violent upheavals will also come with us; they are the *ultima ratio* of peoples and of Tsars. One must be prepared for them, but to call for them without having tried before every other means, to prefer them, is a sign of adolescence and immaturity . . . Should the fateful day (of revolution) come, rush courageously into battle and perish—but don't call for it as a desirable day. If the sun will rise without bloody clouds, it will be much better . . ."

p. 170, l. 24

Herzen, ed. Lemke, *op. cit.*, vol. IX, pp. 453–469

p. 170, l. 28

Kavelin wrote to Herzen on June 19, 1862, from Paris, defending the rights of the Poles to revolution: "They are a conquered people and I understand as well the revolting Pole as I understand the uprising of the Bulgars, the Serbs, or of the Italians against Austria. But whether the nearest road to Poland's liberty is the overthrow of the Russian yoke, that is again another question. I don't think it, I am deeply convinced that it is not. As senseless and abominable as the Russian domination in Poland is (and especially was), nevertheless it is not advantageous for them to throw off our yoke. If the Russian government had the happy idea of giving up Poland, . . . we should witness a strange spectacle: the Poles would be attracted to us, because behind the Polish question there is a much more important one, the Slav question, in which nothing can be done without Russia. By rubbing each other, we may heal ourselves of our crudity and foolishness, but they would heal themselves of the non-Slav saps and scrofulas with which they are swelled up." *Konstantin Kavelins . . . Social-politischer Briefwechsel, op. cit.,* p. 62.

p. 170, l. 35

Kolokol was transferred from London to Geneva after April 1, 1865. The last issue (No. 244–45) appeared on July 1, 1867, exactly ten years after the appearance of the first issue. See on Herzen: Raoul Labry, *Alexandre Ivanovič Herzen, essai sur la formation et le développement de ses idées* (Paris: Bossard, 1928).

p. 171, l. 8

Herzen, ed. Lemke, *op. cit.,* vol. XVI, pp. 25–27, 44–48. See also M. K. Dziewanowski, "Herzen, Bakunin, and the Polish Insurrection of 1863," *Journal of Central European Affairs,* VIII, (April, 1948), pp. 58–78.

p. 171, l. 31

Katkov was editor of the *Russky Vestnik* (Russian Messenger) and after 1862 of *Moskovskie Vedomosti* (Moscow News). A detailed account of his articles and attitudes can be found in S. Nevedensky, *Katkov i ego vremya* (K. and his Time, St. Petersburg: A. S. Suvarin, 1888). See also N. A. Lyubimov, *M. N. Katkov i ego istoricheskaya zasluga* (K. and his Historical Merit, St. Petersburg: Obshchestvennaya Polza, 1889).

p. 172, l. 23
Letter to Nil Alexandrovich Popov (1833–1891), professor of Russian history at Moscow University, of March 17, 1858, in Khomyakov, *Polnoe sobranie sochinenii, op. cit.*, vol. VIII, p. 169 f.

p. 173, l. 23
Its text in Khomyakov, *Polnoe sobranie sochinenii, op. cit.*, vol. I, pp. 377–408. Khomyakov wrote there (p. 407): "Love and favor science not only for the sake of its usefulness, but because it widens and strengthens reason, God's great gift . . . Science demands liberty . . . If one treats it like a mercenary servant, science becomes powerless and sterile . . . That is what we have already experienced ourselves, and what we experience even now."

p. 174, l. 18
Charles de Mazade, "La Russie sous l'Empereur Alexandre II: La politique extérieure de la Russie et le Panslavisme. 1866–1867," *Revue des Deux Mondes,* XXXVIII (May 15, 1868), pp. 405–438. In his above mentioned letter to Prince Gorchakov on censorship in 1857 Tyutchev had written: "The government must mould public opinion. For that purpose the public need not to be taken into legislative councils but there must be an intimate communication between government and people to arouse its spontaneous and unanimous collaboration." Tyutchev referred to the wide circulation in Russia of Herzen's *Kolokol* and demanded the creation of similar journals supporting the government.

p. 175, l. 3
Charles de Mazade, *Revue des Deux Mondes,* 15 October, 1867, p. 1047. Mazade wrote the article as a book review of *Choix de sermons et discours* de Mgr.

Philarète. (Philaret, 1782–1867, Metropolitan of Moscow since 1821, was one of the most influential theologians and orators of Russia of that time). There he wrote also (p. 1050): "The secret of this abasement of the Russian clergy is its complete lack of independence which makes even a Metropolitan of Moscow the first servant of the autocracy. . . . This is the necessary consequence of the whole system, of the disastrous confusion of powers which leaves no room for the independence of the human soul. I really do not know whether there is a more significant spectacle than that of Russia to show to all liberal minds what they must avoid and what they must pursue."

p. 177, l. 3

It was this poem of Tyutchev which contained the famous verse: "And among us in the midst of the Slav family, what a shame, one alone has avoided the hatred of their enemies; he was always and everywhere a traitorous evil-doer to his own. They honor only him, our Judas, with their kisses." This attack upon Poland set the tone for the anti-Polish attitude of the Russian participants. A volume *Bratyam slavyanam* (To our Slav Brothers) which was published for that occasion in Moscow in May, 1867, contained five poems by Tyutchev. Two years later, in 1869, he wrote a poem "To the Czechs on the Anniversary of Hus," which was sent to Prague with the chalice which the Moscow Slav Committee donated to the Czechs, and in March, 1870, he wrote a poem "Hus Burnt at the Stake," always maintaining the attitude that Hussitism was a Czech revival of Orthodoxy. In 1863, at the celebration of the 1,000th anniversary of the arrival of St. Cyril and St. Methodius in Moravia, a movement centering around the Moravian abbey of Velehrad near Ungarisch-Hradisch, started to propagate the Slavic liturgy and the unity of the Slavs under the Roman Pope on the basis of Slav traditions. The Academia Velehradensis was founded in 1907 for the study of the problem.

Another Pan-Slav poet, Apollon Nikolayevich Maikov (1821–1897), Dostoevsky's friend, read a poem at the banquet in which he announced the fulfilment of the task of centuries: the conquest of Constantinople. Maikov was also one of the first to glorify the "misunderstood" Ivan the Terrible.

p. 178, l. 2

Pogodin wrote in his *Polsky Vopros 1831–1867* (Moscow: Tip. Gazetty Russky, 1867), p. 2: "Russia committed no rape, as our enemies charge, made no conquests, as our neighbors say, but merely returned to herself those areas which had belonged to her from time immemorial by right of first occupation, on a par with her native possessions, by the same right by which France possesses Paris and Austria owns Vienna. What is more, Russia once owned other areas which extend a good deal further west and south; that is, Galicia and a part of Moldavia." There is no recognition here of the Ukrainian right to independence of which Herzen spoke; Pogodin's daring Pan-Slav dreams were not realized by Tsarist Russia but by Stalin who annexed Galicia and a part of Moldavia (and Carpatho-Ukraine), areas "once owned" by Russia. Among the Ukrainian delegates from Austria was Josef Livchak, who published afterwards for a short while with Russian support a periodical in Vienna called *Slavyanskaya Zarya* (The Slav Dawn). In that connection Charles de Mazade in *Revue des Deux Mondes* of 15 May, 1868, (*op. cit.*, p. 123) wrote: "It is strange that this (pro-Russian Pan-Slav) propaganda can be conducted under the eyes of the Austrian government which the Moscow newspapers call the foreign oppressor, and that if only half of what happens in Austria would happen in Russia, there would be not enough Siberias to contain those who allowed themselves these dreams of liberation."

p. 179, l. 18

Detailed reports of the Moscow Congress will be found in Milan Prelog, *Pout Slovanů do Moskvy roku 1867*, (The Pilgrimage of the Slavs to Moscow in 1867) tr. by Milada Paulová (Prague: Práce Slovanského Ustavu, no. 5, 1931) and in Julian Klaczko, "Le Congrès de Moscou et la propagande panslaviste," *Revue des Deux Mondes*, XXXVII (1 Sept., 1867), pp. 132–181. In his introduction Klaczko writes: "The action

of individual liberty has diminished in the events
which we witness, . . . and a blind and a wholly material force disintegrates the elements of the European
republic. The purely physiological condition of blood,
of racial origin, is being substituted for the complex
organism created by centuries, for the work of a long and
laborious civilization, and we return to the state of nature by a detour of which the imagination of Rousseau
did not dream, the racial sentiment." Josef Václav Frič,
one of the Czech radicals of 1848, wrote two pamphlets
against the pilgrimage to Moscow, *Die Kehrseite der
slawischen Wallfahrt nach Russland* (The reverse side
of the Slav Pilgrimage to Russia, Prague, 1867) and
Bud' jasno mezi námi! (Let there be clarity between
us, Prague, 1868). The important articles of Ivan
Aksakov on the Slav question which he published in
Den in 1867 were reprinted in vol. I of his *Sochineniya*
(Moscow, 1886) which bears the title "Slovyansky
vopros, 1860–1886."

p. 179, l. 31
Prelog, *op. cit.*, p. 75, reports that even Rieger in the
enthusiasm of a magnificent reception spoke of *one* Slav
nation. The delegates got the impression that "the Russians believe in Pan-Slavism as in a God and that the
whole Slav world will become a federated Russia" perhaps in three years. On the other hand, he reports that
many of the Slav delegates complained that they were
always surrounded by official Russian people and had no
possibility of contacting various peoples and no liberty
of movement. Thus they were not allowed to see any
of the many Westernizing opponents of Slavophilism
and Pan-Slavism.

p. 183, l. 25
Gervinus, *Hinterlassene Schriften* (Vienne: Brau-
müller, 1872), p. 21 f. See Hans Kohn, *Prophets and
Peoples, op. cit.*, pp. 114 ff., 193 ff.

p. 184, l. 23
Rostislaw Fadejew über *Russlands Kriegsmacht und*

Kriegspolitik, ed. by Julius Eckardt (Leipzig: Brockhaus, 1870), pp. V, 35 f. See also by Fadeyev, *Opinion
on the Eastern Question* (London: E. Stanford, 1871)
and *Briefe über die gegenwärtige Lage Russlands*, April
1879–1880 (Leipzig: Brockhaus, 1881).

p. 187, l. 31
    Palacký's "The Idea of the Austrian State" (*Idea
státu rakouského*) was written in 1865 and first published in the political daily *Národ* in April and May.
The separate publication in the same year included also
Palacký's letter of April, 1848, to the Frankfurt Vorparlament. It was reprinted in *Radhost, op. cit.*, vol. III,
pp. 158–230, and ed. by Zdenek V. Tobolka in the *Světová Knihovna*, nos. 558–559. There the quoted passage
(p. 101) is part of the last of the original eight articles.
The article in the *Národ* of November 9, 1864, quoted
in the text, was incorporated by Palacký into his "The
Idea of the Austrian State," pp. 66–73 of the *Světová
Knihovna* edition. There also he wrote (p. 64): "I am
convinced that a dualism in any form whatsoever will
prove within not too long a time destructive for the
whole monarchy, more destructive than a complete
centralization would be." He demanded (p. 34) "that
the Austrian government should be neither German,
nor Magyar, nor Slav, nor Latin, but Austrian in a
higher and general sense, that means on the basis of
equal justice for all its members." "That more than
300 years ago such different peoples have by free
agreements formed the Austrian Empire, I regard as a
in no way small blessing by Divine Providence for all
of them. If it had not happened and if each of these
peoples had kept its full sovereign rights, in how many
and how bloody struggles would they have faced each
other during that time! Perhaps some of them might
even have perished." (p. 29).

p. 188, l. 38
    See on 1867 and its consequences for Austria besides
the standard works by Louis Eisenmann, *Le Compromis
austro-hongrois de 1867, étude sur le dualisme* (Paris:
Société nouvelle de librairie et d'édition, 1904) and

Joseph Redlich, *Das Osterreichische Staats- und Reichs-problem*, 2 vols. (Leipzig: P. Reinhold, 1920, 1926): Robert A. Kann, *The Multinational Empire, National-ism and National Reform in the Habsburg Monarchy*, 2 vols. (New York: Columbia University Press, 1950); Karl Gottfried Hugelmann (ed.), *Das Nationalitäten-recht des alten Osterreich* (Wien: Braumüller, 1934); Oscar Jászi, *The Dissolution of the Habsburg Monarchy* (Chicago: University of Chicago Press, 1929); Arthur J. May, *The Habsburg Monarchy 1867–1914* (Cam-bridge: Harvard University Press, 1951); Hermann Münch, *Böhmische Tragödie. Das Schicksal Mitteleuro-pas im Lichte der tschechischen Frage* (Braunschweig: Westermann, 1949).

p. 190, l. 7
Palacký's last political writings appeared in German translations as *Politisches Vermächtnis* in 1872 and as *Schlusswort* in 1874. Both are reprinted in *Radhost*, *op. cit.*, vol. III, p. 257–317, and edited by J. Borovička in *Světová Knihovna*, nos. 1291–92. The "Testament" of 1872 is important also because it gives an account of the activities of Palacký and his friends for the Czech national movement, and presents a defense of Palacký's views on Russia, on Austria, and on radical and revolutionary thought.

p. 190, l. 24
Danilevsky's *Rossiya i Evropa* appeared in book form in St. Petersburg, 1871; the fifth edition, ed. by N. Strakhov, in 1895. Danilevsky wrote also a two-volume work *Darvininizm* (St. Petersburg, 1885–89); his articles were published as *Sbornik politicheskikh i ekonomich-eskikh statei* (St. Petersburg, 1880). A French sum-mary of "Russia and Europe" was presented in J. J. Skupiewski, *La Russie et l'Europe, coup d'oeil sur les rapports politiques entre le monde slave et le monde germano-romain, d'après la 4e édition russe*, St. Peters-burg, 1889 (Bucarest: Liberté Roumaine, 1890). Sku-piewski pointed out in his Introduction that the Western Slavs and even the Bulgars were in no way so "faithful to Russia" as Danilevsky believed. There exists a German

translation by Karl Nötzel, *Russland und Europa,* eine
Untersuchung über die kulturellen und politischen Be-
ziehungen der slawischen zur germanisch-romanischen
Welt (Stuttgart: Deutsche Verlagsanstalt, 1920). The
German translation contains, however, only ten of the
seventeen chapters of the Russian original. It omits
among others the first two chapters which analyze the
setting of the 1860's in which the book originated.

p. 193, l. 4
   Zarya, 1869, no. 1, pp. 50-52. The second chapter
of Danilevsky's book carries a short poem as motto
which reads: "We hear calumnies, we know insults,
the hydra-headed lies of the newspapers, the brood of
betrayal, envy and fear. Our Russia has no friends!"
No author for these four characteristic lines is given;
they may be from Danilevsky himself.

p. 193, l. 22
   Zarya, 1869, no. 2, p. 57.

p. 195, l. 17
   Zarya, 1869, no. 3, p. 38. The quotation is in the 6th
chapter of Danilevsky's book which like the fifth chapter
was not translated by Nötzel. In the fifth chapter
Danilevsky rejected the idea of a continuous progress
in history. "The thought of an infinite evolution or an
infinite progress belongs to the number of the greatest
stupidities which ever entered men's mind." Once a
civilization declines, mankind follows new paths. "Greek
art became the possession of the whole of mankind, the
possession of the subsequent civilizations, but only their
possession, that means something which they can use
and enjoy—what they can understand but not newly
create or acquire as the Greeks did, and certainly they
cannot progress in that direction."

p. 196, l. 23
   The one exception to this Slav civilization among
the Slavs was according to Danilevsky the Poles. Their
nobility abandoned Slav peacefulness and democracy
and accepted European civilization. Thus it lost "its

whole Slav character, after it had become a renegade to Slavdom in every respect, even so far as to become a tool of the Turks in suppressing the Slavs."

p. 196, l. 25

These political discussions begin with chapter 12, *Zarya*, 1869, no. 8.

p. 197, l. 35

The positive role of Turkey and Islam as a shield protecting the Orthodox Slavs from Europe was also stressed by Konstantin Nikolaevich Leontev (1831–1891) who, however, was not a Pan-Slav nor a Slavophile but a believer in the cultural creativeness of Byzantinism which the Turks for whom he felt strong sympathy shared to a certain extent with the Russians. He also rejected the Slavophile glorification of "humility" and "love." But he was at one with them in the conviction that Russia would solve the social problem, and that the Russians needed an affirmative faith and material security more than they needed rights. In 1890 he wrote to Anatol Alexandrov: "Sometimes I see a Russian Tsar at the head of the Russian movement (of revolutionary socialism) organizing it as Emperor Constantine organized Christianity. But what does such organization mean? Nothing else than constraint, an enlightened despotism, the legitimatization of a chronic violence, applied in adroit and wise doses, a violence which exercises itself upon the personal will of the citizens. It is hardly probable that one could organize this new and rather complex slavery and make it last without a mystic faith. If after Russia's annexation of Constantinople an extraordinary concentration of the Orthodox ecclesiastic bureaucracy should coincide with the development of the mystic faith, and with the inevitable workers' movement, one could guarantee for a long time the political and economic bases of the state." Nicolas Berdaeff, *Constantin Leontieff*, tr. by Hélène Iswolsky (Paris: Desclée de Brouwer, 1937), p. 283 f. He opposed the war against the Turks of 1877 which was undertaken for the "liberation" of the Slavs, and regarded Pan-Slavism as an imitation of European na-

tionalist trends which he rejected. He believed the
fertility of Russia was based upon the mixture of Slav
and Turanian blood and partly even of German blood.
Ibid., pp. 251, 263. But he shared Danilevsky's belief
that Russia was not a state but a world, the bearer of
a new civilization. Therein, he wrote, "I was the disciple
and the fervent adherent of our great Danilevsky whose
thought even today so few people know." *Ibid.*, p. 258.
Yet it should be emphasized that he always rejected all
Slavism. "Russia is not a purely Slav country. Such a
content would be too poor for her universal spirit."
Sobranie sochinenii, 9 vols. (Moscow, 1912) vol. V,
p. 19, See *ibid.* vol. V, pp. 337–353, and vol. VI, pp.
145–193, his "Vostok, Rossiya i Slavyanstvo" (The
Orient, Russia and Slavdom). About him see also I.
von Kolagrivov, *Von Hellas zum Mönchstum* (Regensburg: Pustet, 1948).

p. 201, l. 7

Chapter 14 (*Zarya*, 1869, no. 9) is entitled "Tsargrad" (The City of the Tsar, Constantinople) and
carries as its motto the verse of Tyutchev, calling the
Tsar of Russia to bow before the newly erected altar
of Christ in St. Sophia in Byzantium and to rise as the
Tsar of all Slavs. The geographic extent of the future
Pan-Slav union under the Tsar is found, *ibidem*, p. 21.

p. 206, l. 3

Danilevsky believed Russia was predestined to be
the leader of the movement for the unification of the
Slavs and the bearer of the civilization of the future,
because destiny had spared and preserved her by keeping
her remote. Similarly Germany had been united by its
easternmost member, Prussia, kept for that purpose
remote. It is interesting that Oswald Spengler used the
same argument in singling out Germany as the leader
of the white race against Russia and the colored races:
"Why is the German people the least exhausted of
the white world and therefore the one on which may
be placed the greatest hope? Because his political past
has given it no opportunity to waste its precious blood
and its great abilities. This is the one blessed aspect of

our wretched history since 1500, it has used us spar-
ingly." *The Hour of Decision* (New York: Knopf,
1934), p. 225.

p. 208, l. 34
Koshelev, *Zapiski, op. cit.*, pp. 228–235.

p. 211, l. 22
See on Dostoevsky Hans Kohn, *Prophets and Peoples,
op. cit.*, ch. 5. Dostoevsky edited in 1873 a weekly
Grazhdanin (The Citizen), and in 1876 and 1877 a
monthly one-man-journal *Dnevnik pisatela* (The Diary
of an Author), of which in August, 1880, and shortly
after the author's death in January, 1881, two further
issues appeared. All these articles have been translated
into English by Boris Brasol as F. M. Dostoievsky, *The
Diary of a Writer*, 2 vols. (New York: Scribner's, 1949).
There is a French translation by Jean Zhuzeville, *Le
Journal d'un écrivain*, 3 vols. (Paris: Bossard, 1927).
See also by the same, *Rome et l'internationale*: *une
prédiction de Dostoievski* (Paris: Bossard, 1927). In
Dostoevsky's novels see above all *The Possessed*, part II,
ch. 1, 7; the interesting notes quoted by Ernest J.
Simmons, *Dostoevsky, the Making of a Novelist* (New
York: Oxford University Press, 1940), p. 296 f; and
Dostoevsky's letter to A. F. Blagonravov of December
19, 1880. T. G. Masaryk regarded Dostoevsky as the
central figure for an understanding of modern Russia
and of the Russian revolution. See T. G. Masaryk,
Studie o F. M. Dostojevském, ed. by Jiří Horák (Prague:
Slav Institute, 1932); Jiří Horák, "Masaryk a Dostojev-
skij," *Naše Doba*. XXXVIII (Prague, 1930–31), pp.
324–332, 401–411, 468–476, 535–545, 595–609; Josef
L. Hromádka, "Masaryk und Dostojevskij," *Prager
Rundschau*, I (1931), pp. 97–113.

p. 213, l. 22
"The curious fact is, if one substituted communism
for his (Dostoevsky's) conception of the mission of the
Orthodox faith, and world revolution for his notion of
a Pan-Slavic war against Europe, the identity of his
whole position with that of modern Soviet Russia
would be striking." Ernest J. Simmons, *op. cit.*, p. 327.

p. 215, l. 15

See Olga Novikova, *Skobeleff and the Slavonic Cause* (London: Longman's Green & Co., 1883). There on p. 374 f. the characteristic statement: "Skobeleff admired England, and the English institutions for England, but not for Russia. He would have the Slavonic races develop their destinies as Slavs, and not as Germans or English. Russia has a nobility, but without any political privileges. Skobeleff, like all Russians, was a democrat, and believed, like the overwhelming majority of Russians, that our democracy, required the supreme will of an autocratic concentrated power." See on the period B. H. Sumner, *Russia and the Balkans,* 1870–1880 (Oxford University Press, 1937).

p. 216, l. 14

Like Aksakov, Dostoevsky expected the coming of the proletarian social revolution in Europe, but its waves would break against the Russian shores. Russia would be saved by her better and more progressive social and civic system. "You will ask: what social and civic ideals of our own can we have outside of those of European origin? Well, our social and civic ideals are better, more solid and even—oh, horrible dictu!—more liberal than your European ideals! Yes, they are more liberal because they emanate directly from our people's organism, and they are not a slavishly impersonal transplantation from the West." *The Diary of a Writer, op. cit.,* p. 1004.

p. 216, l. 21

The opposition of the Western liberals to Dostoevsky was sharply expressed after his famous lecture on Pushkin in 1880. Looking without illusions upon the Russian peasants and their communal economy of the *Mir,* so highly praised by the Slavophiles, Gleb Ivanovich Uspensky (1840–1902) wrote: "It is difficult to understand one who in himself reconciles such contradictions." Professor Alexander Dimitrievich Gradovsky of the law faculty of St. Petersburg University (1841–1889) criticized Dostoevsky in an article "Mechty i deistvitelnost" (Illusions and Reality), reprinted in his *Sobranie sochinenii,* VI, pp. 375–383. Dostoevsky answered him in the 1880 issue of his *Diary of a Writer*, *ibid*, pp. 981–1010. Gadovsky wrote: "The speech of the poet does not stand the test of thorough criticism. Poets are poets, but level-headed men always stand on guard, ready to pour a bucket of cold water on the dreamer." See also the sharp criticism of Dostoevsky by his former disciple Vladimir Sergeevich Solovyev in his *Sobranie sochinenii*, 9 vols. (St. Petersburg: Obshchestvennaya Polza, 1901–1903), vol. V, p. 381.

p. 218, l. 7

Samarin was highly critical of the development in Bismarckian Germany. In January, 1876, visiting Berlin, he wrote to Baroness Edita Fedorovna Rahden (1825–1885) that he found Germany ruled on the one hand by the conservative aristocracy (Grossgrundbesitz und Herrenrechte), on the other hand by the Jews. "You certainly know that today almost no Berlin exists, but a new Jerusalem which speaks German." This resulted in politics in the adoration of success and the cult of mammon; in society, in the increase of productivity purely abstractly conceived; and in general life, in an extreme individualism and utilitarianism. "Germany is perhaps the greatest danger which threatens the future of my country, and yet I cannot contemplate without deep pain this dissolution which takes place under the cover of a political power arrived at its zenith. To every Russian who has studied there, at least in my time, Germany is also a kind of fatherland, the milk of which one has sucked for a long time. Unfortunately it is this very Germany which has nourished the men of my age, which disappears." Yurii Fedorovich Samarin, *Perepiska Yu. F. Samarina s Baronessoi E. F. Raden 1861–1867 g.* (Correspondence . . . — the test is in French—Moscow: Mamontov, 1893), pp. 241–243.

p. 218, l. 12

Apollon Maikov glorified Alexander III in a poem written in 1894 after the Emperor's death: "We cherished most in him that even he, the Tsar, had faith in his mission and in the historical mission of the Russian Empire. He proclaimed it without fear. As the sound

of the bell high up in the Kremlin in the tower of Ivan
awakens all the bells around in the wide Russian land
on the festival of the Resurrection, thus the Emperor's
word, in which Russia rose to new life, sounded and
awakened in the people the faith in itself which had
long struggled to be born. It sounded with great might
like the spring thunderstorm which awakens life where
formerly the rigidity and deadness of winter was. What
had been only sentiment and old dim folk-tale, that
became full of life, in armor and conscious of its
strength."

p. 218, l. 15
   On Pobedonostsev see Robert F. Byrnes, "Pobedonostsev's Conception of the Good Society: an Analysis of
his Thought after 1880," *The Review of Politics*, XIII
(1951), pp. 169–190; Friedrich Steinmann and Elias
Hurwicz, *K. P. Pobjedonoszev als Staatsmann der Reak-
tion unter Alexander III* (Königsberg: Osteuropa Verlag,
1933). His *Moskovsky sbornik* (Moscow, 1896) was
translated into English as *Reflections of a Russian
Statesman*, with a preface by Olga Novikoff (London:
G. Richards, 1898); his *K. P. Pobedonostsev i ego kor-
respondenti, pisma i zapiski. Novum regnum* (K.P.P.
and his Correspondents, Letters and Memoranda), 2
vols. (Moscow, 1923) was published in an abridged
French translation, *L'autocratie russe. Mémoires politiques, correspondance officielle et documents inédits*
(Paris: Payot, 1927).

p. 218, l. 30
   Robert F. Byrnes, *op. cit.*, p. 180. See also Konstan-
tine P. Pobedonostsev, "Russia and Popular Education.
A Reply to Prince Kropotkin," *North American Review*,
vol. CLXXIII (1901), pp. 349–354. There are naturally in Pobedonostsev general Russian traits which
sound like Slavophilism: "The difference between the
social spirit and composition of the Anglo-Saxon and
the Russian races is noticeable nowhere so much as in the
church. . . . In all our churches social distinctions are
laid aside and we surrender our positions in the world
and mingle completely in the congregation before the

face of God. . . . The congregation (in an English church) is a congregation of 'ladies and gentlemen' each with a place specially reserved, the rich in separate and embellished pews like the boxes of an opera-house. . . . From its dawn to the present day our Church has been the church of the people, inspired by love and all-embracing, without distinction of class." *Reflections of a Russian Statesman, op. cit.,* p. 206. But his general attitude against parliaments against a free press in the Western sense of the word, against "bourgeois" democracy, were only the echo of what the French Right said about the same time. These arguments were practically the same as those heard from the extreme Left. Yet the fundamental attitude was different. Pobedonostsev warned in his *Reflections* against the utopianism of the Left, therein again echoing the warnings from Burke and de Maistre to Maurras: "In the name of the doctrine for the attainment of an imaginary end —the perfection of the race—will be sacrificed without scruple the most sacred privileges of personal freedom. . . . The terrible emptiness of the moral world will precipitate chaos." The *Moskovsky Sbornik* (Reflections of the Russian Staesman) exists also in a German translation, *K. P. Pobedonoszews Sammlung Moskowitischer Studien über das politische und geistige Leben der Gegenwart, mit Bezug auf Russland;* tr. by C. E. Wohlbrück (Dresden: Pierson, 1904).

p. 219, l. 24
See Theodore H. von Laue, "The Industrialization of Russia in the Writings of Sergej Witte," *The American Slavic and East European Review,* vol. X (1951), pp. 177–190. Witte, however, differed from his German model and his Bolshevik successors by his typically Western bourgeois pacifism. "He always complained that Russia's railways had been built by the generals without regard to economic factors. And as to the current expenses of the army he pointed to the United States, saying that one of the causes of their prosperity was the absence of a large standing army. In short, following a line of thought popular among some of his Western banking friends, he held the economic conse-

quences of militarism to be ruinous. Russian industrialization required peace and a society dedicated to
productive work . . ." (*ibid.,* p. 187). His book *Po
povodu natsionalizma: natsionalnaya ekonomiya i Frid-
rikh List* appeared in a second ed. (St. Petersburg:
Brokgaus-Efron, 1912). See also Stuart R. Tompkins,
"Witte as Minister of Finance, 1892–1903," *Slavonic
and East European Review,* IX, no. 33 (April, 1933),
pp. 590–606.

p. 225, l. 16

See D. Strémooukhoff, *Vladimir Soloviev et son
oeuvre messianique* (Paris: Les Belles Lettres, 1935);
Michael Karpovich, "Vladimir Soloviev on Nationalism," *The Review of Politics,* VIII (April, 1946), pp.
183–191. Solovyev's criticism of Danilevsky and of
Nikolai Strakhov's "Borba s zapadem v russkoi literature" (The Struggle with the West in Russian Literature) is found in the sixth chapter of his "*Natsionalny
vopros v Rossii*" (The National Question in Russia)
in his *Sobranie sochinenii, op. cit.,* vol. V, pp. 76–138.

NOTES TO PART THREE

Page 231, line 5

Onno Klopp (1822–1903), a Hannoverian historian who after 1866 lived in Vienna, complained bitterly how little the Austrian authorities cared about an understanding, on the part of the population, of the idea or the history of the Austrian state. "Hier fehlt das Gemeingefühl. Es ist entsetzlich, sich das auszudenken. Eine Macht, die von der geschichtlichen Darlegung ihres Prinzipes nur moralische Stärkung, nur Vorteil zu erwarten hat, hat nicht bloss eine solche nicht gefördert, sondern gehindert." (A power which has only to expect moral strength and advantages from the historical presentation of its principles, not only does not promote it, but hinders it). Wiard Klopp, *Onno Klopp, Leben und Werken* (Munich: Schnell & Steiner, 1950), p. 97. See also there p. 187, Klopp's remarks against the Austrian alliance with Germany written in 1887.

p. 233, l. 25

See H. Gordon Skilling, "The Partition of the University in Prague," *The Slavonic and East European Review*, XXVII (1949), pp. 430–449. Zdeněk Nejedlý, *T. G. Masaryk*, vol. III (Prague: Melantrich, 1935), pp. 21–97, gives a detailed description of the new Czech university and its professors.

p. 234, l. 6

Masaryk's *Česká otázka. Snahy a tužby národního obrození* (The Czech Question. Efforts and Longings of the National Rebrith) was first published in 1895 and in a second revised edition in 1908. The book offers the best brief history of the Czech national movement, written from the point of view of a disciple of Palacký. In section 33, Masaryk stressed that Palacký regarded as the foremost concrete political goal to establish the Czech relationship with the Bohemian Germans, "who

have inhabited Bohemia jointly with us since the oldest
time," and that he saw therein a practical contribution
to the solution of the humanitarian ideal; he believed
in an Austrian federation against Pan-Germanism and
Pan-Russianism, and within this Austrian federation in
a Czech federation of a part of the German people with
one Slav nation. (Česka otázka, new ed, by Zdeněk
Franta, *Knihy pro každého*, III, nos. 1, 2, Prague: Government Publishing House, 1924, p. 108). The passage
quoted in the text is in section 62, p. 179 f. On page
27 (end of section 6) Masaryk objected to Kollár's over-
emphasis on nationality, wherein he deviated from
Herder: "One can even blame him that he almost completely lost his humanitarianism while he increased the
national longings to the very limit of national exclusiveness, and thereby to injustice."

p. 235, l. 5
See the various points of view in Josef Kaizl, Z *mého
života* (My Life), 3 vols. in 4, ed. by Zdeněk V. Tobolka (Prague: Vilímek, n.d., 1909?); Emanuel Rádl,
Der Kampf zwischen Tschechen und Deutschen, tr.
from Czech by R. Brandeis (Reichenberg: Stiepel,
1928); Alfred Fischel, *Das tschechische Volk*, 2 vols.
(Breslau: Priebatsch, 1928); and Hermann Münch,
Böhmische Tragödie, das Schicksal Mitteleuropas im
Lichte der tschechischen Frage (Braunschweig: Westermann, 1949).

p. 235, l. 31
Schönerer's disciple Karl Hermann Wolf founded
among the Germans in Bohemia a German workers'
party which was later to assume the name of Deutsche
National-Sozialistische Arbeiterpartei. The Pan-Germanism of the Austrian anti-Slavs exercized a strong influence on Hitler. Schönerer himself always boasted that
he came from the common people, "ein Kind des
Volkes, aus der Mitte des Volkes hervorgegangen und
nicht aus den Kreisen der oberen Zehntausend." He
declared that a real man "could not feel at home in a
multi-national state like Austria ("nicht heimisch fühlen
können in diesem Nationalitätenkonglomerat.") He

was one of the first to demand universal suffrage in Austria and like most anti-Semites liked to regard himself as on the extreme Left and radical in his social demands. Every Jew without exception is according to him "inescapably determined by his Semitic blood and Semitic morality and works consciously or unconsciously to undermine the German character." Ferdinand Bilger in his article on Schönerer in *Neue Osterreichische Biographie* 1815–1918, ed. by Anton Bettelheim, vol. V (Vienna: Amalthea-Verlag, 1928), p. 86, stressed the similarity of Schönerer's program with that of the nationalist radicals of 1848 and added: "If we are today after the breakdown of our old state on the road to a union with Germany, so we have to remember Schönerer as the first path-breaker. In the days of his great popularity he carried the national idea constantly and unflaggingly into circles to which until then no glimmer of national consciousness had penetrated."

p. 236, l. 21

See on their theory Robert A. Kann, *The Multi-National Empire, op. cit.*, vol. II, and on Fischhof, Richard Charmatz, *Adolf Fischhof, Das Lebensbild eines Oesterreichischen Politikers* (Stuttgart: Cotta, 1910). Of other books on the subject see Joseph Alexander Freiherr von Helfert, *Fünzig Jahre nach dem Wiener Congresse von* 1814–15. Mit besonderem Hinblick auf die neuesten österreichischen Zustände (Vienna: Karl Czermak, 1865). He demanded a "sound nationality policy" which would preserve the national characters without separation or segregation; he favored Austro-Slavism against the German-Magyar dualism and proposed an active policy in the Balkans, to win the peoples there for Austria. See also Alfred von Kremer, *Die Nationalitätsidee unde der Staat*. Eine kulturgeschichtliche Studie über den Einfluss der nationalen Ideen, besonders auf Staaten mit gemischter Bevölkerung (Vienna: Konegen, 1885); Wenzel Frind, *Das spachliche und sprachlich-nationale Recht in polyglotten Staaten und Ländern* mit besonderer Rücksichtnahme auf Oesterreich und Böhmen vom sittlichen Standpunkte aus beleuchtet (Vienna, 1899).

p. 237, l. 18

Schuselka was born in Budweis, a Bohemian town then predominantly German. Like many Bohemian Germans, his name pointed to Slav descent. Even in the 1840's nationalism was so far advanced that Czech nationalists tried to claim him as a Slav. He wrote then to Count Leo Thun: "Perhaps I really descend on my father's side from Slavs. On my mother's side I come from Gmunden in beautiful Upper Austria. Unfortunately we proletarians have no ancestral records. Nevertheless, I know that I am a German, at least in the third generation. A century ago, my father's family might have been Germanized, not on purpose but in the natural course of events; thus I am really a native German." *Allgemeine Deutsche Biographie*, vol. 34, p. 755.

p. 237, l. 21

His strong opposition to Russia was expressed in his *Deutsche Volkspolitik* (Hamburg: Hoffman & Campe, 1846).

p. 237, l. 27

Oesterreich über alles (Hamburg: Hoffman & Campe, 1848). The book carried a motto from Hegel: "Austria is not a kingdom (Königtum) but an empire (Kaisertum), i.e., an aggregation of many state organizations."

p. 239, l. 27

Deutsch oder Russisch. Die Lebensfrage Oesterreichs, 2nd. ed. (Vienna: Jasper, Hugel & Manz, 1849), pp. V, 13 f, 19, 37, 39 f, 47, 54 f. Several replies to Schuselka's pamphlet appeared, among them *Weder Deutsch noch Russisch sondern Oesterreichisch*, von einem Magyaren (Vienna: Braumüller, 1849) and *Oesterreichs Lebensfrage als Entgegnung auf Schuselkas Deutsch oder Russisch*, von M. F. v. R. (Vienna: Braumüller, 1849).

p. 240, l. 8

Schuselka, *Das Provisorische Oesterreich* (Leipzig: F. W. Grunow, 1850), pp. 68, 87 f.

p. 240, l. 10
Schuselka, *Völker-Einigung. Ein Beitrag zur Versöhnung der Nationalitäten in Oesterreich* (Leipzig: Grunow, 1851).

p. 240, l. 29
Schuselka, *Oesterreich und Ungarn* (Vienna: Friedrich Forster, 1861).

p. 241, l. 1
Editorial "Unser Programm" in *Die Reform*, IV, no. 40 (5 Oct., 1865).

p. 242, l. 37
The *Slovanský přehled* was founded and edited by Adolf Černý. Its publication was interrupted by World War I and after a new start in 1925 it was suppresed in 1939. It was resumed in 1946 with volume XXXII.

p. 243, l. 21
"Il ne tenait qu'aux nouveaux gouvernants de la Serbie d'entrer dans une ère de bon voisinage que bien des raisons semblaient rendre désirable." Émile Haumont, *La Formation de la Yugoslavie* (Paris: Bossard, 1930), p. 551. Haumont was an extreme Serbophile, yet he recognized how much in and after World War I Serbian arrogance did to alienate the Croats. See pp. 665, 682, 687 and 689, 719, 721, 747.

p. 244, l. 29
The position of the Poles in Prussia grew worse after the foundation in 1894 of the Verein zur Förderung des Deutschtums in den Ostmarken (Association for the Advancement of German nationality in the Eastern Marches). The movement was called "Hakatist", from the initials of its three founders, Ferdinand von Hansemann (1861–1900), Hermann Alexander Kennemann (1815–1910), and Heinrich von Tiedemann (1843–1922). Though the movement claimed a purely defensive character, it initiated a "struggle for the soil" and was animated by the feeling described by Gustav Freytag (1816- 1895) in his novel *Soll und Haben* (1855—

the work in three volumes was in its 60th printing in
1904): "Whatever the business that brought me to
these parts, now that I am here, I stand as one of the
conquerors who, for the sake of free labour and human
civilization, have taken the dominion over this soil away
from a weaker race. We and the Slavs—it is an age-old
struggle. And with pride we note that culture, the will
to work, the credit are on our side." Richard Wonser
Tims, *Germanizing Prussian Poland* (New York: Columbia University Press, 1941), points out that though
the movement failed because it was opposed by moderate Germans of all parties and could not be in the atmosphere before 1914 ruthless enough to be effective,
nevertheless it "summed up much that was typical and
symptomatic in the generation that approached 1914."
(p. 282 f.)

The Hungarian government of Kálmán Tisza (1830–
1902) closed in 1875 the Slovak cultural organization,
the Slovenská Matica. Tisza declared on December 15,
1875, in the Hungarian Parliament that no Slovak nationality existed. At the end of the 19th century there
was only one Slovak newspaper in Hungary, *Národnie
Noviny* (National Newspaper), edited by Josef Škultéty
(1853–1948). In 1875 there were in Slovakia 1805 ele-
mentary schools in which Slovak was taught besides
Magyar, in 1905 there were only 241 of these schools.
Under these conditions some of the Slovaks looked to
Russia in a mystical Pan-Slavism, others more realisti-
cally looked to Prague, where in 1896 a Czechoslovak
Union (Českoslovanská jednota) has been founded.

p. 245, l. 37
See on Dmowski W. J. Rose in *The Cambridge History of Poland from Augustus II to Pilsudski* (Cambridge: University Press, 1941), pp. 396–408, and W.
Feldman, *Geschichte der politischen Ideen in Polen seit
dessen Teilungen* (1795–1914) (Munich: R. Oldenbourg, 1917), pp. 343–355, 378–389.

p. 246, l. 35
The most detailed discussion of Neo-Slavism is to

be found in Alfred Fischel, *Der Panslawismus bis zum Weltkrieg, op. cit.*, pp. 439–581. The very informative discussion by Fischel suffers, however, from being written under the immediate impact of World War I. It is true, that, on the outbreak of the war of 1914, the large majority of Poles remained loyal to Russia and that as a result the task of assembling the Russian armies to fight on Polish soil was made easier. (See also W. J. Rose, *op. cit.*, p. 407). This was hardly, however, the results of Pan-Slavism and of Dmowski's policy. The majority of the Czechs and of the Croats remained loyal to the Habsburgs in 1914, too. In both cases the situation changed only in 1917, and then not under the influence of Pan-Slavism but as a consequence of the long duration of the war with its defeats and privations and of the Russian Revolution of March 1917.

p. 247, l. 15

The Sokol movement spread in 1863 to the Slovenes, in 1865 to the Czechs in the USA, in 1867 to the Poles, in 1874 to the Croats and in 1882 to the Serbs. Dr. Tyrš regarded the Sokols in 1869 as a potential national army from the "Šumava (Böhmerwarld) to the Tatra, from the Krkonoš (Riesengebirge) to the Alps." Tyrš followed a program of nationalist progressivism, much influenced by the general mood of the 1860's. Among his slogans were: "Nothing for the individual, everything for the whole (community)." "The reaction is a crime." "The struggle for existence is a natural law." "The future belongs to those who are active." The four F's which characterized the German gymnastic movement ("Frisch, fromm, fröhlich, frei!") were replaced by four S's (Síla, Strength; Svornost, Unity: Svoboda, Liberty: Sláva, Glory). The German gymnastic movement played a great role in the critical period of German nationalism, from 1859 to 1864, when the number of the local associations (Turnvereine) increased from 100 to 1864 and when they met in the German gymnastic festivals (Turnfeste) at Coburg (1860), Berlin, (1861) and Leipzig (1863). The local organizations created in 1860 a permanent central executive committee and in 1868 a national organization, Deut-

sche Turnerschaft. This model was closely followed by
the Sokol which use the word *slet* (to come together fly-
ing) for the gathering of the "falcons." The successor
of Tyrš was Dr. Josef Schreiner (1861–1932) who also
became in 1908 chairman of the newly founded Slav
Sokol Union.

p. 247, l. 30

The strength of the Ukrainian movement lay in Austria. Both the Poles and the Ukrainians enjoyed in
Austria political and cultural liberty and full possibilities
for self-development, withheld completely from them in
"Slav" Russia. In Lemberg (Lviv), Austria, Ukrainian
patriots from Russia founded in 1873 the Shevchenko
Society, later known as the Shevchenko Scientific Society (Naukove tovarystvo imeny Shevchenka). In 1863
the Russian government had forbidden the teaching of
Ukrainian in the schools, the printing of Ukrainian
school texts or popular books or the use of the Ukrainian translation of the Bible. These draconian measures
were strengthened in 1876 when the printing of all
Ukrainian books, Ukrainian performances in theatres,
the singing of Ukrainian songs in concerts and the im-
port of Ukrainian books printed in Austrian Galicia were
forbidden. Mykhailo Dragomanov (1841–1895), then a
professor of history at Kiev University, had just published, together with Vladimir Antonovich (1834–
1909), the *Historical Songs of the Ukrainian People*
(Istoricheskiya piesni malorusskago naroda, 2 vols., Kiev,
1874–75). He went abroad, helped found the Shevchenko Society and published the review *Hromada* in
Geneva before being called to the University of Sofia,
Bulgaria. He was a Europeanized liberal, close to
Herzen, and had a great influence on the Galician
Ukrainians through Ivan Franko (1856–1916), a poet
and leader of the democratic anti-Moscow wing of the
Ukrainians. The Shevchenko Society had its most active
period under the leadership of the Ukrainian historian
Mykhailo Hrushevsky (1866–1934) who was invited in
1894 from Kiev to become Professor of Ukrainian His-
tory in Lemberg and to edit the *Zapysky*, the Journal
of the Shevchenko Society. After World War I he re-

turned to Kiev, where for a short while the Ukrainian
national movement flourished, both under the Ukrainian Centralna Rada, the independent representation of
the Ukrainian people established in 1917, and even in
the period of the Bolshevik NEP. The famous communist literary group Vaplite (Free Academy of Proletarian Literature), headed by Mykola Khvylovy (1893–
1933), the most gifted post-war Ukrainian prose writer,
issued a manifesto demanding that Ukrainian literature
and art "should orient itself toward Western Europe
and turn its back on Moscow." Naturally Khvylovy and
other communist writers had after the end of the NEP
to commit suicide or to disappear in some other way,
and Professor Hrushevsky was forced to emigrate. But
the problem of a Ukrainian nationalism oriented towards the West has apparently not yet ended in the
Ukraine, for the persecution of leading Ukrainian communists by Moscow continued even in 1951. As the
result of World War II the Moscow government succeeded in uniting all Ukrainian territories under its control, thus rendering impossible the situation of before
1914, when the Ukrainians oppressed by Moscow could
develop a free existence in Austria. In spite of the oppression which they suffered between 1919 and 1939
from the "Slav" Polish government, the Polish Ukrainians still had more liberty there for an autonomous development than in the Soviet Union. See for the period
until 1939 the very good bibliography in Michael
Hrushevsky, A History of the Ukraine, ed. by O. J.
Frederiksen(New Haven: Yale University Press, 1941);
also Alexandre Choulguine, L'Ukraine contre Moscou:
1917 (Paris: Alcan, 1935); D. Doroshenko, "Mykhailo
Dragomanov and the Ukrainian National Movement,"
The Slavonic and East-European Review, XVI, no. 48
(April, 1938); Nicholas Czubatyj, "The Modern Ukrain-
ian Nationalist Movement," Journal of Central Euro-
pean Affairs, IV, no. 3 (Oct., 1944), pp. 282–305; John
S. Reshetar, Jr., The Ukrainian Revolution, 1917–1920
(Princeton: University Press, 1952).

p. 249, l. 35
The book by R. Dmowski appeared also in French,

La question polonaise with a preface by Anatole Leroy-
Beaulieu (Paris: Armand Collin, 1909).

p. 251, l. 12

See George Franz, *Erzherzog Franz Ferdinand und
die Pläne zur Reform der Habsburger Monarchie*
(Brünn: Rohrer, 1943) and Robert A. Kann, "Emperor
William II and Archduke Francis Ferdinand in their
Correspondence," *American Historical Review*, LVII,
no. 2 (Jan. 1952). On the stubbornness of the Magyars
and their nationalistic plans even in 1918 see Alexander
Spitzmüller, "L'automne 1918 en Autriche-Hongrie,"
Revue Historique, CCV (1951), pp. 69–77.

p. 251, l. 25

Edvard Beneš, *Úvahy o slovanství. Hlavní problémy
slovanské politiky* (Considerations on Slavdom. The
Main Problems of Slav Policy. Prague: Čin, 1947), p.
159.

p. 252, l. 29

The Byelo-Russians began to organize their national
life in 1905. From 1906 they published a weekly *Nasza
niwa* (Our Country) in Wilna in which they used the
Latin script for Catholic and the Cyrillic script for
Orthodox readers. See Nicholas P. Vakar, *Belorussia.
The Making of a Nation* (Cambridge: Harvard Univer-
sity Press, 1956) It is interesting to note that *A Hand-
book of Slavic Studies* (Cambridge: Harvard University
Press, 1949) which devotes a chapter to the Serbs of
Lusatia and another chapter to their literature hardly
discusses at all the much more important and numerous
Byelo-Russians.

p. 254, l. 25

The most recent book on the origins of World War I
is Luigi Albertini, *Le origini della guerra del* 1914, 3
vols., (Milan: Fratelli Bocca, 1942–43). An English
edition in three volumes began to appear in 1952, (Oxford University Press). See Bernadotte E. Schmitt,
"The Origins of the War of 1914," *The Journal of
Modern History*, XXIV, (March, 1952), pp. 69–74:

"On the main issue he (Albertini) is absolutely clear: the primary responsibility for the outbreak of war in 1914 rests with Germany" or rather with the German general staff. "Neither Sazonov nor the tsar desired war, in Albertini's opinion. The foreign minister's motive in authorizing partial mobilization was not to attack Austria but to dissuade Austria from attacking Serbia, which it did not do." But Albertini stresses also the grave responsibility of the Serb government.

p. 256, l. 15

William Maehl, "The Triumph of Nationalism in the German Socialist Party on the Eve of the First World War," *The Journal of Modern History*, XXIV (March, 1952), p. 40, comments: "Innumerable statements by party leaders had never left doubt that national defense would be the order of the day if Germany were imminently faced with Russian invasion. Regarded by the German worker as a horde of black reaction, a barbaric empire where the splendor of the tsar eclipsed the suffering of a people, despotic Russia was seen as the archfoe of the world proletariat. Beyond this, the German people collectively had always contemplated with nameless terror a Russian inundation of central Europe."

p. 258, l. 2

After All, the autobiography of Norman Angell (New York: Farrar, Straus & Young, 1952), p. 183. Angell was the author of the manifesto which bore the title "Shall we Fight for a Russian Europe?"

p. 259, l. 6

Romain Rolland wrote in the introduction to his *Vie de Beethoven* which appeared as the first of his three "Heroic Lives" in the January, 1903, issue of Charles Péguy's *Cahiers de la Quinzaine*: "The air is heavy around us. Old Europe is stifled by a thick and vitiated atmosphere. A materialism without greatness weighs on the minds and hinders the work of governments and individuals. The world dies suffocated in its prudent and vile egoism. Let us throw open the windows. Let fresh air enter. Let us breathe the breath of heroes.

"Life is stern. It is the daily battle for those who are not resigned to the mediocrity of the soul, and most often it is a sad battle, without greatness, without happiness, fought in solitude and silence. Weighed down by poverty and harsh domestic cares, by excessive and stupid tasks which waste the strength to no purpose, without any hope, without a gleam of joy, most people are separated from each other, without even the consolation of holding out their hand to their brothers in misfortune who ignore them and are ignored by them. They are forced to rely on themselves alone; and there are moments when even the strongest give way under their burden. They call out for help, for a friend . . . Let's revive the people of heroes." Romain Rolland, it is true, called heroes only those who were great of heart and did not triumph by force. There was no nationalism in his words but a conscious universalism. It was much easier, however, to turn to national heroes and to the adoration of force as a way out from the lack of inspiration and greatness, of brotherhood and solitude, felt by so many intellectuals on the European continent in the last two decades before World War I.

p. 259, l. 12
Lord Acton, "Nationality" (1862), reprinted in *The History of Freedom and other Essays* (London: Macmillan, 1907), pp. 270–300.

p. 259, l. 20
Hans Kohn, *Prophets and Peoples, op. cit.*, pp. 92–96.

p. 260, l. 35
Uriel Heyd, *Foundations of Turkish Nationalism* (London: Luzac & Co., 1950), p. 114. See also on Ziya Gökalp, his *Turkish Nationalism and Western Civilization*, tr. and ed. by Niyazi Berkes (London: Allen & Unwin, 1959); Richard Hartmann in *Orientalische Literaturzeitung*, vol. XXVIII (Sept.-Oct.,

1925) pp. 578–610, and Ettore Rossi in *Oriente Moderno*, vol. IV (1924), pp. 574–595.

p. 261, l. 26

Halide Edib in her political novel written in 1910 (a German translation appeared under the title *Das Neue Turan. Ein türkisches Frauenschicksal*, Weimar: Kiepenheuer, 1916) wrote of the new nationalism: "As I listened (to the speeches at a Turanian gathering) my soul was profoundly moved and I felt how deeply the aspirations of the new Turkey are rooted in our forefather's very being; the music welled up from the innermost source of our Turanian blood and carried me away, so that to this day I still seem to hear it, and I realize that we must learn to descend to the springs of life if we would breathe into our political aim the power of inspiration to win the people for its accomplishment." See also Halide Edib, *Memoirs* (London: John Murray, 1917); Alp Tekin, *Türkismus und Pantürkismus* (Weimar: Kiepenheuer, 1915); Ahmed Emin, *The Development of Modern Turkey as Measured by its Press* (New York: Columbia University Press, 1914).

p. 262, l. 6

See Charles W. Hostler, "Trends in Pan-Turanism," *Middle Eastern Affairs*, Jan. 1952, pp. 3–12. During World War II, some of the Pan-Turanian agitators became extreme racialists. See also Charles W. Hostler, *Turkism and the Soviets* (New York: Praeger, 1957); Richard Pipes, *The Formation of the Soviet Union; Communism and Nationalism 1917–1923* (Cambridge: Harvard University Press, 1954); Serge A. Zenkovsky, *Pan-Turkism and Islam in Russia* (Cambridge: Harvard University Press, 1960).

p. 262, l. 18

"Rozanov was the greatest writer of his generation. The Russian genius cannot be gauged without taking him into account, and whatever way they turn out, we must take the responsibility for our great men." D. S. Mirsky, *A History of Russian Literature*, ed. by Francis J. Whitfield, (New York: Knopf, 1949), p. 424.

p. 262, l. 29

"The Revolution called from him (Voloshin) a series of remarkable 'historical' poems on the destinies of Russia . . . 1917 was an elemental effort of Russia to free herself from its outlandish fetters. 'Holy Russia' (in the poem of the same name) wanted to be free, so she . . . 'set fire to her farms and crops, destroyed her ancient abode, and went out into the world humiliated and a beggar . . . Shall I not go on my knees before thee in the mire, blessing the trace of thy bare foot, thou wretched, homeless, drunken Russia—thou fool in Christ?' In another poem (Transubstantiation) he draws a picture of Rome in the 6th century when . . . Papal Rome, 'a new Rome, was born, great and primitive like the elements. Thus the grain of wheat, that it may grow, must dissolve. Dissolve, Russia, and come to new life as the Kingdom of the Spirit!' " *Ibid.*, p. 452.

p. 263, l. 4

Maurice Bowra in *The Cornhill*, Jan. 1944, p. 71.

p. 263, l. 9

George Reavey, *Soviet Literature Today* (London: Lindsay Drummond, 1946) p. 14.

p. 263, l. 13

See *Mayakovsky and His Poetry*, ed. by Herbert Marshall, rev. ed. (London: Pilot Press, 1945). In his "Autobiography. I Myself" Mayakovsky wrote under October, 1917: "To accept or not to accept? For me (as for the other Moscow Futurists) this question never arose. It is my revolution." In his poem "October" he wrote: "Other lands/ old and indifferent./ Their history/ a gaping grave./ But my land's young/ and different/ Free to imagine,/ create and brave." *Ibid.*, p. 130.

p. 263, l. 17

See his "Mystery-Bouffe, an Heroic, Epic and Satyric Representation of our Epoch" (1918) in *Masterpieces of the Russian Drama*, ed. by G. E. Noyes (New York:

Appleton, 1933). In Act 6, Scene 2 (Variant of 1921)
the workers after world-wide victory sing:

> All memory of the past shall perish,
> The bourgeois rule is crushed and lost.
> The earth we hold and we shall cherish.
> We, soldiers of the toilers' host,
> From fields and factories ascend,
> Come from the towns both great and small.
> The world is ours from end to end.
> We, who were naught, today are all.

V. Shchrebina, "Za pravdivoe osveshchenie tvorchestva
V. Mayakovskogo," *Pravda*, 25 March, 1951, attacked
the current Mayakovsky interpretations which regarded
Mayakovsky as a destroyer and not as a true follower of
Russian classical national traditions in poetry and form.

p. 264, l. 38
Bernard Pares, *The Fall of the Russian Monarchy*
(New York: Knopf, 1939), pp. 187–191. Pares gives
the chapter (VII) the title "Slav and Teuton at Grips."
This title is incorrect and misleading. Neither all Slavs
nor all Teutons were at grips. Titles like these play into
the hands of Pan-Slavist and Pan-German chauvinists.

p. 265, l. 11
Count Kokovtsov, *Out of My Past*, tr. from the Russian by Laura Matveev, ed. H. H. Fisher, Stanford:
University Press, 1935), pp. 388, 392. Emperor William
II is reported there to have spoken loosely instead of a
war between Russia and Germany, of a war between
"Slav and German." "Nevertheless I must tell you
frankly that I fear there will be a clash between Slav and
German, and I feel it my duty to apprise you of this
fact." Much was done on both sides to arouse the feeling of a war between Slavism and Germanism.

p. 265, l. 15
Pares, *op. cit.*, p. 188. Grigorii Efimovich Rasputin
(1871–1916) exercised a great influence after 1907 on
the Empress and through her on the political appoint-
ments at the Russian court.

p. 265, l. 32
Maurice Paléologue, *La Russie des tsars pendant la grande guerre*, 3 vols. (Paris: Plon, 1922), vol. I. p. 120.

p. 265, l. 37
Quoted in Pierre Renouvin, *La Crise Européenne et la Grande Guerre*, 1904–1918 (Peuples et Civilisations, XIX, Paris: Alcan, 1934), p. 156. Nikolai Alexeevich Maklakov (1871–1918) was minister of the interior from 1912 to 1915. He was a brother of Vasilii Maklakov. Another former minister of the interior, Peter Nikolaevich Durnovo (1845–1915) who held this office from 1905 to 1906, warned the Emperor in February, 1914, of the dangers to the monarchial regime in Russia in case of a conflict with Germany. See F. A. Golder, *Documents of Russian History*, 1914–1917 (New York: The Century Company, 1927), pp. 3–23.

p. 266, l. 4
On this change of temper in Europe see Hans Kohn, *The Twentieth Century* (New York: Macmillan, 1949).

p. 266, l. 20
See Fr. Smolka, *Autriche et Russie*, with a preface by Henri Martin (Paris, 1869); while the Poles in Russia and in Prussia had no university or institutions of higher learning after 1863, they had two universities in Austria, Cracow, the oldest Polish university, and Lemberg (Lwów), where the University was founded in 1784 and where all the instruction was given in Polish after 1871; Szujski, *Dzieła* (Works), 20 vols. (Cracow: Czas, 1885–1896); Bobrzyński, *Dzieje Polski w zarysie*, 3 vols. (Warsaw: Gebethner & Wolff, 1927–1931).

p. 266, l. 29
Wacław Lednicki, *Life and Culture of Poland as Reflected in Polish Literature* (New York: Roy, 1944), p. 30.

p. 267, l. 6

Krasiński, *Pisma* (Letters), anniversary edition (Cracow: Gebethner & Co., 1912), vol. V-VII, p. 223, quoted in Lednicki, *op. cit.*, p. 37. W. Feldman, *Geschichte der Politischen Ideen in Polen seit dessen Teilungen* (1795–1914) (Munich: R. Oldenbourg, 1917), pp. 389–392.

p. 267, l. 36

See Bronislav Chlebowski, *La Littérature Polonaise au XIXe siècle*, ed. by Manfred Kridl (Paris: Honoré Champion, 1933), ch. XXXI, and W. Feldman, *Die Polnische Literatur der Gegenwart* (Berlin: Karl Curtius, 1916), Book 5, ch. IX. On Wilhelm Feldman (1868–1919) see the postscript by Jiří Horák to his Czech translation of the work, *Současná litteratura polská* (Prague: Laichter, 1936).

p. 268, l. 19

Of the "Wedding" there is a French translation, *Noces*, tr. by M. A. de Lade and G. Lenormand (Paris: Nouvelle Revue Française, 1917). In act II one of the persons of the play, the Journalist, violently rejects peace and demands patriotic madness. "Le trépas est la paix, la paix c'est la mort." "La patrie aura besoin de toute une légion de fous." At the end of Act II turning to the intellectual he commiserates the sad state of Poland:

> Naguère il y avait ici des âmes solides,
> Des risques-tout a moitié fous
> Pour se dévouer ou pour frapper;
> Aujourd'hui rien, plus rien à espérer.
> Vous cherchez des impressions, voilà la mienne:
> Je vous crache au front mon mépris.

In "Deliverance" the poet introduced Mickiewicz' Konrad shouting:

> I call for blood! I wish to bless the knives . . .
> I shall curse the Cross, the emblem of Christ,

If I should deceive the nation through the idea of
    suffering . . .

but Konrad is unable to awake the nation. Everywhere
he finds around him only emptiness; he is isolated. "I
am the prisoner of a single and great idea, in it is my
weakness, in it is my strength."

p. 268, l. 33
W. J. Rose in *The Cambridge History of Poland
from Augustus II to Pilsudski*, 1697–1935 (Cambridge:
University Press, 1941), p. 403.

p. 269, l. 20
The *Cambridge History of Poland*, *op. cit.*, pp. 606–
609, eulogized Pilsudski's anti-French and pro-Hitler
foreign policy. In Hitler and Pilsudski "two personal
rulers faced each other with the game in their own
hands, no longer directly subject to the gusts of popular
passion. . . . It was soon apparent that the German-
Polish treaty (of friendship and non-aggression of January 26, 1934) was to be no mere gesture."

p. 270, l. 4
Czernin, *Im Weltkriege* (Berlin: Ullstein, 1919),
p. 369.

p. 271, l. 18
R. W. Seton-Watson, *Masaryk in England* (Cambridge: University Press, 1942), p. 20.

p. 271, l. 31
  ibid., p. 55.

p. 272, l. 11
  ibid., p. 127 f. In his Conversations with Karel Čapek,
Masaryk on Thought and Life, tr. from the Czech by
M. & R. Weatherall (New York: Macmillan, 1938),
p. 201 ff., Masaryk declared that he could see only one
solution for the small nations—"political cooperation
and reciprocity in economics and culture." As good
examples of what he meant he mentioned the Little En-

tente and the Balkan Entente, weak reeds indeed on which to lean.

p. 272, l. 23
See William J. Rose, "Czechs and Poles as Neighbors," *Journal of Central European Affairs*, vol. XI (1951), pp. 153–171.

p. 273, l. 38
R. W. Seton-Watson, *Masaryk in England, op. cit.,* p. 128.

p. 274, l. 6
ibid., p. 125.

p. 274, l. 19
The Slavonic Review, VI., no. 17 (Dec., 1927) carried an interesting debate about neo-Slavism after World War I. The participants were Paul Milyukov "The World War and Slavonic Policy," Stephen S. Bobchev "The Slavs after the War," V. V. Zenkovsky "The Slavophil Idea Restated," and D. S. Mirsky "The Eurasian Movement." The most interesting statement is that by Zenkovsky, an unregenerate Slavophile of the old school: "Slavdom as a whole has not yet arrived at a consciousness of its historical mission; it is aware more clearly than ever before, that it has such a mission —but is only intuitively aware of it. . . . The historical mission of Slavdom lies . . . in the reconstruction of civilization in a Christian spirit. . . . As long as we remain separate, we are powerless to give the world that which is contained in us. Until we achieve real union . . . we are powerless to do the work entrusted to us by history." See also P. Milyukov, "A New Slavonic Policy," *The Slavonic Review*, vol. VI, no. 18 (March, 1928) and the pro-Western and anti-Slavophile article by the Polish scholar Jan Baudouin de Courtenay in *Le Monde Slave*, July, 1925.

p. 276, l. 2
Emil Ludwig, *Defender of Democracy. Masaryk of*

Czechoslovakia (New York: Robert M. McBride & Co., 1936), p. 132.

p. 276, l. 16

Masaryk, *Sur le Bolshévisme* (Geneva: Sonor, 1921), p. 29. The book appeared in Russian (*O bolshevizme,* Prague: Nasha Ryech, 1921), Magyar, Polish, Bulgarian, Rumanian and Ukrainian as well as in Czech. There is, however, no English translation. Of Masaryk's political writings of the period, the following appeared in Western languages: *Das Neue Europa. Der slavische Standpunkt,* tr. from the Czech by Emil Saudek (Berlin: Schwetschke & Son, 1922)—The English and French texts "The New Europe. The Slav Standpoint" were printed only for private circulation in 1918; *Die Botschaft des Präsidenten Th. G. Masaryk an das tschechische Volk* (Geneva: Sonor, 1919); "The Slavs after the War," *The Slavonic Review,* I (1922).

p. 276, l. 35

In his *The Making of a State: Memories and Observations,* 1914–1918, ed. by H. W. Steed (New York: Frederick A. Stokes, 1927), p. 181, Masaryk wrote that the Bolsheviks "were guilty of much superfluous destruction. Particularly do I blame them for having reveled, after a truly Tsarist fashion, in the destruction of human life." And on page 180: "Uncritical, wholly unscientific infallibility is the basis for the Bolshevik dictatorship, and a regime that quails before criticism and fears to recognize thinking men stands self-condemned." The Czech original *Světová revoluce* (The World Revolution) and the German translation *Die Weltrevolution, Erinnerungen und Betrachtungen,* 1914–1918 (Berlin: Erich Reiss, 1925) appeared early in 1925. It is remarkable that in the beginning of the 1920's Masaryk ascribed to the Russian Soviet regime under Lenin the character of primitive terrorism recalling Ivan IV, the monolithic totalitarianism and the arrogant omniscience of the leadership, which some observers ascribe only to the later development of Stalinism which they regard as a departure from the original spirit of Leninism.

p. 276, l. 39

Festschrift Th. G. Masaryk zum 80. Geburtstage, part II: Th. G. Masaryk als Denker (Bonn: Friedrich Cohen, 1930), p. 5. This Festschrift, which contains a full bibliography of works by and on Masaryk, is the most comprehensive study of Masaryk as political philosopher. Rádl's essay is in French; the late professor of biology at the Czech University of Prague wrote there: "The principal fact is that Masaryk from the beginning began to teach a purely Western philosophy. . . . Thus it came about that the most important Western philosophers have transmitted to us their philosophical method, i.e., have taught us to think in the Western way . . . Leaning firmly on Western civilization to fight against Pan-Slavism and its close relative, Pan-Germanism—two concepts originating in romanticism—and in spite of the full confidence which he had in the critical methods of the West, he felt nevertheless the greatest sympathy for the Slavs in general and for the Russians especially. . . . The reader will not fail, however, to remark that though Masaryk as a writer was passionately interested in the problems of Eastern Europe which he understands very well, he nevertheless never ceases to recommend the Western philosophy and critical analysis as the only way of salvation."

p. 277, l. 13

R. W. Seton-Watson, *Masaryk in England, op. cit.,* pp. 124, 132, 133. On Masaryk and Slavism see Jaroslav Papoušek, "Masaryk i slavyanstvo," *Volya Rossii,* VIII (Prague, 1930), pp. 277–294, and Nikola S. Bobchev, "Masarik i slavyanstvoto," *Slavyanski glas,* XIX (Sofia, 1925), pp. 8–12; XXIV (1930), pp. 19–28. One of Masaryk's main objections to Leninism was based on its non-Western, primitive character. "The life of our fellow-men must be sacred to us, man must respect the personality of his fellow. This principle is the basis of civilization and it must determine the rules of revolution and war. The revolution . . . must try hard to destroy as few human existences as possible. That separates the primitive culture of the Russians

from our Western civilization, they sacrifice too many
lives in their wars and in their revolutions." *Sur le Bolshévisme, op. cit.,* p. 17. "Only the primitive conditions
of Russia . . . made it possible for a vigorous usurper
to bring about the Bolshevist revolution in the chief
towns and establish the rule of a small but organized
minority." *The Making of a State, op. cit.,* p. 180.
See also Fr. Modráček, "Masaryk und der Socialismus,"
Festschrift, op. cit., p. 295.

p. 278, l. 31
    On the historical roots of Leninism see Nikolai Alex-
androvich Berdyayev, *The Origin of Russian Communism* (London: G. Bles, 1937) and *The Russian Idea*
(London: G. Bles, 1947), also *The end of our time*
(London: Sheed & Ward, 1933).

p. 281, l. 23
    "L'Union n'est fédérale qu'en apparence. Les répub-
liques sont soumises en fait à sa tutelle comme elle-
même l'est à la dictature du parti communiste, dont
le comité central et le bureau politique, c'est à dire en
definitive, le sécrétaire général, decident seuls de la
politique à suivre." Paul Milioukov, Ch. Seignobos, L.
Eisenmann, *Histoire de Russie* (Paris: Ernest Leroux,
1933), III, p. 1323 f.

p. 282, l. 12
    Stalin wrote in *Pravda,* October 20, 1920: "The
separation of the borders would undermine the revolutionary might of central Russia. . . . When a life and
death struggle is being waged, and is spreading, between
proletarian Russia and the imperialist Entente, only
two alternatives confront the border regions: either they
join forces with Russia, and then the toiling masses of
the border regions will be emancipated from imperialist
oppression; or they join forces with the Entente, and
then the yoke of imperialism is inevitable. There is no
third solution. So called independence of a so called
independent Georgia, Armenia, Poland, Finland, etc.,
is only an illusion covering up the full dependence of

these governments (if you will excuse me for calling them governments) from this or that group of imperialists."

Staling was then already calling dependence on Russia "liberation" and dependence or alleged dependence on others "imperialism." He wrote then: "We are *for* the separation of India, Arabia, Egypt, Morocco and other colonies from the Entente, for the separation in this case means the freeing of these oppressed countries from imperialism, the weakening of imperialist positions, the strengthening of revolutionary positions. We are *against* the separation of the border territories from Russia, because separation in this case means imperialist slavery for the border territory, the weakening of the revolutionary capabilities of Russia, the strengthening of the imperialist positions."

p. 283, l. 18
See Pokrovsky, *Brief History of Russia,* tr. by D. S. Mirsky, 2 vols. (New York: International Publishers, 1933), I, p. 5, and the excellent article by Anatole G. Mazour and Herman E. Bateman, "Recent Conflicts in Soviet Historiography," *Journal of Modern History,* vol. XXIV (March, 1952), pp. 56–68.

p. 283, l. 28
F. Epstein, *Encyclopaedia of the Social Sciences,* vol. XII, p. 181. See also Fritz Epstein, "Die Marxistische Geschichtswissenschaft in der Soviet Union seit 1927," *Jahrbücher für Kultur und Geschichte der Slaven,* N. S., vol. VI (Breslau, 1930), pp. 78–203; R. Salomon, "Zur Lage der Geschichtswissenschaft in Russland," *Zeitschrift für Osteuropäische Geschichte,* vol. VI (Königsberg, 1932), pp. 385–402; Hans Jonas, "Die Entwicklung der Geschichtsforschung in der Soviet Union seit dem Ausgang des Weltkrieges," *Zeitschrift für Osteuropäische Geschichte,* vol. V (1931), pp. 66–83, 386–396. Pokrovsky's attitude is represented in G. Zaidel and M. Tsvibak, *Klassovy vrag na istoricheskom fronte* (The Class Enemy on the Historical Front), papers and discussions about Tarle and Platonov and their schools

in the joint meeting of the Historical Institute of the Leningrad Section of the Communist Academy and the Leningrad Section of the Association of Marxist Historians (Moscow and Leningrad: Social Economic Government Publishing House, 1931) and Sergei A. Piontkovsky, *Burzhuaznaya istoricheskaya nauka v Rossii* (Bourgeois Historical Science in Russia), (Moscow: Molodaya Gvardiya, 1931). Tsvibak wrote *op. cit.,* p. 68: "Only the science of a rising class can boldly look ahead and predict the future. The Marx-Lenin method has achieved a monopoly position in science because the practice has justified its scientific theses." Tsvibak could apparently in spite of his Marx-Lenin method not foresee that three years later he and his friends would be regarded officially as enemies of the "rising class" on the historical front.

p. 284, l. 30
See Georges Kagan, "La crise de la science historique russe," *Revue Historique,* vol. 65, no. 188 (1940), pp. 1–35; Georg von Rauch, "Die Grundlinien der sowjetischen Geschichtsschreibung im Zeichen des Stalinismus," *Europa Archiv,* V, nos. 19–21 (1950), pp. 3383–88, 3423–32, 3489–94; and the following two publications of the Historical Institute of the Academy of Sciences of the USSR: *Protiv istoricheskoi kontseptsii M. N. Pokrovskogo* (Against Pokrovsky's Concept of History, Moscow, 1939), and *Dvadsat pyat let istoricheskoi nauki v SSSR.* (Twenty Five Years of Historical Science in the USSR, Moscow, 1942). In this book written by V. G. Volgin, E. V. Tarle and A. M. Pankratova the superiority of Soviet historical scholarship is ascribed to the "constant and systematic guidance" by the party and "the particularly great assistance rendered by Stalin himself." The famous article by Stalin and Molotov "On the Teaching of Civic History in the Schools of the USSR," *Izvestia,* May 16, 1934 was translated in *Slavonic and East European Review,* XII (1934–35), p. 204 f. See also S. R. Tompkins, "Trends in Communist Historical Thought," *ibid.,* XII (1934–35), pp. 294–319; B. H. Sumner, "Soviet History," *ibid.,* XVI (1937–38), pp. 601–615, XVII (1938–39),

pp. 151–161; Antoine Florovsky, "La Littérature historique sovietique-russe," *Bulletin d'Information des Sciences Historiques en Europe Orientale*, VI (Warsaw, 1934), pp. 120–186, VII (1935), pp. 5–111.

p. 284, l. 35
Bedny "is the oldest poet of the revolution. His work has been published in Bolshevik periodicals even before the war, and in 1917 he did not have to be converted, or to accept the revolution. He fitted right into it and remained its bard and champion throughout the years. If the institution of a poet laureateship existed in Soviet Russia, no one would contest Bedny's eligibility." Alexander Kaun, *Soviet Poets and Poetry* (Berkeley: University of California Press, 1943), p. 143.

p. 285, l. 14
Journal de Moscou, Nov. 24, 1936, and *New York Times*, Nov. 16, 1936. In view of the attitude of the early 1950's, it might be interesting to find that the official Soviet theory then approved of the Christianization of Russia as "one of the principal factors in the rapprochement of the backward Russian people with the people of Byzantium and, later, with the people of the West, that is to say, with people of higher culture."

p. 285, l. 21
Pokrovsky, *Istoricheskaya nauka i borba klassov* (Historical Science and Class Struggle), a collection of articles and reviews prepared for publication by the Historical Institute of the Communist Academy, 2 vols., (Moscow: Goss. Sotsialno-ekon. izdat., 1933), vol. II, p. 307. The article in *Pravda* was by P. Drozdov, "Istoricheskaya shkola Pokrovskogo (The Historical School of Pokrovsky).

p. 285, l. 31
Tarle had been attacked by Pokrovsky's school at the same time as Sergey Feodorovich Platonov (1861–1933). Tarle, thirteen years younger, lived to witness the restoration of nationalist historiography in Russia.

But even he had to learn the new super-nationalism.
In his book *Bonaparte* (English translation, New York:
Knight Publications, 1937; French translation, Paris:
Payot, 1938) he denied the nationalist character of the
great patriotic war of 1812. "Never did Napoleon, or
his marshals, or their companions in arms, speak of the
war of 1812 as a 'national' war, in the same sense that
they spoke of the Spanish guerrilla war as a 'national'
war. Nor could they compare the two phenomena. The
war in Russia lasted six months . . . the first saw Napoleon constantly victorious. . . . There was not a
single national mass revolt against the French. . . .
There were occurrences of quite a contrary nature, as
when the peasants of Smolensk complained to the
French authorities that their master . . . had been
guilty of betraying the French. . . . The peasants as a
group took no part in these activities. . . . It is clear
that if the Spanish guerrilla warfare may justifiably be
called a national war, it is impossible to apply this
term to any Russian movement in the war of 1812."
No wonder that the reviewer in *Pravda* on June 10,
1937, sharply attacked this "objective" historiography.
But the authorities apparently knew Tarle's potentialities. The next day *Pravda* published a mitigation of its
criticism, and in the following year Tarle published his
Nashestvie Napoleona na Rossiyu. 1812 god (tr. *Napoleon's Invasion of Russia, 1812*, New York: Oxford
University Press, 1942) in which he wrote: "The guerrilla movement that began immediately after the battle
of Borodino . . . could attain success only through the
most active voluntary aid sedulously rendered by the
Russian peasantry. This insatiable hatred toward the
usurpers and . . . oppressors . . . was expressed in the
way in which the Russian peasants joined the army in
1812. . . . According to the unanimous opinion of
the French, absolutely nowhere except in Spain did the
peasants in the villages show such desperate resistance
as in Russia. . . . It was precisely the peasant who
destroyed the magnificent cavalry of Murat, first in the
world, under whose victorious onslaught ran all European armies; it was this very army that the Russian
peasant destroyed. . . . The *entire* war against the in-

vading Napoleon was solidly a national war. . . . It was the people's arm that inflicted upon the greatest commander in world history the irreparable fatal blow." Tarle had discovered the style which from now on was to receive official approval.

E. V. Tarle, "Soviet Historical Research," *Science and Society*, VII (1944), no. 3, p. 230, wrote about Pokrovsky's school. "It was not interested in the personalities who were active in the founding of the great Russian state, exceeding the Roman Empire, the Empire of Charles V, or the Napoleonic Empire; a state embracing half of Europe and half of Asia. I do not accuse all these men of the subjective intention, the conscious desire to destroy all belief in Russia, all patriotism, all respect and love for its great past. . . . But objectively their work was harmful."

See on the trend from 1917 to 1938 Anatole G. Mazour, *An Outline of Modern Russian Historiography* (Berkeley: University of California Press, 1939), pp. 84–98. But in 1951 the vigilant Soviet authorities blamed Tarle's work on Napoleon's invasion of 1812, which reappeared in 1943, for insufficient appreciation of Kutuzov's genius and for Tarle's reliance on non-Russian sources. By not making clear that Kutuzov was much superior to Napoleon as a military genius, Tarle "falsified the figure of one of our great ancestors, whose name counts among those of which our nation is proud." This long article by S. Koshukhov, "K voprosu ob otsenke roli M. I. Kutuzova v otechestvennoi voine 1812 goda" *Bolshevik*, no. 15, (August, 1951) hardly has many parallels even in German national-socialist historical writing.

p. 286, l. 8
The *Istoria SSSR. Kratky kurs*, ed. by Prof. A. V. Shestakov (a textbook for the 4th grade. Moscow: Goss. uchebno-pedag. izdat. Narkomprosa RSFSR, 1945) p. 3, 4. Characteristically the edition, published immediately at the end of World War II, recognized the help rendered to the Soviet Union by Britain and the United States (p. 270) and ends (p. 274): "The heroic

deeds of the Soviet people and above all of the Russian people, which appears as the most prominent people of all the peoples in the Soviet Union have won victory for our land. Thanks to the heroic efforts of the front and of the rear the Soviet people with their great military leader Comrade Stalin at their head could destroy the enemy and save the fatherland from enslavement."

p. 286, l. 19

A French observer, André Pierre, wrote in *Le Temps*, Paris, 5 Sept., 1937: "Je me trouvais à Saint Petersburg quand le tsarisme commemora en 1912 les glorieux souvenirs de la guerre contre Napoleon. En lisant aujourd'hui les journaux de Moscou, j'ai l'impression de revivre les fêtes du centenaire, tant la Russie communiste rejoint la Russie autocratique dans l'exaltation des sentiments qui animèrent les soldats de 1812."

p. 286, l. 37

See André Mazon, *Le Slovo d'Igor* (Paris: Droz, 1940) and above all *La Geste du Prince Igor*, ed. by Henri Grégoire, Roman Jakobson and Marc Szeftel (Annuaire de l'Institut de Philologie et d'Histoire Orientales et Slaves, VIII, New York, 1948) which brings the text, translations into modern Russian, French and English (by S. H. Cross), and commentaries.

p. 287, l. 23

When H. G. Wells visited Russia in July, 1934, he noted: "As I saw one personality after another in Moscow, I found myself more and more disposed to a psychoanalysis of this resistance which is offered to any real creative forces coming in from the West. It is very marked indeed. In a few years, if it is sustained, we may hear Moscow saying if not 'Russia for the Russians,' then at least 'Sovietdom for the followers of Marx and Lenin and down with everyone who will not bow to the prophets,' which, so far as the peace and unity of the world is concerned, will amount to the same thing. There is a strong incorrigible patriotism beneath this Russian situation, all the more effective, because it is disguised." *Experiment in Autobiography* (New York:

Macmillan, 1934), p. 691 f. This was written before
the official rise of the new nationalism and at a time
when the Kremlin declared its eagerness for cooperation
with the West!

p. 291, l. 23
N. S. Timasheff, "Four Phases of Russian Internationalism," *Thought* (New York, March, 1945), pp.
37–54, p. 47. In 1927, at the 15th Congress of the
Russian Communist Party, Stalin declared: "The revolution in USSR is only part of the world revolution,
its beginning and the base for its successful advance."
That was in accordance with Lenin's declaration at the
7th Congress in March, 1918: "International imperialism disposing of the might of capital cannot co-exist
with the Soviet Republic. Conflict is unavoidable and
here is the greatest difficulty of the Russian Revolution,
its greatest historical task, that of provoking the international revolution. *"Sochineniya*, 2nd ed., vol. XXII,
p. 37. See also Waldemar Gurian, "Change and Per-
manence in Soviet Policies," *Thought* (Dec., 1946),
no. 83, pp. 593–622.

p. 292, l. 3
Bolshevik, no. 10, May, 1941, pp. 1–2.

p. 292, l. 7
"Our party is theoretically equipped and united as
no other party on earth because in its activity it leans
on the Marxist-Lennist theory and masters the knowledge of the laws of social development. The duty of
the party and Soviet personnel . . . is unceasingly to
study the theory of Marx and Lenin remembering that
it gives the Party the ability to orient itself in any
circumstance, to foresee the course of events, to understand the inner connections of current developments,
and to recognize not only how and whither events are
now developing, but also how and whither they must
develop in the future." *Bolshevik*, no. 1, Jan., 1945,
p. 10. The bourgeois historian may remark that to
judge from the many trials and executions, the Party
has not been so united in the past nor have the party
members who certainly studied the theory of Marx and

Lenin been able to foresee or evaluate events correctly. To the bourgeois historian, Stalin alone seems to be able "always" to understand and "foresee" events. Other party members don't and they are liquidated not by the class-enemy, but by Stalin. Such a development was certainly not foreseen by Marx or Lenin.

p. 292, l. 11
Stalin, *O velikoi otechestvennoi voine Sovetskogo Soyuza* (On the Great Patriotic War of the Soviet Union), 5th ed. (Moscow: Goss. izdat. polit. literatury, 1946), p. 17. See also in his radio address of July 3, 1941: "Germany suddenly and treacherously violated the non-aggression pact of 1939," *ibid.,* p. 10.

p. 292, l. 38
Ibid., pp. 26 f, 28, 36. Stalin rightly emphasizes in his Order of the Day as National Commissar for Defense on February 23, 1942, that the policy of racial equality of the USSR was a factor of strength in comparison to Hitler's racial policy. *Ibid.,* p. 42.

p. 293, l. 1
Among the many descriptions of the new nationalist fervor see Maurice Hindus, *Mother Russia* (Garden City, N. Y.: Doubleday, Doran & Co., 1943), pp. 93–107; Vera Alexandrova, "Russia is Changing," *American Mercury*, March, 1943, pp. 311–318; Vera Sandomirsky, "Soviet War Poetry," *The Russian Review*, Autumn, 1944. The most popular younger poet Konstantin Simonov (see on him the article by Elena Mikhailova in *Soviet Literature*, Aug. 1946, pp. 46–49) wrote in a famous poem in Nov., 1941, to his friend Alexei Surkov: "I am proud of this dearest of countries, this dear sad country that gave me my birth. I am proud that in Russia my life is to finish, that the mother that bore me was Russian of race, that when seeing me off, in the old Russian manner, she locked me three times in her loving embrace." And Surkov replied: "In the midst of night and darkness we have carefully borne before us the inextinguishable flame of faith in our Russian, our native folk." A fervent Russian patriotism became the theme of all the poems, short stories, novels

and plays, glorifying the Holy Homeland, svyashchen-
naya rodina. The general slogan was "za rodinu, za
Stalina," for fatherland and Stalin.

p. 293, l. 15

See Michael Karpovich, "Soviet Historical Novel,"
The Russian Review, Spring, 1946, pp. 53–63. The
novel by S. Golubov was also translated into English,
No Easy Victories, a novel of General Bagration and
the campaign of 1812, tr. by J. Fineberg (London:
Hutchinson, 1945). A number of Russian war novels
and biographies about historical heroes are available in
English translations, among them S. Sergeev-Tsensky,
Brusilov's Break-Through (London: Hutchinson, 1944);
S. Borodin, *Dmitri Donskoi*, tr. by E. and C. Paul
(London: Hutchinson, 1944); Mikhail Bragin, *Field
Marshal Kutuzov* (Moscow: Foreign Languages Publish-
ing House, 1944); K. Ossipov, *Alexander Suvorov, a
Biography*, tr. by E. Bone (London: Hutchinson, 1944);
R. Wipper (Robert Yuryevich Vipper) *Ivan Grozny*,
tr. by J. Fineberg (Moscow: Foreign Languages Pub-
lishing House, 1947). This book is remarkable because
in it a historian of repute and a man 85 years old tried
to save Ivan's reputation as a reformer and military
strategist of "progressive" importance against moralistic
"liberal" considerations. The book was published in its
Russian original by the Academy of Sciences of the
USSR in 1944. These liberal historians, according to
Wipper, translated "the significant, and on the lips of
Russians extremely majestic, surname Grozny by the
vulgar words Ivan the Terrible." (p. 234). Ivan became
also the hero of a war-time film by S. M. Eisenstein,
for which Sergei Sergeevich Prokofieff wrote the music.
Prokofieff was also the composer of a war-time opera
"War and Peace" dealing with 1812 and with Kutuzov,
a work which he regarded as a distinct war contribution.
See his cable in *The New York Times*, Dec. 2, 1945:
"The Soviet people rose up in defense of their native
land. Every Soviet citizen was eager to make his contribution to the war effort." Alexei Tolstoi also wrote
a play *Ivan Grozny* in two parts (Moscow: Sovetsky
pisatel, 1945).

p. 294, l. 15
The Russian nationalist point of view was expressed
f.i. in Walter Kolarz, *Stalin and Eternal Russia* (Lon-
don: Lindsay Drummond, 1944), p. 48 f. On the
Baltic Republics after the annexation by the Soviet
Union see Czeslaw Milosz, "Die baltischen Völker,"
Der Monat, no. 41 (Berlin: Feb., 1952), pp. 451–466.

p. 295, l. 17
See on the establishment of the autonomy of the
Volga Germans, Rudolf Schilze-Mölkau, *Die Grundzüge
des Wolgadeutschen Staatswesens im Rahmen der rus-
sischen Nationalitätenpolitik* (Munich: Ernst Rein-
hardt, 1931) and Manfred Langhans-Ratzeburg, *Die
Wolgadeutschen, ihr Staats- und Verwaltungsrecht in
Vergangenheit und Gegenwart*, zugleich ein Beitrag
zum bolschewistischen Nationalitätenrecht (Berlin: Ost-
Europa-Verlag, 1929).

p. 298, l. 15
Istoriya SSSR, vol. III (for tenth grade), 2nd ed.
(Moscow: Goss. uchebno-pedag. izdat., 1941), p. 29.
The quotation regarding Stalin's attitude is from Lav-
rentii Pavlovich Beria, *K voprosu ob istorii bolshevist-
skikh organizatsii v Zakavkazie* (To the Question regarding the History of the Bolshevik Organizations in
Trans-Caucasia), 5th ed. (Moscow: Goss. izdat. polit.
literatury, 1939), p. 56. In the new edition of the
Istoriya SSSR, 1946, vol. III, p. 45, the text has been
changed and Stalin's speech after the victory over
Japan on Sept. 2, 1945, is quoted. On p. 29 the military
technology of the Tsarist army is blamed for its backwardness. "In Port Arthur there was even no wireless
telegraph, though it had been invented already in 1895
by A. S. Popov." The textbook for the ninth grade,
Novaya Istoriya, 1870–1918, ed. by Prof. V. M. Khvos-
tov and Prof. L. I. Zubak (Moscow: Goss, uchebno-
pedag. izdat., 1946), p. 125, put the new view briefly:
"Thus began the Russo-Japanese war. It was an acquisi-
tive imperialistic war. Russian Tsarism was defeated—
Tsarism and not the Russian nation. For Russia was
much stronger than Japan and could have defeated her,

but the Tsarist government prepared itself badly for the war." This invincibility under a better government than that of the Tsars was expressed in a pamphlet by N. M. Korobkov, *Mikhail Kutuzov* (Moscow: Military Publishing House of the National Commissariat for Defense, 1945), p. 5, written especially for officers: "We are on the road to a new growth of the power of our country. Prepared historically to great feats, our army and our new Stalinist military art surpass everything that Russian history has ever known. But we do not forget our great ancestors, we do not forget the heroic past of our nation. (Their) memory is a faithful guarantee of the great future to which the genius of a leader (genialny vozhd), Generalissimus Stalin, leads the country on new paths."

The text in the pamphlet by Beria, mentioned above, reveals the switch from "socialism" to "nationalism" in Stalin's line. Two official translations into English exist. L. Beria, *On the History of the Bolshevik Organizations in Transcaucasia*, tr. from fourth Russian ed. (New York: International Publishers, 1939) and tr. from seventh Russian ed. (Moscow: Foreign Languages Publ. House, 1949). This speech by Stalin's faithful fellow countryman and follower helped establish the official legend about Stalin's activities in his younger years. Stalin's attitude in 1905 is discussed on pp. 44–46 of the 1939 ed. (pp. 71–73 of the 1949 ed.): "In January, 1904, the Russo-Japanese War broke out. The Bolsheviks of Transcaucasia, headed by Comrade Stalin, consistently pursued Lenin's line of 'defeat' for the Tsarist government, constantly urging the workers and peasants to take advantage of the military embarrassments of Tsarism and to fight for the revolutionary overthrow of the autocracy. The All-Caucasian Committee of the RSDLP (Russian Social Democratic Labour Party, the Bolshevik organization), the Tiflis and Baku Committees of the RSDLP issued a number of leaflets exposing the imperialist predatory character of the Russo-Japanese War on the part of both warring powers and calling for the defeat of Tsarism. One of the leaflets . . . said: 'However much they may call us non-patriots and the enemies at home, let the autocracy . . . remember that the RSDLP represent 99% of the population of Russia. . . . Their brothers are being driven into the jaws of death to shed the blood of the sons of the Japanese, a brother people! . . . We want this war to be more lamentable for the Russian autocracy than was the Crimean War. . . .' Day in and day out the Bolsheviks urged the soldiers to support the revolutionary struggle of the people against Tsarism."

p. 301, l. 17

A good discussion of the Slav peoples in and after World War II is in Albert Mousset, *The World of the Slavs* (London: Stevens & Sons, 1950), a revised edition of the French original, published in 1946.

p. 302, l. 5

Testifying before the House Committee on Un-American Activities Judge Blair F. Gunther of the Court of Common Pleas, Pittsburgh, accused the American Slav Congress of being "the most dangerous fifth column operating among our Slav population. Its chief aim is to subvert millions of Slavic Americans operating in our basic industries in order to cripple our national defense apparatus. It gives every evidence of Moscow direction and control." The Congress was listed as a subversive agency by the Attorney General of the United States on Sept. 21, 1948. On June 25, 1949, the House Committee on Un-American Activities found that the Congress changed its keynote at the end of World War II "from super-patriotism to outright treason." The Committee charged that the embassies of the USSR and of the Slav states cooperated actively with the American Slav Congress. It drew its main support from groups in Pittsburgh, Detroit, Chicago, Cleveland and New York. Among the chief leaders were named Leo Krzycki, George Pirinsky, and Louis Adamic. A number of American Slav organizations, above all the Polish-American Congress and the Slovak League of America, were reported to be hostile to the Congress and loyal to the United States.

p. 303, l. 35
Christo Gandev in *Slavyansko bratstvo*, sbornik
(Slav Brotherhood. A Symposium), Biblioteka Izvori
(Sources), no. 2 (Sofia: Publications of the Propaganda
Ministry, 1945).

p. 308, l. 15; p. 310, l. 3
Some wide-spread pamphlets, characteristic of this
Soviet patriotism are: P. Moskatov, *Geroichesky rabochy
klass nashei rodiny* (The Heroic Working Class of our
Fatherland), 2nd ed. (Moscow: Gossud. izdat. polit.
liter., 1946); S. G. Kolesnekova, *O sovyetskom patri-
otizme* (On Soviet Patriotism) (Moscow: Gossud. izdat.
polit. liter., 1947); L. A. Leontyev, *Proiskhozhdenie i
kharakter vtoroi mirovoi voiny* (The Origin and Character of the Second World War), printed in 100,000
copies (Moscow: Pravda, 1946); I. Mints (the well
known historian), *Velikaya otechestvennaya voina so-
vyetskogo soyuza* (The Great Patriotic War of the Soviet
Union), printed in 500,000 copies (Moscow: Gossud.
izdat. polit. liter., 1947). Leontyev quotes on p. 7
Stalin's article "On the article of Engel's 'The Foreign
Policy of Russian Tsarism' " which he published in
Bolshevik, 1941, no. 9, and in which he strongly criticized Engels for having overlooked the much worse and
dangerous foreign policy of British imperialism which
in its conflict with German imperialism was mainly
responsible for World War I. Mrs. Kolesnikova starts
her pamphlet with a quotation from Lenin (*Sochineniya*,
vol. XXIII, p. 290) that patriotism is "one of the
deepest human feelings, fortified by centuries and
thousands of years of individualized (or isolated) fatherlands," and she concludes with a verse from the National Anthem of the Soviet nation: "Through storms
the sun of liberty radiated to us,/ and the great Lenin
illuminated for us the road,/ Stalin made us grow
—in loyalty to our nation,/ he has inspired us to
work and heroic deeds." See also P. Vyshinsky, "So-
vyetsky patriotizm i ego velikaya sila," (Soviet Patriotism
and its Great Strength), *Bolshevik*, 1947, no. 18, pp.
28–29, and G. F. Alexandrov, "Kosmopolitizm-ideolo-
giya imperialisticheskoi burzhuazii," (Cosmopolitanism,

the Ideology of the Imperialistic Bourgeoisie), *Voprosy
filosofii*, 1948, no. 3, pp. 174 ff.

p. 311, l. 15
Georg von Rauch, "Die sowjetische Geschichtsforschung heute," *Die Welt als Geschichte*, 1951, no. 4,
(pp. 249–262), p. 258.

p. 312, l. 3
Mrs. Nechkina's article "K voprosu o formule neimen-
shee zlo" (On the Question of the Lesser Evil), *Voprosy
istorii*, 1951, no. 4, pp. 44–48, was in the form of a
letter to the editor and was specially recommended by
the editor. Yet her volume in the *Istoriya SSSR*, 2 vols.,
2nd ed. (Moscow: Goss sots.-ekon. izdat. 1947-49) had
been censored in *Voprosy istorii*, 1950, no. 7, for insufficient understanding of Tsarist colonial policy, because
she had not recognized the reactionary, pro-British and
pro-Turkish character of the independence movement
of the Caucasian peoples under Shamyl against Tsarism.

p. 312, l. 35
Voprosy Istorii, 1951, no. 1, pp. 155–156. The thesis
had been defended on June 26, 1950.

p. 313, l. 11
Review of *Progressivnoe vliyanie velikoi Russkoi natsii
na rozvitie Yakutskogo naroda*, pt. 1, ed. by A. I. Nov-
gorod (Yakutsk: Yakutskoe Goss. izdat., 1950) in *Voprosy istorii*, 1951, no. 1, p. 140.

p. 313, l. 25
I. Kon, "K voprosu o spetsifike i zadachakh istori-
cheskoi nauki," *Voprosy istorii*, 1951, no. 6, pp. 48–64.
The quote is *ibid.*, p. 63.

p. 314, l. 1
Article "Pan-Slavism" in *Bolshaya Sovyetskaya Entsiklopediya*, vol. 44 (Moscow: Ogiz, 1939), cols. 68 f.
The reference to Marx and Engels there is to *Sochineniya*, VII, 277.

p. 314, l. 21
Anatole G. Mazour and Herman E. Bateman, *Journal of Modern History*, XXIV (March, 1952), p. 64.

p. 314, l. 30
See review in *Slavyane*, August, 1947, pp. 51 f. and in general Elizabeth Valkenier, "Soviet Impact on Polish Post-War Historiography, 1946–1950," *Journal of Central European Affairs*, vol. XI, January, 1952), pp. 372–396; V. Korolnik, J. Miller and M. Misko, "Polskaya istoricheskaya nauka na VII Vrotslavskom sezde 1948 goda," *Voprosy Istorii*, 1949, no. 2, pp. 108–127; and Roman Werfel, "Konferenz polnischer Historiker," *Für dauerhaften Frieden, für Volksdemokratie* (the official Cominform organ, Bucharest, March 6, 1952). According to this Marxist Polish historian, his colleagues at the congress realized "the profound community of fate which bind the Polish people in past and present in many fields with the Russian, Ukrainian and Byelo-Russian peoples, with the Czech and Slovak peoples and with the peoples of the Danubian basin." The right spirit was expressed in the monthly *Bolgarskaya Kulturnaya Khronika* (Sofia, Dec., 1951) which began an article "Pod solntsem sovyetskoi kultury" (Under the Sun of Soviet Culture): "Soviet culture is the richest in ideas, the most democratic and the most humane in the world. . . . More and more brilliantly the sun of Soviet culture illumines the whole globe. The culture of the people's democracies also develops under its powerful influence."

p. 315, l. 4
Joseph Stalin, *Marxism and the National and Colonial Question*, tr. from the Russian ed. prepared by the Marx-Engels-Lenin Institute (New York: International Publishers, n.d., 1935?), pp. 167, 168, 301.

p. 315, l. 21
The future nationalist trend of Lenin's revolution had been foreseen by some Russian nationalists who published the symposium *Smena vekh* (The Change of Guide-Posts) in Prague, 1921. See especially Nikolai

Vasilyevich Ustryalov, *Pod znakom revolyutsii* (Under the Sign of Revolution), 1st. ed. (Kharbin: Russkaya Zhizn, 1925), 2nd enlarged ed. (Kharbin: Poligraph, 1927). Ustrialov writes there in the introduction, p. V: "No doubt, the motherland is being rebuilt and rises again." The articles were written between 1921 and 1926. They are divided into two sections. Natsional-Bolshevism, political articles, and *Russkie dumy*, sketches to the philosophy of our time. Some articles are remarkable for Russian nationalism in the 20th century, especially "National Bolshevism" pp. 47–53 (originally published Sept. 18, 1921); "Of the Future Russia," pp. 132–135; "The Nationalization of the October," pp. 212–218; "Russia and Blok's Poetry," pp. 346–356; and "Of the Russian Nation," pp. 374–393, written originally for a *Vseslavyansky Sbornik*, a Pan-Slav Symposium, published by the Union of Slav Committees in Zagreb in honor of the 1000th anniversary of the Kingdom of Croatia.

p. 316, l. 12

The lecture by Kovalov was regarded as so important, that it was published in English by *Soviet Monitor*, issued by Tass Agency, London, no. 8815, August 13, 1947. The greatness of the Russian national past was praised by Vladimir Yermelov, "Veliky russky narod" (The great Russian nation), *Slavyane*, 1945, no. 10, pp. 6–10: "The history of the Russian nation is the history of legendary epic heroic deeds. The heroic battles which the Russian nation fought for the freedom and independence of its motherland, were at the same time battles for the freedom and independence of other nations." Referring to the wars of Alexander Nevsky, of Ivan the Terrible, of 1812, and of 1877, the author pointed out that the Russian nation never brought oppression to other peoples but only liberty. "Such are the Russian national traditions."

p. 317, l. 6

The struggle against cosmopolitanism began with an article in *Pravda* on Jan. 28, 1949. "Ob odnoi anti-patrioticheskoi gruppe teatralnikh kritikov" (About an anti-patriotic Group of Theatre Critics) and in *Kultura i zhizn* of Jan. 30, 1949, "Na chuzhdikh pozitsiakh" (On Foreign Positions). From that time on everybody was violently attacked who did not proclaim the unique originality and absolute priority of everything Russian. Stalin's articles on linguistics began to appear on June 26, 1950, as a contribution to a discussion started by *Pravda* on May 9, 1950, about the theories of Nikolai Yakovlevich Marr (1864-1934), a Georgian like Stalin, whose recognition as official and leading Marxist philologist had been assured by Stalin and who was now completely repudiated by the same Stalin. See Clarence A. Manning, "Soviet Linguistics and Russian Imperialism," *The Ukrainian Quarterly*, VIII, no. 1, (1952), pp. 20-27.

p. 318, l. 18

Kopecký stressed the point of supreme loyalty of all workers to the Soviet Union: "Wherever the question arises whether the working people prefer the land in which they live but in which they are exposed to class exploitation, growing misery and oppression, or the Soviet Union, they will always decide for the Soviet Union, even should they be exposed to the greatest terror of capitalist and pseudo-socialist patriots. The working masses of France, Italy and other capitalist lands have already taken this decision. They declare that they will never bear arms against the Soviet Union and the people's democracies and that they will greet the Soviet army as liberator, when the Soviet army should oppose the aggressor. Yes! The just character of such a war puts on the effort of the peoples, which lead such a war, the seal of sacred patriotism."

p. 320, l. 28

"Protiv ideologicheskikh izvrashchenii v literature," (Against Ideological Perversions in Literature), *Pravda*, July 2, 1951, and "Ob opere Bogdan Khmelnitsky" (about the Opera Bogdan Khmelnitsky), *ibid.*, July 20, 1951. On July 10, *Pravda* printed an apology by Sosyura: "I think (your) criticism fully justified. I have deeply recognized that the Soviet Ukraine is unthinkable, detached from the powerful growth of our state of many nationalities; for the Ukraine achieved its happiness thanks to the fraternal help of the great Russian people and the other peoples of our motherland."

p. 321, l. 19
In *Pravda Ukrainy*, July 15, 1951. The same paper reported on July 22, that the Ukrainian Society for the Dissemination of Political and Scientific Knowledge complained that "too few lectures are being given about the eternal friendship of the Russian and Ukrainian peoples and about the struggle against Ukrainian bourgeois nationalism and cosmopolitanism."

p. 322, l. 13
See report in *Manchester Guardian* by Alexander Werth from Moscow, Oct. 26, 1947.

p. 322, l. 35
See Solomon M. Schwarz, "Revising the History of Russian Colonialism," *Foreign Affairs*, April, 1952, pp. 488–493; Mark Alexander, "Tensions in Soviet Central Asia," *The Twentieth Century*, Sept., 1951, pp. 192–200; and above all M. H. Ertuerk, "Was geht in Turkestan vor?" *Ost-Probleme*, 1950, pp. 1010–1016.

p. 323, l. 3
"Ob antimarksistskoi otsenke dvizheniya myuridisma i Shamilya v trudakh nauchnykh sotrudnikov Akademii," (About the Anti-Marxist Appreciation of Myuridism and of Shamil in the Works of the Scientific Collaborators of the Academy), *Vestnik Akademii Nauk SSSR*, no. 11, Nov. 1950; E. Adamov and L. Kutakov, "Iz istorii proiskov inostrannoi agentury vo vremya kavkazskikh voin" (From the History of the Intrigues of Foreign Agents at the Time of the Caucasian Wars), *Voprosy Istorii*, no. 11, No., 1950. The most criticized book was that by R. Magomedov, *Borba gortsev za nezavisimost pod rukovodstvom Shamilya* (The Struggle of the Mountaineers for the Independence under Shamil's Leadership), (Makhach-Kala: Daghestan Section of the Acad-

emy of Sciences of the USSR, 1939). The author was especially blamed for the "horrifying assertion" that this war of independence formed part of the international revolutionary movement.

p. 323, l. 36
See "Ob epose Altamych" (About the Epos A.), *Literaturnaya Gazeta*, Feb. 14, 1952; and "O reaktsionnoi sushchestnosti eposa Gesser Khan," (About the Reactionary Nature of the Epos G. K.), *Kultura i Zhizn*, Jan. 11, 1951.

p. 324, l. 29
"Za marksistko-leninskoe osveshchenie voprosov istorii Kazakhstana," (For the Marxist-Leninist Elucidation of the Questions of the History of K.), *Pravda*, Dec., 26, 1950.

p. 326, l. 28
See Otto Friedman, *The Break-up of Czech Democracy* (London: Gollancz, 1950) pages 97, 24, and Stephen Borsody, *The Triumph of Tyranny. The Nazi and Soviet Conquest of Central Europe* (New York: MacMillan, 1960) Chaps. XIV and XV. How strong the illusions about the new Slavism in the West were after World War II, can be seen from A. J. P. Taylor, *The Course of German History* (New York: Coward-McCann, 1946) p. 9: "The Slav people have come of age; none of them will again pass under German tutelage—nor under Anglo-Saxon tutelage either. The peoples of Western Europe, and finally of the United States as well, have learned that they can employ the German to enslave the Slav only at the price of being enslaved themselves. Sooner than pay this price, Western civilization—and particularly its two great powers, England and America—have recognized the Slavs as equals; this is the meaning of the Anglo-Soviet alliance of 1942, and of the present collaboration between the three great powers." It is doubtful whether the United States ever wished to employ the Germans to enslave the Slavs. The United States took the lead in 1918 in recognizing the independence and equality of the Slavs,

the Czechs, the Poles, the Yugoslavs. The danger of an Anglo-Saxon tutelage over the Slavs did probably never exist. The danger of a Russian tutelage over the Slavs did exist in modern history and was realized after World War II.

BIBLIOGRAPHY

This short general bibliography supplements the references in the Notes. With few exceptions, only books, not articles, are included.

The reader interested in contemporary developments in the Soviet Union will be greatly helped by three periodicals publishing translations from Russian sources, *The Current Digest of the Soviet Press*, a weekly publication by the Joint Committee on Slavic Studies; *Soviet Press Translations*, a biweekly published by the University of Washington in Seattle; and *Ost-Probleme*, a weekly published by the USIS, Press Division, Bad Godesberg; and reviewing also the publications of all communist satellite countries. Useful services will also be rendered by Charles Morley, *Guide to Research in Russian History* (Syracuse University Press, 1951), Leonid I. Strakhovsky, ed., *A Handbook of Slavic Studies* (Harvard University Press, 1949); Milivoy Stoyan Stanoyevich, ed., *Slavonic Nations of Yesterday and Today, Select Readings and References* (New York: H. W. Wilson, 1925); Robert J. Kerner, *Slavic Europe, a Selected Bibliography in the Western European Languages* (Harvard University Press, 1918) and *The Foundations of Slavic Bibliography* (The University of Chicago Press, 1916).

Lubor Niederle, *La Race Slave, statistique, démographie, anthropologie*, tr. from Czech by Louis Léger (Paris: Alcan, 1911).

Alexander Nikolaevich Pypin, *Panslavism v proshlom i nastoyashchem* (Panslavism in Past and Present), a series of articles which appeared originally in *Vestnik Evropy*, Sept. to Dec., 1878 with a continuation on

"Literary Panslavism" in June, August and Sept., 1879. In revised ed. by V. V. Vodovozov (St. Petersburg: Kolos, 1913).

Andrei Nikolaevich Sirotinin, *Rossiya i slavyane* (Russia and the Slavs, St. Petersburg: M. M. Stasyulevich, 1913).

Orest Fiodorovich Miller, *Slavyanstvo i Evropa* (Slavdom and Europe, Articles and Speeches, 1865–1877, St. Petersburg: Blagosvetlov, 1877).

Miloš Weingart, ed., *Slované. Kulturní obraz slovanského světa* (The Slavs. A Culture Picture of the Slav World), 3 vols. (Prague: Vesmír, 1927–1929) The first vol. of this work is by Jaroslav Bidlo, *Dějiny Slovanstva*, (A History of the Slavs), an attempt at a short synthesis of Slav history, divided in four parts: Origins of Slav States and Nations; Slavs as Equal Competitors of the European Nations in Politics and Culture; Political and Cultural Decline of the Slavs; Renaissance and Liberation of Slav Nations. There is an important bibliography.

Louis Léger, *Le Panslavisme et l'intérêt français* (Paris: Flammarion, 1917).

Louis Léger, *Souvenirs d'un slavophile*, 1863–1897 (Paris: Hatchette, 1905).

Wacław Lednicki, "Panslavism" in Feliks Gross (ed.), *European Ideologies* (New York: Philosophical Library, 1948), pp. 808–912.

Alfred Fischel, *Der Panslawismus bis zum Weltkrieg, éin geschichtlicher Ueberblick* (Stuttgart: Cotta, 1919). Edvard Beneš. *Uvahv o slovanství, hlavní problemy slovanské politiky* (Reflections on the Slavs. The main Problems of Slav Policy. Prague: Čin, 1947). There is a French translation, *Où vont les Slaves?* (Paris: Notre Temps, 1948).

Antonin Pimper, *O nacionalismu a novém slovanství* (On Nationalism and the New Slavdom. Prague: Legie, 1930).

Wolf Giusti, *Il panslavismo* (Milan: Instituto per gli studi di politica internazionale, 1941).

Emil Deckert, *Panlatinismus, Panslavimus und Panteu-tonismus in ihrer Bedeutung für die Politische Weltlage* (Frankfurt a.M.: H. Keller, 1914).

Eduard Winter, *Russland und die slavischen Völker in der Diplomatie des Vatikans 1878–1903* (Berlin: Aka-demie-Verlag, 1950). Leo XIII hoped for the unity of the churches and for friendship with Russia, while Pobyedonostsev suspected that "the Curia is a revolu-tionary element; it is the representative of Europe, of the hated West."

Eduard Winter, *Der Panslavismus nach den Berichten der österreichisch-ungarischen Botschafter in St. Peters-burg* (Prague: Deutsche Akademie der Wissenschaften, Phil.-Hist. Klasse XVII, 1944).

Reinhard Wittram, "Die russisch-nationalen Tendenzen der achtziger Jahre im Spiegel der österreichisch-ungarischen diplomatischen Berichte aus St. Peters-burg," in Walther Hubatsch, Ed., *Schicksalswege deutscher Vergangenheit* (Düsseldorf: Droste Verlag, 1950) pp. 321–351. "There was no question then in Russia of any general Pan-Slav or nationalist chauvinist trends," p. 334.

J. Grüning, *Die russische öffentliche Meinung und ihre Stellung zu den Grossmächten 1878–1894* (Berlin & Königsberg: Osteuropa Verlag, 1929).

S. A. Korff, *Russian Foreign Relations during the Last Half Century* (New York: Macmillan, 1922).

William Thomas Steed, ed., *The M. P. for Russia, Reminiscences and Correspondence of Mme. Olga Novikoff* (London: A. Melrose, 1907).

G. Ghikas, *Botschafter von Navikov über den Pan-slavismus und die orientalische Frage* (Vienna: Stern, 1907).

Jos. Pervolf, *Slavyane, ikh vzaimniya otnosheniya i svyazi* (The Slavs, their Mutual Relations and Ties), 3 vols. (Warsaw, 1886–1893).

J. L. Seifert, *Die slavische Friedfertigkeit* (Forschungen zur Völker-psychologie und Soziologie, Leipzig, 1927).

Thomas Jaritz, *Uber die grössten Teils slavische Ab-stammung der Bewohner deutscher Länder* (Villach: F. F. Hoffman, 1853). For German-Slav peace, because half of the original inhabitants of Germany were Slavs. "Two fraternal peoples should divide the common heritage."

Count Adam Gurowski, *Le Panslawisme, son histoire, ses véritables elements réligieux, sociaux, philosophiques et politiques*, vol. I (Florence, 1848).

Rudolph Vrba, *Russland und der Panslavismus, statistische und social-politische Studien*, 2 vols. (Prague: Selbstverlag, 1913). A defense of Russia against alleged plans of the Jewish plutocracy to fight Russia under the pretext of Panslavism. "Panslavism does not exist in reality. It is only the pretext for war against Russia."

Andrzej Baumfeld, *Polska myśl mesjaniczna* (The Polish Messianic Thought. Warsaw: E. Wende, 1910).

Marjan Zdziechowski, *Mesjaniści i Słowianofile; szkice z psychologii narodów Słowianskich* (Messianists and Slavophiles; Studies in the psychology of the Slav Nations. Cracow: Gebethner, 1888).

Wacław Lednicki, *Poland and the World* (New York: Polish Institute of Arts and Sciences, 1943).

Wacław Lednicki, *Life and Culture in Poland* (New York: Roy, 1944).

Wilhelm Feldman, *Deutsche, Polen und die russische Gefahr* (Berlin: K. Curtius, 1915).

Oscar Halecki, *Borderlands of Western Civilization* (New York: Ronald Press, 1952).

Oscar Halecki, *The Limits and Divisions of European History* (London: Sheed Ward, 1950).

Nicholas Chubaty, "The Ukrainian and Russian Concepts of the History of Eastern Europe," Shevchenko Scientific Society, *Proceedings of the Historical-Philological Section*, vol. I (New York and Paris, 1951).

Walter Kolarz, *Myth and Realities in Eastern Europe* (London: Lindsay Drummond, 1944).

Walter Kolarz, *Russia and her Colonies* (London: George Philip & Son, 1952).

Alexander Brückner, *Die Slaven und der Weltkrieg* (Tübingen: Mohr, 1916).

Jozef Aloizy Reitzenheim, *La Pologne parmi les Slaves et ses Rapports avec la Question d'Orient.* (Paris: Ledoyen, 1854).

Frederick Thomas Buller, *Apollyon and the Reaction of the Slavonians, with a Review of the Political State of Europe under the Action of the Contending Principles* (London: Partridge & Oakey, 1847).

Prosper Vallerange, *Le Panlatinism, Confederation Gallo-Latin et Alto-Gaulois* (Paris: Passard, 1862).

Heinrich Wuttke, *Polen und Deutsche; politische Betrachtungen* (Schkeuditz: Blomberg, 1846).

Roman Sembratovich, *Le tsarisme et l'Ukraine.* Preface by Bjoernsterne Bjoernsen (Paris: Cornély, 1907).

Axel Schmidt, *Russlands Weltverteilungsplan* (Jena: Diederichs, 1917).

S. Harrison Thomson, "A Century of a Phantom, Panslavism and Western Slavs," *Journal of Central European Affairs*, XI (1951), no. 1, pp. 57–77.

Paul Milyukov, "World War and Slavonic Policy," *Slavonic Review*, VI (1927–28), pp. 268–290.

Richard Charmatz, *Zarismus, Panslawismus, Krieg.* (Vienna: Anzengruber-Verlag, 1915).

Vladimir Clementis, *Panslavism, Past and Present*, tr. from the Slovak by Paul Selver (London: Czechoslovak Committee for Slav Reciprocity, 1943).

Albert Mousset, *Le Monde Slave* (Paris: Editions Françaises et Internationales, 1946).

A. Gedeonoff, *Panslawismus eine Weltgefahr?* (Münster i.W.: Libertas-Verlag, 1950).

Lucien Laurat, *La linguistique et l'imperialisme russe* (Paris: Les Isles d'or, 1951).

Klaus Mehnert, *Weltrevolution durch Weltgeschichte.*

Die Geschichtslehre des Stalinismus (Kitzingen: Holzner Verlag, 1950).

Anatole Leroy-Beaulieu, *La France, la Russie et l'Europe* (Paris: Calman Levy, 1888).

Everard de Choiseul-Gouffier, *La Russie et le Panslavisme*, 3rd ed. (Nancy: Serdoillet, 1871).

Charles Loiseau, *Le Balkan slave et la crise autrichienne* (Paris: Perrin, 1898).

René Henry, *Questions d'Autriche-Hongrie et question d'Orient*, 2nd ed. (Paris: Plon-Nourrit, 1903).

André Chéradame, *L'Europe et la question d'Autriche au seuil du XXe siècle*. 4th ed. (Paris: Plon-Nourrit, 1906).

Victor Bérard, *The Russian Empire and Czarism*, tr. by Frederick Greenwood (London: D. Nutt, 1905).

Jan Kucharzewski, *The Origins of Modern Russia* (New York: Polish Institute of Arts and Sciences, 1948).

Alexander von Schelting, *Russland und Europa im russischen Geschichtsdenken* (Bern: Francke, 1948).

Fritz Lieb, *Das westeuropäische Geistesleben im Urteile russischer Religionsphilosophie* (Tübingen: Mohr, 1929).

Fritz Lieb, *Russland unterwegs, der russische Mensch zwischen Christentum und Kommunismus* (Bern: Francke, 1945).

Bernhard Schultze, *Russische Denker, ihre Stellung zu Christus, Kirche und Papsttum* (Vienna: Herder, 1950).

Nicholas Zernov, *Three Russian Prophets, Khomiakov, Dostoevsky, Soloviev* (London: SCM Press, 1944).

Ernst Benz, *Die Ostkirche im Lichte der protestantischen Geschichtsschreibung von der Reformation bis zur Gegenwart* (Freiburg & Munich: Karl Alber, 1952).

Paulin Gérard Scolardi, *Krijanich, Messager de l'Unité des Chrétiens et Père du Panslavisme* (Paris: Picard, 1947).

Josef Dobrovský, *Dobrovský's Slavin*. Mit einem An-
hang "Der böhmische Cato" (Prague: Von Mayegg,
1934).

A. Selishchev, *Vzglyady Karla Gavlichka na Rossiyu. K
istorii slavyanskogo vzaimootnoshenii v politike 19go
veka* (Karel Havlíček's Views on Russia. A Contribution to the History of Slav Interrelationships in Nineteenth Century Politics. Kazan, 1913).

Karel Kazbunda, *Pout Čechů do Moskvy 1867 i ra-
kouská diplomacie* (The Czech Pilgrimage to Moscow
in 1867 and the Austrian Diplomacy. A Publication
from the Archives of the Czechoslovak Ministry of
Foreign Affairs. Prague: Orbis, 1929).

Count Vladimir A. Bobrinsky, *Prazhsky Syezd. Che-
khiya i Prikarpatsky Rus* (The Prague Congress. Che-
khia and Carpathian Russia. St. Petersburg: Svyet,
1909).

Viktor Mikhailovich Chernov, *Marksizm i slavyanstvo*
(Petrograd, 1917).

D. Merejkowsky, *Le Tsar et la Révolution* (Paris:
Mercure de France, 1907). "Sooner or later there will
be a clash between Europe and the Russian Revolution, not between one or the other European people
but between the whole of Europe and the Russian
revolution—or rather anarchy. . . . The Russian revolution is as absolutist as the autocracy, which it rejects."

Helen Iswolski, *Der neue Mensch im Russland von
heute* (Luzerne: Vita Nova Verlag, 1936).

Sir John Maynard, *Russia in Flux before October* (London: Gollancz, 1941).

Vladimir Weidlé, *La Russie absente et présente* (Paris:
Gallimard, 1949).

W. Lednicki, *Poushkine et la Pologne. A propos de la
trilogie antipolonaise de Poushkine.* (Paris: Leroux,
1928).

V. Z. Zavitnevich, *Russkie slavyanofili i ikh znachenie
v dele uyasneniya idei narodnosti i samobytnosti* (The
Russian Slavophiles and their Importance in the Eluci-

dation of the Idea of Nationality and of National O-
riginality. Kiev: Samonenko, 1915).

Nikolai Leontyevich Brodsky, *Rannie slavyanofili: A. S.
Khomyakov, I. V. Kireevsky, K. S. i I. S. Aksakovy*
(Moscow: Istor-Lit. Biblioteka, no. 5, 1910). Important
texts and comments on the early Slavophiles.

Semion Afanasevich Vengerov, *Peredovoi boets slavyano-
filstva, Konstantin Aksakov* (The Foremost Fighter
for Slavophilism K. A. St. Petersburg: Prometei, 1912).

Yuri Feodorovich Samarin, *Okrainy Rossii* (Russia's
Borderlands), *Sochinenia,* 9 vols. (Moscow: D. Samarin,
1878–1911), vols. 8 and 9.

N. O. Lossky, *History of Russian Philosophy* (New
York: International University Press, 1951).

N. Byelozersky, A. I. Gertsen, *slavyanofilstvo i zapadniki*
(Herzen, Slavophilism and the Westernizers. St. Petersburg: Sev. knigo-izdat., 1905).

Pavel Nikolaevich Milyukov, *Razlozheniye slavyano-
filstva: Danilevsky, Leontyev, Vl. Solovev* (The Disintegration of Slavophilism. Moscow: Kushnerev,
1893).

S. Voznesensky, *Russkaya literatura o slavyanstve*
(Petrograd. Karbasnikov, 1915). A Bibliography of
Russian literature about the Slavs.

D. H. Sumner, *Russia and the Balkans, 1870–1880*
(Oxford: Clarendon Press, 1937).

N. M. Druzhinin (ed.), *Slavyansky sbornik: slavyansky
vopros i russkoe obshchestvo v 1867–1878 godakh*
(Moscow: Lenin Public Library, 1948). Important collection from the manuscript division of the library on
the Slav problem and Russian society in the years 1867–
1878.

Razumnik Vasilevich Ivanov-Razumnik, *Istoriya russkoi
obshchestvennoi mysli. Individualizm i meshchanstvo v
russkoi literature i zhizni XIX veka* (History of Russian
Social Thought. Individualism and Citizenship in the
Russian Literature and Life in the 19th Century), 2
vols. (St. Petersburg: M. M. Stasyulevich, 1907).

Richard Hare, *Pioneers of Russian Social Thought. Studies of non-Marxian Formation in 19th Century Russia and of its Partial Revival in the Soviet Union* (London: Oxford University Press, 1951).

V. A. Pushkin, *Skobelev o nemtsakh. Ego zavety slavyanstvu* (Skobelev about the Germans. His Legacy to the Slavs. Petrograd: I. D. Sytin, 1914).

Pierre Koutouzow, *Les vrais intérêts du monde slave et la paix européenne. Réponse au général Skobelew.* (Berlin: R. Wilhelmi, 1882).

Alfred Portier d'Arc, *L'esprit national russe sous Alexandre III* (Paris: Charpentier, 1890).

Nikolai Sevastyanovich Derzhavin, ed., *Trudy Instituta Slavyanovedeniya Akademii Nauk SSSR.* (Publications of the Slavistic Institute of the Academy of Sciences of the USSR), vol. I, 1932; vol. II, 1934. Volume II, pp. 189–230 contains K. A. Pushkarevich, "Balkanskie slavyane i russkie isvoboditeli" (The Balkan Slavs and the Russian Liberators. The Slav Committees and the Events in the Balkans before the Russian-Turkish War of 1877–78), and on pp. 247–260, V. N. Korablev, "Lyudevit Gaj" (To the 60th Anniversary of his Death).

Uchenye zapiski Instituta Slavyanovedeniya Akademii Nauk SSSR (Scholarly Essays of the Slavistic Institute of the Academy of Sciences of the USSR), vol. I, 1949; vol. II, 1950. Vol. I contains on pp. 57–84 I. I. Udartsov, "Iz istorii slavyanskogo sezda v Prage v 1848 g." (From the History of the Slav Congress in 1848). Vol. II contains articles to the 5th anniversary of the liberation of Bulgaria and the establishment of a people's democracy there; to the 5th anniversary of the Slovak uprising of 1944; and to the 100th anniversary of the Bulgarian revolutionary poet Christo Botev (1848–1876).

Josef Macůrek, Dějiny východních Slovanů (The History of the Eastern Slavs), 3 vols. (Prague: Melantrich, 1947). Excellent bibliography especially also on Ukrainian and Byelo-Russian history.

Josef Jirásek, *Rusko a my. Dějiny uztahů československo-ruských od nejstarších dob až do r. 1914* (Russia and

We. A History of Czechoslovak-Russian relations from oldest times to 1914), 4 parts (Prague: Miroslav Stejskal, 1946).

Slovanská vzájemnost 1836–1936, Symposium to the 100th anniversary of Kollár's book, ed. by Jiří Horák (Prague: Czech Academy of Sciences and Arts, 1938).

Wolf Giusti, *Un contributo allo studio dell' ideologia panslava - la figura di Svatopluk Čech* (Trieste: Editrice Università, 1950). See on the same author also Arne Novák, *Sv. Čech, dílo a osobnost* (Sv. Čech, his Work and Personality), 2 vols. (Prague: Vesmír, 1921–1923), and Jednota Svatopluka Čech, *Svatopluku Čechovi. Sborník* (A Symposium to S. C., published by the S. C. Union, Prague, 1949).

Edvard Beneš, *Paměti. Od Mnichova k nové válce a k novém vitězství* (Memoirs: From Munich to the New War and the New Victory. Prague: Orbis, 1947).

T. G. Masaryk, *Les Slaves après la guerre* (Prague: Orbis, 1923).

Rudolf Nadolny, *Germanisierung oder Slavisierung. Eine Entgegnung auf Masaryks Buch Das Neue Europa* (Berlin: O. Stollberg, 1926).

Jerzy Pogonowski, *Ilyrizm i słowiańszczyzna, studja nad odrodzeniem Chorwackiem* (The Illyrian and Slav Movements, a Study of Croat Renaissance. Lwów: Księgarnia naukowa, 1924).

Thomas Čapek, *The Slovaks of Hungary, Slavs and Panslavs* (New York: Knickerbocker Press, 1906).

Paul Milyukov, "Eurasianism and Europeanism in Russian History," *Festschrift Th. G. Masaryk zum 80. Geburtstage*, part I (Bonn: Friedrich Cohen, 1930), pp. 225–236.

Esper Esperovich Prince Ukhtomsky, *Puteshestvie na vostok E. I. V. Gossudarya naslednika Tsesarevicha 1890–1891* (The Journey to the Orient of H. I. H. the Crownprince 1890–1891), 3 vols. in 6 parts (St. Petersburg, 1893–97).

Michael Pap, "Soviet Difficulties in the Ukraine," *The Review of Politics*, vol. XIV (April, 1952), pp. 204–232.

Theodore I. Geshkoff, *Balkan Union* (New York: Columbia University Press, 1940).

Robert J. Kerner and Harry N. Howard, *The Balkan Conferences and the Balkan Entente 1930–1935* (Berkeley: University of California Press, 1936).

L. S. Stavrianos, *Balkan Federation: A History of the Movement toward Balkan Unity in Modern Times* (Northampton, Mass.: Smith College Studies in History, vol. XVII, 1942).

N. Lenin, *Izbrannie stati po natsionalnomu voprosu* (Selected Articles on the National Question), 2nd ed. (Moscow: Goss. izdat., 1925).

Leninizm i natsionalny vopros (Leninism and the National Question. Handbooks for the Activists and Propagandists of the Party, no. 7) (Rostov on the Don: Severny Kavkaz, 1931).

El. Drabkina, *Natsionalny i kolonialny vopros v tsarskoi Rossi* (The National and Colonial Question in Tsarist Russia. Moscow: Communist Academy, 1930). A very important bibliography.

N. N. Popov, *Natsionalnaya politika sovetskoi vlasti* (The Nationality Policy of the Soviet State. Moscow: Goss. izdat., 1927), 6th ed. (Charkov: Proletar, 1931).

M. C. Reikhel (ed.), *Sovetsky federalizm*. A Symposium (Moscow: Goss. izdat., 1930).

Edige Kirimal, *Der nationale Kampf der Krimtürken* (Emsdetten in Westfalen: Lechte, 1952).

Roman Smal Stocki, *The Nationality Problem of the Soviet Union and Russian Communist Imperialism* (Milwaukee: Bruce, 1952).

Jakob Jatzwank, *Sorbische Bibliographie* (Berlin: Akademie Verlag, 1952).

V. Burian et alii, eds., *Slovanský sjezd v Bělehradě v 1946* (The Slav Congress in Belgrade in 1946), Library of the Slav Committee, no. 1 (Prague: Orbis, 1947).

Michael Karpovich, "A Forerunner of Lenin: P. Ň. Tkachev," *Review of Politics*, vol. VI (1944), pp. 336–350.

N. Rjasanoff, *Karl Marx über den Ursprung der Vorherrschaft Russlands in Europa*, tr. from the Russian by A. Stein. Ergänzungshefte zur Neuen Zeit, no. 5, 1908–09 (Stuttgart: Paul Singer, 1909). R. criticizes Marx but supports Engels: "Engels behielt recht. Er wies schon damals vollkommen richtig nach, dass der Hauptgrund der europäischen Hegemonie Russlands in der Grundmaxime der ganzen äusseren Politik Katherina II lag—dass Russland die anderen europäischen Mächte sich nach Möglichkeit untereinander zerfleischen und schwächen liess," p. 61.

Karl Marx & Friedrich Engels, *The Russian Menace to Europe* (Glencoe, Illinois: Free Press, 1952).

Raymond L. Garthoff, "The Stalinist Revision of History: the Case of Brest-Litovsk," *World Politics*, (Oct., 1952).

Harry Pross, "Deutschnationale Aspekte in der jüngsten SED-Publizistik," *Ost-Probleme*, Vol. IV, 39 (Sept. 27, 1952).

Merle Kling, *The Soviet Theory of Internationalism* (St. Louis: Washington University, 1952).

F. Barghoorn, "Stalinism and the Russian Cultural Heritage," *Review of Politics*, vol. VI (1944), pp. 336–350.

G. Fedotov, "Russia and Freedom," *The Review of Politics*, vol. VIII, (1946), pp. 12–36. One of the most thoughtful and penetrating essays on the meaning and chief trends of Russian history.

Waldemar Gurian, *Bolshevism: An Introduction to Soviet Communism*, (Notre Dame, Indiana: The University of Notre Dame Press, 1952).

Harry Pross, "Ideologie und Staatsraison," *Ost-Probleme*, vol. VII, no. 12 (1955).

Josef Matl, *Das Slawentum zwischen Ost und West* (Klagenfurt: Austria, 1950).

Nicholas V. Riasanovsky, *Russia and the West in the Teaching of the Slavophiles. A Study of Romantic Ideology* (Cambridge, Mass.: Harvard University Press, 1952).

Georg von Rauch, *Russland: Staatliche Einheit und Nationale Vielheit* (Munich: Isar Verlag, 1953).

Herbert Ludat, *Der Europäische Osten in abendländischer und sowjetischer Sicht* (Köln-Braunsfeld: Rudolf Müller, 1954).

Otto Forst de Battaglia, *Zwischen Europa von der Ostsee bis zur Adria* (Frankfurt a.M.: Verlag der Frankfurter Hefte, 1954).

Emanuel Sarkisyanz, *Russland und der Messianismus des Orients* (Tübingen: Mohr, 1955).

Hans Kohn, *The Mind of Modern Russia. Historical and Political Thought in Russia's Great Age* (New Brunswick, N.J.: Rutgers University Press, 1955).

Peter Scheibert, *Von Bakunin zu Lenin*, vol. I: Die Formung des radikalen Denkens in der Auseinandersetzung mit deutschem Idealismus und französischem Bürgertum (Leiden: E. J. Brill, 1956).

Michael Boro Petrovich, *The Emergence of Russian Pan-Slavism, 1856–1870* (New York: Columbia University Press, 1956).

Hildegard Schaeder, *Moskau das Dritte Rom. Studien zur Geschichte der politischen Theorien in der slawischen Welt* (Darmstadt: Wissenschaftliche Buchgesellschaft, 1957).

Otokar Odložilik, "Congresses of Slavic Youth, 1890–1892," *The Annals of the Ukrainian Academy*, vol. V (1958), pp. 1327–1357.

Hans Uebersberger, *Oesterreich zwischen Russland und Serbien. Zur Südslawischen Frage und der Entstehung des ersten Weltkrieges* (Graz: Böhlau, 1958).

Werner Conze, *Polnische Nation und deutsche Politik im ersten Weltkrieg* (Graz: Böhlau, 1958).

Nicholas V. Riasanovsky, *Nicholas I and Official Nationality in Russia, 1825–1855* (Berkeley: University of California Press, 1959).

Index

HANS KOHN was born in Prague, Czechoslovakia, September 15, 1891. He came to the United States in 1933, after having received his doctorate in jurisprudence from the German University of Prague in 1923. He taught history at the New School of Social Research, New York City, in 1933; became Professor of History, Smith College, 1934–41, Sydenham Clark Parsons Professor of History, 1941–9; and has been Professor of History at the City College of New York since 1949. In 1935, and again in 1937–8, he was visiting professor at Harvard. Professor Kohn has frequently lectured at other institutions, such as the universities of California, Colorado, and Minnesota, the Naval War College, and Mount Holyoke College. He is the author of numerous books, including: *A History of Nationalism in the East* (1929); *The Idea of Nationalism: A Study in its Origins and Background* (1946); *Prophets and People: Studies in Nineteenth Century Nationalism* (1946); *German History: Some New German Views* (1954); *The Mind of Modern Russia: Political and Social Thought in Russia's Great Age* (1955); *Nationalism, Its Meaning and History* (1955); *The Making of the Modern French Mind* (1955); *Nationalism and Liberty: the Swiss Example* (1956); *Basic History of Modern Russia: Political, Cultural, and Social Trends* (1957); *The Mind of Germany: The Education of a Nation* (1960). *Pan-Slavism* was originally published in 1953.

THIS BOOK is set in Electra, a Linotype face designed by W. A. Dwiggins. The book was composed, printed, and bound by The Colonial Press Inc. Paper manufactured by S. D. Warren Company, Boston. Cover design by MUNI LIEBLEIN.

VINTAGE RUSSIAN LIBRARY

VINTAGE POLITICAL SCIENCE
AND SOCIAL CRITICISM

VINTAGE HISTORY
EUROPEAN

VINTAGE HISTORY
AMERICAN

A free catalogue of VINTAGE BOOKS will be sent to you at your request.
Write to Vintage Books, Inc., 501 Madison Avenue, New York 22,
New York.

VINTAGE BIOGRAPHY AND AUTOBIOGRAPHY

VINTAGE WORKS OF SCIENCE
AND PSYCHOLOGY

A free catalogue of VINTAGE BOOKS will be sent to you at your request. Write to Vintage Books, Inc., 501 Madison Avenue, New York 22, New York.

VINTAGE HISTORY AND CRITICISM
OF LITERATURE, MUSIC, AND ART

PB-11964
17

For a free catalogue, write to Vintage Books, Inc., 501 Madison Avenue New York 22, New York.